DESTINATION AMERICA

DESTINATION AMERICA

Chuck Wills

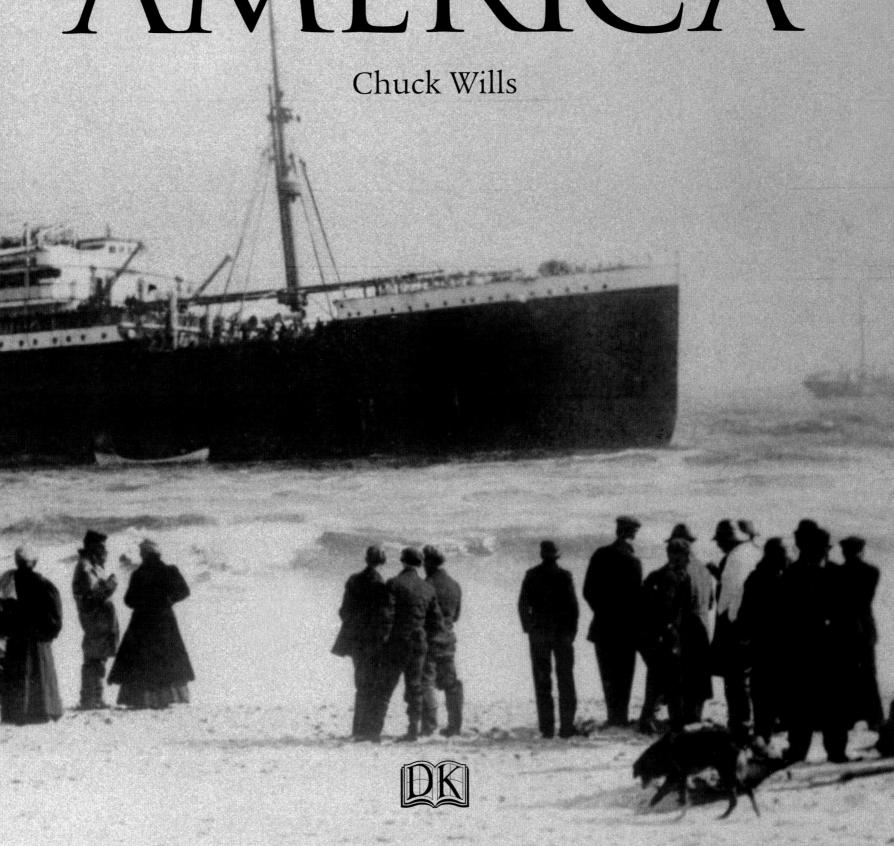

DK

LONDON, NEW YORK, MELBOURNE, MUNICH, AND DELHI

Project Editor   Anja Schmidt
Assistant Managing Art Editor   Michelle Baxter
Editorial Assistant   Michelle Kasper
Designer   Mark Johnson Davies
Design Assistant   Jee Chang
Picture Researcher   Chrissy McIntyre
DTP Coordinator   Milos Orlovic
Production Manager   Ivor Parker
Project Director   Sharon Lucas
Creative Director   Tina Vaughan
Category Publisher   Andrew Heritage
Publisher   Carl Raymond

Published in Great Britain in 2006 by
Dorling Kindersley Limited
80 Strand, London WC2R 0RL

2 4 6 8 10 9 7 5 3 1

A Note on Sources and Figures

While *Destination America*'s creative team strove to use the most
reliable sources and up-to-date scholarship for the figures
and dates in the book, there is considerable disparity in both
contemporary and historical sources about how many
immigrants from various groups came to the United States, and
when, as well as the number of their descendants today, and so
on. The text necessarily reflects this situation. For numbers or
percentages of Americans of particular ancestral groups,
we generally have used the latest available data from the U.S.
Census Bureau—but because ancestry is self-selected by Census
respondents, these figures must also be considered inexact.

A CIP catalogue record for this book is available from
the British Library

ISBN 1 4053 0752 8

Colour reproduction by
Colourscan, Singapore

Printed in China by
Hung Hing Offset Printing Company Ltd

Discover more at
www.dk.com

Quotes and excerpts throughout this book are
taken from the PBS television series by David
Grubin. The four programmes' titles that are
attributed throughout the book are: "The
Golden Door," "The Earth is the Lord's,"
"The Art of Departure," and "Breaking
Free: A Women's Journey."

CONTENTS

INTRODUCTION

In Paul Mazursky's 1984 movie comedy *Moscow on the Hudson*, Robin Williams plays a Russian musician who defects to America in Bloomingdale's in New York City. His character soon finds himself with an Italian-born girlfriend, an immigration lawyer who fled Castro's Cuba, and a circle of friends who come from around the world. "Everyone I meet here," he marvels, "is from somewhere else."

Williams's character is speaking specifically about New York City in the 1980s, but the line is equally applicable to contemporary America as a whole. The one thing that unifies the 295 million people living in the United States today is that at some point in the last half-millennium, they or their ancestors came here from someplace else.

The sole exception is the Native Americans—who lost almost an entire continent to the new arrivals—but as far as forensic anthropology can determine, even the Native Americans are newcomers in terms of prehistoric human migration. For the rest of us, the distance from our immigrant roots concerns relative chronology: whether our ancestors came ashore via Plymouth Rock, or Ellis Island, or through the International Arrivals facility at JFK Airport.

PUSHING AND PULLING

Scholars of immigration use the terms "push" and "pull" to describe the motivations that brought immigrants to the United States— "push" being the factors that drove them from their native countries (political or religious persecution, overpopulation, unemployment), and "pull" being the factors that attracted them to America (availability of land, job opportunities, religious tolerance).

All of these factors, whether "push" or "pull," have to do with American freedom—economic, political, religious, and creative. This theme of freedom is what makes this book, and the television series that it accompanies, different from other histories of American immigration. Instead of structuring our story in terms of specific periods of immigration, or focusing on the experience of immigrants from particular groups, we have sought to show how the desire for freedom is the unifying element through five

THE PULL OF FREEDOM
Immigrants and refugees have demonstrated great ingenuity, as well as great courage, in their efforts to get to America—like these Cuban refugees, attempting to reach Florida in 2003 aboard a raft powered by a 1951 Chevrolet truck.

centuries of immigration to America. For most immigrants, however, the "pull" of America was not limited to one single type of freedom. The whole package was what mattered. The United States was not only the first modern nation to free itself deliberately from the fetters of colonialism and to repudiate feudal notions of privilege, it was also a society that guaranteed its inhabitants "certain inalienable rights," in the words of the Declaration of Independence, including freedom of religion, the press, and assembly, plus political representation and equality under the law, as part of its basic governmental framework.

In combination with abundant land and an economic system that rewarded entrepreneurial spirit, these guarantees made America the destination of millions for whom a thirst for liberty was bound up with a hunger for material betterment. The Eastern European Jews who arrived in the late 19th and early 20th centuries are a case in point: they came to America not only to escape the anti-Semitic violence of the pogroms, but also to opt out of a society that limited their educational and professional opportunities and restricted even where they could live. Much the same is true of today's immigrants from Asia, Africa, the Caribbean, Latin America, and the Middle East, who seek not only a living wage, but also a refuge from the lawlessness and hatreds of their homelands.

THE HANDS THAT BUILT AMERICA

Freedom's promise was not always fulfilled. While precise numbers cannot be determined, some immigrants eventually returned to their native countries out of homesickness or disillusionment; others never intended to stay in the first place. Historically, the "pull" that drew many immigrants to America has been the opportunity to make money to send home to

FREEDOM TO PROTEST
Freedom of speech and freedom of assembly in action: thousands of protestors against the Vietnam War march down Pennsylvania Avenue in Washington, D.C., on November 15, 1969.

those who stayed behind: in the 21st century, there are villages in, say, Ecuador and the Dominican Republic, that depend on remittances from husbands, fathers, sons, and daughters in America in the same way that villages in Ireland and Sicily did more than a century ago. And many immigrants, now and then, have come to America mainly in hopes of accumulating enough savings to return home and live comfortably. But these immigrants were, and are, in the minority. Most came, and still come, to stay, with no greater goal than to be accepted as Americans.

At the same time, America's welcome to immigrants has never been unconditional. The mainly German and Irish arrivals of the first big wave of immigration, from about 1815 to 1860, endured considerable (if unofficial) opposition from "Nativists." As President John F. Kennedy— the great-grandson of Irish immigrants—put it, "The Irish were the first to endure the scorn and discrimination later to be inflicted, to some degree at least, on each successive wave of immigrants by already settled 'Americans.'"

Discrimination became a matter of national policy in the various laws that, for all intents and purposes, outlawed immigration from Asia in the late 19th and early 20th century, while the arrival of the next big wave of immigrants— this time mainly from Southern and Eastern Europe—ultimately sparked the immigration

SUCCESS STORY
Austrian-born Daniel Spitzer stands in front of his shoe store on New York City's Lower East Side around the turn of the 20th century. He came to America alone, age 14, in 1880; when he died in 1932, he owned real estate throughout the city.

restrictions of the early 1920s, which remained in place for four decades. In our own era, the impact of illegal immigration—according to the U.S. Census Bureau, there were at least 7 million such immigrants at the turn of the 21st century—is an increasingly controversial issue.

But however difficult and dangerous the journey, the immigrants still come. And without their labor, and that of their millions of predecessors, America as we know it would not exist. As the Irish rock group U2 expressed it on the soundtrack to another immigration-themed movie—Martin Scorsese's 2002 epic *The Gangs of New York*—immigrants provided "The Hands that Built America."

A very incomplete inventory of those building hands would include the Irish and Chinese who laid the railroad tracks that knitted the country together . . . the Poles and Finns and Welsh who forged the steel to make those rails, and who mined the coal to power the trains that ran along them . . . the Germans and Scandinavians and Russians who raised the wheat and meat to feed those miners and factory workers, and who turned the western Plains into the world's breadbasket . . . the African slaves and their descendants who cropped cotton in the scorching fields of the South . . . the French-Canadians and Armenians who spun that cotton into thread in the mills of New England . . . and the Jews and Italians and Puerto Ricans who wove that thread into clothing in the sweltering sweatshops of New York City.

Immigrant contributions have been intellectual as well as physical. American freedom of expression and inquiry turned the United States into one of the world's most dynamic nations in terms of scientific and cultural achievement—in great part due to immigrants who came seeking to use their talents to the fullest, fleeing intractable political and creative repression, and often their very lives were in danger in the face of unreasoning racial and religious bigotry. Again, a very incomplete list of these immigrants includes names like Einstein and Fermi, Arendt and Nabokov, Gropius and Mies, Stravinsky and Weill, Wilder and Dietrich . . .

A NATION OF IMMIGRANTS—AGAIN

Destination America appears at a significant time in the history of American immigration. More so than at any period in the last 100 years, the United States in the first decade of the 21st century is a nation of immigrants. The liberalization of immigration policy in 1965 and subsequent legislation opened the floodgates for a vast new wave of immigrants, one that has brought millions of people to America from parts of the world from which entry was previously denied or severely limited—especially South and East Asia and the Middle East—while half of all immigrants in recent years have come from Latin America. In 2002, the U.S. Census Bureau pegged the country's foreign-born population at 11.5 percent, not far off the historic high of 15 percent in 1910.

This influx is changing life in the United States in ways that will not be fully apparent for a long time, but its impact can already be felt across the entire nation, not just in major cities like Los Angeles and New York (in both cities the foreign-born population numbers more than one third), but in places like Maine, Nebraska, and Wisconsin—the adopted homes, respectively, of many Somali, Mexican, and Laotian Hmong newcomers. One recently reported statistic—that salsa has exceeded ketchup as the country's best-selling condiment—speaks volumes.

If I require further proof of how the latest immigrants are changing American society, I need only to get up from my computer and run the day's errands. I buy a magazine at a Pakistani newsstand, purchase the dinner vegetables at a Korean deli, and stop for a falafel at a Yemenite restaurant. I take a call on my cell phone from a buddy in Los Angeles—a public-school teacher who tells me that in his classroom of 31 kids, only two speak English at home. If my tasks take me far outside my neighborhood, I may return home in a taxi driven by someone from Nigeria, or Macao, or somewhere in what used to be the Soviet Union. In the lobby I pick up the letters deposited by a Jamaican mail carrier, and chat with my Filipino neighbors in the elevator to my floor.

I share with all these people a common identity as an American. Our desire to make a decent living while living in a free society unites us across superficial barriers of ethnicity, culture, and language. They came here for much the same reasons that brought my own forebears, many years ago, across the sea from England, Ireland, and Germany. *Destination America* is our story, and the story of our nation.

Chuck Wills
New York City, 2004–05

BUILDING AMERICA
A skyscraper rises above Manhattan in this 1908 photograph. The preceding year saw 1.3 million people arrive in the United States—the peak year for immigration. Many of them helped build America.

1

SETTLING
AMERICA

They have come from all over the world. Their faces

have changed, not their reasons: flight from poverty,

persecution, war. Drawn by the shimmering promise

of America, immigrants have been coming since

America's beginning, for a better life, for their very

survival. Whole communities transplanted

themselves in search of liberty and land. They

reached for a future denied them at home. America

meant opportunity—as it still does today.

"The Golden Door"

INDEPENDENCE DAY
Fireworks explode over the U.S. Capitol in Washington, D.C.,
celebrating America's birthday—July 4th, or Independence Day.
Although the signing of the Declaration of Independence was not
finished until August of 1776, July 4th was chosen as the official
anniversary of the United States' independence because that was
the day the 13 colonies voted on the Declaration's final draft.

COMING TO AMERICA

The settlement of North America from the 1500s to the 1800s is the story of the interaction of three distinct groups: the Native Americans, who would ultimately be pushed to the continent's margins by warfare, disease, and the land-hunger of the second group, the European settlers. Five European powers—Spain, France, England, the Netherlands, and Sweden—established major colonies in North America from the late 1500s to the mid-1700s, with England's colonies breaking away to establish the United States of America. The third group consisted of unwilling immigrants—enslaved Africans.

In a sense, even the Native Americans—the indigenous peoples that the first European explorers misnamed "Indians"—were immigrants to North America. The American continents were the last of the Earth's major landmasses to be inhabited by humans, initially by peoples from Asia, somewhere between 35,000 and 15,000 years ago.

The first significant European presence in North America began with the voyages of Christopher Columbus and other explorers around the turn of the 16th century. These early expeditions were part of a wider age of exploration in which Europe began projecting its power around the world, with Spain and Portugal in the lead.

National rivalries were a major factor in the settlement of North America. In 1494, Pope Alexander VI divided all newly discovered lands between Spain and Portugal, but the other European powers were not about to be excluded from the New World. Both England and France claimed territory in North America on the basis of exploratory voyages in the 1490s. The Reformation (*see pp 60–61*), which put Protestant England in conflict with Catholic Spain, added a religious dimension to the scramble to establish outposts in North America.

Beyond national and religious rivalries, the lure of mineral wealth drew adventurous Europeans to the New World. Having toppled the indigenous empires of the Aztecs in Mexico and the Incas in Peru, Spanish conquistadores shipped huge quantities of gold and silver back across the Atlantic. Inspired by the hopes of finding yet more treasure, the expeditions of Nuñez Cabeza de Vaca, Hernando de Soto, and Francisco Coronado trekked through the present-day southwest and southeast United States from 1528 to 1542. Reports of "Cities of Gold" proved to be wishful thinking, but these expeditions extended the boundaries of Spain's empire well into North America.

In the 1600s, colonization of North America began in earnest, with the French in Canada and the Mississippi Valley, the Spanish in the southwest, and the English along the Atlantic coast, with a Dutch enclave in the Delaware and Hudson River valleys. The early settlers included fortune-seekers, people fleeing poverty in their homelands, religious refugees, and growing numbers of African slaves (*see pp 32–33*).

In the mid-1700s, Britain defeated France to become the dominant power in North America, but the Revolutionary War (*see pp 36–39*) brought a new nation, the United States of America, into being.

PATTERNS OF SETTLEMENT

Until relatively recently, popular histories tended to frame the story of the nation's settlement in terms of the movement from east to west, with the (mostly) Northern European inhabitants of the Atlantic coast spreading through the interior and finally reaching the Pacific. It is now acknowledged that the reality is more complex, and that the lands that would become the United States were explored, and to a certain extent settled, from south to north and from north to south as much as from east to west. For example, the missionaries, traders, and trappers of French Canada ranged across the West and into the Rocky Mountains many decades before Lewis & Clark's famous 1803–1806 expedition. It is also instructive to remember that Spanish colonists founded Santa Fe, New Mexico, in 1610, a decade before the Pilgrims landed at Plymouth, Massachusetts, while in September 1781—just as the Continental Army prepared to besiege the British forces at Yorktown, Virginia, in the last great battle of the Revolutionary War—44 settlers from Mexico arrived at the site of the present-day city of Los Angeles, California. America's settlement, then, was a multicultural, multidirectional process from the beginning.

COLUMBUS ARRIVES
This colored woodcut is the first visual depiction of Christopher Columbus's arrival in the New World. Published in Florence, Italy, in 1493, it accompanied verses by poet Giuliano Dati that paraphrased the explorer's report to King Ferdinand of Spain.

VOYAGES OF EUROPEAN EXPANSION

The Portuguese found sea-lanes through the Atlantic and Indian oceans to India. Ferdinand Magellan's global circumnavigation revealed a western route through the Strait of Magellan and across the Pacific Ocean. The Spanish, taking a westward route, found the Caribbean islands and the Americas. English and French mariners sought northern passages to Asian markets and their voyages paved the way for the establishment of European settlements in North America.

Voyages of European expansion 1492–1597

→ Viking expeditions	→ English expeditions
→ Spanish expeditions	→ French expeditions
→ Portuguese expeditions	→ Dutch expeditions

AMERIGO VESPUCCI

1451–1512

Like Christopher Columbus, Amerigo Vespucci was born in Italy, but he made his fame and fortune under the Spanish flag (he also worked for Portugal on occasion). As a merchant and official, Vespucci was involved with the business side of Columbus's expeditions, which apparently inspired him to begin explorations of his own. Between 1497 and 1512, he made several voyages to the New World, but just how many are still debated. His accounts of the new lands, however, were widely read, and he was among the first Europeans to grasp that the newly discovered land masses were not parts of Asia but an entirely new world. In 1507, German mapmaker Martin Waldseemuller published a widely reproduced map that labeled the New World "America," from the Latinized form of Vespucci's name, because he believed Vespucci the first European to reach the New World. The name stuck, despite Vespucci's relative obscurity.

AN UNEVEN EXCHANGE

The opening of contact between the Old World and the New World began a process that historian Alfred Crosby dubbed the "Columbian Exchange"—the movement of biological life-forms between the Americas and Europe. From the New World came crops like potatoes, corn, and tobacco, while the Old World sent wheat, sugar, and rice back across the Atlantic. Europeans also brought domestic animals, like cattle, horses, and sheep, whose use would affect the lifeways of indigenous groups. This exchange had a profound impact on the ecosystems of both worlds and on the daily lives of their inhabitants.

But the exchange also brought European diseases that devastated the indigenous peoples of the New World, whose immune systems had no resistance to microbes that caused such contagious diseases as smallpox and measles. Warfare, mistreatment, and enslavement by Europeans took many Native American lives, but disease caused far more deaths. The indigenous population of the Americas probably dropped by two-thirds between roughly 1500 and 1800. Some historians believe that up to 90 percent of the total Native American population perished from European diseases.

Many early settlements tried to maintain good relations with the local people—a pragmatic consideration when the settlers were, at first, a vulnerable minority. Unfortunately, conflict became widespread—and often devastating to both sides—throughout the Colonial era, for a variety of reasons, but especially because of the settlers' seemingly unquenchable hunger for land. Many Native American groups resisted the tide of white settlement, others moved westward to evade it, but that tide eventually proved inexorable.

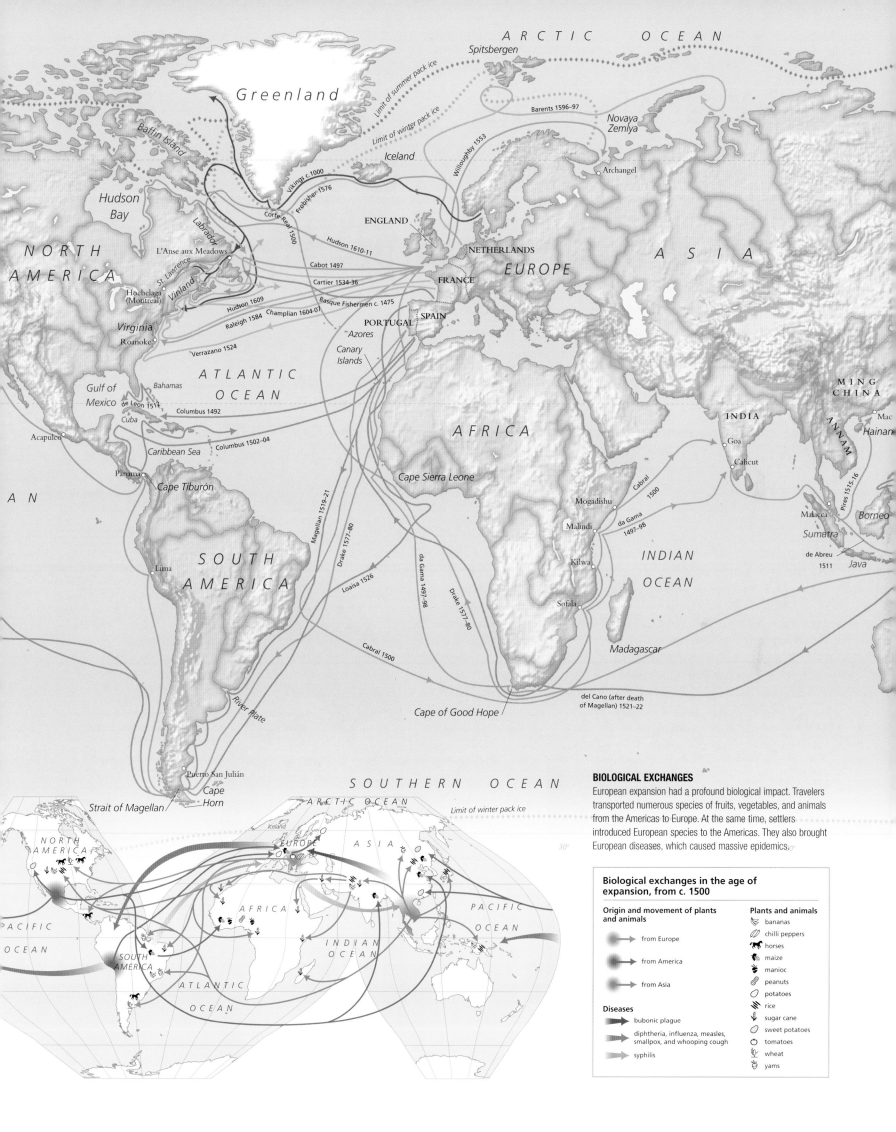

ARCTIC OCEAN

Spitsbergen

Greenland

Limit of summer pack ice

Limit of winter pack ice

Barents 1596–97

Novaya Zemlya

Willoughby 1553

Archangel

Baffin Island

Iceland

Hudson Bay

Vikings c.1000

Frobisher 1576

Corte-Real 1500

Hudson 1610-11

ENGLAND

NORTH AMERICA

Labrador

L'Anse aux Meadows

St. Lawrence

Cabot 1497

NETHERLANDS

EUROPE

ASIA

Cartier 1534-36

FRANCE

Hochelaga (Montreal)

Vinland

Hudson 1609

Basque Fishermen c. 1475

Raleigh 1584

Champlian 1604-07

PORTUGAL

SPAIN

Virginia

Roanoke

Verrazano 1524

Azores

Canary Islands

MING CHINA

Gulf of Mexico

Bahamas

ATLANTIC OCEAN

de Leon 1513

Columbus 1492

Cuba

Acapulco

Caribbean Sea

Columbus 1502–04

INDIA

Goa

Mac

Hainan

AFRICA

Calicut

ANNAM

Panama

Cape Tiburón

Cape Sierra Leone

Cabral 1500

Pires 1515–16

Malacca

Borneo

Magellan 1519–21

Drake 1577–80

Mogadishu

da Gama 1497–98

Sumatra

Malindi

SOUTH AMERICA

Lima

da Gama 1497–98

INDIAN OCEAN

de Abreu 1511

Java

Loaisa 1526

Kilwa

Drake 1577–80

Sofala

Cabral 1500

Madagascar

River Plate

del Cano (after death of Magellan) 1521–22

Cape of Good Hope

Puerto San Julián

Cape Horn

SOUTHERN OCEAN

Strait of Magellan

ARCTIC OCEAN

Limit of winter pack ice

BIOLOGICAL EXCHANGES

European expansion had a profound biological impact. Travelers transported numerous species of fruits, vegetables, and animals from the Americas to Europe. At the same time, settlers introduced European species to the Americas. They also brought European diseases, which caused massive epidemics.

Iceland

NORTH AMERICA

EUROPE

ASIA

PACIFIC OCEAN

AFRICA

PACIFIC OCEAN

SOUTH AMERICA

INDIAN OCEAN

ATLANTIC OCEAN

30°

Biological exchanges in the age of expansion, from c. 1500

Origin and movement of plants and animals

→ from Europe

→ from America

→ from Asia

Diseases

⟹ bubonic plague

⟹ diphtheria, influenza, measles, smallpox, and whooping cough

⟹ syphilis

Plants and animals

🍌 bananas

🌶 chilli peppers

🐎 horses

🌽 maize

🍠 manioc

🥜 peanuts

🥔 potatoes

🌾 rice

sugar cane

🍠 sweet potatoes

🍅 tomatoes

🌾 wheat

yams

The First Americans

Two hundred centuries ago the world was locked in an Ice Age. As ice sheets spread across the northern hemisphere, sea levels dropped, creating a "land bridge" that connected Asia and North America across the 60-mile-wide Bering Strait, which now separates Siberia from Alaska. At some point, bands of hunters—pursuing prey like the now-extinct woolly mammoth—crossed over this land bridge to become the first settlers in what would become the United States of America.

Archaeologists call this land bridge Beringia. The term "land bridge" conjures up images of skin-clad hunters picking their way across a narrow ribbon of dry land, but in fact Beringia extended, at times, about 1,000 miles from north to south.

The question of when the first human beings crossed from Asia to America is fiercely debated. For many years it was widely accepted that the earliest evidence of human habitation in North America were arrowheads embedded in mammoth bones found near Clovis, New Mexico, which date to about 11,000 years ago. In the 1970s, however, excavations at the Meadowcroft Rockshelter in western Pennsylvania seemed to show a human presence as far back as 16,000 or 17,000 years ago. Recent finds at Monte Verde in Chile and other sites in North and South America have only heightened the debate.

So has the discovery of Kennewick Man, a 9,000-year-old, nearly complete human skeleton found in Washington in 1996. Scientists believe that Kennewick Man's remains indicate Caucasoid racial origin (from Europe, West Asia, or North Africa) rather than Mongoloid (from Northeast Asia), raising the possibility that prehistoric peoples from several parts of the world may have reached the Americas. Kennewick Man supports a growing consensus among archaeologists that the peopling of the Americas was a more complex process than previously thought.

How these Paleoindians, as archaeologists named them, spread across the Americas, and how long it took them to do so, is also open to debate. During the early migration period, much of North America was covered by two vast ice sheets—the Laurentian and Cordilleran—with a narrow corridor between them. Some archaeologists believe Paleoindian bands migrated through this corridor; others believe the corridor was impassable and that the Paleoindians first moved south along the ice-free west coast of North America, and then eastward into the interior of North America and southward into Central and South America. Recently, archaeologists have conjectured that Paleoindians made their way south not only on land, but also by boat along the Pacific Coast. Not until the ice sheets receded, however, were Paleoindians able to settle the northern reaches of North America.

By 1500—when the contact period between Europe and the Americas began—the descendants of the Paleoindians lived everywhere from the Canadian Arctic to the tip of South America. These Native

KENNEWICK MAN
This model *(left)* is an artist's reconstruction of the Kennewick Man, based on the shape of his skull *(above)*. The discovery led to a conflict between Native American groups, who claimed the remains for burial, and scientists who wanted to keep them for study.

CLOVIS POINTS
Paleoindians of the Clovis Culture lived in present-day Arizona, New Mexico, and Texas. They used spear points like the ones shown here to hunt big game, including the woolly mammoth. These so-called "Clovis points" were made of flint, jasper, or chalcedony.

MEADOWCROFT ROCKSHELTER
Excavated between 1973 and 1978, Pennsylvania's Meadowcroft Rockshelter yielded more than 2,000 stone tools and the remains of about 1,000 animals. While its exact age remains a source of controversy, it may be the oldest human habitation in North America.

Beringia: Humans cross into the Americas, across the Bering land bridge created by lower sea levels during the last Ice Age, by 15,000 BCE

Old Crow
Bluefish Cave
Beringia
Dry Creek
Mackenzie
Cordilleran Ice Sheet
Ice corridor opened from 11,300 BCE
NORTH AMERICA
Columbia River
Kennewick
Lake Missoula
Chipp
Wilson Butte Cave
Lake Lahontan
Lake Bonneville
Missouri
Shrive
Lamb Spring
Mesa Verde
Kimmswoci
Calico Hills
Clovis
San Diego
Early human settlers hunt North American megafauna (mastodons, mammoths and many other species) as climate changes make such animals ex
Rio Grande
Gulf of Mexico
Appalac
Valsequillo
Central America
El Bosque
Caribbe
PACIFIC OCEAN
El Inga
Andes
Guitarrero Cave
Pikimachay

The first American settlers

➤	possible colonization route
◆	major site 100,000–12,000 BCE
	extent of ice sheet 18,000 BCE
	extent of ice sheet 10,000 BCE
	coastline 18,000 BCE
	ancient river
	ancient lake

THE FIRST AMERICAN SETTLERS
The first human settlers crossed the Bering land bridge about 25,000 years ago, but progress south may have been blocked by ice sheets. The melting of the ice over the next millennia isolated settlers from Asia, as Beringia was flooded by seawater, but land passages opened for travel south.

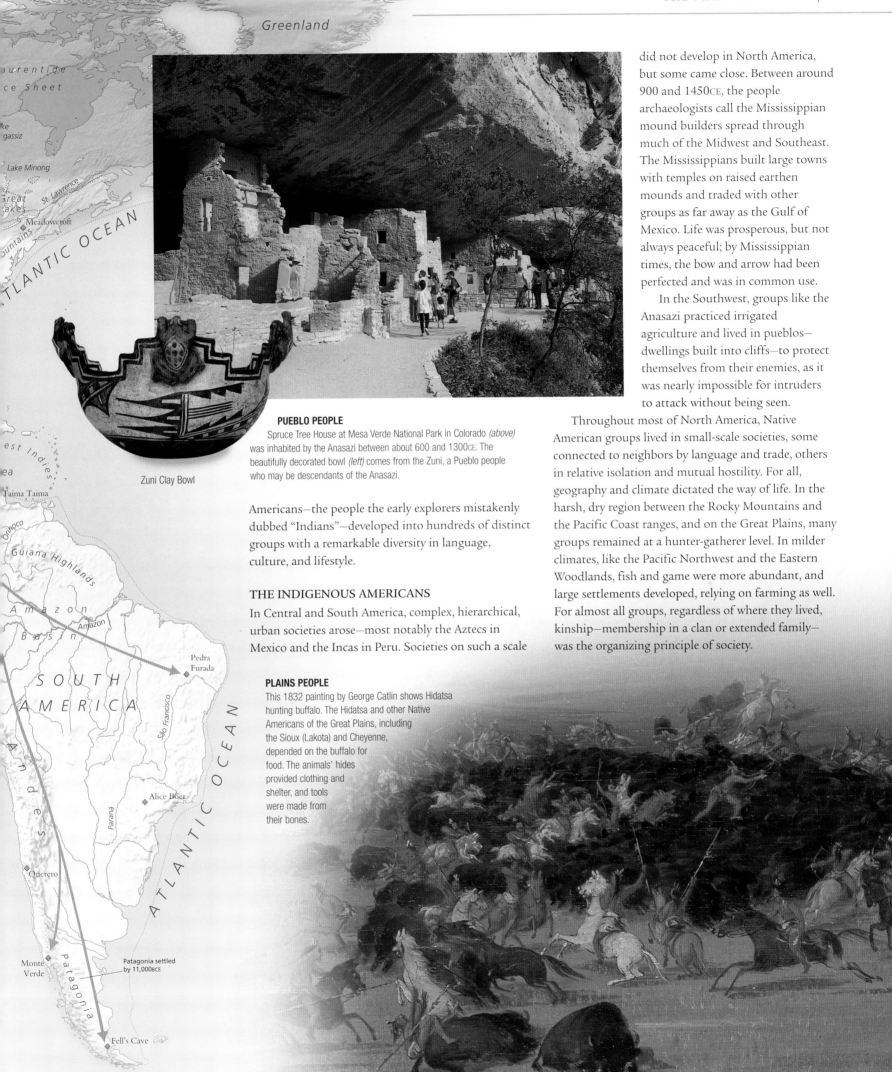

did not develop in North America, but some came close. Between around 900 and 1450CE, the people archaeologists call the Mississippian mound builders spread through much of the Midwest and Southeast. The Mississippians built large towns with temples on raised earthen mounds and traded with other groups as far away as the Gulf of Mexico. Life was prosperous, but not always peaceful; by Mississippian times, the bow and arrow had been perfected and was in common use.

In the Southwest, groups like the Anasazi practiced irrigated agriculture and lived in pueblos—dwellings built into cliffs—to protect themselves from their enemies, as it was nearly impossible for intruders to attack without being seen.

Throughout most of North America, Native American groups lived in small-scale societies, some connected to neighbors by language and trade, others in relative isolation and mutual hostility. For all, geography and climate dictated the way of life. In the harsh, dry region between the Rocky Mountains and the Pacific Coast ranges, and on the Great Plains, many groups remained at a hunter-gatherer level. In milder climates, like the Pacific Northwest and the Eastern Woodlands, fish and game were more abundant, and large settlements developed, relying on farming as well. For almost all groups, regardless of where they lived, kinship—membership in a clan or extended family—was the organizing principle of society.

PUEBLO PEOPLE
Spruce Tree House at Mesa Verde National Park in Colorado *(above)* was inhabited by the Anasazi between about 600 and 1300CE. The beautifully decorated bowl *(left)* comes from the Zuni, a Pueblo people who may be descendants of the Anasazi.

Zuni Clay Bowl

Americans—the people the early explorers mistakenly dubbed "Indians"—developed into hundreds of distinct groups with a remarkable diversity in language, culture, and lifestyle.

THE INDIGENOUS AMERICANS

In Central and South America, complex, hierarchical, urban societies arose—most notably the Aztecs in Mexico and the Incas in Peru. Societies on such a scale

PLAINS PEOPLE
This 1832 painting by George Catlin shows Hidatsa hunting buffalo. The Hidatsa and other Native Americans of the Great Plains, including the Sioux (Lakota) and Cheyenne, depended on the buffalo for food. The animals' hides provided clothing and shelter, and tools were made from their bones.

WHO CAME FIRST?

For hundreds of years people have argued over just who "discovered" America. In the Middle Ages it was widely believed throughout Europe that an Irish priest, St. Brendan the Navigator, had sailed to a new land far to the west. A 15th-century Welsh poem celebrated the exploits of Prince Madog ab Owain Gwynedd, who was said to have led 10 shiploads of his countrymen across the Atlantic. Today, some contend that the ancient Phoenicians or Egyptians reached North America thousands of years ago. In his 2003 book, *1421: The Year the Chinese Discovered America*, Gavin Menzies argues that America was discovered from the opposite direction—by Chinese sailing across the Pacific. The evidence for all these claims, however, is slim.

Bone Scraper

Fishing Basket

HUNTING AND FISHING TOOLS

Early North Americans used the bone scraper *(top)* to remove flesh from animal skins, like buffalo. The finely woven basket is a fish trap used to catch fish like salmon.

It is now accepted that the Vikings, who had already colonized Iceland and Greenland, reached North America's east coast around 1000CE, when Leif Eriksson journeyed to a land he named Vinland—though Vinland's location has never been definitively established. Until recently, the main evidence for the Viking presence in North America was found in the chronicles known as the *Icelandic Sagas,* written mainly in the 13th and 14th centuries, which include accounts of the explorations of Leif Eriksson and other Viking voyagers. When the *Sagas* were finally translated into English in the mid-19th century, their publication sparked speculation among American scholars that the Vikings might have beat Christopher Columbus to the New World by roughly 500 years. So did the discovery of various Viking relics that were found as far west as Minnesota, although these have largely been discredited by archaeologists.

In 1960, a Norwegian archaeological team found definite evidence of a Viking settlement from about the time of Eriksson's voyage at L'Anse Aux Meadows in Labrador, Canada—the first European outpost in the Americas. Finally, some historians believe that Basque fishermen plied the waters off Newfoundland well before 1492, sometimes going ashore to dry their catches of cod—but they did not report their activities in order to keep the rich fishing grounds for themselves.

CORN

Over the course of several thousands of years, the first settlers of the Americas began to grow food crops to supplement their hunting and gathering. One of the staple foods for many groups was corn (*Zea mays*), the cultivated form of a wild grass, called teosinte, which grew in southern Mexico and Central America. Archaeologists believe corn cultivation began in Mexico around 7,000 years ago; it reached North America perhaps 5,000 years later. Corn transformed the lives of many Native Americans by providing a reliable food supply that could be dried for use in the winter—something that encouraged many migratory groups to establish permanent settlements.

Zea mays

CANADIAN CANOE BUILDERS

An 1863 photograph *(below)* depicts Montagnais in Quebec building a birch-bark canoe, which was slim and portable. In the opinion of some historians, Montagnais bands in Labrador may have encountered Viking explorers—which would make them the first Native Americans to come in contact with Europeans.

THE VIKINGS

North America's first European settlers came from what are now Denmark, Norway, and Sweden around the 9th century CE. The Norse, or Vikings (the latter comes from a Scandinavian word for "pirate"), terrorized Europe for more than two centuries in seaborne quests for plunder. Organized into small bands under chieftains, Viking raiders took to the sea because of a lack of arable land at home. The Vikings' success was due in large part to their superior maritime technology: their chief vessel, the longship (which reached 115 feet in length), was powered by both oars and sails and could navigate the open sea or travel up inland rivers.

RAIDING AND TRADING

The Vikings were settlers and traders as well as raiders. With a presence in the Byzantine Empire and control over much of Britain and Ireland, the Vikings sailed across the Atlantic, settling in Iceland in the late 9th century, and in Greenland about a century later.

Around 980, Bjarni Herjulfsson sighted land to the west of Greenland. Twenty years later, Leif Eriksson, son of Erik the Red, the discoverer of Greenland, set out to find that land. Eriksson and his crew confirmed Herjulfsson's discovery, sailed south, and wintered over at the mouth of a river. Returning to Greenland, Eriksson described the region as having a mild climate in which grapes grew, so the Vikings named it Vinland. Historians are unsure of Vinland's exact location; it may have been as far south as modern-day Cape Cod.

VIKINGS IN VINLAND

Leif Eriksson inspired several attempts to establish outposts in Vinland over the next two decades. Leif's brother Thorvald landed somewhere on the North American coast, where he and his crew fought with native inhabitants they called "Skraelings." Sometime between 1010 and 1015, an Icelander, Thorfinn Karlsefni, arrived with more than 150 settlers, including Leif's half-sister, Freydis. The settlers traded cloth for furs with the Skraelings, but after relations between the two groups turned hostile, the Vikings sailed for Greenland. Among them was Snorri, the young son of Karlsefni and his wife Gudrid—the European child born in the Americas.

OSBERG SHIP
Discovered in 1904, this remarkably well-preserved Viking longship is now housed in a museum in Oslo, Norway. Around seventy feet long and built of oak planks, it dates from the early 9th century CE.

VIKING WEAPONS
The Viking arsenal included spears, six to ten feet long and tipped with iron points like the one at left. Swords, like those at right, were forged of both iron and crude steel and were about three feet long.

L'ANSE AUX MEADOWS
Based on Icelandic shelters, these reproductions of Viking huts are built of sod over a wooden frame. The original settlement may date from Leif Eriksson's voyage, or from the later expedition led by Thorfinn Karlsefni.

Spanish Settlers

Thanks to Christopher Columbus's 1492 voyage, Spain was the first European power to gain a foothold in the Americas. Motivated by the desire to win souls for Christianity (by force if necessary) and by lust for gold and glory, Spanish conquistadores toppled native empires in Central and South America and made the first forays into what would become the United States.

In the beginning, it was about spices—a necessary luxury on European tables in the 15th century, when, in one historian's words, "even in the rich houses, the meals came putrid to the table." Pepper, cloves, nutmeg, and other spices came from the so-called Spice Islands (modern-day Indonesia) through Arab and Venetian middlemen. This galled the rising maritime nations of Portugal and Spain. A ruthlessly ambitious, Italian-born sea captain, Christopher Columbus, assured King Ferdinand and Queen Isabella of Spain that there was a shortcut to the riches of Asia—by sailing westward across the Atlantic Ocean.

The Spanish monarchy bankrolled a three-ship expedition, which left Palos, Spain, on August 3, 1492. On October 12, a lookout sighted land—probably modern-day Watling Island in the Bahamas. By January 1496 Columbus was back in Spain, convinced he had reached China or, at least, Japan. He ventured across the Atlantic three more times before his death in 1506, and he died believing he had found a sea route to Asia. Other expeditions soon proved that he had instead reached a vast unknown land.

THE SPANISH SPREAD OUT

The Caribbean served as the springboard for Spanish exploration and settlement of the mainland. In 1512, Juan Ponce de León sailed from Puerto Rico to Florida, although he thought the peninsula was an island. The Spanish returned to Florida in 1528 when a party led by Pánfilo de Narváez landed at Tampa Bay. Under constant attack from the local Native Americans, the expedition built boats and tried to reach Mexico. Almost all perished.

SPANIARDS IN THE SOUTHWEST
Frederick Remington painted this 1898 depiction of the Coronado expedition on the march. The Grand Canyon in present-day Arizona was among the natural wonders encountered by Coronado and his company.

COMMEMORATING COLUMBUS
Modern replicas of Columbus's three vessels—the *Nina*, *Pinta*, and the *Santa Maria*—were built by the Spanish government and sailed along the Florida coast in 1992 to mark the 500th anniversary of the explorer's first voyage to the New World. Columbus's flagship, the *Santa Maria*, was 87 feet in length, the *Nina* was 74 feet, and the *Pinta* was 70 feet—and the fastest.

The surviviors, led by Nuñez Cabeza de Vaca, came ashore near Galveston, Texas, beginning an odyssey that ended six years later when Cabeza de Vaca and three other survivors reached a Spanish outpost in northern Mexico.

Cabeza de Vaca reported that the Native Americans he had encountered spoke of Cibola—seven magnificent "cities of gold"—a tale that inspired two further expeditions that filled in much of the map of the southern North American continent. The first began in 1539, when Hernando de Soto's expedition got as far west as Oklahoma and as far north as Tennessee. Most importantly, he discovered the Mississippi River in 1541. The second expedition was in 1540, when Francisco Vázquez de Coronado led 300 Spaniards north from Mexico in search of Cibola and its mythical gold. One of Coronado's scouting parties sighted the Grand Canyon, and the expedition got as far north as Kansas before turning back to Mexico.

FROM CONQUEST TO COLONIES

Spain's first attempt at establishing a permanent settlement in Florida ended in disaster. In 1559, Tristán de Luna landed at Pensacola with about 1,500 men, but two years later the colony—ravaged by disease, hurricanes, and fighting with the Native Americans—was abandoned. But in 1565, Admiral Pedro Menéndez de Avilés founded St. Augustine at the mouth of Florida's St. John's River. Established as a military outpost guarding Spanish shipping in the Gulf of Mexico, St. Augustine is today the oldest continuously inhabited community of European origin in the United States.

The defeat of the Spanish Armada in 1588 and competition from other European powers halted Spain's colonizing efforts in eastern North America, but the Spanish continued to expand north from Mexico into Texas and the southwest. In 1598, Juan de Oñate founded the first settlements in New Mexico, including a regional capital at Santa Fe in 1610. He served as the first Governor-General of New Mexico.

In 1767, the Spanish emperor's expulsion of the Jesuits from Spain's colonies led the government to ask the Franciscan Order to replace them as missionaries in Baja (lower) California. A Franciscan monk, Junipero Serra, was appointed head of these missions, and in 1769, he founded a mission at San Diego, California, the first settlement in what would become America's most populous state.

HERNANDO DE SOTO
Born in Barajas, Spain, around 1496, Hernando de Soto did not survive the expedition he began. He died of fever in May 1542, along the Mississippi River.

SPANISH FORT
Fort Matanzas is a military outpost constructed by the Spanish in the 17th and 18th centuries to protect ships approaching St. Augustine. The fort was built using *coquina*—a type of limestone composed of fossilized shellfish.

ESTAVANICO
c.1503–1539

One survivor of the Narváez expedition was an African known by his Spanish name, Estavanico. Estavanico was sold into slavery and became a servant of Andrés de Dorantes, an officer with whom he endured years of Native American captivity and grueling travel trying to reach Spanish territory. Estavanico proved invaluable to their survival—he could quickly learn languages, and the Native Americans admired his ability to heal the sick. In 1539, Estavanico was sent with a priest to search for Cibola. He reached a pueblo of the Zuni people in New Mexico, where he was killed.

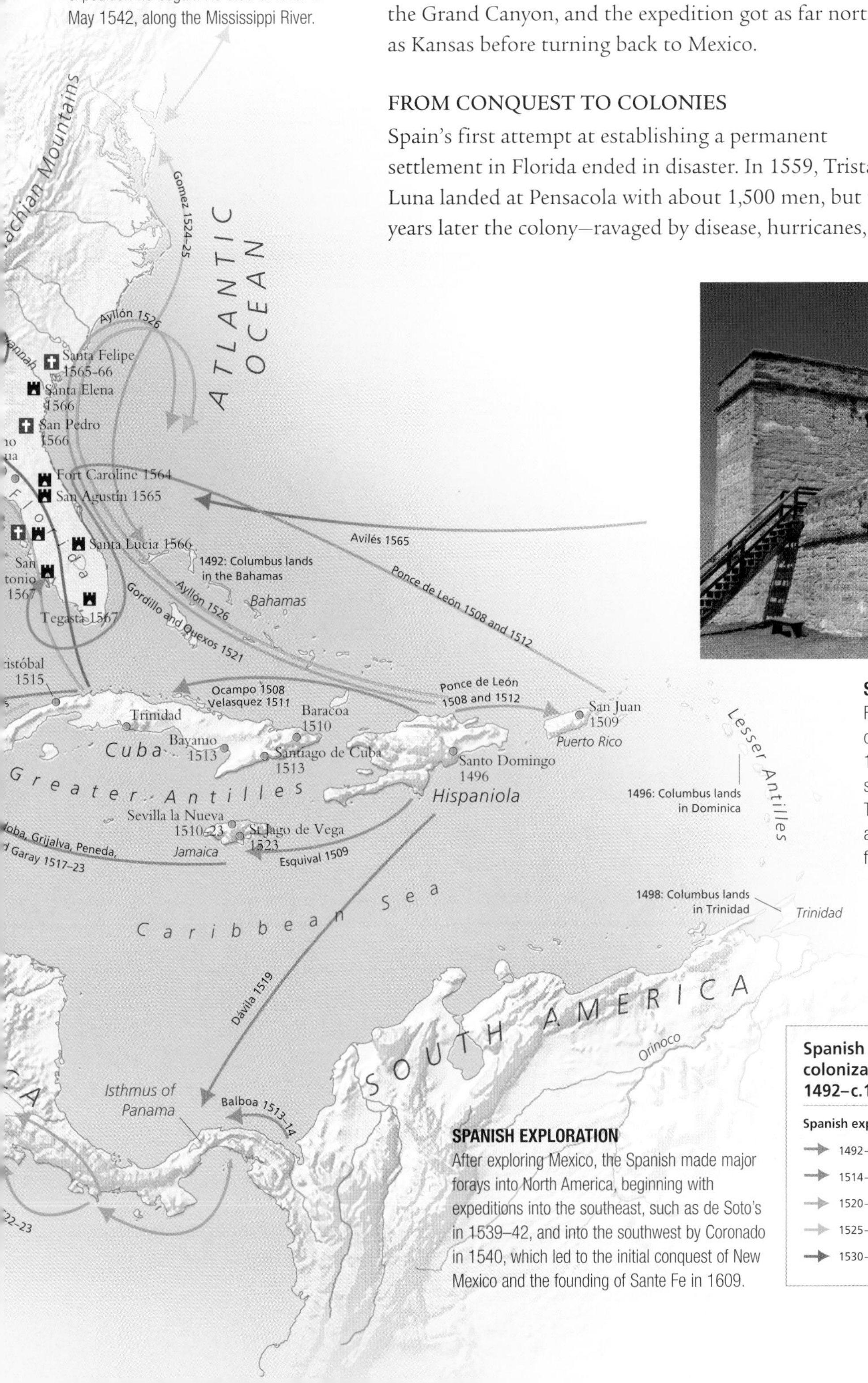

SPANISH EXPLORATION
After exploring Mexico, the Spanish made major forays into North America, beginning with expeditions into the southeast, such as de Soto's in 1539–42, and into the southwest by Coronado in 1540, which led to the initial conquest of New Mexico and the founding of Sante Fe in 1609.

Spanish exploration and colonization in the New World 1492–c.1600

Spanish expansion	Spanish settlement
1492–1514	● Spanish town
1514–20	⊞ fort
1520–25	✠ Jesuit mission
1525–30	silver mine
1530–1600	1632 date of foundation

Map labels: Appalachian Mountains, Gomez 1524–25, ATLANTIC OCEAN, Ayllón 1526, Santa Felipe 1565–66, Santa Elena 1566, San Pedro 1566, Fort Caroline 1564, San Agustin 1565, Santa Lucia 1566, 1492: Columbus lands in the Bahamas, Avilés 1565, Ayllón 1526, Gordillo and Quexos 1521, Bahamas, Ponce de León 1508 and 1512, Tegasta 1567, San antonio 1567, Cristóbal 1515, Ocampo 1508, Velasquez 1511, Trinidad, Bayano 1513, Baracoa 1510, Santiago de Cuba 1513, Cuba, Greater Antilles, Sevilla la Nueva 1510–23, St Jago de Vega 1523, Jamaica, Esquival 1509, Santo Domingo 1496, Hispaniola, Ponce de León 1508 and 1512, San Juan 1509, Puerto Rico, 1496: Columbus lands in Dominica, Lesser Antilles, Garay 1517–23, Grijalva, Peneda, Dávila 1519, Caribbean Sea, 1498: Columbus lands in Trinidad, Trinidad, Isthmus of Panama, Balboa 1513–14, SOUTH AMERICA, Orinoco

French Settlers

France had more success than Spain in establishing a network of permanent settlements in eastern North America. With the St. Lawrence River serving as a gateway, and the lakes and rivers of the continent's interior providing highways for trade and settlement, New France extended from the Canadian Arctic to the Gulf of Mexico, comprising much of the modern-day southeast and midwest states.

The idea of reaching Asia by sailing westward persisted after Columbus; however, the focus shifted to finding a navigable passage through the "New World" to the riches of the East. In 1524, King Charles I of France dispatched an Italian captain, Giovanni da Verrazano, to find such a passage. Verrazano sailed up the east coast from the Carolinas to Newfoundland, discovering New York Harbor along the way. He failed to find the "Northwest Passage," but the voyage gave France a claim in North America.

A decade later, Jacques Cartier sailed up the St. Lawrence River and returned to France with two Native Americans. They told tales of Saguenay, an inland city rich with gold and precious stones. Like Cibola in the Spanish southwest, Saguenay didn't exist, but as Cibola had with the Spanish, the tales prompted France to send out more expeditions.

In 1535, Cartier sailed up the St. Lawrence again, this time as far as Montreal. After enduring a miserable winter at Quebec, the surviors returned to France empty-handed. Cartier made one more fruitless voyage up the St. Lawrence in 1541.

The newly discovered land lacked gold, but it teemed with another valuable commodity—animal furs, especially beaver pelts, which the Native Americans eagerly traded for metal tools and other European goods. By the end of the 16th century, there were French trading posts along the St. Lawrence, and, in 1604, the French established a settlement they called Acadia on the shores of the Bay of Fundy.

In 1608, the mariner Samuel de Champlain sailed from France with 32 settlers and founded what would become the city of Quebec. Champlain also explored the surrounding area and helped France's Indian allies, especially the Hurons, in their long-standing conflict with the Iroquois to the south. Quebec struggled in its early years, and for a time was captured by the English, but the colony finally prospered, with French farmers cultivating land along the St. Lawrence and fur traders ranging through much of the interior.

LASALLE AND LOUISIANA

In 1677, René-Robert Cavelier, *Sieur* (Lord) de La Salle won King Louis XIV's permission to extend New France far to the south. La Salle and a small party journeyed down the Mississippi River to the Gulf of Mexico, claiming the land on both sides for France and naming it Louisiana in honor of the king. In 1702, Jean-Baptiste Le Moyne de Bienville arrived with orders to establish permanent settlements in the region. Sixteen years later, Bienville founded New Orleans; by 1730 the city had 8,000 inhabitants.

CASSETTE GIRLS

French colonial authorities believed that family life was critical in maintaining stable permanent settlements. With single men forming the majority of colonists in the early years of New France, the French government actively recruited young unmarried women for the colonies to provide the settlers with wives. In 1663, for example, the first of more than 700 female orphans, *Les Filles de Roi* (Daughters of the King), arrived in Montreal. The French also deported a shipload of prostitutes to Louisiana in 1721. A few years later, the French took a different tack by arranging passage for hundreds of *Filles de Cassette* (Cassette Girls—so-called because they brought their possessions in a small trunk) to New Orleans and Mobile. The *Filles de Cassette* were young women "of good character," and they were chaperoned by nuns of the city's Ursuline convent.

LA SALLE
La Salle followed up his successful voyage down the Mississippi with an attempt to plant a French colony at the river's mouth. It proved a failure, and La Salle was killed by his own men in 1687.

THE FUR TRADE
The administrators of New France were careful to maintain good relations with the Native Americans, both to preserve the lucrative fur trade and to build alliances against the English colonies to the south.

Map labels (partial):

James Bay

peg

rt Maurepos
34

Fort St. Charles
1732

Fort St. Pierre
1731

Fort Kaministikwia

Fort Michipicton
1730

Lake Superior

St. Esprit
1665

Chouart and Radisson 1659–1660

Sault Ste. Marie
1668

Allouez 1665–67

St. Ignace 1672

PAYS D'EN HAUT

Fort St. Croix
1680

Michilimackinac
1697

Fort La Baye
1718

Joliet and Marquette 1672–73

Lake Huron

Fort Rouille (Toronto)
1749

d'Huillier
1700

Lake Michigan

Fort Pontchartrain
(Detroit)
1701

Fort Presqu'Isle

Fort Beauharnais
1727

Lake Erie

Fort St. Joseph
1680

Hennepin 1680

Fort Crèvecoeur
1680

Fort St. Louis
1682

Fort Duquesne
1754

Fort Orléans
1718

Fort Vincennes
1732

Fort Miami
1704

de Léry 1729

Missouri River

Cahokia 1698

Kaskaskia 1703

Ohio River

The Illinois Post 1700

Fort Massac 1758

Fort Chartres 1718

St. Genevieve 1732

Missouri River

Fort Arkansas 1686

de La Salle 1684–87

Fort Prudhomme
(Memphis) 1682

Fort Tambeché
1736

Natchitoches
1714

Fort Rosalie
1716

Fort Toulouse
1736

Fort Condé
(Mobile) 1710

Batton Rouge 1720

Maurepos (Biloxi)
1699

New Orleans
1718

Florida

Gulf of Mexico

Yucatan Peninsula

LOUISIANA

INDIAN TERRITORY

Appalachian Mountains

Tadoussac
1600

Albanel 1671–72

Acadia

Gulf of St. Lawrence

Cape Breton Island

Quebec
1608

Trois Rivières
1634

Montreal 1642

NEW FRANCE

St. Lawrence River

La Chine

Lake Champlain

Montreal
1689

Champlain 1609–16

Fort Orange 1624
(Albany 1664)

Fort Niagara
1679

Lake Ontario

Fort Le Boeuf
1679

Boston

Newport

New York

Philadelphia

Richmond

Jamestown

Charleston

Halifax
1749

NOVA SCOTIA

Champlain

Bay of Fundy

Verrazano 1524

ATLANTIC OCEAN

Ottawa River

Cartier

CARTIER

Born in St. Malo, Brittany, in 1491, Jacques Cartier gave Canada its name when he used an Iroquois Native American name for village, *kanata*, to describe the area surrounding the French settlement at Stadacona (now Quebec).

CHAMPLAIN

Prior to the 1608 expedition that established Quebec, Samuel de Champlain explored and mapped much of the northeast coast of North America, from the St. Lawrence River southward to Martha's Vineyard in present-day Massachusetts.

The French also established outposts in the "Illinois Country" south of the Great Lakes, while hardy *voyageurs* (canoeists) and *coreurs de bois* (forest runners) traveled as far west as the Rocky Mountains in their search for furs.

THE LEGACY OF NEW FRANCE

Despite the lure of the fur trade and generous land grants to colonists, the French government had little success in luring permanent settlers to New France. Still, the missionaries, trappers, and traders of New France explored much of what would become the United States, and this legacy survives in place names from Terre Haute, Indiana, to Baton Rouge, Louisiana. New France also lives on in the heritage of many Americans; in the 2000 census, more than 2.3 million Americans claimed French-Canadian ancestry.

VOYAGEURS

The *voyageurs* used canoes like the one shown in this painting to transport trade goods along New France's vast network of rivers and lakes. An 18th-century Jesuit missionary wrote that the *voyageurs* "are not scared to paddle five or six hundred leagues [up to 2,000 miles] in a canoe, live for a year or 18 months on corn and bear fat and sleep under shelters made of roots or branches."

VERRAZANO

Giovanni da Verrazano's 1524 voyage is commemorated by the Verrazano Bridge, which links the New York City boroughs of Brooklyn and Staten Island.

FRENCH EXPLORATION

By the mid-16th century, French expeditions traced the Atlantic coast in detail and then moved north in search of new routes to Asia. Champlain, aided by Iroquois and Montagnais, explored the St. Lawrence River and the Great Lakes from 1609 to 1616.

French exploration and colonization of North America

French expansion

- → 1500–1600
- → 1600–1650
- → 1650–1675
- → 1675–1700
- → 1700–1750

○ French settlement
○ Non-French Settlement

1632 date of foundation

THE LOST COLONY

England was a small, poor nation compared to France and Spain when the great age of exploration began around 1500. Although England would prove the most successful of all the European powers in establishing colonies in North America, its first efforts met with failure, capped by the disappearance of an entire colony.

EARLY ENGLISH VENTURES

When news of Columbus's discoveries reached England, King Henry VII commissioned mariner John Cabot of Bristol (born Giovanni Caboto in Italy) to sail westward. In 1497, Cabot's ship, the *Matthew*, made landfall in North America. The exact location is not known, but it was probably on Newfoundland or the Labrador coast. Cabot returned to England convinced, like Columbus, that he had reached Asia.

Eighty years later, Queen Elizabeth I granted soldier Sir Humphrey Gilbert a patent to colonize "remote heathen and barbarous lands"; the patent

THE BAPTISM OF VIRGINIA DARE
Born to Elinor White Dare, the daughter of John White, and her husband Ananias Dare, Virginia was the first child of English parentage born in what would become the United States.

MODERN *MATTHEW*
In 1997, a replica of John Cabot's ship *Matthew* sailed from Bristol, England, to Newfoundland, Canada, to mark the 500th anniversary of the original voyage. Very little is known about Cabot, but his 1497 voyage had profound consequences for the settling of North America.

JOHN WHITE, GOVERNOR AND PAINTER
White's 1585 painting of Native Americans "sitting at meat," as captioned by Thomas Hariot in *A Briefe and True Report,* is just one of his numerous watercolors depicting native life.

stipulated that colonists "shall enjoy all the privileges of . . . persons native to England" and be governed according to English law. In 1583, Gilbert sailed with seven ships. After reaching Newfoundland, the fleet sailed south, but a storm sank Gilbert's vessel and the expedition was abandoned.

SIR WALTER RALEIGH'S SCHEME

With Gilbert's death, his half-brother, Sir Walter Raleigh—soldier, courtier, poet, and businessman, as well as explorer and colonizer—inherited his patent. In 1584 Raleigh sent a scouting expediton that landed at Roanoke Island, in Albermarle Sound off the coast of North Carolina. The Englishmen named the land Virginia in honor of Elizabeth, England's "Virgin Queen."

A year later, 108 men under the command of Richard Grenville and Ralph Lane arrived at Roanoke. The settlers spent most of their time looking for gold and became dependent on the increasingly resentful local Native Americans for food. When Sir Francis Drake stopped at Roanoke on the return leg of his voyage around the world in 1586, the settlers caught a ride back to England. Among this party was John White, a noted explorer and talented artist. He made numerous watercolor paintings of the local Native Americans, animals, and plant life, many of which were published in Thomas Hariot's book *A Briefe and True Report of the New Found Land of Virginia.*

In May 1587, Raleigh tried again, sending out a party of 89 men, 7 women, and 11 children, with John White as governor. The colony ran into trouble immediately. The Native Americans, embittered by their experience with the earlier settlers, were mostly hostile and refused to provide food. Supplies ran low. In August, White sailed back to England to organize support for the settlement.

THE LOST COLONY

Unfortunately for the Roanoke colonists, England was now preocuupied by its conflict with Spain. It took White three years to mount a relief expedition, and when he landed at Roanoke, in August 1590, he found the settlement ransacked and the settlers—who

THE FIRST FORT
The members of 1585 expedition to Roanoke Island built an "earthen fort" for protection. This modern reproduction—part of the Fort Raleigh National Historic Site—was constructed in 1950 after extensive archaeological research.

VANISHED SETTLERS
This 19th-century print depicts John White returning to find that the colonists have vanished. In a 1593 letter to historian Richard Hakluyt, White appealed "to the merciful help of the Almighty" for "the relief of my discomfortable company of planters in Virginia."

included White's daughter and granddaughter—gone. The only clues to their fate were the letters "CRO" carved on a tree and the word "CROATOAN" carved into a doorpost. Croatoan was the name of an island about a hundred miles south of Roanoke; the settlers may have tried to flee there in the hope of finding refuge with a friendly Native American tribe. Stormy weather prevented White's ship from reaching Croatoan. He sailed back to England, leaving behind one of history's most tantalizing mysteries. No creditable trace of the settlers has ever been found. It is most likely that starvation and Native American attacks killed them all, although some believe a few survivors may have been kidnapped by, or found refuge with, local Native American tribes.

After his unsuccessful relief expedition, White retired to Ireland, where he died in 1593. Today, White's artwork is an invaluable record of North America at the dawn of European settlement.

English Settlers

England established its earliest successful North American colonies in the first three decades of the 17th century. In Virginia, a plantation society emerged, underpinned by the labor of indentured servants (*see pp 138–139*) and slaves imported from Africa. To the north, in what soon became known as New England, Puritans from Old England made their vision of a righteous society in the wilderness a reality.

In April 1606, newly-crowned King James I of England granted a charter to the Virginia Company of London, giving the company the right to colonize Virginia—defined as all the land in North America between, roughly, South Carolina and Connecticut. This was a new kind of colonial enterprise: a joint-stock company, charged with making a profit for its shareholders, rather than a monopoly by a government, royalty, or individual.

In 1607, the company landed 104 men and boys at the mouth of the James River (both the river and the settlement they built on its banks were named for the king). In one historian's words, the settlers "represented a cross-section of contemporary English life," from adventurous young aristocrats to poor laborers from the countryside and the streets of London.

For years, Jamestown teetered on the brink of disaster. Disease claimed many lives; hunger claimed even more. Only the timely arrival of a relief fleet in 1610 saved the colony from abandonment. Tobacco cultivation, which would eventually put the colony on a sound economic footing, began in 1612.

The year 1619 saw several important "firsts" for the colony: the first women colonists arrived; a House of Burgesses—the first democratically elected assembly in North America—was established; and the first documented African slaves were imported into the colony (*see pp 32–33*). Jamestown endured a devastating Indian attack in 1622, however, and a settlers' rebellion in 1676. But by the time Williamsburg replaced Jamestown as Virginia's capital in 1699, the colony was prospering.

THE "NOXIOUS WEED"

Native Americans throughout the New World had used tobacco for thousands of years before the arrival of the first Europeans; one of the first references to it came from an English sea captain who visited the French Huguenot settlement in Florida (*see pp 62–63*) and described how the Native Americans "have a kind of herb dried [which they] do suck the smoke thereof, which smoke satisfieth their hunger." Native tobacco was generally too harsh for the European palate, but in 1612, John Rolfe of Jamestown began growing a smoother hybrid version imported from the Caribbean, and when samples reached England, it was an immediate hit. King James I himself opposed the habit, writing a pamphlet, *A Counterblaste to Tobacco*, in which he inveighed against the "black stinking fume," but even the King was powerless to halt his subjects' growing addiction to the "noxious weed." The importance of tobacco exports to the success of the early English colonies in the South cannot be underestimated. By the 18th century, tobacco—known as "country money"—was even used as currency in the Tidewater region.

Tobacco label

FREEDOM FOR WOMEN
Pocahontas

Her real name was Matoaka; "Pocahontas"—which means "playful girl" in the Algonquian language—was a nickname given to her by her father, Powhatan, leader of Virginia's Native Americans. In 1608, when Pocahontas was about 13 years old, Powhatan's warriors captured Captain John Smith, leader of the colony at Jamestown. Powhatan ordered Smith killed, but Pocahontas begged her father to spare the Englishman's life.

The only account of this famous episode comes from Smith's own writings, so we do not know if this is really how it happened.

What is certain is that from then on, the young woman's life was linked to the Jamestown settlement, and vice versa. Pocahontas brought much-needed gifts of food to the settlers, and her friendship with the Englishmen kept the peace with Powhatan. Smith wrote that she was "the instrument to preserve this colony from death, famine, and utter confusion." After Smith returned to England, relations between the settlers and the Native Americans soured. Pocahontas became a pawn in that conflict in 1613, when Captain Samuel Argall kidnapped her in a bid to force concessions from Powhatan. By the time her father ransomed her, Pocahontas had fallen in love with settler John Rolfe. The couple married in 1614, with Powhatan's blessing.

In 1616, Pocahontas (now known as Lady Rebecca), Rolfe, and their baby son Thomas traveled to England, where Pocahontas was an immediate sensation both at court and with the public. In the somewhat patronizing words of one contemporary observer, Pocahontas "not only accustom[ed] herself to civility, but still carried herself as the daughter of a King, and was accordingly respected by persons of Honour." She died of smallpox the following year while sailing back to Virginia.

Map labels

Davis 1585–87

1497: Cabot raises English flag on northern tip of Newfoundland

Hudson Bay

Severn Factory

RUPERT'S LAND

James Bay

Fort Albany 1670

Eastmain

Rupert House 1668

Moose Factory 1671

Lake Superior

Ottawa River

Lake Huron

Lake Michigan

Lake Ontario

Lake Erie

Detroit

Niagara

Lake Champlain

St. Lawrence River

Montreal

NEW ENGLAND

Labrador

Newfoundland

Gulf of St. Lawrence

Cape Breton Island

Acadia

NOVA SCOTIA

Halifax 1749

Cabot 1497

1713: to Britain via Treaty of Utrecht

Portsmouth 1639

Salem 1629

Providence 1636

Plymouth 1620

Newport

New Haven 1637

New York 1664

Philadelphia 1682

Baltimore 1729

Appalachian Mountains

Smith 1608

Fort Necessity 1754 1639 (to Newport)

Batts and Fallam 1671

Charlottesville 1744

Richmond 1733

Williamsburg 1699

Jamestown 1607

Roanoke

Ohio River

Fort Chiswell 1758

Needham and Arthur 1673

Charlotte 1750

New Bern 1710

Wilmington 1730

INDIAN TERRITORY

LOUISIANA

Mississippi River

Fort Augusta 1735

Woodward 1674, 1685

Georgetown 1735

Charleston 1672

Fort King George 1721

Savannah 1733

New Orleans

Raleigh 1584

ATLANTIC OCEAN

ENGLISH EXPLORATION AND COLONIZATION

This map shows all the English expeditions, from John Cabot in 1497 through John Davis in 1587, as well as the English settlements and when they were founded.

English exploration and colonization of North America

Symbol	Period	
→	1450–1500	English settlement
→	1500–1600	Non-English Settlement
→	1600–1650	1632 date of foundation
→	1650–1673	
→	1674–1700	

FIRST MASS

Father Andrew White, an English Jesuit priest, celebrated the first Roman Catholic Mass in English North America on March 25, 1634, on an island in the Potomac River. White was among the 128 colonists who sailed from England in two ships, the *Ark* and the *Dove*, to establish Maryland, which was named for Queen Henrietta Maria, wife of King Charles I of England.

The next English colony in the south was Maryland, established in 1634 on land granted to George Calvert, Lord Baltimore, by King Charles I. The colony was intended to be a haven for English Roman Catholics, but it also attracted Puritan and Anglican settlers. To keep the peace between these groups, in 1649 the colony's assembly passed a law—popularly known as the Toleration Act—which mandated religious freedom for all colonists "professing to believe in Jesus Christ." As in Virginia to the south, Maryland's economy was based mainly on tobacco.

The Carolinas were settled for economic rather than religious reasons. In 1663, King Charles II granted the land between Virginia and Spanish-ruled Florida to eight English "proprietors"; in return, the proprietors promised to establish a colony that would export goods like rice and indigo back to England.

JAMESTOWN SETTLEMENT

This modern painting by Sidney King provides an aerial view of Jamestown in 1614—the year John Rolfe married Pocahontas and shipped the first cargo of Virginia tobacco to England. Around this same time, the colony began expanding from the original settlement, the "Old Town," into the "New Town" to the east.

THE PILGRIMS AT PLYMOUTH

In the early 17th century, a group of Separatists—Calvinist Protestants who believed the Church of England was insufficiently "reformed"—moved from England to the Netherlands. In 1620, with support from London investors, a group of these Separatists—known to history as the Pilgrims—sailed for North America aboard the *Mayflower*. (There were only about 35 Pilgrims in the party; 77 other colonists were recruited by the investors.)

The Pilgrims were supposed to settle within the Virginia Company's territory, but instead they landed at Plymouth, Massachusetts, on December 21, 1620, after pledging to govern themselves through "just and equal laws." The Pilgrims landed at the worst possible time of year—winter. They spent their first months living in crude earthen shelters, and hunger, cold, and disease claimed many lives. The colony might well have perished without the help of the Native Americans, who introduced the Pilgrims to one of their staple foods—corn—and showed them how to cultivate it. (The Pilgrims also benefited from the fact that many of the local people, the Wampanoags, had died in a smallpox epidemic, leaving plenty of cleared land for the newcomers.) In the autumn of 1621, the Pilgrims and the Native Americans had a feast to celebrate the colony's first harvest—the origin of America's Thanksgiving holiday.

Thanks to farming and fishing, Plymouth Plantation—as the Pilgrims named their settlement, which extended from Cape Ann south through Cape Cod to Nantucket—prospered to the extent that, in 1627, they were able to pay back the English investors who had bankrolled the venture. Although the Pilgrims are revered today as the founders of New England, the Plymouth settlement would soon be subsumed by a much larger wave of immigrants—the Puritans.

PLYMOUTH ROCK
This 19th-century engraving is a romanticized depiction of the landing of the Pilgrims at Plymouth in 1620. According to tradition, the Pilgrims stepped ashore on a large rock—today enshrined as a monument—although the first recorded reference to the rock appeared more than a century later.

THE *MAYFLOWER*
The Pilgrims planned to sail from England aboard two ships, the *Mayflower* and the *Speedwell*, but the latter vessel proved unseaworthy and returned to port, leaving the *Mayflower* to continue alone. The settlers endured 66 storm-tossed days at sea before finally making landfall on the Massachusetts coast.

PURITAN CHURCH
This clapboard "meeting house," or church, in Midway, Georgia, is spare both inside and out, reflecting the Puritan's opposition to any distracting ornamentation.

JOHN WINTHROP
In his famous sermon *A Model of Christian Charity*, John Winthrop proclaimed that the Puritan colony must be "a City upon a Hill."

"CITY UPON A HILL"

The Pilgrim settlement at Plymouth was just a prelude to a major wave of immigration from England. Like the Pilgrims, the Puritans were Calvinists who were uncomfortable with the Church of England; the Puritans hoped to "purify" the church from within. In 1629, however, facing increasing persecution from the established church, a group of Puritan leaders met at Cambridge University and agreed that they would be better off in North America, where they would be free to live according to the Biblical precepts that they believed should be the basis of civil society.

An advance party of Puritan settlers founded Salem, Massachusetts, later that year. The great migration began in earnest in 1630, when about 1,000 Puritans settled on the site of present-day Boston, establishing the Massachusetts Bay Colony under the governorship of John Winthrop, who wanted his "City upon a Hill" to be an example of righteousness to the world. Another 10,000 or so English Puritans emigrated over the next decade. By the mid-1640s, the colony, including outlying settlements, numbered more than 40,000 people. The Massachusetts Bay Colony was run along strict Calvinist lines. The Puritans had no tolerance for other religious viewpoints, but their stern faith gave them the strength to settle the New England wilderness and to crush Native American efforts to resist their expansion.

THE GROWTH OF NEW ENGLAND

That expansion intensified in 1638, when clergyman Thomas Hooker led about 100 Puritans westward from Boston—the capital of the Massachusetts Bay Colony—into the Connecticut River Valley. In that same year, another clergyman, John Davenport, founded a settlement he called "a new haven" on Long Island Sound. Together with several other communities, the new outposts eventually comprised Connecticut. Meanwhile, assorted traders, adventurers, and Puritans established an English presence in what would become Vermont, New Hampshire, and Maine.

A colony of a different kind was Rhode Island. Founded in 1636 by Roger Williams, a minister who had been banished from Massachusetts because of his ideas on freedom of worship, it was the first colony to guarantee religious tolerance, and it provided a refuge for Quakers, Baptists, Jews, and other non-Puritans.

ROGER WILLIAMS
Declaring "forced worship stinks in God's nostrils," Roger Williams—memorialized here in a statue in Providence, Rhode Island's Roger Williams Park—founded Providence in 1638, on land given to him by the Narragansett Native Americans, whom he befriended after his banishment from Massachusetts in 1936.

OLD STATE HOUSE
A 1791 engraving shows Boston's Old State House, seat of government for the colony and, later, the state of Massachusetts. The building was completed in 1713 to replace the original "Town House," which had burned down several years earlier.

Dutch and Swedish Settlers

Two other nations, the Netherlands and Sweden, also established colonies in North America during the 17th century. Sweden's impact would be minimal, and the Dutch colony of New Netherlands lasted only about a half-century before its conquest by the English. Dutch religious toleration and encouragment of immigration, however, would have important consequences for the United States.

HENRY HUDSON
On his final voyage in 1609, Hudson sought the Northwest Passage again, this time sailing under the English flag via the Canadian Arctic, but his crew mutinied and set him and his son adrift in a small boat. They were never seen again.

MINUIT BUYS MANHATTAN
According to legend, Canarsie Native Americans sold Manhattan to Peter Minuit for $24 of trade goods, mostly glass beads. In fact, most Native American peoples had no understanding of land ownership; they probably thought they were selling the right to hunt and fish on the island.

In 1609, an English sea captain in the service of the Dutch Republic, Henry Hudson, sailed the *Half-Moon* into New York Harbor and up the broad Hudson, which he hoped would be a navigable passage from North America to Asia. Five years later, the Dutch established Fort Orange as a fur-trading post; in 1624, the Dutch sponsored a group of Protestant Walloons (French-speakers from what is now Belgium) who settled at Beverwick—the first permanent settlement in the New Netherlands.

A small island at the mouth of the Hudson had some potential as a seaport, so in 1626 Peter Minuit of the Dutch West India Company purchased Manhattan Island from the local Native Americans in history's most celebrated real-estate deal.

In its early years, Manhattan was a rowdy port town, and settlement of the surrounding areas was hampered by conflict with the Native Americans. A strong-willed governor, Peter Stuyvesant, arrived in 1647 to impose some discipline on the populace and make peace with the Native Americans. Stuyvesant's authoritarian style, however, did not go over well in what was already a freewheeling multicultural community; in 1654, for example, an official account reported 18 languages being spoken in the streets.

Stuyvesant's attempts to enforce the orthodoxy of the Dutch Reformed Church also met with opposition from residents who included "Papists [Catholics], Mennonites, and Lutherans among the Dutch

THE FUR TRADE

As with the French in Canada, the lure of wealth from furs was originally the motive behind the Dutch colonization efforts. And as in Canada, the fur of the beaver was prized above all others; glossy and water-repellent, the beaver's pelt produced a fine felt that was used to trim outer garments, or made into hats. The Iroquois Native Americans controlled the fur trade in the Hudson River Valley, which is why the first Dutch outposts in New Netherlands were upriver rather than on the coast. The demand for beaver pelts was so great that by the late 1600s the beaver were mostly gone from the region, forcing the Native Americans and the traders to move continually westward in search of fresh sources. The beaver's importance to the early economy of New Netherlands is commemorated by the presence of a beaver on the Seal of the City of New York.

City of New York Seal

[and] also many Puritans and Independents . . ." according to another contemporary account. Eventually Stuyvesant was forced to introduce a more democratic government, and when he attempted to block immigration of Quakers and Jews, the directors of the Dutch West India Company ordered him to allow religious tolerance of anyone "moderate, peaceful, and inoffensive."

NEW SWEDEN

Another nation, Sweden, established a colony on the southern banks of the Delaware River. In 1638, two shiploads of Swedish settlers built Fort Christina (named for Sweden's 12-year-old Queen) near present-day Wilmington, Delaware. Eventually some 600 Swedes and Finns immigrated to New Sweden, establishing small settlements of farms in Pennsylvania, Maryland, Delaware, and New Jersey. Sweden's presence in North America was short-lived. The Dutch considered the Swedes to be trespassers on their territory, and in 1655 Peter Stuyvesant sent an

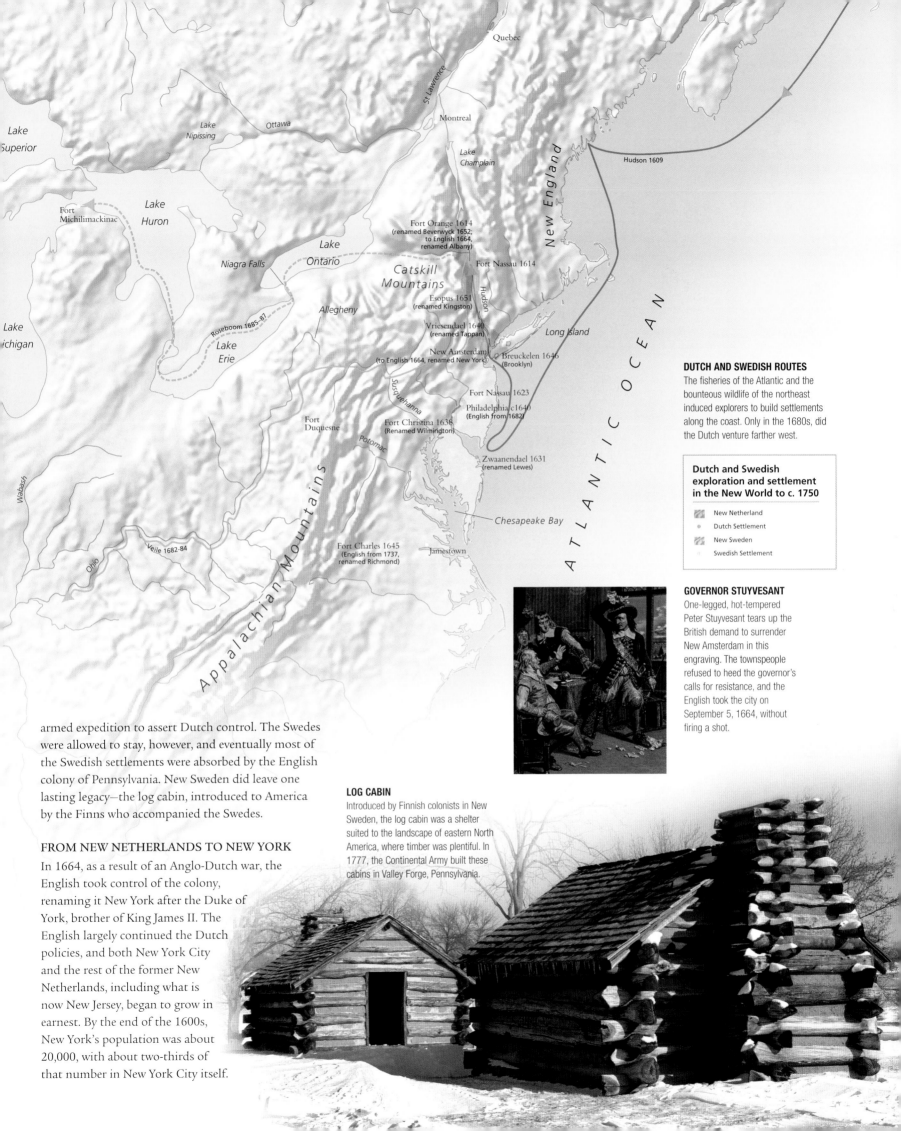

Quebec

Montreal

Lake Superior

Lake Nipissing

Ottawa

Lake Huron

Fort Michilimackinac

Lake Michigan

Lake Erie

Niagra Falls

Lake Ontario

Roseboom 1685-87

Allegheny

St Lawrence

Lake Champlain

New England

Hudson 1609

ATLANTIC OCEAN

Fort Orange 1614
(renamed Beverwyck 1652;
to English 1664,
renamed Albany)

Fort Nassau 1614

Catskill
Mountains

Esopus 1651
(renamed Kingston)

Hudson

Vriesendael 1640
(renamed Tappan)

New Amsterdam
(to English 1664, renamed New York)

Breuckelen 1646
(Brooklyn)

Long Island

Susquehanna

Fort Nassau 1623

Philadelphia c1640
(English from 1682)

Fort
Duquesne

Fort Christina 1638
(Renamed Wilmington)

Potomac

Zwaanendael 1631
(renamed Lewes)

Chesapeake Bay

Waabash

Veile 1682-84

Ohio

Appalachian Mountains

Fort Charles 1645
(English from 1737,
renamed Richmond)

Jamestown

DUTCH AND SWEDISH ROUTES

The fisheries of the Atlantic and the bounteous wildlife of the northeast induced explorers to build settlements along the coast. Only in the 1680s, did the Dutch venture farther west.

Dutch and Swedish exploration and settlement in the New World to c. 1750

- New Netherland
- Dutch Settlement
- New Sweden
- Swedish Settlement

GOVERNOR STUYVESANT

One-legged, hot-tempered Peter Stuyvesant tears up the British demand to surrender New Amsterdam in this engraving. The townspeople refused to heed the governor's calls for resistance, and the English took the city on September 5, 1664, without firing a shot.

LOG CABIN

Introduced by Finnish colonists in New Sweden, the log cabin was a shelter suited to the landscape of eastern North America, where timber was plentiful. In 1777, the Continental Army built these cabins in Valley Forge, Pennsylvania.

armed expedition to assert Dutch control. The Swedes were allowed to stay, however, and eventually most of the Swedish settlements were absorbed by the English colony of Pennsylvania. New Sweden did leave one lasting legacy—the log cabin, introduced to America by the Finns who accompanied the Swedes.

FROM NEW NETHERLANDS TO NEW YORK

In 1664, as a result of an Anglo-Dutch war, the English took control of the colony, renaming it New York after the Duke of York, brother of King James II. The English largely continued the Dutch policies, and both New York City and the rest of the former New Netherlands, including what is now New Jersey, began to grow in earnest. By the end of the 1600s, New York's population was about 20,000, with about two-thirds of that number in New York City itself.

SLAVERY AND THE TRIANGLE TRADE

On August 20, 1619, a Dutch ship with a cargo of African slaves dropped anchor off Jamestown, Virginia (*see pp 26–27*). In desperate need of labor for the colony's tobacco fields, the colonists bought 20 slaves from the Dutch. It was the start of slavery in North America; almost four centuries later, Americans continue to struggle with the legacy of that August day.

THE BIRTH OF THE PECULIAR INSTITUTION

The first Africans in the English colonies were considered more like indentured servants (*see pp 138–139*) than slaves. In the latter part of the 1600s, however, true slavery—meaning that the Africans' offspring, as well as the Africans themselves, were

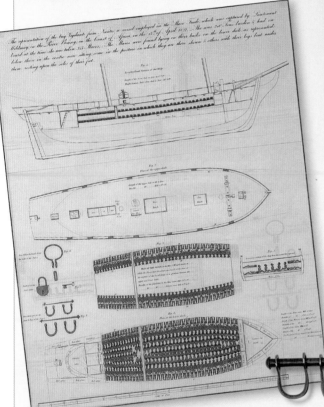

considered permanent "property" of their "master"—became established in custom and then in law. There were slaves in all the colonies, but the "peculiar institution" (as later apologists called it) of property took hold in Virginia, Maryland, and the Carolinas.

THE TRIANGLE TRADE AND THE MIDDLE PASSAGE

From 1500 to the mid-19th century, as many as 10 million Africans were forcibly brought to the Americas. The vast majority went to the Caribbean or to South America. Several hundred thousand were brought directly to North America, many arriving via the 18th-century commercial system known as the "Triangle Trade."

On the first leg, European ships carried trade goods to the West African coast. These goods were exchanged for slaves, who were generally captives taken in wars between different African peoples. (By the 17th century, slaves were purchased in Africa for about $25 and sold in the Americas for about $150.) On the second leg—the Middle Passage—the slaves

SLAVE SHIP
A diagram of an 18th-century slave ship shows how Africans were packed—and often held in place with the ankle restraints shown below—in the vessel's holds. A 1788 inquiry by the British Parliament found that one ship, the *Brookes*, crammed more than 600 slaves into spaces intended for 450.

Ankle Restraints

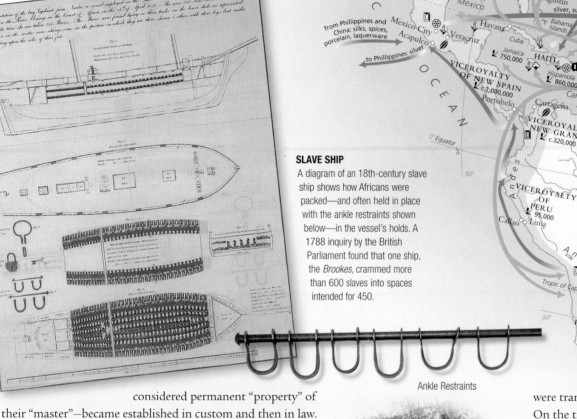

were transported across the Atlantic for sale. On the third leg, ships returned to Europe with sugar, tobacco, and rum.

The Middle Passage was a horrific experience that generally claimed the lives of between 10 and 20 percent of each human cargo. By the time the Africans were loaded onto the slave ships, they were already suffering from malnutrition and disease after the long forced march from the interior. Aboard ship, they were usually packed in as tightly as possible, often head-to-foot and chained in place. Many slaves were crippled for life as a

PLANTATION SLAVES
The more fortunate slaves became house servants or craft workers, but most were employed as field hands cultivating cotton, tobacco, indigo, rice, or—like those shown in this 19th-century photograph—sugar cane.

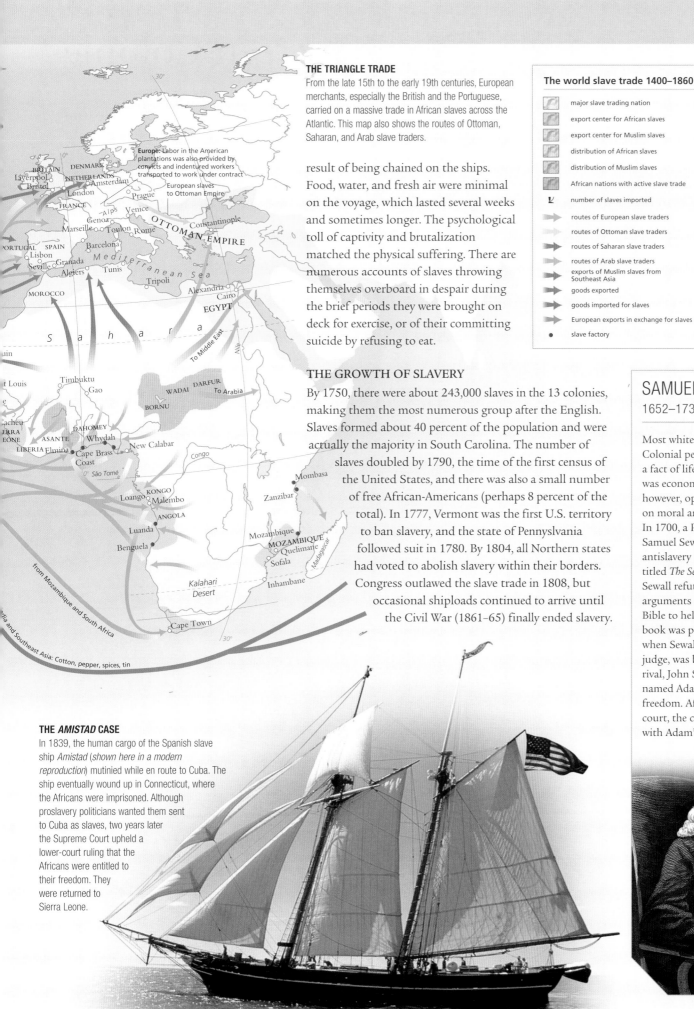

THE TRIANGLE TRADE

From the late 15th to the early 19th centuries, European merchants, especially the British and the Portuguese, carried on a massive trade in African slaves across the Atlantic. This map also shows the routes of Ottoman, Saharan, and Arab slave traders.

Europe: Labor in the American plantations was also provided by convicts and indentured workers transported to work under contract

European slaves to Ottoman Empire

The world slave trade 1400–1860

	major slave trading nation	**Goods produced using slaves**	
	export center for African slaves	cocoa beans	
	export center for Muslim slaves	coffee	
	distribution of African slaves	cotton	
	distribution of Muslim slaves	diamonds	
	African nations with active slave trade	gold	
	number of slaves imported	silver	
		sugar	
	routes of European slave traders	tobacco	
	routes of Ottoman slave traders	**Other goods traded**	
	routes of Saharan slave traders	dyestuffs	
	routes of Arab slave traders	furs and hides	
	exports of Muslim slaves from Southeast Asia	pepper	
	goods exported	silk and textiles	
	goods imported for slaves	spices	
	European exports in exchange for slaves	tin	
		Goods imported for slaves	
	slave factory	salt cod	

result of being chained on the ships. Food, water, and fresh air were minimal on the voyage, which lasted several weeks and sometimes longer. The psychological toll of captivity and brutalization matched the physical suffering. There are numerous accounts of slaves throwing themselves overboard in despair during the brief periods they were brought on deck for exercise, or of their committing suicide by refusing to eat.

THE GROWTH OF SLAVERY

By 1750, there were about 243,000 slaves in the 13 colonies, making them the most numerous group after the English. Slaves formed about 40 percent of the population and were actually the majority in South Carolina. The number of slaves doubled by 1790, the time of the first census of the United States, and there was also a small number of free African-Americans (perhaps 8 percent of the total). In 1777, Vermont was the first U.S. territory to ban slavery, and the state of Pennyslvania followed suit in 1780. By 1804, all Northern states had voted to abolish slavery within their borders. Congress outlawed the slave trade in 1808, but occasional shiploads continued to arrive until the Civil War (1861–65) finally ended slavery.

from Mozambique and South Africa

...la and Southeast Asia: Cotton, pepper, spices, tin

THE *AMISTAD* CASE

In 1839, the human cargo of the Spanish slave ship *Amistad* (*shown here in a modern reproduction*) mutinied while en route to Cuba. The ship eventually wound up in Connecticut, where the Africans were imprisoned. Although proslavery politicians wanted them sent to Cuba as slaves, two years later the Supreme Court upheld a lower-court ruling that the Africans were entitled to their freedom. They were returned to Sierra Leone.

SAMUEL SEWALL
1652–1730

Most white Americans of the Colonial period accepted slavery as a fact of life. For one thing, slavery was economically important. Some, however, opposed the institution on moral and religious grounds. In 1700, a Puritan minister, Samuel Sewall, published the first antislavery tract in the colonies titled *The Selling of Joseph,* in which Sewall refutes some of the common arguments for slavery, using the Bible to help make his case. The book was published during a time when Sewall, also a Massachusetts judge, was battling his proslavery rival, John Saffin, over a slave named Adam, who was seeking his freedom. After several years in court, the case finally ended with Adam's release.

The Thirteen Colonies

The first decades of the 18th century saw the rapid growth of the English colonies in North America, thanks to a combination of a high birthrate, the growth of the slave population, and immigration—mostly from the British Isles, but including growing numbers of Germans and other groups. The era also saw the people of North America increasingly drawn into the imperial conflicts of the European powers.

B y 1750, England had 13 American colonies, with a population of about 1,170,000 people. The original colonies in New England, the South, and New York were joined by Pennsylvania, founded by Quakers (see pp 66–69) in 1682, and Georgia, established as a haven for Britain's poor by General James Oglethorpe in 1733.

The growth of the English colonies far outstripped that of the other European possessions in North America. In 1750, there were only about 10,000 settlers in Spain's colonies, with half in New Mexico and the remainder split between Florida and Texas. French Canada's non–Native American population was about 50,000, with another 3,000 French settlers in Louisiana and 2,000 scattered throughout the Mississippi Valley and the "Illinois Country" south of the Great Lakes.

New France's population might have been small, but its territory was vast, as was the wealth it generated from the fur trade. The British government coveted this wealth, and it was also concerned with the threat that the French and their Native American allies posed to the western frontiers of its American colonies. Throughout the 17th and 18th centuries, France and England went to war several times, with each nation's colonies taking part; in 1704, French soldiers and Huron Native Americans attacked Deerfield, Massachusetts, killing more than 50 people and taking another 100 captive, while, in 1745, troops from New England captured the French fort at Louisbourg, which guarded the mouth of the St. Lawrence River.

EMPIRES IN CONFLICT

These small wars finally culminated in a major conflict—called the French and Indian War in North America, and the Seven Years War in Europe—which eventually spread around the world. The prelude came in 1755, when a young Virginian colonel, George Washington, was dispatched to the Ohio River Valley to shut down a French outpost, Fort Duquesne. A year later, King George II formally declared war on France.

The conflict went badly for the British at first, but General James Wolfe captured Canada's capital, Quebec, in a daring assault in September 1759. It was not until 1763, however, that the French agreed to peace terms. In the treaty that ended the war, France ceded Canada to Britain, while Spain (which had come into the war on Britain's side) got Louisiana. Britain was now the undisputed master of North America from the Atlantic to the Mississippi.

Paradoxically perhaps, the British victory in the French and Indian War put Britain and its North American colonies on the path to conflict. First, the British government declared the area beyond the Appalachian Mountains off-limits to settlement. The intent was to mollify the Native Americans of the continent's interior, and thus avoid disrupting the fur trade. This restriction was deeply resented by

The Thirteen Colonies

- - - Borders of the Thirteen Colonies
• British settlement with date of foundation
Proclamation Line of 1763

Density of population
settlement growth by 1660
settlement growth by 1700
settlement growth by 1760

Map labels:
RUPERT'S LAND
NOVA SCOTIA (to Britain 1713)
QUEBEC (created 1763)
NEW FRANCE
MAINE (to Massachusetts)
New England
Lake Huron
Lake Ontario
Lake Erie
Portland 1632
NEW HAMPSHIRE
Boston (to Massachusetts 1691)
Providence 1636
MASSACHUSETTS
NEW YORK
Newport 1639
New Haven
(to Connecticut 1664)
RHODE ISLAND
CONNECTICUT
New Amsterdam 1625 (acquired from Dutch 1664)
PENNSYLVANIA
NEW JERSEY
Philadelphia 1682
Wilmington 1730
Baltimore 1729
DELAWARE
Annapolis 1649
Charlottesville 1744
MARYLAND
VIRGINIA
Williamsburg 1699
INDIAN RESERVATION
NORTH CAROLINA
ATLANTIC OCEAN
SOUTH CAROLINA
Georgetown 1735
Charleston 1672
GEORGIA
Savannah 1733
WEST FLORIDA created 1764
(to Britain 1763-83; to Spain 1783)
Gulf of Mexico
FLORIDA
Cuba
St. Lawrence

GENEROUS GENERAL
Soldier and humanitarian James Edward Oglethorpe envisioned Georgia as a place where debtors, petty criminals, and the poor could make a fresh start. The colony banned slavery at first, although that ban was lifted by Parliament in 1749. The colony was also intended to serve as a barrier to Spanish expansion from Florida.

THE ZENGER TRIAL

A 1733 court case in New York set a powerful precedent for freedom of speech in the future United States. At its center was John Peter Zenger, a printer who had emigrated from Germany about 20 years earlier. Zenger's newspaper, *The New-York Weekly Journal*, published a series of articles that criticized the colony's governor, William Cosby. Zenger did not actually write the articles, but the fact that he had printed them was enough for Cosby to order Zenger thrown in jail for "seditious libel." At the trial, Zenger's lawyer, Andrew Hamilton, persuaded the jury that the articles were not libelous because they were factual, and Zenger was freed after eight months in jail, during which his wife, Anna, kept his printing press in operation. Zenger went on to become the official printer of both New York and New Jersey.

The New-York Weekly Journal

Americans in the southern colonies, who were already looking to the lands that would one day become Tennessee and Kentucky, as well as the Ohio River Valley, as a natural arena for expansion and economic opportunities.

Second, the mainly Protestant citizens of the 13 colonies were alarmed by the Quebec Act. Passed by Parliament in 1774, the law extended the boundaries of Quebec into Native American territory and guaranteed religious tolerance to the French-speaking Roman Catholics of Canada.

Third, the war cost Britain a lot of money. To recoup these costs and to provide for the colonies' defense, Parliament began imposing direct taxes on the colonies for the first time.

Finally, the struggle against the French and Native Americans led to stirrings of national pride among Americans. Although most colonists were of British descent and considered themselves loyal subjects of the Crown, many began to chafe at their status as "second-class citizens" within the British Empire, while others like the Irish, German, and Dutch felt no particular loyalty to Britain in the first place. Slowly but surely, the stage for revolution was set.

THE DEATH OF WOLFE
American artist Benjamin West's 1770 painting shows the British general, James Wolfe, mortally wounded on the battlefield following his successful assault on Quebec. The French commander, the Marquis de Montcalm, also died of wounds the following day.

"Now, God be praised, I will die in peace!"

General James Wolfe on his deathbed

The Revolutionary War

Independence was not a goal at the start of the Revolutionary War. The majority of the American colonists considered themselves loyal subjects of King George III and only wanted their rights as British citizens. The breach between the colonists and the Crown, however, proved too wide to be healed peacefully, and after eight years of war a new nation—the United States of America—emerged.

The first signs of conflict between the colonists and the British government came in the 1760s, when Americans grew increasingly resentful of taxes imposed by Parliament. Besides the economic burden, there was a principle involved: growing numbers of colonists felt it was wrong to pay these taxes when they had no representatives in Parliament—a sentiment summed up by the famous rallying cry of the prominent Sons of Liberty: "No taxation without representation."

CRISPUS ATTUCKS
1723–1770

On the night of March 5, 1770, a rowdy mob of Bostonians began taunting a group of British soldiers. Insults gave way to rocks and snowballs, and several of the soldiers fired into the crowd, killing three people; two others later died of their wounds. The first person to fall in the "Boston Massacre," as the Patriots labeled it, was a sailor, Crispus Attucks, of African and Indian ancestry. Attucks is considered the first person to die in the struggle for American independence; a monument in his honor was erected on Boston Common 118 years later.

THE STAMP ACT
Passed by Parliament in 1765, the Stamp Act imposed a tax on printed matter ranging from property deeds to playing cards. In opposition to the act, the *Pennsylvania Journal* sarcastically suggested affixing this stamp *(right)* to imported goods.

BOSTON TEA PARTY
Crudely disguised as Mohawks, a Patriot mob heaved 342 chests of tea into Boston Harbor on December 16, 1773, to protest the British East India Company's monopoly on the sale of that beverage in the colonies. Parliament retaliated by closing the port of Boston to trade.

BATTLE OF LEXINGTON
Seven hundred British regulars faced about 70 Patriot militia—known as "Minutemen" for their ability to turn out quickly to defend their homes—at Lexington, Massachusetts, on April 19, 1775. No one knows who fired the first shot of the war, but the brief clash left eight Patriots dead.

In the 1770s, American "Patriots" began to form into organizations like the Sons of Liberty to oppose British policies. When Patriots dumped a shipload of tea into Boston Harbor in 1773 to protest the British East India Company's monopoly, the British responded by shutting the port down and sending troops. The more radical Patriots began to arm. In April 1775, a British force left Boston to seize armaments in Lexington and Concord. They met prepared resistance from Patriots, and the war was on.

FROM LEXINGTON TO SARATOGA

Help came from the rest of the colonies and a regular fighting force—the Continental Army—formed under the command of George Washington. The Patriots managed to drive the British out of Boston in March 1776. When a last-ditch effort to make peace failed, a Continental Congress with delegates from all 13 colonies convened in Philadelphia. Around July 4, the delegates began signing a Declaration of Independence. Drafted largely by Virginian Thomas Jefferson, the document asserted that "these United Colonies are, and of right ought to be, FREE AND INDEPENDENT STATES . . ."

Making independence a fact took seven more years of war. Although most of the battles ended in defeat or a stalemate for the Patriots, Washington managed to keep his army in the field and fighting, even when its numbers dwindled down to a few thousand.

In August 1776, British forces inflicted a serious defeat on the Continental Army in the Battle of Long Island, and the British occupied New York City the following month. The Continentals took some revenge at Trenton, New Jersey, on December 26, when they overwhelmed a force of

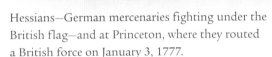

Hessians—German mercenaries fighting under the British flag—and at Princeton, where they routed a British force on January 3, 1777.

The tide began to turn in 1777 when the Patriots defeated a British force at Saratoga, New York. The victory convinced France, Britain's traditional enemy, to support the Patriots with troops and arms.

The Revolutionary War was also a civil war. Patriot leader John Adams later observed that only one-third of the American population actively supported the Patriot cause; another third tried to remain neutral, and the remaining third stayed loyal to Britain. In the South, there was a parallel guerrilla war between Loyalist and Patriot irregulars. On the frontier, the mostly pro-British Native Americans attacked settlements, and Patriot forces retaliated in kind against Native American communities.

African-Americans fought on both sides. The British promised escaped slaves their freedom if they volunteered for service. The Patriots made no such offer, but free African-Americans served in the regiments of the Continental Army and in the ships of the Continental Navy.

The response of the largest colonial immigrant group, the Germans, was mixed. Many were Mennonites (see pp 74–77) or members of other religious sects who opposed all war, and some endured persecution from Patriots for their stance. Others eagerly took up arms for the Patriot cause.

THE SIGNERS
This painting by Jonathan Trumbull depicts the committee that drafted the Declaration of Independence (*from left to right:* John Adams, Roger Sherman, Robert Livingston, Thomas Jefferson, and Benjamin Franklin) presenting the document to the Continental Congress.

THE DECLARATION OF INDEPENDENCE
Its ink badly faded, the original Declaration of Independence now resides in the National Archives in Washington, D.C. Four days after its signing in Philadelphia, General George Washington ordered the document read aloud to the troops of the Continental Army in New York City to gear them up for battle.

THE BRITISH SURRENDER

Humiliated by his defeat at Yorktown, General Lord Charles Cornwallis did not attend the surrender ceremony, instead deputizing one of his subordinates. To add insult to injury, the British officer offered his sword to the French general, rather than Washington.

J. HECTOR ST.JOHN DE CRÈVECOEUR

1735–1813

What is an American? This is the question Hector St. John de Crèvecoeur set out to answer in his 1782 book Letters From an American Farmer. Born in France in 1735, de Crèvecoeur settled in New York State in 1765. Despite harassment from both sides in the Revolutionary War (his wife was a Loyalist), Crèvecoeur set forth an optimistic vision of the United States as a place where people from all backgrounds would achieve a common identity: "He is an American, who, leaving behind him all his ancient prejudices and manners, receives new ones from the new mode of life he has embraced [and] the new government he obeys . . . Here individuals of all races are melted into a new race of man, whose labors and posterity will one day cause great changes in the world."

SARATOGA TO INDEPENDENCE

The victory at Saratoga and the consequent entry of France—and also Spain and the Netherlands—into the war ultimately guaranteed a Patriot victory, but the winter of 1777–78 found the Continental Army in a desperate state. The troops made camp at Valley Forge, outside British-occupied Philadelphia. While the weather was relatively mild—contrary to the popular legend—food, medicine, clothing, and every other necessity were in short supply, and hunger, disease, and desertion thinned the army's ranks. Washington wrote to the increasingly ineffectual Continental

> "What then is the American, this new man?"
>
> J. Hector St. John de Crèvecoeur

LOYALIST ENCAMPMENT

Loyalist refugees from the Revolutionary War make camp along the St. Lawrence River in this 1784 painting by English artist James Peachey. The descendants of these "United Empire Loyalists" make up a large percentage of today's English-speaking Canadians, especially in the Maritime Provinces.

Congress that unless something was done, the Continentals would have to "starve, dissolve or disperse." Despite that gloomy prediction, the nucleus of the army managed to survive battles with the British at Monmouth, New Jersey, and along the Brandywine River in Pennsylvania, in the spring of 1778.

The focus of the fighting then shifted to the southern colonies. Loyalist sentiment was strong in the region, leading to vicious partisan warfare, especially in the overmountain country beyond the Tidewater. Although the British commander in the south, General Lord Charles Cornwallis, scored several victories over the Continentals and local militia, losses forced him to take refuge at Yorktown, Virginia—not far from Jamestown—in the summer of 1781.

Reinforced by French troops, Washington's Continentals marched south to take advantage of this opportunity. After a French fleet in Chesapeake Bay succeeded in keeping British reinforcements from reaching Yorktown, the Patriots and French dug in their artillery and put the stranded British garrison under siege. On October 18, after continuous bombardment and infantry assault, Cornwallis surrendered. For the first time in modern history, a colonial people had defeated its rulers. In recognition, the British military band played a popular tune called "The World Turned Upside Down" as Cornwallis's men marched out to lay down their arms.

It would take two more years of sporadic fighting and tense negotiations by American peace commissioners Ben Franklin, John Adams, and John Jay, however, before American, British, and French representatives finally hammered out the Second Treaty of Paris, on April 15, 1783, which ended the war and officially recognized the existence of a new nation—the United States of America.

FREEDOM FOR WOMEN
Founding Mothers

ANNE HUTCHINSON

Born Anne Marbury in Alford, England, in 1591, Hutchinson and her husband immigrated to Massachusetts in 1634. There, Hutchinson held weekly meetings at her house to discuss the sermons preached by the colony's ministers and other religious matters. She quickly became embroiled in the growing conflict between different factions—the so-called Antinomian Controversy—that held differing views on the nature of salvation. The colony's religious and civil leaders (who, of course, were largely one and the same) accused Hutchinson and her supporters of heresy and banished them from the colony. For a time Hutchinson lived in Rhode Island, which she helped settle in 1638. After the death of her husband, she moved to what is now Pelham Bay in the Bronx, where she and most of her family were killed in a Native American raid in 1643.

MARGARET BRENT

Sometimes called "America's first feminist," Margaret Brent arrived in Maryland from England in 1638. Through shrewd land deals, she expanded her original 70 acres of property into more than a thousand, making her one of the colony's largest landowners. She also served as an adviser to the colony's governor, Leonard Calvert, who made her the executor of his estate on his deathbed. After his death, Brent formally requested two votes in Maryland's assembly—one in her role as Calvert's executor, and one for herself. (Brent was aware that if she were a man, her status as a landowner would have qualified her for the vote.) The colony's royal proprietor, Lord Baltimore, angrily denied Brent's request, upon which she moved to Virginia.

ABIGAIL ADAMS

A brilliant writer, a capable businesswoman, and a keen judge of people, Abigail Smith Adams might have had a significant political career of her own if she had been born in 1944 instead of 1744. The daughter of a Quincy, Massachusetts minister, she married a rising lawyer, John Adams, in 1764. Twelve years later, with John Adams now a prominent Patriot leader, she famously wrote to him that in drafting the Declaration of Independence Congress should "remember the ladies and be more generous and favourable to them than your ancestors." Abigail ably managed the family's farm and business interests during the Revolutionary War, while John was in Europe on diplomatic missions, and during his presidency, from 1801 to 1804, she served as the nation's second First Lady.

Westward Expansion

The sheer physical size of the United States was a major factor in the growth of immigration: the nation offered plenty of land to newcomers, much of it good farmland, along with abundant natural resources. America was bigger than most European nations at the time it achieved independence, and in less than a century it expanded clear to the Pacific and beyond.

The 1783 treaty that ended the Revolutionary War set the new nation's western border at the Mississippi River; Spain retained Florida and the lower Mississippi Valley. Most of this new nation's 900,000-square-mile area was occupied solely by Native Americans, but a growing number of white settlers were moving west through the passes of the Appalachian Mountains.

In 1803, the United States doubled in size with the Louisiana Purchase, when French Emperor Napoleon Bonaparte, having acquired the vast territory from Spain, sold it to the United States at a price that worked out to four cents an acre. The purchase moved the nation's border west to the Rocky Mountains. Northern expansion was out of the question after the War of 1812, when Canada successfully fended off an American invasion.

THE NORTHWEST ORDINANCE

The Northwest Ordinance, passed by Congress in 1787, established measures for the settlement and government of the Northwest Territory—what is now the states of Illinois, Indiana, Michigan, and Wisconsin. It set up procedures for achieving statehood and guaranteed freedom of religion and other civil rights to residents there, including Native Americans. Key among its provisions was a ban on slavery in the region, even though northeastern states such as

ALASKA AND HAWAII
Texas (267,277 square miles in land area) lost its long-held status as America's biggest state when Alaska (656,425 square miles) achieved statehood in January 1959, eight months before Hawaii became the 50th state.

KENTUCKY PIONEERS
An 1851 painting by George Caleb Bingham depicts the great frontiersman Daniel Boone leading the first party of settlers into Kentucky in 1775. Six years before, Boone and five companions had blazed a trail from Virginia to Kentucky through the Cumberland Gap in the Appalachian Mountains.

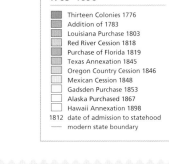

The map shows the following states with their statehood dates:

NORTH DAKOTA 1889 · MINNESOTA 1858 · SOUTH DAKOTA 1889 · WISCONSIN 1848 · MICHIGAN 1837 · VERMONT 1791 · MAINE 1820 · NEW HAMPSHIRE 1788 · MASSACHUSETTS 1788 · NEW YORK 1788 · RHODE ISLAND 1790 · IOWA 1846 · OHIO 1803 · PENNSYLVANIA 1787 · CONNECTICUT 1788 · NEBRASKA 1867 · ILLINOIS 1818 · INDIANA 1816 · NEW JERSEY 1787 · DELAWARE 1787 · WEST VIRGINIA 1863 · MARYLAND 1788 · DISTRICT OF COLUMBIA 1788 · KANSAS 1861 · MISSOURI 1821 · KENTUCKY 1792 · VIRGINIA 1788 · OKLAHOMA 1907 · TENNESSEE 1791 · NORTH CAROLINA 1789 · ARKANSAS 1836 · SOUTH CAROLINA 1788 · MISSISSIPPI 1817 · ALABAMA 1819 · GEORGIA 1788 · TEXAS 1845 · LOUISIANA 1812 · FLORIDA 1845

HOW AMERICA BECAME WHOLE
The map above explains how America grew from 1783 to 1896, from purchases to annexations, and includes the year each state was granted statehood.

The growth of the US, 1783–1898

- Thirteen Colonies 1776
- Addition of 1783
- Louisiana Purchase 1803
- Red River Cession 1818
- Purchase of Florida 1819
- Texas Annexation 1845
- Oregon Country Cession 1846
- Mexican Cession 1848
- Gadsden Purchase 1853
- Alaska Purchased 1867
- Hawaii Annexation 1898
- 1812 date of admission to statehood
- — modern state boundary

New York and New Jersey still permitted slavery. The question of whether new states would be slave or free would be a divisive political issue, and ultimately one of the major causes of the Civil War.

FROM SEA TO SHINING SEA

The next big territorial acquisition came through war. In 1836, American settlers in the Mexican province of Texas successfully fought for independence; after nine years as an independent republic, Texas joined the United States in 1845. Partly as a result of the U.S. annexation of Texas, the United States and Mexico went to war in April 1845, a conflict that ended in a decisive American victory. In the Treaty of Guadeloupe Hidalgo, signed in February 1848, Mexico

ceded California and New Mexico to the United States. Meanwhile, the United States and Great Britain both claimed the "Oregon Country" of the Pacific Northwest. Eventually the two nations signed the Oregon Treaty dividing up the region in 1846.

In 1853, Secretary of State William Gadsden negotiated with Mexico the purchase of the land that now forms southern Arizona and New Mexico.

Together, the acquisitions of the 1840s and 1850s added another 1.25 million square miles to the United States, pushed the nation's western border to the Pacific, and filled in the outline of the continental United States as it exists today.

AMERICA OVERSEAS

Secretary of State William Seward bought Alaska from Russia in 1867, and in 1898 the United States acquired an overseas empire from Spain following the Spanish-American War. Spain ceded Guam and the Philippines (*see pp 182–183*)—the latter a U.S. colony until it achieved independence in 1946—and Puerto Rico in the Caribbean (*see pp 174–175*). In 1917, Puerto Ricans were granted U.S. citizenship. Also in 1917, the United States, fearful of German expansion and eager for a naval base to help protect the Panama Canal, bought several Caribbean islands from Denmark for $25 million, and St. Croix, St. John, and St. Thomas became the U.S. Virgin Islands.

In Hawaii, U.S. minister John L. Stevens conspired with other non-Hawaiians to overthrow Queen Liliuokalani. In 1893, Marines were sent ashore from an American warship in Honolulu Harbor, and Liliuokalani was forced to surrender. Five years later, the United States annexed the islands as a territory. Both Alaska and Hawaii became states in 1959.

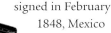

LOUISIANA PURCHASE TREATY
The Louisiana Purchase consisted of three separate agreements between the United States and France: a treaty of cession and two agreements concerning the transaction's monetary exchanges. The closed volume (*left*) is the French copy of one of the later agreements. The purchase cost $15 million.

LEWIS & CLARK EXPEDITION
A postage stamp (*above*) commemorates the bicentennial of the Lewis & Clark Expedition. President Jefferson dispatched his private secretary, Meriwether Lewis, and an army officer, William Clark, to lead an exploratory expedition through the newly acquired Louisiana Territory. Setting out from St. Louis, Missouri, in August 1803, the party reached the Pacific Coast in November 1805 and returned in August 1806.

PRESCIENT PURCHASE
Secretary of State William Seward's (*second from left in this painting by Emanuel Leutze*) purchase of Alaska was derided by some Americans, who believed that the territory—which they dubbed "Seward's Icebox"—was a useless wasteland. However, Alaska's mineral wealth alone has paid back the purchase price countless times over.

EUROPEAN EMIGRATION

Between 1815 and 1915, some 30 million Europeans arrived in the United States. For many it was a long and arduous journey. In the early part of the century, just getting to a port of embarkation might mean days or weeks of travel on foot, by rivercraft, or in horse-drawn vehicles. Because regularly scheduled departures were rare in the age of sail, immigrants often had to wait in port for days or weeks before their ship departed.

In Northern Europe, many immigrants departed from Dutch or German ports like Amsterdam and Bremen. Later, when immigration from Central and Eastern Europe was on the rise, immigrants often had to travel down the Danube River to Black Sea ports like Constanta and Varna. From there, they had to endure weeks or months at sea aboard sailing ships subject to the vagaries of wind and weather.

The spread of the railroads across Europe in the mid-1800s greatly shortened travel time to embarkation ports, while the introduction of steamships cut passage time from weeks to days, in the case of the fastest ships. Ships also increased in size, some carrying more than 1,000 immigrants in steerage class.

Except in places where immigration was restricted—like the Russian Empire—it was fairly easy to travel from an obscure European village to the United States by the late 19th century. A potential immigrant contracted with a shipping company agent, often a local cleric or teacher, who informed the head office at the departure port. The agent then received a departure date and ticket voucher, which he passed along to the immigrant, who boarded a train for the port city. If the port of embarkation was Bremen, immigrants could almost step directly from the train onto their ship—the city had railroad track leading right onto the docks.

Between 1882 and 1917, the U.S. government introduced laws regulating immigration. In 1891, for example, Congress barred from admission those "suffering from a loathsome or a dangerous contagious disease" and those "convicted [of] a misdemeanor involving moral turpitude" like anarchists and polygamists. As a result, steamship lines became increasingly careful about whom they let on board. Immigrants had to have their papers checked and their health inspected before departure. Sometimes immigrants had to spend several days awaiting boarding, during which they were lodged and fed by the steamship company.

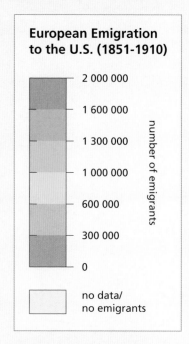

European Emigration to the U.S. (1851-1910)

— 2 000 000
— 1 600 000
— 1 300 000
— 1 000 000
— 600 000
— 300 000
— 0

number of emigrants

no data/
no emigrants

KEY TO EUROPEAN EMIGRATION
The shaded areas correlate to the number of emigrants leaving Europe during the time period indicated on each separate map. English-speaking people formed the largest group of immigrants to America during this time, followed by German speakers.

EUROPEAN EMIGRATION TO THE U.S. 1851–1860

Although the Irish potato blight receded in 1850, the effects of the famine continued to spur Irish emigration into the 20th century. Still facing poverty and disease, the Irish set out for America where they reunited with relatives who had fled at the height of the famine.

EUROPEAN EMIGRATION TO THE U.S. 1861–1870

The growing population of Prussia and the independent German states outstripped the available land. Industrialization could not provide decent-paying jobs, and political rights were limited. Dissatisfied with the lack of land and opportunity, many Germans left.

EUROPEAN EMIGRATION TO THE U.S. 1871–1880

In 1871, Prussian Chancellor Otto von Bismarck united the German states to form the German Empire. Whereas previous German immigrants had been mainly from Northern Germany, under Protestant Prussian rule, they came from southern, predominately Catholic, states.

EUROPEAN EMIGRATION TO THE U.S. 1881–1890

A new surge of Irish emigration resulted from more crop failures and increasing political and religious strife. Emigration from England (and to a lesser extent Scotland and Wales) continued, mainly by skilled laborers seeking work in America's industries and farmers seeking land.

EUROPEAN EMIGRATION TO THE U.S. 1891–1900

Italian emigration was fueled by dire poverty. Life in Southern Italy, including the islands of Sicily and Sardinia, offered landless peasants little more than hardship, exploitation, and violence. Even the soil was poor, yielding little, while malnutrition and disease were widespread.

EUROPEAN EMIGRATION TO THE U.S. 1901–1910

The anti-Semitic violence of the Russian pogroms drove millions of Jews out of the Russian Empire. In the Austro-Hungarian Empire, people emigrated to escape army conscription and ethnic tensions, such as the forced assimilation of Hungary's minority groups.

Early Immigration

Between the end of the Napoleonic Wars in 1815 and the start of World War I, some 60 million Europeans left their native continent—the greatest mass migration in human history. Many emigrated to the colonies the European powers acquired around the world during this era. For about 30 million of these people, however, the United States was the destination.

CARD-CARRYING NATIVIST
A certificate from around 1845 declares the bearer to be a member of the Native American Republican Association of Philadelphia—one of the many anti-immigrant societies that sprang up as the number of immigrants rose sharply in the mid-1800s.

The first major wave of immigration to the United States lasted from 1815 until the end of the Civil War in 1865; most of those who came during this period were English, Irish, and German. The second major wave, from the end of the Civil War to roughly 1890, brought another ten million, still mostly people from Northern Europe.

NATIVISM AND KNOW-NOTHINGS

For most of the 19th century there was no real regulation of immigration; not until 1890 did the federal government take over immigration policy from the individual states. During this period, anyone who could pay his or her passage could come to the United States. The Constitution provided a naturalization process for those who decided to become citizens.

This *laissez-faire* approach did not, however, mean that immigrants were universally welcomed. Even during the Colonial Era, some Americans feared non-English immigrants would establish, in the words of no less a personage than Benjamin Franklin, "their language and manners to the exclusion of ours." Writing about German immigration to Pennsylvania in 1751, Franklin asked, "Why should Pennsylvania, founded by the English, become a colony of Aliens . . ."

In the mid-1800s, the United States was still—apart from its slave population—a largely homogenous nation of Anglo-Saxon Protestants. Resentment towards large numbers of Germans and Irish immigrants (the latter mostly Roman Catholic)

fostered a Nativist movement that found expression in occasional mob violence and through anti-immigrant political groups like the Know-Nothing Party of the 1850s, which won 43 Congressional seats in the 1854 election.

Immigrants, however, were welcomed into the ranks of the Union Army during the Civil War; historians estimate that a third of the soldiers who fought for the North were of foreign birth, most of them German, Irish, or English. The forces of the Confederacy, however, did not include many foreign-born troops, because the South—with little industry and a slave-based, agricultural economy—attracted relatively few immigrants.

The first federal restrictions on immigration were aimed solely at Asians. Pressure from Nativist groups in California led to the first significant federal immigration law—mandatory residency permits for Asian immigrants. Seven years later, in 1882, Congress passed the Chinese Exclusion Act (*see pp 154–155*), which practically halted Chinese immigration.

FERTILE FIELDS
The availability of cheap, or even free, land in the West (like this wheat field in South Dakota, *c.*1880) was a powerful impetus to 19th-century immigration, particularly among Germans, Scandinavians, and other Northern Europeans.

RUN-OFF ELECTION
With the crude ethnic stereotyping typical of the era, a Nativist cartoon from the 1850s depicts caricatures of whiskey-drinking Irish and beer-guzzling German immigrants stealing a ballot box. Indignation at the supposed drinking habits of immigrant groups—and their potential political power—fueled Nativist sentiment.

URBANIZATION AND IMMIGRATION
The growth of the railroads and industrialization transformed the North American landscape. The economic boom turned the continent into a magnet for thousands of immigrants. Inventions and innovations abounded; cities arose across the continent, supporting factories that expanded because of the demands of the Civil War.

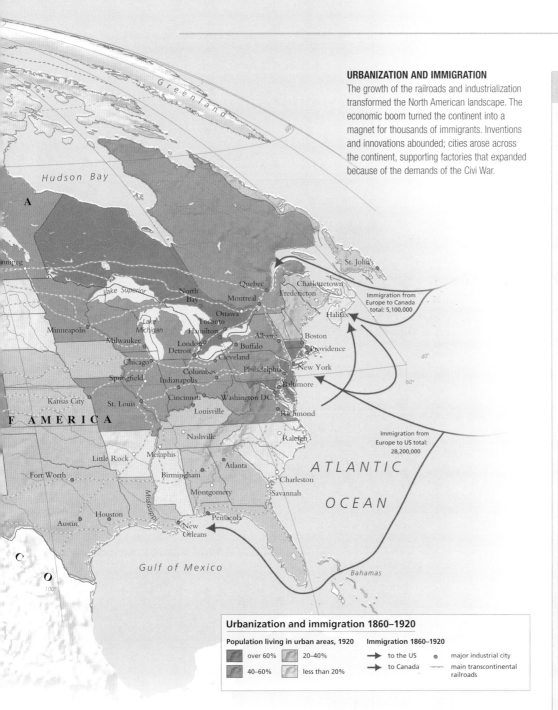

Immigration from Europe to Canada total: 5,100,000

Immigration from Europe to US total: 28,200,000

Urbanization and immigration 1860–1920

Population living in urban areas, 1920
- over 60%
- 40–60%
- 20–40%
- less than 20%

Immigration 1860–1920
- → to the US
- → to Canada
- ● major industrial city
- main transcontinental railroads

ENGLISH ONLY?

The United States doesn't have, and has never had, an official language. Some have claimed that the Continental Congress considered making German the new nation's language in order to sever linguistic ties with Britain. (This is a myth, however; its source is likely a 1795 episode in which Germans in Virginia unsuccessfully petitioned Congress to print copies of federal laws in their language.)

Throughout the 19th century, American public schools in many communities offered instruction both in English and in the language spoken by the local "majority minority"—for example, French in Louisiana, and German in many of the cities of the Midwest. When immigration increased before the turn of the 20th century, critics charged that these dual systems would hamper the "Americanization" of immigrant children, and gradually public schools

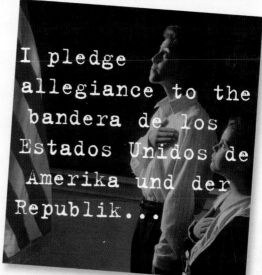

U.S. ENGLISH
An advertisement produced by U.S. English, which claims to be "the nation's oldest, largest citizens' action group dedicated to preserving the unifying role of the English language in the United States," asks "Will is come to this?"

adopted an English-only policy. The removal of the German language was expedited by anti-German sentiment associated with World War I. Between 1917 and 1922, most of the states dropped the language from their school curricula.

This early, English-only movement faded away, but revived again in the 1970s. Proponents claimed that making English the sole language of government and public education was crucial to provide a "common ground" in an ever more ethnically diverse United States. Critics charged that English-only supporters were motivated more by old-fashioned Nativism and, in particular, by unease over the growing presence of the Spanish language as the numbers of Americans of Hispanic ancestry rose rapidly. (By the turn of the 21st century, it was estimated that at least 20 million Americans spoke Spanish as their primary language.)

In 1981, Senator S. I. Hayakawa of California introduced a bill that would have amended the Constitution to establish English as the nation's official language, but the bill never went to vote. As of 2005, 25 states have declared English their official language, while two states, Hawaii and New Mexico, are now bilingual.

TRANSPORTATION

Until recent decades, emigrants bound for America had to endure a transoceanic journey that was always uncomfortable, frequently dangerous, and sometimes deadly. The fact that so many people were willing to endure the hardships involved in getting to America is a powerful testimony to their courage and determination.

THE AGE OF SAIL

Until the mid-1800s, the only way to get from Europe to America was by sailing ship. The westward passage took an average of six weeks, but bad weather could double that time. Immigrants were usually packed into the lowest deck of the ship, above the steering gear that controlled the ship's rudder—this is the source of the term "steerage," which became synonymous with immigrant passage even after steamships replaced sailing ships by the late 19th century. In many cases, passengers were confined to that area of the ship and not allowed to leave it.

Steerage accommodations were cramped, with crude bunks for sleeping and only canvas partitions for privacy. On some ships, passengers had to bring their own food; on ships that provided rations, the food was often poor in both quality and quantity. In 1850, a British official reported that on most ships

JOURNEY'S END
Irish immigrants disembark at the Battery on the southern tip of Manhattan Island in this 1847 painting by Samuel Waugh. (The Chinese junk in the background is a creative embellishment of the artist's.)

STEERAGE PASSENGERS TAKE THE AIR
In 1911, a U.S. Immigration Commission report found that on most ships, "The open deck space reserved for steerage passengers is usually very limited, and situated in the worst part of the ship, subject to the most violent motion, to the dirt from the stacks and the odors from the hold."

"[T]he bread is mostly condemned bread ground over with a little fresh flour . . . and rebaked." The water was almost always just as foul.

Crowded and unsanitary accommodation, lack of ventilation, and bad food and water made ships breeding grounds for diseases like typhus and cholera, especially the "coffin ships" carrying emigrants fleeing the potato famine in Ireland (*see pp 144–145*). In 1847 alone, typhus killed 7,000 passengers on transatlantic voyages. A year later, Congress passed the American Passenger Act, which established health and safety standards for ships carrying immigrants to America.

KEEPING IT CLEAN
British Public Health officials spray disinfectant aboard a ship about to sail for the United States. Shipboard outbreaks of cholera and other diseases greatly declined when sail gave way to steam on the Atlantic run.

THE AGE OF STEAM

The arrival of steamships after around 1850 greatly reduced passage time; by the 1870s, the average transatlantic crossing took two weeks. The great wave of European immigration that began around 1880 overlapped with the rise of major steamship lines—Cunard and White Star in Britain, Hamburg-Amerika and Norddeutscher-Lloyd in Germany, and Holland-Amerika in the Netherlands—all of which competed for immigrant fares. By 1900, the average price of a steerage ticket was about $30. Many immigrants traveled on prepaid tickets sent by relatives already in America; others bought tickets from the small army of traveling salesmen employed by the steamship lines.

A relatively few number of ports served the immigrant trade. Most Central and Eastern Europeans embarked from Hamburg or Bremen in Germany. For Italians, it was usually Genoa or Naples; for those from the British Isles, Liverpool, or Queenstown (now Cobh) in Ireland. Before boarding their ship, emigrants went through a processing that included being bathed and "de-loused." The steamship lines also made sure all passengers had their paperwork in order because the United States fined shipping companies for each passenger denied entry.

Conditions in steerage varied from ship to ship. Aboard the biggest Atlantic liners, which could carry as many as a 1,000 steerage passengers, accommodations were spartan but clean, with adequate sanitation, food, and even recreational facilities. There were still plenty of older, smaller, slower ships, however, where steerage remained dirty, overcrowded, and unhealthy. On all ships, families were segregated from single people, and single people were segregated by sex. For many steerage passengers, the lack of privacy in the dormitory-style cabins was the worst part of the voyage. Steerage passengers attempted to relieve the boredom and anxiety of the voyage with card games, dances, conversation, and endless rechecking of their entry documents.

THE JET AGE

By the time the next major period of immigration began in the mid-1960s, aircraft had replaced ships as the main mode of long-distance transportation. The immigrants' journey to America was now a matter of days or hours, instead of weeks or even months at sea. In addition,

AIRBORNE ARRIVALS
Eighty-two refugees arrive at Miami, Florida, from Varadero Airport in Cuba on December 1, 1965. On November 6, 1965, Cuba and the United States formally agreed to to start an airlift for Cubans who wanted to go to the United States. Two such "freedom flights" occurred each week between 1965 and 1973.

LINE UP FOR ENTRY
International arrivals wait to be fingerprinted and photographed at San Francisco International Airport in January 2004, after the start of the US-VISIT program—one of the new security measures enacted post-9/11.

changes in immigration policy now allowed immigrants to obtain their entry visas and other paperwork at U.S. consulates in their home countries, eliminating the kind of processing that took place at Ellis Island (*see pp 48–53*). Today, New York's John F. Kennedy Airport is the major point of entry—84,860 people arrived with immigrant visas in the 2003 fiscal year.

Ellis Island

For about 12 million immigrants between 1892 and 1954, the gateway to the United States was a small island in New York Harbor—Ellis Island. Nearly half of all contemporary Americans have at least one ancestor who passed through its Great Hall. A restored Ellis Island now stands as a symbol of the great age of immigration to the United States, drawing more than two million visitors a year.

LADY LIBERTY

Generations of immigrants would remember with emotion their first sight of the Statue of Liberty as their ship steamed into New York Harbor. A gift from the people of France to the people of the United States, the bronze statue, officially known as "Liberty Enlightening the World," was dedicated on October 28, 1886. Designed by French sculptor Frédéric Auguste Bartholdi, the statue measures 151 feet from the top of its pedestal base to the tip of the torch.

CASTLE GARDEN
Some 8 million immigrants passed through Castle Garden in its 35 years of operation—about three-quarters of all immigrants during that period. The facility was operated jointly by New York State and the federal government until the opening of Ellis Island.

The opening of Ellis Island overlapped with the start of a third major wave of immigration to the United States, which began around 1890 and ended with the outbreak of World War I in 1914. During this quarter-century, about 15 million people arrived—more than a million a year, on average, from 1905 to 1914—and most of them came through Ellis Island. In its origins, this wave was different than those that came before. For the first time, the majority of immigrants came not from Northern Europe, but from Central, Southern, and Eastern Europe—people from Italy, Poland, the Austro-Hungarian Empire, and Russia, including more than two million Jews.

From 1855 to 1890, immigrants arriving in New York had disembarked at Castle Garden, a former fort at the southern tip of Manhattan Island. In the 1880s, the rising number of immigrants began to exceed Castle Garden's capacity. In 1890, the federal government authorized the construction of a new station offshore, on a three-acre island previously used as a picnic spot. Landfill would later extend the island to approximately 27 acres.

Ellis Island opened for business on January 1, 1892, when, accompanied by her two brothers, 15-year-old Annie Moore of Ireland became the first immigrant admitted through the new facility. In 1897, a fire burned the original buildings to the ground. Expanded and rebuilt with fireproof masonry buildings, Ellis Island reopened in 1900. The immigration restrictions of the 1920s sent the facility into a decline. From 1924 on, it was used as a military training center, and to house "enemy aliens" during World War II and refugees afterward. The facility closed completely in 1954.

The Russians have long made heavy propaganda use of Ellis Island. They call it a concentration camp, which, of course, is outrageous. No one mistreats us here. Our jailers—nearly all of them, anyway—are very kindly people, who go to extraordinary lengths, within the system, for which they don't pretend to be responsible, to make our stay here as little like a nightmare as they can. There is a movie here every Tuesday and Thursday night; the children get milk six times a day and go to school three hours a day. We are kept warm and fed generously—nothing like the Colony, I assure you, but more than enough. But I will tell you, it is hard to not be depressed at the realization that within the American government, which has rightly been honored so long as the guardian of individual freedom and human dignity, there is one agency that can seize a man and bring him to this place.

George Voskovec, Czechoslovakian playwright and actor, detained at Ellis Island in 1951, under the Internal Security Act of 1950

ELLIS ISLAND
By 1906, Ellis Island had grown to three separate but connected islands, as shown in this aerial view. Most of the landfill used to expand the island came from the excavation of New York City's subway system.

PROPER PAPERWORK
Steamship companies had to pay for the return passage of immigrants denied entry, so company officials were usually careful to make sure that steerage passengers had proper paperwork, like the passport at left, and could meet health standards.

STEERAGE ARRIVALS
Most immigrants crossed the ocean in steerage, the cheapest of the classes offered by the transatlantic steamship lines. First- and second-class passengers could land directly from the Manhattan piers; steerage passengers, like those shown at right, were ferried to Ellis Island.

IMMIGRANTS AWAIT THEIR RELEASE FROM ELLIS ISLAND
Crowded to almost three times its capacity, the immigration station at Ellis Island, New York, was closed temporarily on September 24, 1920, until the congestion could be relieved. Meanwhile, thousands of incoming immigrants were held aboard the vessels on which they arrived. Hundreds of immigrant families had no sleeping quarters, and the station facilities' employees were taxed to the utmost.

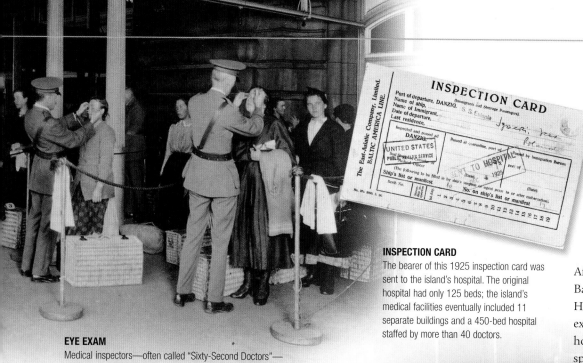

INSPECTION CARD

INSPECTION CARD

The bearer of this 1925 inspection card was sent to the island's hospital. The original hospital had only 125 beds; the island's medical facilities eventually included 11 separate buildings and a 450-bed hospital staffed by more than 40 doctors.

EYE EXAM

Medical inspectors—often called "Sixty-Second Doctors"—check immigrants' eyes for trachoma. Widespread in Southern Europe around the turn of the 20th century, the disease was infectious and could cause blindness. More immigrants were excluded for trachoma than for any other disease.

A decade later Ellis Island became part of the Statue of Liberty National Monument, but it was not until the mid-1980s that a serious restoration effort began, overseen by the National Park Service, but funded by private donations. The island opened to the public in 1986, and four years later the magnificently restored Main Hall began a new life as the Ellis Island Immigration Museum.

ISLAND OF JOY, ISLAND OF SORROWS

After dropping their baggage off in the island's Baggage Hall, immigrants lined up to enter the Great Hall of the Registry Room—the main part of the examination process, which took an average of five hours. As the immigrants filed through this immense space, inspectors of the U.S. Public Health Service quickly examined them for signs of infectious diseases

IMAGES OF IMMIGRANTS

Augustus Sherman worked as a clerk on Ellis Island from its opening in 1892 until his death in 1925. He was a talented amateur photographer, who took several hundred remarkable photographs of newly arrived immigrants, like the Romanian trio shown here. Sherman's photographs provide a matchless portrait of the diverse people who passed through the island on their way to becoming Americans.

GREAT HALL

The Great Hall of the Registry Room was a 200-by-100-foot space divided into 12 aisles. The tags worn by the immigrants listed the name of the ship they arrived on, so that inspectors could cross-check their names against the ship's passenger list.

or mental and physical disabilities, several of which—from tuberculosis to "feeble-mindedness"—could deny an immigrant entry to the United States.

Those who passed this preliminary examination—usually about 90 percent on a typical day—proceeded to the far end of the Great Hall. There, U.S. Immigration inspectors asked each adult immigrant 29 questions, ranging from name, age, and occupation to whether or not there was a job waiting for them in the United States. (A "yes" to that question could lead to an immigrant's being denied entry as per an 1865 law that forbade contract labor.) After 1917, immigrants also had to prove basic literacy in English or in their native language.

After inspection, immigrants descended from the Registry down the "Stairs of Separation," so called because they marked the parting of ways for many families and friends with different destinations. Immigrants were directed toward the railroad ticket office and trains to points west, or to the island's hospital and detention rooms. Those immigrants bound for a ferry to Manhattan met their friends or relatives at the "Kissing Post," where many joyous and tearful reunions occurred.

Those who were detained might have to endure a stay that could last weeks, and accommodations were in constant shortage. From 1900–08, dormitories consisted of two long, narrow rooms; each slept 300 people in triple-tiered bunks that were raised to convert the rooms into daytime waiting areas.

For a small number of would-be immigrants and their families, however, Ellis Island was an "island of sorrows." Most of the detainees held for medical or other reasons eventually passed their examinations and were allowed to land. About 2 percent, however, were deported back to their homelands.

THE DINING HALL
The detainees in this photograph are women and children who arrived unaccompanied by husbands or male relatives. They weren't allowed to leave until their safety could be guaranteed by a letter, telegram, or train ticket from a male relative already in America.

ALL ABOARD
Immigrants with destinations beyond New York City took a ferry to the railroad terminal across the Hudson River at Jersey City, where they continued their journey by rail. The immigrant who held this ticket traveled across the continent to California.

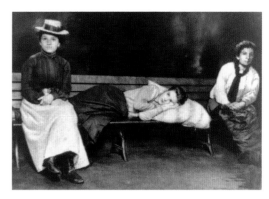

ENTRY DENIED
Passengers classified as "undesirable" await deportation to their homelands. Inspectors screened for polygamists, people with prison records for crimes involving "moral turpitude," and all "persons suffering from a loathsome or contagious disease."

NEW YORK CITY'S MELTING POT
By the 1920s, the diversity of nationalities on Manhattan reflected that of the population of the United States as a whole. Many immigrants found comfort in ethnic neighborhoods filled with people from their homeland.

Ethnic neighborhoods in Manhattan c.1920

African-American	Irish
Chinese	Italian
Czech, Hungarian	Jewish
French	Scandinavian, Finnish
German	Syrian, Turkish, Armenian, Greek

Closing the "Golden Door"

As the number of immigrants increased from the 1890s on, an increasingly vocal anti-immigration movement gathered strength. Some opponents of unrestricted immigration were organized labor leaders who feared that union members would lose their jobs to immigrants willing to work for lower wages. Ironically, some of these labor leaders—like Samuel Gompers, head of the American Federation of Labor—were immigrants themselves.

WEEPING LIBERTY
This newspaper cartoon protests the passage of the Alien Registration Act of 1940, also known as the Smith Act. The law required aliens over the age of 14 to be fingerprinted.

Other Americans were more concerned with the social consequences of immigration. The early 1900s was a time when many people believed in the inferiority or superiority of different ethnic groups. Proponents of immigration "reform" declared that the newest immigrants—Slavs, Italians, and Jews—were mentally and physically inferior to the descendants of the mainly Northern European immigrants who had come before. They believed the newcomers would never become "true Americans"; as writer Madison Grant argued in his 1916 best seller, *The Passing of the Great Race*, immigration was causing the "mongrelization" of America. Today these attitudes would be labeled as racist, but at the time they were widespread not only among the public, but also among prominent intellectuals and politicians.

World War I slowed immigration, but the Russian Revolution of 1917 fueled fears that immigrant radicals would try to incite revolution in

ILLEGAL IMMIGRATION

Immigration remains controversial in the 21st century. Some Americans contend that the federal government's attempt to distinguish between political and "economic" refugees is unfair and perhaps racist, because it tends to exclude people from Haiti and the war-torn countries of Africa. And in the wake of the 9/11 attacks, fears that terrorists might enter the country have complicated the admission of many immigrants.

But the biggest concern is over illegal immigration, particularly from Latin America, and especially from Mexico. The border between the United States and Mexico is simply too long and porous to patrol effectively—even though the U.S. Border Patrol turns back some 1 million illegal immigrants each year. In 2003, the U.S. Immigration and Naturalization Service estimated that there were 7 million illegal immigrants in the United States, about 70 percent of them from Mexico. Other estimates put the total at 10 million or higher.

Some argue that illegal immigrants provide an economic benefit by doing the kind of low-wage, unskilled labor that native-born Americans are increasingly unwilling to do. Others believe illegal immigrants have a negative economic effect because they consume taxpayer-supported public services, like medical care and education.

U.S. BORDER PATROL
U.S. Border Patrol officers use aircraft, all-terrain vehicles (*shown here*), and even horses in their effort to intercept illegal aliens crossing the long U.S.-Mexican border.

the United States. When the rate of immigration picked up again in 1921, Congress began to set quotas for admission based on national origin. This movement culminated in the passage of the Johnson-Reed Act of 1924, which not only reduced the number of immigrants permitted to enter the United States each year, but was also an attempt to "freeze" the ethnic makeup of America by basing each nation's annual quota on the number of immigrants living in America prior to World War I. (The quotas were for European nations; immigration from the Eastern Hemisphere was already restricted by existing laws.)

The Smith Act, named after its sponsor, Virginia Representative Howard Smith, required some 3.5 million immigrants who had not been naturalized as citizens to register with the Immigration and Nationalization Service. The law was passed as a "National Security" measure in response to the outbreak of World War II in Europe.

In later years, some exceptions were made—for "displaced persons" following World War II, for foreign nationals married to U.S. servicemen, and for refugees from Communism during the Cold War. Largely as a result of the Smith Act, however, the percentage of

ON THE LOSING SIDE
This Vietnamese girl was photographed on arrival at San Francisco International Airport in September 1977, after Congress allowed political refugees to immigrate from South Vietnam.

Americans of foreign birth or parentage declined (from a high of 14.3 million in 1930 to a low of 9.6 million in 1970). But new laws would change that.

IMMIGRATION SINCE 1965

In 1965, Congress passed a sweeping new immigration law. The Immigration Act of 1965 did away with the old quota system that favored Europe, replacing it with

FLOATING TO FREEDOM
Since 1991, the volunteer pilots of *Hermanos al Rescate* (Brothers to the Rescue) have patrolled the waters between Florida and Cuba, saving more than 4,000 refugees—including the passengers on this raft—from possible death.

> "Once upon a time there was no such thing as an illegal immigrant to America. If you could get here, you could stay here."
>
> "The Golden Door"

a "family preference" system; legal immigrants to America could now sponsor relatives from their countries of origin. Subsequent laws permitted increased immigration of political and religious refugees from Cuba, Vietnam, the former Soviet Union, and other nations. For example, after the fall of South Vietnam in 1975, thousands of Vietnamese who were at risk of persecution under the new Communist regime were allowed into the United States as refugees.

For the first time in America's history, the majority of immigrants are from Asia and Latin American, rather than from Europe. The 2000 Census found that about 10 percent of today's Americans were born in a foreign land.

CHINESE NEW YEAR
Chinese-American children, in traditional dress, wave American flags at a New Year celebration in Los Angeles. Despite immigration restrictions that lasted for 60 years, the Chinese are the largest Asian ethnic group in America, numbering more than 2.3 million in 2000.

2

FREEDOM TO WORSHIP

Persecuted for their religious beliefs, a long line

of men and women have taken refuge in America ever

since the Pilgrims landed at Plymouth Rock. From

the Anabaptists fleeing Switzerland and Germany

in the 18th century, to the Hasidic Jews fleeing

Eastern Europe after World War II, to the Tibetans

who come today, their numbers have been small, but

they have always come—bearing witness to the idea

of America as a haven for immigrants in search

of religious freedom.

"The Earth Is the Lord's"

ORTHODOX WEDDING
A groom (still in coat) dances after his Orthodox Jewish wedding in Baltimore, Maryland. Orthodox Judaism is characterized by a strict adherence to Jewish law and tradition. Between the early 1880s and the early 1920s, nearly 2.5 million Jews arrived in America from Central and Eastern Europe, the majority of them fleeing persecution in Russian-ruled territory.

THE EARTH IS THE LORD'S

Following the desire for a better material life for themselves and their children, the desire for religious freedom probably motivated more immigrants to come to America than any other concern—and the two desires have often been inextricably linked. In the words of historian Will Durant, "For men came across the sea not merely to find new soil for their plows but to win freedom for their souls, to think and speak and worship as they would."

The founding of European colonies in North America coincided with the Protestant Reformation—one of the watershed events of human history. The Reformation not only split Europe along Catholic and Protestant lines, it also spawned a variety of religious groups whose members often suffered persecution from civil and religious authorities alike. This persecution varied widely from country to country, both in form and in the degree of severity. In some places, members of minority faiths resented paying taxes to support the established church and being forced to attend worship services; in other places, refusing to conform to the local religion meant death.

To those suffering from harassment or maltreatment in the Old World, the New World offered space to create new societies in which they could worship without interference—like the Pilgrims and Puritans who founded New England.

At the time, however, the idea that freedom of worship was a fundamental human right was in its infancy. Many of those who came to the colonies seeking the freedom to practice their particular faith were quick to deny that freedom to those whose beliefs were different—most notably the New England Puritans, who banished, punished, and sometimes executed Quakers (see pp 66–69) and other non-Puritans.

One of those banished from Puritan Massachusetts was Roger Williams, one of the first great figures in the history of religious freedom in what would become the United States. Williams believed that because no one can truly know which religion is "acceptable" to God, everyone should be free to worship according to his or her own conscience—something he called "soul liberty." Williams, who founded Rhode Island in 1636, put the idea into practice; the colony quickly became a haven for Quakers, Jews, and other "dissenters."

Later in the 1600s, Quaker leader William Penn established Pennsylvania, which welcomed immigrants of many faiths, while in the New Netherlands (soon to be New York), the Dutch government adopted a policy of religious tolerance—not so much out of philosophical principle, but because it was good for business.

CONGRESS SHALL MAKE NO LAW . . .

In Europe, the Reformation led to a series of deadly and devastating wars of religion that brought even more refugees, like the Huguenots (pp 62–64), to the colonies. The suffering caused by these European conflicts, as well as the intellectual advances of the 18th-century Enlightenment, led the founders of the United States to make freedom to worship the law of the land in the First Amendment to the Constitution: "Congress shall make no law respecting an establishment of religion or prohibiting the free exercise thereof" [in other words, there would be no state-supported church, as in Britain], while the document's Article VI barred "religious tests" for public office. And although the majority of Americans—then and now—profess Christianity, the new nation confirmed separation of church and state in a 1797 treaty with the Muslim state of Tripoli in North Africa, which stated, "The government of the United States is not, in any sense, founded on the Christian religion."

This guarantee inspired countless immigrants to make their way to the United States, often at great risk and hardship—from Jews escaping anti-Semitic pogroms in the 19th-century Russian Empire to Tibetans fleeing the Communist Chinese occupation of their homeland in the 1990s. As a result, the United States became the most religiously diverse nation on earth, with some 2,000 distinct religious groups by the early 21st century. Its example fostered the growth of religious freedom in other nations, and continues to provide hope to those suffering persecution for their beliefs around the world.

BURNING BULL

In 1520, Pope Leo X officially condemned German monk Martin Luther for heresy; Luther responded by publicly burning the bull (papal edict) outside the town gate at Wittenberg, Germany. Luther's break with the church hierarchy sparked the Protestant Reformation—which would soon affect the settlement of America.

THE REFORMATION

At the start of the 16th century, virtually all of Western Europe's Christians were united in the Roman Catholic Church. By the end of the century, however, Rome's religious monopoly was shattered. The Reformation—a turning point in human history—divided Europe between Catholic and Protestant states, with profound consequences not just for the Old World, but for the New World as well.

LUTHER'S CHALLENGE

During the intellectual ferment of the Renaissance, some European thinkers came to believe that the Church had strayed from its Biblical roots, becoming corrupt. At the same time, many rulers resented the drain of wealth from their territories to Rome.

In 1517, a German monk, Martin Luther, openly questioned Pope Leo X's authorization of the sale of indulgences—essentially, promises of forgiveness of sins in return for cash. Although Luther's original intent was simply to spark a theological dialogue, rather than to start a separate church, the papacy sensed a threat and quickly tried to silence him.

The son of a miner, Luther had studied law before becoming a monk. His anxieties over his own salvation persisted until, through Bible study, he came to believe that Christians were saved only by faith, and not

through a combination of faith and good works, as the Roman Catholic Church taught. He also believed that Christians should be able to read the Bible in their own language, and while in hiding from Church authorities, he produced the first translation of the Bible into German. The new technology of the printing press rapidly spread Luther's teachings throughout Europe. And although Luther was condemned by Rome, he had powerful protectors among the German nobility. Eventually, Lutheranism took hold in much of Northern Germany, in the Scandinavian nations, and in pockets elsewhere in Europe.

THE REFORMATION SPREADS

Next to Luther, the most influential figure of the Reformation was John Calvin, a French lawyer. In his *Institutes of the Christian Religion* (1536), Calvin

EUROPEAN RELIGIONS

Although Lutheran, Catholic, and Anabaptist ideas spread throughout Europe, the Roman Catholic Church largely succeeded in suppressing the Reformation in much of the continent by the mid-1500s; afterwards, Protestantism was mostly concentrated in Northern Europe. This map shows the breakdown of religion in Europe around 1590, including the different strands of Protestantism.

The religious map of Europe 1590

- almost exclusively Catholic, with just minimal Protestant presence in northern areas
- overwhelmingly Catholic, with appreciable Protestant minority
- Catholic majority, but with very strong Protestant minority
- exclusively or overwhelmingly Protestant, with only slight Catholic presence in places
- Protestant majority, with some Catholic presence
- mainly Catholic, with strong Greek Orthodox presence
- Greek Orthodox, with significant Muslim presence in some areas of the Balkans
- Muslim majority

frontier of Holy Roman Empire 1590

Calvinist locally dominant Protestant denomination

ETERNAL CITY

Pope Leo X, who reigned from 1513 to 1521, nearly emptied the papal treasury through personal extravagance, patronage of the arts, and the desire to complete the construction of St. Peter's Basilica *(below)* in Rome.

THE COUNTER-REFORMATION
The Council of Trent got its name from the Italian city in which members of the Roman Catholic hierarchy periodically gathered, from 1545 to 1563, to define the Church's doctrines and practices in defense against the Reformation.

saw Mary's sister, Elizabeth, as their savior, and several uprisings were made in her name. As a result, Mary imprisoned her in the Tower.

Mary died in 1558 and Elizabeth became queen. She restored the Church of England, but as ruler of a people who by now were weary of religious strife, the Church pursued a "middle way" during her reign: the Church of England was Protestant in the sense that it rejected the authority of the pope and embraced many of the theological doctrines of the Reformation, but it retained elements of Catholic organization and ritual.

REFORMERS IN AMERICA

This made the church insufficiently "reformed" in the eyes of some Protestants. Influenced by the doctrines of John Calvin, these Puritans—so-called from their desire to "purify" the church—grew restive under the Anglican hierarchy. In the 1620s, Puritan leaders like John Winthrop began to see England's territory in North America as a place where they could live and worship according to their own rights (see pp 28–29).

In America, a policy of religious tolerance was encouraged by many new settlers. The Dutch, for example, transplanted to their American colonies a policy of religious tolerance, which had arisen after the mostly Protestant Netherlands had succeeded in gaining independence after a long and bloody struggle against their Spanish Catholic rulers. Their colonies became a haven for settlers of many faiths, including Jews. Many of the Pilgrims, who preceded the Puritans to America, had lived in the Dutch city of Leiden for a time before sailing to New England. There they were exposed to further Dutch standards of toleration, which impressed them favorably.

laid out an intellectually rigorous form of Protestantism, which he put into practice as ruler of the Swiss city of Geneva. The Calvinist strain of Protestantism eventually won a wide following throughout Europe, especially in the Netherlands, France, and Scotland.

In the wake of Luther and Calvin came even more radical reformers like the Anabaptists (see p 74), who sought to interpret the Bible literally and to live according to its precepts. By rejecting all forms of civil and religious hierarchy, the Anabaptists and other radical sects came under harsh persecution from Lutherans, Calvinists, and Catholics.

The Reformation came to England in 1543, when King Henry VIII proclaimed himself head of the Church of England. Henry's motivations were dynastic, not theological—he had even published a pamphlet condemning Luther. But when the pope refused to allow him to divorce his first wife, who had failed to bear him a male heir, Henry broke with Rome and set up a national church, the Church of England, with the monarch as its head.

Henry's death in 1547 touched off almost a century and a half of religious unrest in the British Isles—turmoil that played a major role in the settling of North America. In 1553, Mary Tudor, a staunch Roman Catholic, succeeded to the throne following the death of Henry's son, Edward VI. Mary's determination to restore England to Catholicism led to the execution of more than 300 Protestant clergy, and earned her the nickname "Bloody Mary." The persecuted Protestants

JOHN CALVIN
1509–1564

Of all the varieties of Protestantism that emerged in the 16th century, Calvinism had the greatest influence on the development of what would become the United States. Calvin's doctrines were central to the faiths of the Pilgrims and Puritans, who settled in New England; the French Huguenots, who found refuge in the English colonies; and the Dutch, who founded New Netherlands. Calvin stressed the utter dependence of the individual human upon God in everything. Although individuals could do nothing to affect their own salvation—because God predestined the fate of all souls—Calvinism held that people should strive to lead virtuous lives.

Huguenots

Despite the monarchy's efforts to halt the spread of Protestantism in France, the Reformed doctrines of John Calvin won many adherents in the mid-1500s. These French Protestants became known as "Huguenots." There are several theories about the origin of the name; many sources believe it derives from a Flemish term, *Huis Genooten* or "house fellows," used to describe early Protestants who worshiped secretly in one another's houses.

First migration	**1640s**
Migrated from	**France**
Approx. number in USA	**6,000 (1725)**
Settlement	**South Carolina; New Rochelle and New Paltz, New York; Pennsylvania; Boston, Massachusetts; Virginia**

HUGUENOT FORTRESS
Built during the 14th century, this castle served as a Huguenot stronghold during the Wars of Religion. It is located in Beuvreuil, near the town of Dampierre-en-Bray in Northern France.

By 1561, there were more than 2,000 Huguenot congregations throughout France, with over a million members, or about 15 percent of France's total population. The Huguenots were most numerous in Southern France, although there were communities throughout the country. The new faith proved especially attractive to merchants and craftspeople in the nation's cities, yet it also won many converts from the nobility. Although the French government granted a measure of toleration to the Huguenots in 1560, their rapidly growing numbers—and the political and economic power they wielded—alarmed many Catholic French leaders, as did Huguenot vandalism of Catholic churches in some communities. In March 1562, tensions boiled over when a Catholic mob murdered a group of Huguenots at Vassy. A month later, the Huguenot leadership announced that they were taking up arms in their own defense.

FRENCHMEN IN FLORIDA

In 1562, Admiral Gaspard de Coligny, the Huguenot leader, sent an expedition commanded by Jean Ribault and René de Laudonniere to North America to reconnoiter sites for a possible Huguenot colony. The explorers landed in Florida at the mouth of the St. John's River (the site of present-day Cape Canaveral), and left a small party near what is now Parris Island, South Carolina, although that settlement was quickly abandoned. In 1654, the French returned and built a fort at the St. John's River site, which they named Fort Caroline after France's King Charles IX. A year later, a Spanish force commanded by

ST. BARTHOLOMEW'S DAY
Church bells signaled the beginning of the slaughter of Huguenots in Paris on August 23, 1572. The attack was authorized by King Charles IX at the urging of his mother, Catherine de Médicis.

MASSACRE AT FORT CAROLINE
Spanish soldiers under the command of Admiral Pedro Menéndez de Avilés attacked the French Huguenots at Fort Caroline in what is now Florida. The Spanish commander posted a sign over the bodies of those killed: "I do this not as to Frenchmen, but as to Lutherans."

Pedro Menéndez de Avilés destroyed the fort and killed all the settlers, including some 350 people, led by John Ribault, who had the bad luck to arrive just weeks before the Spanish attack. The Spanish built St. Augustine (*see pp 20–21*) on the site.

THE WARS OF RELIGION

The attack at Vassy began a period known in France as the Wars of Religion—eight separate conflicts over 35 years that collectively devastated the nation. The low point, for the Huguenots, came in August 1572 with the St. Bartholomew's Day Massacre and its aftermath, which left as many as 70,000 Huguenots dead in Paris and other cities. Among those killed was Admiral de Coligny. The Huguenots continued fighting for 26 more years, however, in the hope of either putting a Huguenot on the throne, or at least winning tolerance for their religion and recognition of their political rights.

The Wars of Religion finally ended in 1598, five years after Prince Henry of Navarre became King Henry IV. Originally a Huguenot, Henry had converted to Catholicism in order to become king, but, in 1698, he proclaimed the Edict of Nantes, which granted the Huguenots religious and political freedom. As a *quid pro quo* for the Catholic hierarchy, however, the edict restricted the establishment of Huguenot congregations in predominantly Catholic parts of the country. Henry IV was a popular monarch with both his Catholic and Protestant subjects; the

> "...we grant to those of the said Religion power to build Places for the Exercise of the same, in Cities and Places where it is granted them..."
>
> Edict of Nantes

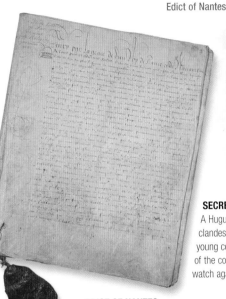

EDICT OF NANTES
Named for the town in Brittany in which it was proclaimed, Henry IV's edict allowed Huguenots to remain in control of the towns they had occupied during the Wars of Religion, but tolerance was not established in Paris.

SECRET WEDDING
A Huguenot pastor clandestinely marries a young couple, while a member of the congregation stands on watch against local authorities.

edict was respected during his reign and, to a lesser extent, during that of his son Louis XIII. When Louis XIV became king in 1643, however, a new period of persecution of the Huguenots began. The archetype of the "absolute monarch," Louis believed that the Huguenots represented a political threat to France's national unity.

In the early 1660s, Louis barred Huguenots from public office, banned nationwide gatherings of Huguenot leaders, and authorized the destruction of Huguenot churches, which, supposedly, were not specifically protected by the Edict of Nantes. With Louis's support, the Catholic hierarchy also stepped up efforts to reconvert Huguenots to Catholicism. The *dragonnade*—which involved quartering soldiers in Huguenot households, and sometimes forced conversions—was a particularly hated tactic.

Finally, in 1685, Louis revoked the Edict of Nantes, replacing it with the Edict of Fontainebleau. Its directives were sweeping: both public and private Protestant worship was forbidden, Protestant clergy were ordered to convert to Catholicism within two weeks or leave the country, and Huguenot parents would henceforth have to have their children baptized by Catholic priests and raised in the Catholic faith.

The new edict forbade Huguenots to leave the country on pain of imprisonment. Despite this, 200,000–400,000 Huguenots managed to flee.

GASPARD DE COLIGNY
1584–1646

Gaspard de Coligny, a man of noble birth, was the Admiral of France by 1552. Taken prisoner by the Spanish in 1557, he was released in 1559, the same year he publicly announced his conversion to Protestantism. Prominent from the outset of the Wars of Religion, he became the major Huguenot leader, negotiating the Treaty of Saint-Germain in 1570, which ended the first phase of the conflict. Reconciled with King Charles IX and Catherine de Médicis, Coligny returned to the court in 1571 and became the king's favorite adviser. Coligny's influence distressed Catherine who ordered his assassination. He escaped a first attempt, but fell in his home two days later during the St. Bartholomew's Day Massacre.

HUGUENOTS IN NORTH AMERICA

The Huguenot migration from France was one of the first great movements of religious refugees in modern times. Many went to England; others settled in Germany, Switzerland, the Netherlands, or in the Dutch colony of Cape Town in South Africa. Because the Huguenot refugees tended to be hard-working, well-educated, and highly skilled, they were generally welcomed wherever they settled. The Huguenot exodus amounted to a "brain drain" for France, and some historians believe the loss of so many productive citizens contributed to the economic problems that would eventually lead to the French Revolution.

We remained in London three months, waiting for a passage to Carolina. Having embarked, we were sadly off: the spotted fever made its appearance on board our vessel, of which disease many died, and among them our aged mother. Nine months elapsed before our arrival in Carolina. We touched at two ports—one a Portuguese, and the other an island called Bermuda, belonging to the English, to refit our vessel, which had been much injured in a storm. Our Captain having committed some misdemeanor, was put in prison, and the vessel seized. Our money was all spent, and it was with great difficulty we procured a passage in another vessel. After our arrival in Carolina, we suffered every kind of evil. In about eighteen months our elder brother, unaccustomed to the hard labor we had to undergo, died of a fever. Since leaving France we had experienced every kind of affliction—disease, pestilence, famine, poverty, hard labor. I have been six months together without tasting bread, working the ground like a slave; and I have even passed three or four years without always having it when I wanted it. God has done great things for us, enabling us to bear up under so many trials. I should never have done, were I to attempt to detail to you all of our adventures. Let it suffice that God has had compassion on me, and changed my fate to a more happy one. For which glory be unto him.

From a letter by Judith Manigault, who emigrated from France through the Netherlands to London and then America in 1685

Several thousand Huguenots—the exact number cannot be determined—eventually settled in the English colonies in North America.

Even before 1685, however, there were small numbers of Huguenots in the colonies. The first Huguenots arrived in the New Netherlands in the 1640s, settling in the Hudson River Valley. In 1678, after the New Netherlands had become New York, 12 Huguenot families received a land grant of some 40,000 acres and established the town of New Paltz. Huguenots also originally settled New Rochelle, in present-day Westchester County, New York. The town took its name from La Rochelle, one of the major Huguenot strongholds in France.

The Huguenots were especially important in the development of South Carolina. In 1680, the colony's leaders brought a small group of Huguenots over in an effort to start a silk-making industry. Many followed after 1685; these settlers and their descendants played a major role in establishing the slave-based plantation economy that flourished in the colony.

The Huguenots who arrived after the revocation of the Edict of Nantes came at a fortunate time. With the colonial economy and population expanding rapidly, their skills in metalworking and cabinetmaking were much needed and often well-rewarded. Many also excelled as merchants, including Peter Faneuil, son of Huguenot settlers in New Rochelle, who gave the city of Boston the original Faneuil Hall in the 18th century. Another Bostonian, James Bowdoin—grandson of Pierre Baudouin, who arrived in America in 1687—held important government posts during and after the Revolutionary War, and founded Bowdoin College.

HUGUENOT HOUSE
This is one of the original six stone houses built by the Huguenot settlers in New Paltz, New York, the earliest of which dates to 1692. The town's Huguenot Street became a National Historic Landmark District in 1985.

CHARLESTON'S FRENCH CHURCH
Huguenots assimilated easily to colonial life. One of their few existing symbols in early America is the French Protestant Church in Charleston, South Carolina, which holds a service in French every year to commemorate the Edict of Nantes.

PAUL REVERE
1734–1818

At some point in the early 1700s, a teenaged Huguenot named Apollos de Revoire arrived in Boston. Changing his name to Revere, he prospered as a silversmith, a craft he passed on to his son Paul, who became one of the city's leading citizens—and, in the run-up to the Revolutionary War, an ardent Patriot. Revere was an engraver, as well as a silversmith, and his propaganda work for the Patriot cause—like his depiction of the "Boston Massacre" of 1770—did much to stir up anti-British sentiment. Revere became enshrined in American folklore in 1863, thanks to Henry Wadsworth Longfellow's poem "Paul Revere's Ride," a romanticized account of his ride to warn the countryside that British troops were marching out of Boston to seize Patriot supplies.

JESUITS

In 1534, a Spanish ex-soldier, Ignatius Loyola, founded a new Roman Catholic religious order—the Society of Jesus, or Jesuits. Highly disciplined and centrally organized, the order quickly became active in a number of fields, including missionary work in the New World. Within 20 years, some 1,000 Jesuits were afield in Africa, Asia, and the Americas.

The first Jesuit missionaries arrived in New France in 1625. Known to the Native Americans as the "Black Robes" because of their apparel, the Jesuits went on to explore much of present-day North America in their effort to convert the Native Americans to Roman Catholicism; they ranged as far south as Arizona and as far west as Oregon, but were especially active in the Great Lakes region.

If the Jesuits proved successful as explorers, their success as missionaries was mixed, at best. The Native Americans grasped that when the Black Robes appeared, diseases like smallpox often followed, and many Jesuits were tortured or killed. On the other hand, French fur traders resented the Jesuits' campaign to stop them from plying the Native Americans with alcohol. By the mid-1700s, the Jesuit presence in North America was in decline.

The Jesuits, however, left a lasting legacy in the form of the *Jesuit Relations*. Each Jesuit missionary in North America was required to send home an annual report detailing his activities. These were published annually in Europe in an attempt to create interest in (and support for) the order's activities. With their highly detailed accounts of the landscape, wildlife, and people of North America in the 1600s and 1700s, the *Jesuit Relations* are one of the major sources of information about the early years of French colonization.

SOLDIER TO SAINT
Ignatius Loyola devoted his life to the Church while recovering from wounds suffered in a battle in 1521. He was canonized by Pope Gregory XV in 1622, sixty-six years after his death.

THE *JESUIT RELATIONS*
The frontispiece of an early edition of the *Jesuit Relations* for 1688 and 1689, published in Paris by Sébastien Cramoisy from 1632 to 1672. The English translation of the documents—completed between 1896 and 1901—runs to more than 18,000 pages. Historian Reuben Gold Thwaites undertook the monumental task of translating the *Jesuit Relations*.

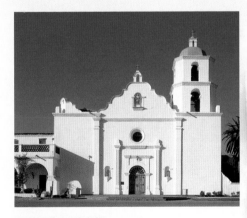

FRANCISCAN MISSION
The Jesuits' successors as missionaries, the Franciscans (named after St. Francis of Assisi), established a chain of missions in what is now California during the 18th century. Shown above is Mission San Luis Rey de la Francia, founded in 1798, near the present-day city of San Diego.

BLACK ROBE BEATIFICATION
Jesuit priests and Mohawks gather in upstate New York in 1925 to celebrate the beatification of Father Isaac Jogues, a French Jesuit missionary put to death by the Mohawks in 1646. They regarded Jogues as a sorcerer and blamed him for crop blights and epidemics. He was canonized five years later.

Quakers

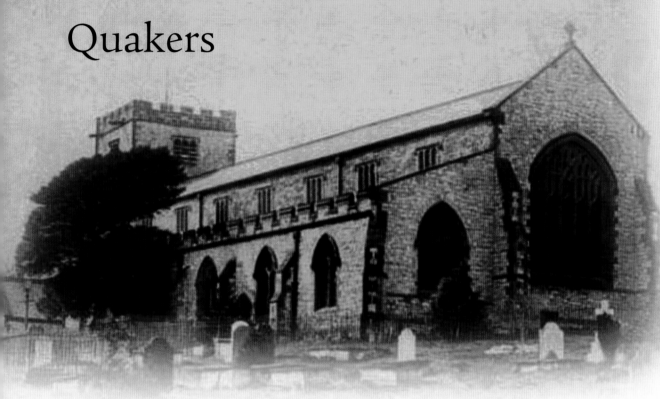

First migration	**1656**
Migrated from	**England**
Approx. number in USA	**125,000 (2005)**
Settlement	**Maryland; Massachusetts; New Jersey; North Carolina; Pennsylvania; Rhode Island; South Carolina**

ST. MARY'S CHURCH
In this parish church in Ulverston, in Cumbria, Northern England, George Fox announced to the startled congregation that "God was come to teach His people by His Spirit, and to bring them off from all their old ways, religions, churches, and worships."

FIRST FRIEND
George Fox was born in Leicestershire, England, in 1624. As a young man, Fox experienced revelations that he developed into the basic beliefs of the Society of Friends in the 1640s.

In the mid-1600s, in an England beset by religious controversy and civil war, a group formed that rejected clerical hierarchy, ceremonial ritual, and any kind of rigid theology, in favor of a faith based purely on a direct relationship between the individual and God. Considered a threat to both civil and religious authority, the Quakers were persecuted in both England and New England before founding a colony of their own.

Originally a Puritan offshoot known as "the Seekers," the Quaker movement coalesced around Swarthmoor Hall in Lancashire, in Northern England, around 1650. The movement's leaders, most prominently George Fox, preached a simple form of Christianity that forbade warfare, swearing oaths, and class distinctions. Spurning formal services, they worshipped in small groups, or meetings, with every member free to speak when moved by "the Inward light." According to Fox, the term Quaker was first applied by an anti-Quaker judge who "[called] us Quakers because we bid them tremble at the word of God." The early Quaker practice of interrupting others' church services to "rebuke" the worshippers contributed to their unpopularity. The Quakers contemptuously called churches "steeple-houses."

To emphasize equality before God, members called one another "friend"—and, around 1650, the group adopted the name the Society of Friends.

Fox and his associates traveled across England, spreading the Quaker message. By the 1660s, there were perhaps 60,000 Quakers in England, concentrated in the North, the West Country, and London.

AN UNFRIENDLY RECEPTION FOR THE FRIENDS

The Quakers' radical religious and social beliefs earned them persecution from all sides. During Oliver Cromwell's Puritan Commonwealth, they were

SWARTHMOOR HALL
Built in 1586, in Lancashire, England, this house was home to Judge Thomas Fell and his wife Margaret, who hosted George Fox after his arrival in Ulverston in 1652. The Fells became ardent supporters of Fox, and Swarthmoor Hall served as a headquarters for the Quaker movement for years. Margaret—who is often called "the Mother of Quakerism"— married Fox after Thomas Fell's death.

denounced for "blasphemy" and accused of plotting against the government. After King Charles II restored royal rule in 1660, the leaders of the established Church of England condemned them for refusing to attend services or to contribute financially to the Church—both of which were required by law. The relative equality of men and women among Quakers was also shocking. At least 15,000 Quakers were jailed in England between 1652 and 1689; several

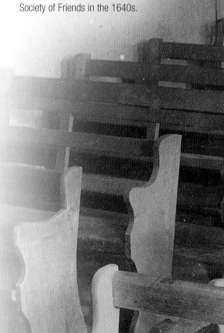

hundred died of mistreatment in prison or in mob attacks. George Fox was thrown in jail eight times between 1649 and 1673, but he lived to see Quakers achieve official toleration in England following an act of Parliament in 1689.

It was the same in New England. The first Quakers—Ann Austin and Mary Fisher—arrived in Boston in 1656 and were quickly thrown out by the Massachusetts Bay Colony's leaders for disrupting Puritan services. Persecution only stimulated the Quakers. Two were hanged in Boston in 1659 after ignoring orders to stay out of the colony. Two others, including Mary Dyer *(see side panel)*, met the same fate over the next two years.

Still, Quakers established communities in Cape Cod, Massachusetts, and in Newport, in tolerant Rhode Island, where the ship *Woodhouse* arrived in 1657 with a group of English Friends. Quakers also managed to settle in Dutch-ruled New Amsterdam and its surrounding areas *(see pp 30–31)*, as well as in New Jersey, the Carolinas, and Maryland. George Fox himself toured the colonies from 1671 to 1673.

FRIENDS UNDER THE LASH
A 1661 law of the Massachusetts Bay Colony called for Quakers to "be stripped naked from the middle upwards, and tied to a cart's tail and whipped through the town"—a punishment depicted in this 19th-century print. Some were also branded on the shoulder with the letter "R"—for "Ranter."

" Why should any man have power over any other man's faith, seeing Christ Himself is the author of it?"

George Fox

ORIGINAL MEETING HOUSE
Between 1688 and 1690, George Fox built a Meeting House located a short distance from Swarthmoor Hall. The spare interior reflects the Friends' disdain for decoration and any other distraction from "the Inward Light." .

MARY DYER
C.1610–1660

Born May Barrett in England around 1610, Dyer and her husband immigrated to Massachusetts around 1635. Dyer became a supporter of Anne Hutchinson *(see p 39)* and as a result was banished to Rhode Island. In 1652, Dyer returned to England and became a Quaker after meeting Fox. Five years later, she returned to the colonies to spread the Quakers' doctrines. For defying Massachusetts' ban on Quakers, she was sentenced to hang in 1659 and was reprieved while literally on the gallows. Nevertheless, she defied the law again the following year, and this time she was hanged. In her last words, she told the crowd that she had returned to Boston "desiring you to repeal the unrighteous and unjust law made against the innocent servants of the Lord." Dyer's death fulfilled that mission; a lingering guilt over her execution eventually led the colony's leaders to ease the anti-Quaker laws.

This statue of Mary Dyer sits in front of the Massachusetts Statehouse, facing the Boston Common where she was hanged.

PENN'S "HOLY EXPERIMENT"

William Penn *(see opposite)*, one of the most prominent converts to Quakerism, was the son of an admiral. In 1681, King Charles II granted Penn a huge expanse of land along the Delaware River to cancel a debt he owed to Penn's deceased father. Penn took this opportunity to launch what he called a "Holy Experiment"—a new colony in which not only Quakers could settle, but other persecuted religious groups could go to find refuge and the freedom to worship.

Later that year, Penn's cousin, William Markham, led the first settlers to Pennsylvania ("Penn's Woods" in Latin), where they laid out a city called Philadelphia ("City of Brotherly Love" in Greek). Penn arrived in the colony in 1682, and in one of the few instances of fair dealing between settlers and Native Americans, he negotiated a treaty with the local people, the Leni Lenape, that allowed the two groups to live in peace. The French philosopher Voltaire reportedly said that it was the only treaty between colonists and Native Americans that was "never sworn to and never violated," as Quakers do not believe in swearing oaths.

The colony's growth was phenomenal. By 1685, there were about 9,000 settlers, and, by 1690, Philadelphia exceeded New York City in population. The original Quaker settlers were joined by Anabaptist refugees from Germany and Switzerland *(see pp 74–75)*, and later by large numbers of Scots-Irish *(see pp 140–141)*, who were looking for a better life in America and who pushed the colony's frontier westward to the Allegheny Mountains. On the eve of the Revolutionary War, Pennsylvania was home to 250,000 non-Native Americans, about a third of them German-speaking.

THE QUAKER INFLUENCE

Quaker dominance in Pennsylvania declined after the Revolutionary War, although Quaker families still formed Philadelphia's commercial elite. (The Quakers had nothing against business, and many became wealthy merchants and manufacturers.)

From its earliest days, Quakerism stressed that the "Inward light" must also find expression in service to others, and so throughout American history, Quakers have devoted themselves to philanthropy, education, and progressive social causes. Quakers were especially

QUAKER MEETING HOUSE
The Friends Meeting House, built by Quakers in 1775, is the oldest public building in the Mount Holly Historic District of New Jersey. It is still used for weekly Quaker meetings as well as musical programs, plays, art shows, and workshops.

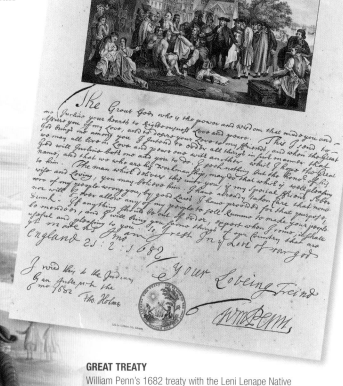

GREAT TREATY
William Penn's 1682 treaty with the Leni Lenape Native Americans *(reproduced above)* began a period of good relations between Pennsylvania's settlers and native inhabitants that lasted for about 70 years. In the 1830s, Edward Hicks—a Quaker himself—painted this view of Penn presenting his treaty to the Lenape at Shackamaxon, Pennsylvania, in June 1682. Penn *(the figure with outstretched arms)* shows the Delaware Native Americans a chest of jewels and a bolt of fabric, while other settlers bring more chests from a boat at the shoreline.

active, for example, in the antislavery movement. As early as 1688, a group of German Quakers made one of the first formal protests against slavery in the colonies, and while some Pennsylvania Quakers did own slaves, they came under great pressure from their fellow Quakers to renounce the practice. Quakers then went on to take the lead in organizing abolitionist societies in the late 1700s.

Quakers have also figured prominently in pacifist and antiwar activities. The Quaker refusal to bear arms—the "peace testimony"—earned them harassment and sometimes imprisonment in times of war. In 1917, Quakers formed the American Friends Service Committee to provide alternatives to military service for conscientious objectors during World War I. The AFSC, which won a Nobel Peace Prize in 1947, continues to work for peace and social justice in the United States and throughout the world. Today, about 100,000 Americans profess the Quaker faith.

WILLIAM PENN
1644–1718

William Penn converted to Quakerism at the age of 23, after witnessing a traveling minister. A religious nonconformist in his younger years, he had been expelled from Oxford for protesting compulsory chapel attendance. Dissatisfied with the Anglican Church, he desired a more personal religious experience and was drawn to the Quaker conviction of individual enlightenment. His devotion to Quakerism led to a break with his father and to problems with civil authorities. Penn was imprisoned for a time in the Tower of London, where he wrote his most famous work, *No Cross, No Crown,* in 1689. Alexander Milne Calder's statue of William Penn *(left)* stands atop Philadelphia's City Hall, surveying the city Penn envisioned as a "green country town." From 1894, when the statue was completed, until 1986, when the Liberty Place complex opened nearby, the city's real-estate moguls honored an unwritten agreement not to construct any building higher than "Billy Penn's Hat."

PEACE TESTIMONY
During the 2004 Democratic National Convention, the American Friends Service Committee protested the war in Iraq by placing 907 pairs of boots—representing each of the U.S. servicepeople who had died in the conflict thus far—in Boston's Copley Square.

VIETNAM PROTEST
A delegation from the Board of the American Friends Service Committee (Quakers) visited the White House to continue a discussion of Vietnam policy with top administration officials, while supporters held a "meeting for worship" on the sidewalk outside of the Executive Mansion. Dr. Henry Kissinger, special advisor to President Nixon—himself of Quaker descent—met with the Quaker delegation.

MORMONS

The desire for freedom to worship in the United States led not only to immigration from abroad, but internal migration as well. In the first half of the 19th century, a new and uniquely American religion—the Church of Jesus Christ of Latter-Day Saints, more popularly known as the Mormons—emerged in western New York State. From 1831 to 1847, the Mormons moved three-quarters of the way across the continent. Today, there are more than 2.5 million Mormons in America, and they comprise about three-quarters of the population of Utah.

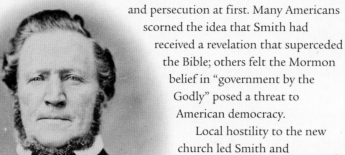

BRIGHAM YOUNG
Born in Vermont in 1801, Brigham Young became a Mormon in 1832. He served as the governor of the Utah Territory from 1849 to 1857, when President James Buchanan removed him from office.

AMERICAN REVELATION

In 1827, Joseph Smith, of Palmyra in western New York State, announced that the angel Moroni had guided him to a buried set of golden plates engraved in "reformed Egyptian," which the 21-year-old Smith then translated into English with the aid of special glasses. According to Smith, the plates revealed that ancient Israelites had traveled to North America thousands of years earlier. Further revelations led Smith to found a new sect in 1830, which became known as the Mormons, from the faith's principal scripture, *The Book of Mormon*.

The early 1800s was a time of religious ferment in the United States. Mormonism was just one of several new sects to spring up in those years, and it was among the most successful and enduring, although the "saints" endured much hostility and persecution at first. Many Americans scorned the idea that Smith had received a revelation that superceded the Bible; others felt the Mormon belief in "government by the Godly" posed a threat to American democracy.

Local hostility to the new church led Smith and thousands of his followers to leave New York State for Kirtland, Ohio, in 1831, and then to Independence, Missouri, two years later. Proslavery Missourians suspected the Mormons of spreading antislavery propaganda, however, and, in 1839, the Mormons moved again, this time building their own city, Nauvoo, in Illinois, and Joseph Smith became the mayor. The growing number of Mormons, and their consequent political power, led to continual trouble between the Mormons and their non-Mormon neighbors (who they called "Gentiles")—a conflict that culminated with the murder of Joseph Smith and his brother Hyrum.

The brothers had been jailed in Carthage, Illinois, after they destroyed the printing press used by a rival, anti-polygamy (plural marriage) Mormon faction. Although the governor of Illinois guaranteed their safety, a mob stormed the jail and killed them on June 27, 1844.

TOWERING TEMPLE
Salt Lake City's Mormon Temple was dedicated in 1893, 44 years after construction began. Only practicing Mormons are permitted inside, but non-Mormons can visit the Temple's famous Tabernacle, which features a 12,000-pipe organ.

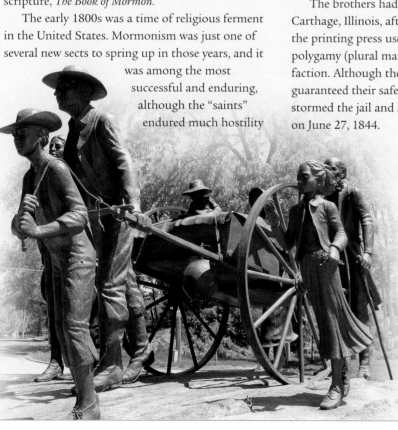

MORMON TRAIL
This is a statue at the Mormon Trail Visitor Center in Florence, Nebraska, where Mormon pioneers spent the winter of 1846–47 on their way to Utah. Most of the pioneers walked the entire distance, carrying their belongings in handcarts like the one shown in this monument.

charter would be revoked, so the mainstream Church of Latter-Day Saints repudiated polygamy. Utah became a state in 1896.

CONVERTS

In 1849, two years after Young established Deseret, the Church founded the Perpetual Emigrating Fund Company to assist Mormons in Illinois who wanted to migrate to Utah. Gradually, as the company's resources and range expanded, it became instrumental in gathering converts to Utah from abroad. By providing immigrants with loans to cover the cost of the voyage, the fund aided 26,000 Europeans, roughly 36 percent of the estimated 73,000 Mormon converts to arrive in Deseret, between 1852 and 1887—predominately from England and the Scandinavian countries.

Missionary work is still a fundamental aspect of a young Mormon's life. As of 2005, there were 56,000 Mormons participating in missions and spreading the faith worldwide. As a result, the Church of Jesus Christ of Latter-Day Saints is the fastest growing denomination in the world.

THE ROAD TO DESERET

Leadership of the movement passed to Brigham Young, who decided that the Mormons could live in peace only by moving to the unorganized territory of the Far West. At the same time, he pledged that the murderers of Joseph Smith would pay for their crime: "I swear by the eternal Heavens that I have unsheathed my sword, and I will never return it until the blood of the Prophet Joseph is avenged."

In 1847, Young led an advance party of 150 settlers to the shores of Great Salt Lake in present-day Salt Lake City, Utah. Over the next couple of years, 15,000 Mormons made the 1,100-mile trek from the Nebraska Territory to the new settlement, which they named "Deseret." Thrifty, industrious, and well-organized, the Mormons thrived, establishing settlements throughout the region and prospering through farming and selling their produce to pioneers and gold-seekers traveling to California.

Mormon experimentation in self-government was short-lived, however. In 1850, the federal government organized the Utah Territory, which included Deseret. Seven years later, federal troops arrived after the Mountain Meadows Massacre, a deadly clash between Mormons and "Gentiles," in this case an emigrating group from Arkansas headed for Nevada. Although the Mormons deny the connection, some historians believe they encouraged Paiute Native Americans to attack the group as they rested in Mountain Meadows.

By 1860, the territory had a non-Native American population of 40,000. This should have qualified Utah for statehood, but the Mormons sanctioned polygamy, a practice most Americans found repugnant. In 1890, the U.S. Supreme Court decided that the Church's

SOUND THE TRUMPET
Trumpeters open the annual pageant—held every summer since 1934—at Hill Cumorah near Palmyra, New York. To the left is the gold leaf–covered statue of the Angel Moroni, who, according to Mormon theology, led Joseph Smith to the hiding place of the golden plates from which he translated *The Book of Mormon*.

The Plain People

In the wake of Martin Luther's challenge to the Roman Catholic Church, even more radical reformers emerged. These Protestants became known as Anabaptists, from their belief that Christians must be baptized as adults rather than infants ("ana" means "again" in Greek). The movement began in Switzerland in 1525 and quickly spread through German-speaking Europe and into Moravia (now part of the Czech Republic).

First migration	1600s
Migrated from	Holland, Germany, Switzerland, Russia
Approx. number in USA	330,000 (2005)
Settlements	Pennsylvania; Iowa; Ilinois; Kansas; Ohio; Michigan; Indiana; South Dakota

ANABAPTISTS

The Anabaptists also took the New Testament's instruction "Do not be conformed to this world" (Romans 12:2) literally, believing that Christians should reject the authority of the state and live in communities that emulated those of the early Christians, including holding property in common and refusing to pay taxes or fight in wars. The most radical Anabaptists believed that Christ's second coming was imminent, so they felt they were bound by no earthly laws at all.

For denying both accepted religious doctrines and the authority of civil governments, the Anabaptists were persecuted by religious and political authorities alike. Most of the movement's early leaders were killed and their followers driven out of their communities. Persecution didn't stem the spread of the movement: after putting more than 300 Anabaptists to death in the Palatinate region of Germany, the local ruler said, "What shall I do? The more I kill, the greater becomes their number."

In Westphalia, Germany, a particularly radical Anabaptist group managed to win control of the city of Münster, but when they began persecuting non-Anabaptists a combined Lutheran-Catholic army crushed them in 1535.

The Anabaptist belief that Christians should be baptized only upon confession of faith influenced the leaders of the Baptist movement that emerged within 17-century Protestantism, including Roger Williams, founder of Rhode Island (*see pp 28–29*)

MENNONITES

Anabaptism became the wellspring of several religious movements, including the Baptists, Quakers (*see pp 66–69*), and Mennonites. Menno Simons, a former Roman Catholic priest, founded this last group in the Netherlands around 1528.

MENNONITE MARTYRDOM
Condemned for membership in "the assembly of the reprobated sect of the Mennonists, or Anabaptists," Anneken Hendriks met a fiery death in Amsterdam in 1571, as depicted in this 1685 engraving by Jan Luiken.

ANABAPTIST HOMETOWN
This is a 15th-century painting of Zurich, Switzerland, by Hans Leu. The first Anabaptist meeting took place in the village of Zollikon, just outside the city, in January 1525.

GERMANTOWN MEETINGHOUSE
Mennonite settlers at Germantown, Pennsylvania, constructed this fieldstone meetinghouse in 1770 to replace their original place of worship, a "little log church" built in 1708. It is still in use.

TRADITIONAL DRESS
Mennonite spectators enjoy a rodeo in Arcadia, Florida, in 1996. Members of more conservative Mennonite groups adhere to a strict dress code—wome"s heads must always be covered in public, for example—but Mennonites do not believe in separation from the wider world.

Mennonites later established communities in Germany, Poland, and Russia.

A few Dutch Mennonites arrived in New Netherlands in the 1600s, but the first significant Mennonite community in America was Germantown, Pennsylvania, founded in 1683. William Penn encouraged Mennonite immigration to the colony, and thousands arrived from Germany over the following decades.

The Mennonites cherished the religious freedom they found in Pennsylvania, but they were deeply opposed to one aspect of life in the colonies—slavery. In February 1688, the Germantown Mennonites gathered at the home of Rigert Worrels and drafted a pamphlet condemning slavery, arguing that "though [the slaves] are black, we cannot conceive there is more liberty to have them slaves . . . those who steal or rob men, and those who buy or purchase them, are they not all alike?" The "Germantown Protest," as it came to be called, is considered the first public protest against slavery by a religious group in America.

THE GERMAN MAYFLOWER

In 1997, the U.S. Senate recognized October 6th as "National German-American Day" in honor of the first significant group of German immigrants—the 13 families who arrived in Philadelphia on that day in 1683. These Mennonite families, for the most part interrelated by blood or marriage, had established strong ties with the Quakers in their hometown of Krefeld, near the Dutch border. Attracted by the prospect of a retreat from persecution, they bought land from William Penn, becoming participants in his Holy Experiment. The man credited for having organized this venture is Francis Daniel Pastorius, an agent for the Frankfurt Company, who arranged the land deeds and sailed ahead to attend to the business. For five pounds, one-half fare for children, the 13 families set sail on July 24, 1683, aboard the *Concord*, later termed the *German Mayflower*. Upon arrival, these 33 men, women, and children founded Germantown, Pennsylvania, the first permanent Mennonite settlement in the United States and "The Gateway of American Mennonitism."

> "America treated us like no European country treated us. They always found a way to tolerate us. Like anybody else, you were a citizen."
>
> John Ruth, Mennonite Minister/Historian

Pennsylvania was the main destination for most German and Swiss Mennonite immigrants until the early 19th century, when Mennonites fleeing the Napoleonic Wars arrived in Iowa and Illinois.

The next wave of Mennonite immigrants to the United States came from Russia in the 1870s. Descendants of German Mennonites who had been invited to settle in Russia by the Empress Catherine the Great in the 18th century, they left Russia after the government made males liable for military service in the early 1870s. About 10,000 arrived between 1873 and 1880; the Midwest, especially Kansas and Iowa, was the destination for most.

Today, about 330,000 Americans profess the Mennonite faith, in several groups. Pacifism, a commitment to social justice, and active missionary work remain at the center of Mennonite life.

AMISH

In the 1690s, there was a split in the Mennonite movement in Europe when followers of Jakob Ammon formed a conservative group that became known as the Amish. The first immigrants arrived in Pennsylvania around 1727; their descendants still live there, particularly in Lancaster County, and there are other Amish communities in Ohio, Michigan, and Indiana.

The Old Order Amish live much like their 18th-century ancestors—wearing somber clothes, speaking a dialect of German, favoring horse-drawn buggies over cars, and limiting the use of modern technologies like electricity and the telephone. The Amish way of life is a determination to live according to the original principles of their faith. Self-sufficiency is the hallmark of the Amish community: the Amish

do not pay or collect Social Security benefits. Most do not accept Medicare or Medicaid, or carry health insurance; the community pools funds for members who cannot afford to pay medical bills on their own.

There are probably 80,000 Old Order Amish in the United States today. While farming remains an Amish economic mainstay, recent years have seen an upsurge in Amish entrepreneurship, with often family-run businesses making and selling a variety of products, especially furniture and small buildings like sheds.

AMISH FARMER
An Amish boy operates a horse-drawn mower in Lancaster County, Pennsylvania. Amish farmers do make use of some machinery, but horses rather than engines usually provide the power.

BARN RAISING
A barn raising is probably the most familiar example of Amish communal life. The entire community participates, with the men doing the carpentry, the women cooking a meal, and the children running errands. The barn is usually built in a day.

HUTTERITE APPAREL
Women plant flowers at a Hutterite colony in North Dakota. Hutterite women wear long dresses, aprons, and kerchiefs, often brightly colored or patterned. Hutterite men wear black shirts and pants, and, like the Old Order Amish, grow beards after marriage.

HUTTERITES

A smaller Anabaptist-derived group, the Hutterites, formed in Moravia in the 1520s. The Hutterites, who lived communally and held all property in common, were originally from Switzerland, southern Germany, and the Tyrol (the border region between Austria and Italy). Many were skilled craftsworkers, and they were invited to settle in Moravia by Moravian nobles in exchange for their wares. They took their name from Jakob Hutter, an early leader who was burned at the stake in Austria in 1536.

In one writer's words, the story of the Hutterites is one of "continued persecution, martyrdom, and flight" over the next several hundred years. Religious and political turmoil drove them, in turn, from Moravia to Hungary, Romania, and finally Russian-ruled Ukraine. In the 1870s, they came to the United States, driven by the same "Russification" policies that motivated Russia's Mennonites to immigrate.

The Hutterites settled in South Dakota, where they lived in peaceful isolation for nearly 40 years. When the United States entered World War I, however, the Hutterite community fell victim to anti-German hysteria and opposition to their staunch pacifism. Many fled over the border to Canada, although most later returned to the United States.

Initially, the Hutterite immigrants to North America were divided into three groups: The Schmiedeleut, Dariusleut, and the Lehrerleut. (A schism among the Schmiedeleut in the 1990s led a faction known as the Committee Hutterites to split off from the main group.) Members of these groups live communally in settlements called colonies, each with about 150 people. When a colony's population exceeds this number, a new colony is established.

Today there are some 20,000 Hutterites in the United States and Canada. They continue to live in communal settlements, making a living through farming, raising livestock, and more recently, light manufacturing.

THANKING GOD
Hutterite children pray before a meal in a communal dining room. Hutterite families tend to be large, with as many as 10 children. In some Hutterite colonies, children leave school at age 16; in others, they attend public high schools and can go on to college.

JAKOB HUTTER
UNKNOWN–1536

In 1528, a group of persecuted Anabaptists from Germany, Switzerland, and Austria found sanctuary in Austerlitz, Moravia. However, ethical questions and power struggles threatened to divide the community and Jakob Hutter, an Anabaptist preacher, arrived to help smooth out internal difficulties. A charismatic leader, he was also an exceptional organizer and worked throughout Austerlitz teaching a communal lifestyle. It was this Austerlitz community that later developed into the Hutterites. As for Hutter, King Ferdinand of Austria placed a price of 40 guilders on his head and, in 1535, Hutter and his wife were captured and brought to trial. Despite torture, Hutter refused to renounce his beliefs and was burned alive at the stake in 1536. His wife escaped, but was executed two years later.

BURNING STAKE
Hutter went to his death tied to a stake like this replica from the Bruderhof Museum, etablished by a modern Christian community with Anabaptist roots.

First migration	1735
Migrated from	Germany; Russia
Approx. number in USA	40,000 (2005)
Settlement	Georgia; Nazareth and Bethlehem, Pennsylvania; New Jersey; Maryland; Winston-Salem, North Carolina; Florida; District of Columbia

OLD MORAVIA
The town square of Telc in southwestern Moravia, now part of the Czech Republic, is lined with 400-year-old buildings, including Town Hall.

MORAVIAN WORSHIPPERS
Worshippers at a Moravian Church in Charlotte, North Carolina, hold candles aloft while singing "Silent Night" at the conclusion of the traditional Christmas Eve service, which begins with a Love Feast—a simple meal shared by the congregation.

Moravians

Another Protestant group that put down roots in the United States was the Moravians. Unlike the Mennonites, Amish, and Hutterites, the Moravians did not derive from the Anabaptist movement. (For the purposes of this discussion, "Moravian" refers to members of the Moravian Church rather than inhabitants of the Moravian region of Central Europe.)

PERSECUTION
Mounted Catholics attack Moravian farmers in this print. Systematic persecution of the Moravians began in the mid-1540s, driving many to leave their homelands for Poland. By 1557, there were three provinces of the Church: Bohemia, Moravia, and Poland.

The Moravians instead trace their roots back to the followers of Jan Hus of Bohemia—the region that today comprises most of the Czech Republic. Hus's teachings anticipated Luther's, and he was burned at the stake by Catholic authorities in 1415. Hus's followers, the Unitas Fratrum ("United Brethren" in Latin), went underground for the next two and a half centuries. By 1467, the Moravians, as they eventually became known, established their own ministry and espoused a warm, personal faith in Christ, with similarities to the Mennonites and Quakers, although their worship was more in keeping with traditional Christianity. In the late 1600s, many Moravians immigrated to the Lutheran states of Germany, encouraged by the growth of Pietism, a movement within Lutheranism that promoted beliefs similar to their own. Many settled at Herrnhut, the estate of a Pietist Lutheran nobleman, Count von Zinzendorf.

In 1735, a group of Moravians from Herrnhut sailed across the Atlantic to establish a settlement in the newly founded colony of Georgia. A year later, another group set out; on the ship was John Wesley, a young Church of

England clergyman. A terrible storm blew up, and the Moravians' calm and trust in God in the face of danger led Wesley to re-examine his own faith, setting him on the path to found the Methodist Church.

The Georgia settlement was unsuccessful because the pacifist Moravians refused to take part in fighting against the Spanish to the south. In 1749, the British government confirmed the right of Moravians to settle in its North American colonies. Moravians soon founded the towns of Nazareth and Bethlehem in Pennsylvania, while others settled in New Jersey and Maryland. Another group, led by Bishop Augustus Spangenberg, settled a 100,000-acre tract that is now Winston-Salem, North Carolina.

Music played a great part in Moravian life, both in worship and as an everyday activity. From Germany they brought the tradition of the *Collegium Musicum*—a community orchestra performing both secular and sacred music. The first was established in Bethlehem in 1744, and it had the first American performance of works by composers like Franz Haydn.

JOHN WESLEY
The Moravian faith had a profound impact on John Wesley during his time in Georgia and upon his return to England. On May 24, 1738, Wesley was at a gathering of Moravians in London when he experienced a religious awakening—"I felt my heart strangely warmed," in his words—which inspired him to establish the Methodist Church.

Our common way of living was this: From four in the morning till five, each of us used private prayer. From five to seven we read the Bible together, carefully comparing it (that we might not lean to our own understanding) with the writings of the earliest ages. At seven we breakfasted. At eight were the public prayers. From nine to twelve I usually learned German and Mr. Delamotte Greek. My brother writ sermons, and Mr. Ingham instructed the children. At twelve we met to give an account to one another what we had done since our last meeting, and what we designed to do before our next. About one we dined. The time from dinner to four, we spent in reading to those whom each of us had taken in charge, or in speaking to them severally, as need required. At four were the Evening Prayers; when either the Second Lesson was explained (as it always was in the morning,) or the children were catechised, and instructed before the congregation. From five to six we again used private prayer. From six to seven I read in our cabin to two or three of the passengers, (of whom there were about eighty English on board), and each of my brethren to a few more in theirs. At seven I joined with the Germans in their public service; while Mr. Ingham was reading between the decks to as many as desired to hear. At eight we met again, to exhort and instruct one another. Between nine and ten we went to bed, where neither the roaring of the sea, nor the motion of the ship, could take away the refreshing sleep which God gave us.

An excerpt from Wesley's journal kept during his voyage to America. The ship left Gravesend, England, on October 21, 1736.

The 18th-century Moravians believed they had a special mission to bring the Gospel to the Native Americans, and carried out extensive missionary work, which was financed by each Moravian community. The number of Native American converts was small, however, due partly to the opposition the missionaries faced from land-hungry white settlers and from traders who wanted to preserve the lucrative but destructive trade in alcohol.

Jews

Although Jewish immigration into what would become the United States began in the mid-1600s, Jews were a small minority until anti-Semitic persecution in Eastern Europe drove millions to seek safety in America. Today, the United States is home to some 6 million Jews—more than any other nation, including Israel.

First migration	1654
Migrated from	**Brazil; Germany; Poland; Russia; Ukraine; Lithuania; Austria; Hungary; Romania; Czech Republic; Slovak Republic; Syria**
Approx. number in USA	**6 million (2005)**
Settlement	**Every major city in America**

The Diaspora—the dispersal of the Jewish people from their Biblical homeland—began with the Babylonian Exile in the 5th century BCE and accelerated after Rome crushed a Jewish revolt and destroyed Jerusalem in 70CE. By the late Middle Ages, Europe's Jews comprised two main groups: the Sephardic Jews, who lived under Muslim rule in the Iberian Peninsula (modern Spain and Portugal), and the Ashkenazic Jews, who lived in Western Europe.

The Muslim rulers of Spain and Portugal were tolerant toward the Jewish population. Over the centuries, however, Christian states gradually gained control of the Iberian Peninsula. In 1492—on the same day that Christopher Columbus set sail on his first voyage—the Spanish monarchy banished all Jews who refused to convert to Christianity. Portugal followed a few years later. Hundreds of thousands of Jews who refused to convert fled to the Muslim-ruled regions of North Africa and the Middle East. To further this ethnic cleansing, Spain and Portugal instituted the Inquisition, a religious commission charged with rooting out any practicing Jews and other "heretics."

In the rest of Europe, Jews lived a precarious existence. Condemned by the Roman Catholic Church for the murder of

JEWISH GHETTO
Photographed below is part of Venice's Jewish ghetto as it appears today. Founded in 1516, it is the oldest such district in Europe. The term "ghetto" is thought to derive from the Italian word *gettare*, meaning metalwork—a trade practiced by many of the district's early inhabitants.

WAILING WALL
Jews pray at the Western, or Wailing, Wall in Jerusalem. Believed to be the only surviving remnant of the Temple of Jerusalem, which was destroyed by the Romans in 70CE, the Wall is of great significance for Jews around the world.

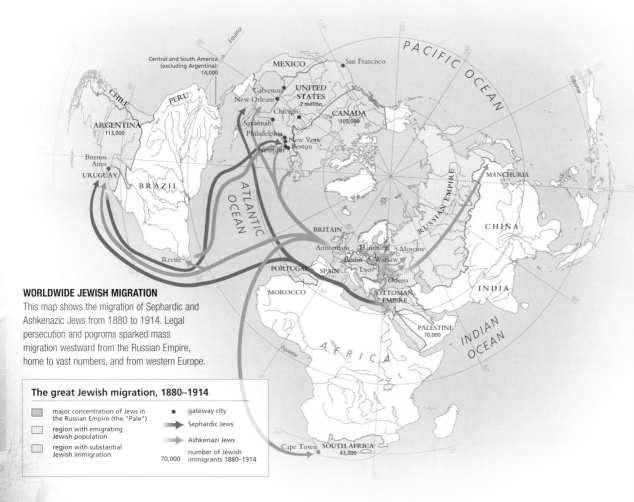

WORLDWIDE JEWISH MIGRATION
This map shows the migration of Sephardic and Ashkenazic Jews from 1880 to 1914. Legal persecution and pogroms sparked mass migration westward from the Russian Empire, home to vast numbers, and from western Europe.

The great Jewish migration, 1880–1914

- major concentration of Jews in the Russian Empire (the "Pale")
- region with emigrating Jewish population
- region with substantial Jewish immigration
- gateway city
- Sephardic Jews
- Ashkenazi Jews
- 70,000 number of Jewish immigrants 1880–1914

HIJACKED

For about 30 years, a rich Jewish community thrived in Recife, Brazil, under religious freedoms allowed by Dutch occupation. In 1654, the Portuguese won back the colony, and most Jews, remembering the Inquisition, planned to return to the Netherlands. Sixteen ships sailed; however, one unfortunate ship, called variously the *St. Charles* or *St. Catherine*, was captured by Spanish pirates. In turn, the Spaniards were attacked by a French privateer, who guaranteed the Jews' safety—for a price. According to city council minutes, upon arrival in New Amsterdam, the French captain Jacques de la Motte brought suit against the "23 souls . . . who must pay equally." By court order *(below)*, their possessions were sold at auction, but two of the Jews were confined to jail, the proceeds having failed to fulfill their debt.

Christ, they were at the mercy of local rulers. In 1290, England expelled all its Jews, and they were not welcome to return until nearly 300 years later. In most communities, Jews had to live in designated districts, or ghettos, and their rights to own property, to do business with non-Jews, and to participate in political life were restricted. Ghettos were also frequently the target of mob violence. Eventually many Western European Jews migrated to Eastern Europe.

SEPHARDIC IMMIGRATION

Of all the European powers in the 17th century, the Netherlands was the most tolerant toward Jews, so many Jews of Sephardic background moved to Amsterdam and other Dutch cities. From there, a few Jews probably crossed the Atlantic to settle in New Amsterdam, but the first significant Jewish migration into the colony was in 1654.

In September of that year, the ship *Santa Catarina* arrived in New Amsterdam with 23 Jews on board. They were refugees from the Dutch colony at Recife, Brazil. Recife had come under Portuguese rule, and the Jews feared the Portuguese would bring the Inquisition with them. New Amsterdam's governor, Peter Stuyvesant, did not want the Jews in the colony, but his

superiors in the Dutch West India Company overruled him. The refugees from Recife established Shearith Israel, the first Jewish congregation in America.

Over the next 150 years, more Jews followed. Most were Sephardic; many became prominent merchants in coastal cities, from Newport, Rhode Island, to Savannah, Georgia. By the end of the 18th century, there were between 1,500–2,500 Jews living in America.

TOURO SYNAGOGUE

This photograph shows the elegant interior of Touro Synagogue in Newport, Rhode Island. Completed in 1763 to serve a mostly Sephardic congregation, the magnificent building was designed by Peter Harrison, one of the most celebrated American architects of the colonial era.

CENTRAL SYNAGOGUE
Founded in 1839, New York's Central Synagogue has long been one of the city's leading Reform congregations. The sanctuary was built in 1872.

GERMAN JEWS

The next wave of Jewish immigration was Ashkenazic in origin and mainly from Germany and regions of Europe with a strong German presence, including parts of modern-day Poland. They spoke Yiddish, a combination of medieval German and Hebrew, which developed among Ashkenazim around 1100.

While Jews in the German states had made some social gains in the 18th and 19th centuries—Prussia granted citizenship to Jews in 1812, for example—these very gains led to anti-Semitism in many places. Some German states enacted strict laws governing their Jewish communities: in the words of one historian, "The life of the Jews was highly regulated to ensure that the state extracted as much value as possible from them; laws were issued addressing employment, family life, residence, and communal affairs."

German Jews who chafed under these restrictions began arriving in the United States in the 1830s. Some remained in the East Coast cities, while others moved inland and settled alongside non-Jewish German immigrants in the Midwest and, to a lesser extent, the South. In the wake of the California Gold Rush, some went west: the first Jewish congregation in San Francisco (named Shearith Israel, like New York's first synagogue) met for worship in 1849.

Most of the early German Jewish immigrants were single men who worked as traveling peddlers. Some managed to build their initially modest businesses into major enterprises, including August Belmont, Otto Kahn, Solomon Loeb, and Paul Warburg, who established major banks, and Isidor Straus, who made Macy's the world's largest department-store chain before tragically going down with the *Titanic*. German

ISAAC MAYER WISE
1819–1900

The most prominent American Jew of his time, Rabbi Isaac Mayer Wise was a pioneer in the spread and organization of Reform Judaism in America. He left his native Bohemia in 1846 to preach in New York, where he made a number of controversial reforms, including the introduction of Confirmation, a mixed choir, and family pews. Throughout his career as a rabbi and editor of two Jewish publications, Wise strove to fashion a unified American Judaism. While he ultimately failed to unite the Orthodox and Reform movements, he did make massive strides towards the unification of Reform Judaism by establishing the Union of American Hebrew Reform Congregations, Hebrew Union College, and the Central Conference of American Rabbis.

BILINGUAL BARGAINS
Daniel Spitzer stands outside his shoe store—hung with signs in English and Hebrew—on Manhattan's Lower East Side. The crowded neighborhood (it had an astonishing population density of 375,000 people per square mile in 1910) was the center of Jewish life in New York City in the late 19th and early 20th centuries.

GALVESTON

Around the turn of the 20th century, wealthy Jews of German origin decided that too many new arrivals from Eastern Europe were staying in East Coast cities. They came up with the "Galveston Plan" to recruit Jewish immigrants to bypass Ellis Island in favor of the port of Galveston, Texas, from which they would resettle in the Midwest. The program began in 1907 under a Galveston rabbi, Henry Cohen; only about 10,000 immigrants passed through before World War I shut it down.

LONE STAR OF DAVID
Some Galveston immigrants disembark on July 1, 1907.

GRANT AND THE JEWS
A political cartoon from 1882 accuses ex-President Ulysses S. Grant of hypocrisy for speaking at a meeting protesting persecution of Jews in Russia; 20 years earlier, when Grant was a Union commander in the Civil War, he excluded Jews from territory occupied by his forces.

Jews also brought with them the Reform movement, which de-emphasized strict observance of biblical laws in favor of a form of Judaism more suited to the modern world. The leading reform figure in the United States was Isaac Mayer Wise, who established the Union of American Hebrew Reform Congregations in 1873.

EASTERN AND CENTRAL EUROPEAN JEWS

The German Jewish immigration was just a prelude to a huge wave of immigration of Jews from Central and Eastern Europe. This wave began in the early 1880s, crested in the early 1900s, and receded only with World War I and the immigration restrictions of the early 1920s. In this period of roughly 40 years, between 2 and 2.5 million Jewish immigrants arrived in the United States.

They came, mainly, from the Pale of Settlement. This was a vast stretch of Russian-ruled territory stretching from Lithuania to the shores of the Black Sea in the south, including Russian Poland and Ukraine. With a few exceptions, all Jews in the Russian Empire were restricted to this area from the late 18th century onward. In addition to Jews from the Pale, the major wave of immigration also included Jews from the Austro-Hungarian Empire, which included Romania and what are now the Czech and Slovak Republics.

Czar Alexander III's "Temporary Laws" of 1881, which placed even more restrictions on the Jews and tacitly encouraged non-Jewish Russians to persecute Jews in their communities, sparked this massive immigration. The result was a wave of pogroms (*see pp 198–199*) that convinced Jews that they would never be able to live and worship freely under Russian rule.

The Eastern European Jews differed from earlier Jewish immigrants. Most came as entire families from the *shtetls* (self-contained Jewish communities) of the Pale. They spoke Yiddish, followed the Orthodox form of Judaism, and many sought to preserve the customs and traditions of their homeland in the United States.

About 60 percent of the Eastern and Central European Jewish immigrants settled in cities like Boston, Chicago, and especially New York; by 1920,

THEN AND NOW.—1862 AND 1882.

"Oh, now you weep, and I perceive you feel
The dint of pity. These are gracious drops."

almost half of the 3.5 million Jews in the United States lived in New York, mostly on the Lower East Side, and they comprised about a quarter of the city's population.

ANTI-SEMITISM IN AMERICA

In 1790, President George Washington assured the congregation of Touro Synagogue in Newport, Rhode Island, that the new nation would "give to bigotry no sanction, to persecution no assistance." While Washington's promise has largely held true, anti-Semitism has been an ugly reality in the United States from time to time. In 1862, for example, during the Civil War, General Ulysses S. Grant ordered all Jews "as a class" expelled from the area under his command in a misguided attempt to halt illegal trading in Confederate cotton. After protests from Jewish citizens who pointed out that many Jews were fighting in the Union Army, President Lincoln quickly rescinded the order. In the 1910s and 1920s, automaker Henry Ford financed the publication of viciously anti-Semitic books and newspapers. Less virulent but more prevalent forms of anti-Semitism included quotas for Jewish admissions to some universities; "restricted" clubs, resorts, and hotels that barred Jews; and the attempts of some communities to keep Jews from buying homes through covenants on real-estate sales. Most of these discriminatory practices were successfully challenged in the courts, but they persisted for much of the 20th century.

"For many Jews, America was their only hope, their last refuge."

"The Earth Is the Lord's"

LIGHTING THE MENORAH
The lighting of the National Hanukkah Menorah in Lafayette Park, near the White House, marks the start of the eight-day festival—a tradition that began in 1979, when President Jimmy Carter first lit the *shammash* (the middle candle used to light the menorah's other eight candles).

HASIDIC JEWS

Like the Amish (*see p 76*), America's Hasidic Jews (who number about 200,000, concentrated mainly in Brooklyn, New York) spark curiosity as a people seemingly living in the past in the midst of modern society.

Hasidism (sometimes spelled Chasidism) comes from the Hebrew for "pious ones." The movement began around 1740, in a region of Southeast Poland that is now in Ukraine. Hasidim's spiritual father was Israel Ben Eliezer, also known as Ba'al Shem Tov, or "The Master of the Good Name." A manual laborer, rather than a rabbi, Eliezer believed that Jewish spiritual life had become too focused on formal study of the Scriptures at the expense of direct, ecstatic connection with God, especially through prayer. God, preached Eliezer, was everywhere, and so every act, no matter how mundane, should reflect joy in God's creation.

This championing of emotion over reason led to opposition from conservative religious authorities, whom the Hasidim called *Mitnageddim* (opponents).

PURIM
A holiday celebrating the foiling of an anti-Jewish plot in the 5th century BCE, Purim is a time for children to wear costumes. The distinctive dress of the Satmar Hasidim includes a wide fur hat, the *shtreimel*, worn on *Shabbes* (the Sabbath).

So did the exuberant nature of Hasidic worship, which included dancing and singing, and the claims that some Hasidic leaders, known as *Tzaddiqs* (righteous ones), had mystical powers and could perform miracles. Despite this opposition, Hasidic communities were established throughout Eastern Europe.

Like many once-radical religious groups, the Hasidim became intensively conservative over time. Leadership became hereditary, with *rebbes* (rabbis) governing their followers in communities known as "courts." The Hasidim resisted modernization, not only adhering strictly to traditional Jewish law but also maintaining the customs, even the clothes, of their 18th-century forebears.

For 200 years, the Hasidim existed within the greater context of Orthodox Judaism in Eastern Europe. Then the movement all but perished in the Holocaust.

SUKKOT
Non-Jews often confuse Ultra-Orthodox Jews—like the men shown here, celebrating the start of the festival of Sukkot in Hebron, Israel—with Hasidic Jews, but there are significant differences between them, as well as among the several Hasidic communities.

SUBWAY SHUL
A Lubavitcher man reads his daily prayers on a New York City subway. In contrast with the Satmar, the Lubavitch style of dress is more modern. Dress for all Hasidic women is not formulaic, as it is for men, but stresses modesty.

HASIDIM IN AMERICA

There were Hasidim among the Eastern European Jews who immigrated to the United States in the late 19th and early 20th centuries, but the movement became

40,0000 Hasidim in America, but over the next four decades that number quadrupled, thanks to the high birthrate of Hasidic families. The vast majority of Hasidim now live in three Brooklyn neighborhoods— Boro Park, Crown Heights, and Williamsburg—with outposts in suburban and upstate counties.

There are at least a dozen Hasidic communities today. The three largest are the Satmar, who take their name from Satu Mar in Hungary; the Bobover, from Galicia in what is now Ukraine; and the Chabad Lubavitch, originally from Russia. The groups disagree over issues like the amount of contact permissible with non-Jews. The main divisions are between the insular Satmar and the more "worldly" Lubavitchers.

The Hasidim have found freedom to worship and live according to their traditions in America, but not without occasional problems with their non-Jewish neighbors. In 1991, a young African-American boy died in a car accident involving a Lubavitcher motorcade. Hours later an African-American mob murdered a visiting Jewish scholar from Australia. The incident

> "You can choose what you want here, but one of the choices is not to become part of the mass culture, and that's what Hasidim are choosing."
>
> Joshua Halberstam, Author/Grandson of one of the first Hasidic spiritual leaders in Brooklyn

firmly established with the arrival of Holocaust survivors after World War II. (Others went to Canada, Australia, and Israel). In 1960, there were only about

touched off four nights of rioting in the Crown Heights neighborhood of Brooklyn—the worst such episode in the city in decades.

STRIFE AND HEALING
Left: Congressman Major Owens meets with Ben-Tzion Meltzer, Executive Director of CARE, a group formed to heal the rifts between the communities. *Below:* Riot gear-clad police in Crown Heights on August 21, 1991.

MENACHEM SCHNEERSON
1902–1994

Born into a scholarly Jewish family in Ukraine, Schneerson married the daughter of the Lubavitcher *rebbe* in 1928. He was studying at the Sorbonne in Paris when the Germans invaded, but he and his wife reached New York in 1941. A decade later, he succeeded his father-in-law as the Lubavitcher *rebbe*. By then, the group was devastated by the Holocaust, but Schneerson rebuilt it into a worldwide organization with more than 1,400 outreach centers. He was as renowned for his hard work as for his piety—it is said he did not take a day off in 42 years. By the time of his death, some of his followers were convinced that he was *Moshiac* (the Messiah).

Tibetan Buddhists

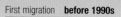

First migration	before 1990s
Migrated from	**Tibet**
Approx. number in USA	**7,500 (2002)**
Settlement	**Minneapolis-St. Paul, Minnesota; New York City; Madison, Wisconsin; San Francisco, California**

POTALA PALACE
Completed at the end of the 17th century, the massive Potala Palace towers more than 400 feet over the Lhasa River Valley. The palace was both the Dalai Lama's residence and the seat of Tibet's government until the Chinese occupation.

MONASTIC MUSIC
A Tibetan monk plays a drum and a *kangling*, a short horn-like instrument made from a human thighbone. Instrumental music and chanting are central to Tibetan Buddhist services.

In 1949, four years of civil war in China ended with the victory of Mao Zedong's People's Liberation Army over Chiang Kai-shek's Nationalist forces. On October 1st of that year, Mao proclaimed the establishment of the People's Republic of China in Beijing. The world's most populous nation was now a Communist state, with ominous consequences for Chinese who dared to assert their religious beliefs.

Tibet is one of the most rugged and isolated places in the world. Its 500,000 square miles include most of the mountains and plateaus of the Himalayan mountain range between India and China. This beautiful but harsh region is also the home of one of the world's most intensely religious societies.

Buddhism came to Tibet by way of China in the 7th century CE. Between the 10th and 13th centuries, a system of government known as Lamaism evolved in Tibet, with a Dalai (supreme) Lama serving as the nation's political and religious ruler. After the death of each Dalai Lama, leading Buddhist monks searched for a male child whom they believed to be his reincarnation. Another Lama—the Panchen Lama—served as a kind of regent until the new Dalai Lama reached maturity.

China asserted control over Tibet in the 18th century, but the Lamas retained power internally. Tibet remained resolutely isolationist—not a single European managed to enter the capital, Lhasa, during the entire 19th century—and devoted to its unique traditions.

PRAYER WHEELS

Left: Mani, or prayer wheels, which contain copies of the mantra *Om Mani Padme Hum,* which Tibetan Buddhists believe encapsulates the entire essence of the Buddha's teachings. *Above:* A row of prayer wheels along the walls of a monastery in Lhasa.

Handheld Prayer Wheels

Tibetan society was feudal, with a mostly peasant population working land owned by the monasteries, virtually untouched by the modern world.

Tibet's isolation was breached in 1904, when British forces captured Lhasa and forced the Lamas to open the nation's border with India. Just a few years later, however, Britain ceded control of Tibet back to China and, after the Chinese Revolution of 1911–12, Tibet declared its independence .

CHINESE IN TIBET

Tibet retained its independence for nearly four decades, although there was sporadic fighting with Nationalist Chinese forces along its borders.

In 1949, Mao Zedong came to power in China. To China's new rulers, Tibet represented everything that communism opposed. It was a determinedly feudal, pre-industrial land in which religious devotion permeated virtually every aspect of the lives of its 6 million people. Besides these ideological and social issues, the Chinese asserted that they had a historical right to overlordship of Tibet. In 1950, Chinese forces moved into Eastern Tibet, easily overwhelming the nation's tiny and ill-equipped army. The Dalai Lama appealed to the United Nations for help, but his plea fell on deaf ears.

The following year, the Chinese government pressured the Dalai Lama's representatives into signing what they called the "Plan for the Peaceful Liberation of Tibet." The plan created the Tibet Autonomous Republic (TAR), to be ruled jointly by Chinese and Tibetan authorities. In September 1951, Chinese forces marched into Lhasa. The 14th Dalai Lama—who was just 17—remained in the Potala Palace, but with Chinese troops and Communist officials close by. The agreement, however, did not apply to all of historical

GELEK RINPOCHE

A Buddhist monk, Gelek Rinpoche escaped over the Himalayas when he was 19 years old, just after the Chinese invasion of Tibet in 1959.

"In the middle of the night, I wake up by gun sounds. All the monks start getting up, saying, 'Now the war broke out.' By four or four thirty, I begin to see a bunch of people on horseback, running out of the summer palace, toward the south. And then a cannon hits them, and all the dust goes in the air and then I think not all of them got killed. When the dust settled down you begin to see there's again running and then it was a clear sign that the summer palace is completely gone. My choice is whether I continue to stay here or leave but I don't know where I can contact my parents; they're in Lhasa, [which is] completely surrounded. They are only six miles away, but still there's no way to contact. By evening, every monk's going without carrying any belongings, just put on the shoes and left. When they reach the formal Indian/Tibetan border, lots of Tibetans try to climb the mountain straight, but they couldn't climb and people fell down. But I remembered my parents saying you have to go zigzag, and then cut wherever the lowest peak is. I think maybe two, three hundred people went before me and came back. So I said, 'Let's cut this way, zigzag.' Finally I cross the Tibetan border, exactly at midnight into the Indian territory. And that is my final goodbye to my homeland. The moment I have opportunity, I came here, and I'm very happy to be in [my] new home. I'm really very proud to be American citizen. My admiration to America is not American power. It is the freedom and the individual rights. That's why I took a shelter here, all the way from Tibet, escaping persecution of religion."

Tibet. Part of Eastern Tibet was under direct Chinese rule, and when the Chinese imposed sweeping land reforms, guerrilla warfare against the Chinese broke out in 1956—reportedly with help from the U.S. Central Intelligence Agency. The guerrilla fighting soon spread into Central Tibet, as did many refugees.

Tibetans were also alarmed by the Chinese policy of importing ethnic Chinese settlers into Tibet—a procedure that threatened to make the Tibetans a minority in their own land. In addition, they resented the drain of resources from Tibet into China, and Communist hostility to their religion, which included closing monasteries and imprisoning monks and nuns.

LITTLE RED BOOK

Mao Zedong, ruler of the People's Republic of China (1949–76), published his favorite aphorisms in the *Little Red Book,* which had a distribution of millions of copies, including in Portuguese, as shown here.

INVASION

In a rare photo from the 1950 Chinese "liberation" of Tibet, soldiers ferry a vehicle across a river aboard a raft, while engineer troops construct a bridge upstream. Estimates of the number of troops used in the operation range from 35,000 to 80,000.

When Chinese officials openly insulted the Dalai Lama in 1959, an anti-Chinese uprising began in Lhasa. Chinese forces quickly moved in to crush the revolt. The Dalai Lama fled to Dharamsala in Northern India, where he set up a government-in-exile. The Chinese installed the Panchen Lama in his place.

The Chinese government then began a program of repression that amounted to genocide. Exact figures are hard to determine—all foreigners were banned from Tibet between 1961-63—but probably more than a million Tibetans died as a result of the Chinese occupation. In their effort to denationalize Tibet, women were forcibly sterilized, children were taken from their homes and sent to China, and any resistance—whether violent or nonviolent—was met with torture, imprisonment, and execution. In addition to the human toll, the Chinese destroyed 6,000 monasteries and many priceless cultural artifacts.

The situation in Tibet improved somewhat in the late 1970s, but unrest continues today as Tibetans continue to demand independence and the return of the Dalai Lama, who became a worldwide symbol of Tibet's ordeal, especially after he won the Nobel Peace Prize in 1989.

INTO EXILE
The 14th Dalai Lama (riding the white horse) crosses the Zsagola Pass in the Himalayas during his escape from Tibet. In a 1997 interview, the Dalai Lama said, "I only escaped from Tibet because I feared my people would resort to desperate violence if the Chinese took me as their prisoner."

TIBETANS IN INDIA
A Tibetan refugee prepares food at Kalimpang, India. An estimated 80,000 Tibetans fled to India in the years after the 1959 uprising; today, there are more than 60 separate Tibetan refugee settlements in India.

CELEBRITY CONNECTIONS

Attracted by the Tibetan culture, religion, and emphasis on nonviolence, celebrities use their fame to raise awareness of conditions in Tibet. In 1994, the Beastie Boys, a New York hip-hop trio, donated song royalties to launch the Milarepa Fund, a nonprofit organization that produced the Tibetan Freedom Concerts. In 1996–2001, these benefit concerts raised more than $2.3 million and brought together some of music's biggest stars to call for the freedom of Tibet and promote nonviolence.

To introduce Americans to Tibetan culture, Grateful Dead drummer Mickey Hart produced an album of the Tibetan Gyuto monks, whose traditional and sacred music has been suppressed in Tibet. Richard Gere, the celebrity most commonly associated with the cause, has utilized his success to draw media attention to the Tibetans' struggle for over a decade. He also started the Gere Foundation, a nonprofit organization that provides assistance for groups working to preserve the cultural identity of the Tibetan people and restore their independence.

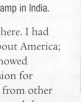

TSERING

A Tibetan refugee who fled when she was in her early 20s, Tsering left behind her parents and daughters. The daughters eventually made it to a refugee camp in India.

"I came through Solu Khumbu. The journey took 34 days to get to Nepal. It was a very hard journey—like going through hell. We didn't have food or water so we almost died from hunger. We tried to eat ice and therefore got blisters in our mouth. And our tongue would get stuck on the ice and when pulling it off blood would come out. I made an acquaintance in Nepal who pitied me, and therefore helped me make a passport. And instead of sending his own daughter to work in Hong Kong, as was actually intended, he sent me out of compassion. So in that way I came to Hong Kong where I worked as a babysitter for a month and then I came straight here. I had heard about America; that it showed compassion for refugees from other countries and that everyone in America is equal. My father knew about these things—so he would tell us. Here everyone has rights and it's a free country. Everybody here is intelligent and educated. Nobody is being discriminated against and tortured. Here people don't tell you to stand up when you are sitting down, or sit down when you are standing up. Here, it's not like it is in Tibet. Nobody tells you what to do."

Despite concerns that assimilation into American society would lead to the loss of Tibetan cultural identity, these Tibetan exiles remain determined to preserve their heritage even as they take their place as Americans. In the words of one Tibetan in Minnesota: "There are so many Tibetans in Minneapolis that our Tibetan traditions and culture may be able to survive. We can maintain our own identities here."

MONKS IN MANHATTAN
Tibetan monks arrive at New York City's Carnegie Hall for the annual Tibet House benefit concert on February 26, 2001. Held every year since 1990 during the Tibetan New Year, the concerts have featured such performers as David Byrne, Philip Glass, Lou Reed, and Patti Smith.

THE TIBETAN RESETTLEMENT PROJECT

About 130,000 Tibetans fled the country during and after the 1950 Chinese invasion, most winding up in refugee camps in India and Nepal. Only about 500 Tibetans managed to reach the United States before the 1990s.

In 1990, at the urging of the Dalai Lama, Congress passed a special bill authorizing permanent immigration visas for 1,000 Tibetans living in India and Nepal. In 1992–93 these Tibetans were resettled across the country under the auspices of the Tibet-U.S. Resettlement Project (TUSRP), privately funded by the Tibetan government-in-exile and various American pro-Tibet organizations. The Tibetan government-in-exile oversaw the selection process to ensure that the visa recipients represented a cross-section of Tibetan exile society.

Within a few years, the original 1,000 immigrants were joined by about 3,500 relatives admitted through the "family preference" system (*see p 55*). In addition to the Tibetans of the TUSRP, by the early 2000s, an estimated 2,000 Tibetans had come to the United States on tourist or student visas and remained as undocumented aliens hoping to gain asylum. The largest concentrations of Tibetans live in the twin cities of Minneapolis-St. Paul, Minnesota, and the New York City area.

HAPPY *LOSAR*
Tibetans mark *Losar* (New Year) outside Lhasa on February 5, 2005—the start of the Year of the Wood Bird in the Tibetan calendar. The weeklong celebration includes the making and display of new prayer flags like the ones shown here.

First migration	1999
Migrated from	**China**
Approx. number in USA	**10,000 (2002)**
Settlement	**New York; New Jersey; Boston, Massachusetts; Philadelphia, Pennsylvania; Houston and Dallas, Texas; Seattle, Washington; Chicago, Illinois; California**

Falun Gong

In recent years, worldwide attention has focused on Falun Gong, a Chinese spiritual movement whose practitioners have met with widespread persecution by the Chinese government, which labels it an "evil cult." Official Chinese harassment of Falun Gong followers in the United States led to unanimous condemnation from Congress in 2002.

THE CHAIRMAN WATCHES
A portrait of Mao Zedong looks down on Tiananmen Square in Beijing, China's capital. The Falun Gong protest in April 1999 drew more than 10,000 people, making it the largest protest in the square since the massive pro-democracy demonstrations in 1989.

Falun Gong, also known as *Falun Dafa* (from the Chinese words for "Wheel of Dharma" or "Wheel of the Law"), first emerged in China in 1992. The movement's leader, Li Hongzhi (*see side panel*), taught that mental and physical well-being could be achieved by meditation and the exercises of *Qi Gong* ("Working of Energy"), a practice with deep roots in China.

In its early years, Falun Gong was promoted by the Chinese government. In 1999, however, the official attitude toward the movement changed radically. The Chinese government declared Falun Gong guilty of "false teachings" and threw about 1,000 teachers and practitioners in jail. In April of that year, Falun Gong practitioners staged a protest in Beijing's Tiananmen

Square, which fueled the official crackdown and led to the arrest of more than 100 of the movement's leaders.

Why the crackdown? First, Li Hongzhi mixed the traditional exercises with teachings that drew on elements of Buddhism, Taoism, and Western New Age thinking, including a belief in extraterrestrials. These ideologies clashed with the Chinese government's image of the nation as a modern, forward-thinking society. Second, China's state-run medical establishment opposed Falun Gong because its

DRIVEN UNDERGROUND
Left: A policeman forcibly removes a Falun Gong member from Tiananmen Square during a September 1999 protest. Peaceful protests continued in 2000.
Above: Falun Gong practitioners meet in secret in a Beijing suburb in February 2000. Those who exercise in public are routinely subject to arrest.

followers believe the practice can cure diseases. Third, and most importantly, the movement's popularity and rapid growth in the 1990s led the Chinese government to consider Falun Gong a threat to its authority. By 2000, Falun Gong claimed a membership of 70 million in China, more than the total membership of the Chinese Communist Party, although official Chinese sources claimed the true number was much lower. A second wave of repression began in 2001, and Falun Gong sources claim that as of 2004, more than 1,500 practitioners had died of torture and maltreatment in Chinese prisons, with hundreds of thousands more detained in jails and "re-education" camps.

FALUN GONG IN AMERICA

Falun Gong claims a membership of 30 million outside China, although this figure cannot be verified. The exact number of followers in America is unknown, but there are groups in 45 states. What is known is that the Chinese government's anti-Falun Gong campaign has reached into the United States itself. Practitioners who have immigrated to America have reported intimidation, including death threats, from Chinese officials in local embassies and consulates; others have been detained while visiting China. Falun Gong has sought to have the U.S. State Department ban the admission of Chinese officials who have participated in their persecution.

LI HONGZHI
c.1951–

The founder of Falun Gong was born in China's Jilin province in 1951 or 1952 and he became intensely interested in Buddhism, Taoism, and other religions as a child. He is reported to have worked as a musician and a store clerk before devoting himself to *Qi Gong* in the late 1980s. After founding Falun Gong, Li published the movement's bible, *Zhuan Falun*, in 1996. Li gained U.S. citizenship in 1997 and moved to New York City in 1998, shortly before the Chinese government crackdown began. He continues to direct Falun Gong's worldwide activities and to spread the movement's message through videotapes, audiotapes, and the Internet.

WANTED MAN
An image from Chinese television announces the arrest warrant for Li Hongzhi for "spread[ing] superstition and fallacies . . . resulting in the deaths of practitioners."

CAPITOL DEMONSTRATION
Falun Gong members gather at the Capitol in Washington, D.C., in July 1999 to protest the Chinese government's request, via Interpol, that America extradite Li Hongzhi to face criminal charges—a request that was denied. Three years later, Congress passed a resolution condemning the official persecution in China and anti–Falun Gong activities in the United States.

Muslims

Immigration from the Islamic world is a fairly recent phenomenon in the United States, but it is a phenomenon that is having a major cultural impact. There may be as many as 7 million Muslims in America today, more than three-quarters of them immigrants from predominantly Islamic countries. Islam is now thought to be America's fastest-growing faith, and Muslims are poised to become the nation's largest non-Christian minority.

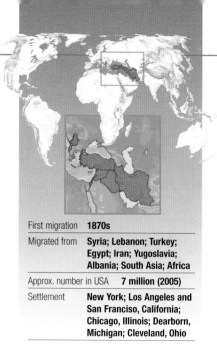

First migration	1870s
Migrated from	**Syria; Lebanon; Turkey; Egypt; Iran; Yugoslavia; Albania; South Asia; Africa**
Approx. number in USA	**7 million (2005)**
Settlement	**New York; Los Angeles and San Franciso, California; Chicago, Illinois; Dearborn, Michigan; Cleveland, Ohio**

Islam ("submission to the will of God" in Arabic) was the last of the three great monotheistic faiths to be founded. It began in the 7th century CE when Muhammad, a merchant of Mecca (in what is now Saudi Arabia), received a revelation that he was the final messenger, or prophet, of God. Muhammad transcribed subsequent revelations into the *Qu'ran*, or Koran, Islam's holy scriptures.

Over the next centuries, the new faith spread rapidly, through conversion and conquest, from the Arabian Peninsula across much of the Mediterranean world, southward into Africa, and eastward to India, China, and what is now Indonesia. Islam also made inroads into Europe, including the Balkans and modern-day Spain and Portugal. Western Europe, however, managed to resist Muslim expansion.

During the Middle Ages, the Crusades pitted European Christians against Muslims for control of Jerusalem and other places holy to both faiths, while Christian rulers drove the Muslims from Spain and Portugal at the end of the 15th century. Both episodes fostered a mistrust between the Western and Islamic worlds that persists, in some forms, to this day. Like most religions,

Islam was also subject to internal divisions; the source of division was a dispute over Muhammad's successor as leader of the faith, which separated Muslims into the minority Shi'ites and the Sunni majority.

EARLY ISLAMIC IMMIGRATION

Muslims were present in the New World from the dawn of European exploration and settlement (*see Estavanico, p 21*), but the first group of Muslim immigrants in the present-day United States came against their will. Some historians estimate that as

KA'BAH
The holiest spot in Islam, the *Ka'bah* lies within the Great Mosque in Mecca. Muslims believe it contains a fragment of rock given to Adam by God. One of Islam's fundamental tenets requires all Muslims to make the *Haj* (pilgrimage to Mecca) at least once in their lifetime.

QU'RAN
Muslims consider the *Qu'ran* to be the Word of God as revealed to the Prophet Muhammad and regard it as the ultimate authority for Islamic law and worship. This copy, from Morocco, is bound in sheepskin and finely decorated with gold leaf.

SYRIAN STREET
A grocer displays *marcouk*, traditional Syrian bread, in his store on Washington Street in New York City. By 1920, New York was home to half of America's Syrian and Lebanese population.

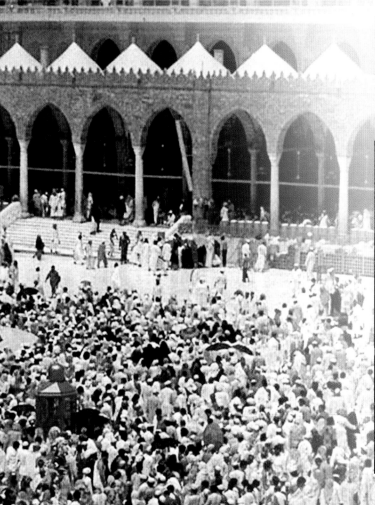

RUG TRADE
Early Muslim immigrants were often crudely stereotyped. A 1950 Chicago guidebook, for example, described the city's "Arabic quarter": "Arabs sell tapestry and rugs, wholesale and retail. . . . You will find no orgies out of the Arabian Nights here."

many as 20 percent of the slaves brought from West Africa to America were Muslims, yet they were unable to practice their faith in the plantations of the South.

Modern Muslim immigration began in the mid-1870s, largely from Syria and Lebanon, then parts of the Ottoman (Turkish) Empire, which ruled much of the Middle East. Many of these immigrants were young men seeking to avoid conscription into the Turkish Army. Like the German Jews (*see pp 80–83*), many initially worked as traveling peddlers, especially in the South. The most prosperous opened stores in cities and brought their families over. The first Arab

immigrants arrived in New York City in 1870; by the turn of the 20th century there was a thriving Muslim community centered around Washington Street in downtown Manhattan.

The collapse of the Ottoman Empire after World War II brought another influx of Muslim immigrants, but immigration from the Middle East largely halted with the immigration restrictions of the 1920s.

LATER ISLAMIC IMMIGRATION

The next wave came in the late 1940s, when Muslims from the communist nations of Yugoslavia and Albania arrived among the displaced persons admitted after World War II and with the start of the Cold War. Unlike the Muslims who arrived during the Ottoman era, these immigrants sought the freedom to practice their religion in addition to economic betterment.

Muslims remained a tiny minority in the United States, however, until the immigration reform of 1965 (*see pp 54–55*), which ended the official preference for Europeans. By some estimates, more than half of the total post-1965 immigrants from the Middle East and Asia were Muslim. Many came because of religious and political turmoil, including the Arab-Israeli wars, the Iraqi persecution of its Kurdish minority, "ethnic cleansing" in the former Yugoslavia, and most recently, ethnic strife in sub-Saharan Africa.

Iranian immigration is a special case. The Iranian Revolution of 1979 deposed the pro-American rule of the Shah and established a rigidly Islamic government under Ayatollah Khomeini. In one of the biggest demonstrations in human history, more than 3 million Iranians took to the streets of Tehran to welcome the return of their religious leader on February 1, 1979. On the other hand, more than 100,000 Iranians fled the country for the United States. Some were Iranian Jews, but the majority were Iranian Muslims who had ties to

The Ebrahimis at a family wedding in 1953.

FREEDOM FOR WOMEN

Ferdows Naficy and Her Daughters

Ferdows Naficy yearned for a new life away from the confines of the traditional landowning family she had married into 14 years earlier, at first to continue her university education, and later to build a life for herself and her three children. Her daughter Mahnaz Afkhami believes Ferdows needed to be independent: "I think my mother wanted to prove that on her own, without any support, any privilege, any connection to anything other than her own capabilities as a woman and as a person, she could do what she wanted to do. And America was a place where that was possible." When Ferdows arrived, she knew no English and worked to support herself in a restaurant and a cannery. Over the next several years, she brought her daughters over, earned a Master's degree, and started a successful career in linguistics.

Ferdows's elder daughter, Mahnaz, was brought over to go to school when she was 15—the younger, Farah Ebrahimi, when she was ten. The girls eventually returned to Iran, both determined to make a difference. Mahnaz, working for women's rights, was appointed Minister of State for Women's Affairs within the Shah's regime. Farah supported a movement to overthrow the Shah. In 1979, the revolution did occur, but with it came violence and the elimination of women's rights. Both sisters escaped to America, where, continuing her work as a women's rights advocate, Mahnaz founded an organization dedicated to advancing gender equality in the Muslim world. According to Mahnaz, her mother's example was an inspirational one: "I think that what I take from mother is her belief in her own agency, belief in her own autonomous existence, and rights as a female human being; and, the fact that her optimism resulted in formulating a way of life for herself, which was ultimately fruitful and satisfying." Adds Farah, "She's really someone to be proud of from any generation, in any country. But to have been who she is from where she came, and to have done it, is a small miracle."

TEACHER
Ferdows Naficy enters her classroom at the Defense Language Institute in Monterey, California.

SISTERS
Farah Ebrahimi *(left)* lost her husband to the revolution. She and her sister Mahnaz Afkhami *(right)* were united in America after years of political differences.

the Shah's regime or who were otherwise unwilling to live under the repressive rule of the Shi'ite *mullahs* (religious authorities). By the early 21st century an estimated 1 million Iranian-Americans lived in the United States, the majority in the New York and Los Angeles metropolitan areas.

The pace of Muslim immigration increased greatly in the 1990s. At the beginning of the decade, Muslims represented only about one-tenth of one percent of immigrants entering the United States. At the turn of the 21st century, the figure was about 45 percent. The United States' Arab population doubled during these years, rising from about 860,000 in 1990 to nearly 1.2 billion. Unlike previous waves of Arab immigration, this wave was made up predominantly of Muslims, and more than half were born in, or were born to parents from, Egypt, Lebanon, and Syria. The number of mosques in America nearly doubled as well, to about 2,000 in 2001; most also function as classrooms, libraries, conference centers, bookshops, and social halls.

Political, ethnic, and religious strife continues to drive Muslim immigration. Many Muslim immigrants from India, for example, have come to America to escape tensions between that nation's Hindus and Muslims, while thousands of Iraqi Kurdish refugees—who faced reprisals from Saddam Hussein after the Gulf War of 1991—were resettled in the United States in the mid-1990s.

WOMEN VOTING IN IRAN
Iranian women show their identity cards as they line up to vote in a 1979 election. In 1979, the ruling shah was forced out of the country by conservative Muslim forces and Iran became an Islamic republic, led by Ayatollah Ruhollah Khomeini. Women were forced to wear the *chador* and to be separated from men in public spaces.

ADAPTING TO AMERICA

As a relatively new group on the American scene, Muslim immigrants face difficulties similar to those faced by earlier arrivals. Like the Irish and Chinese before them, for example, their religion and cultural traditions are unfamiliar to many native Americans, a situation that has sometimes led to unofficial discrimination—on the part of employers, for example, who refuse to recognize Islamic religious holidays.

Muslim immigrants also face a more serious challenge—the bigotry of some Americans toward Islam in general, fueled by the rise of Islamic fundamentalism abroad and the actions of terrorists. The 9/11 attacks have compounded this situation. A 2004 study by Cornell University, for example, found that 44 percent of Americans favored some curtailment of civil liberties for American Muslims. Post-9/11 security concerns are likely to have an impact on the number of new Muslims immigrants.

DIRECTIONAL AID
Because praying must be done while facing toward Mecca, Muslims have used devices like the sundial compass (above) to determine the correct direction.

DRIVEWAY PRAYER
The divisions between different Muslim groups (Shia, Sunni, etc.), and along ethnic lines within these groups, are evident in this 2001 photo, which shows members of a predominantly Afghan mosque in Queens, New York, praying in the driveway outside the mosque, following a dispute between Northern and Southern Afghani members.

> "Coming in order to be an independent woman in this country was a huge motivation for many women to come."
>
> Mahnaz Afkhami, Iranian Immigrant

THE NATION OF ISLAM

Nearly a quarter of America's Muslim population is African-American. Most worship as orthodox Muslims. From the 1930s to the 1980s, however, many belonged to a homegrown offshoot, the Nation of Islam, often called the "Black Muslims." The movement gained a widespread following after 1930, when an Arab immigrant, W. D. Fard, began to preach that African-Americans needed to turn away from Christianity and embrace Islam—although the form of Islam taught by Fard and his African-American successor, Elijah Muhammad, differed from conventional Islam in many ways. With the rise of the African-American civil rights movement after World War II, the Nation of Islam grew in popularity in African-American communities. The movement stressed the necessity of self-help and moral conduct, but it also rejected integration of the races because of the inherent "evil" of the white race. The movement reached its height in the early 1960s under the leadership of the brilliant Malcolm X. After making a pilgrimage to Mecca (a religious requirement for Muslims), where he saw Muslims of all races worshipping together, Malcolm X began to turn toward orthodox Islam; he was assassinated in 1965. Malcolm's successor, Wallace D. Muhammad (Elijah Muhammad's son) continued the trend toward orthodox Islam and dissolved the movement in 1985, although a splinter group led by Louis Farrakhan retains the name and the earlier separatist beliefs.

CALL FOR UINTY
Malcolm X addresses a crowd in Harlem during the June 29, 1963, Unity Rally.

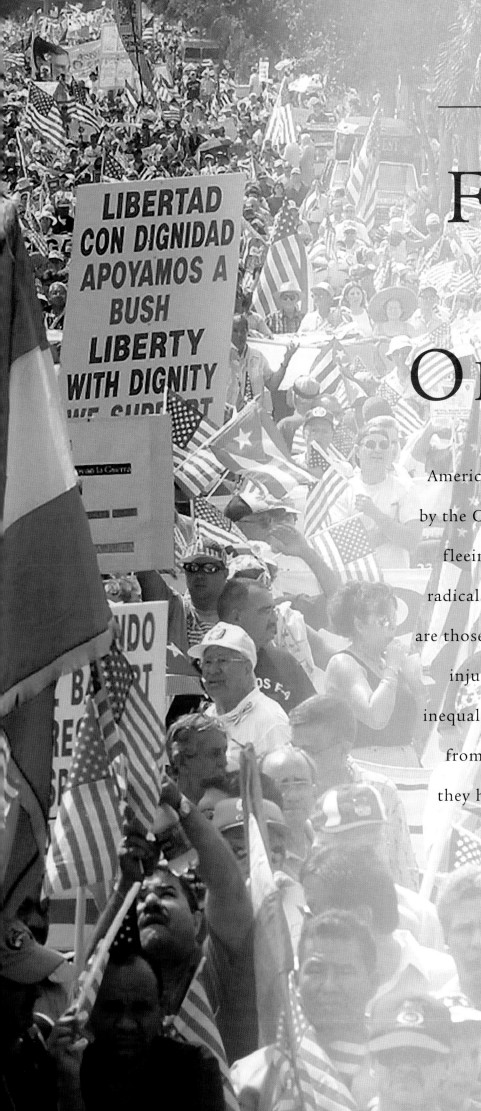

3

FREEDOM FROM OPPRESSION

America, governed under the freedoms established

by the Constitution, has been a sanctuary for people

fleeing oppression. Dissidents, troublemakers,

radicals, they have been labeled many things. They

are those who have taken a stand against tyranny and

injustice; those who have spoken out against

inequality, often in the face of intimidation. Barred

from their homelands as enemies of the state,

they have come to America—a haven where their

voices will not be silenced.

EXILES IN PROTEST
Several thousand members of more than 100 Cuban exile groups
march in protest down Calle Ocho, the street at the heart of
Miami's Little Havana, in March of 2003. They were opposed to an
upcoming conference between moderate Cuban exile groups and
Cuban government officials. In the decades following Fidel Castro's
1959 coup, more than 1 million Cubans fled to the United States.

A POLITICAL CHOICE

In 1649, after years of civil war, England became a commonwealth and King Charles I lost his head to an executioner's ax. Eleven years later, Charles I's son was restored to the throne. Three of the judges who had condemned the new king's father to death—William Goffe, Edward Whalley, and John Dixwell—promptly set sail for Boston. Despite Charles II's furious demands for their return, the three regicides managed to evade capture with the connivance of Puritan clergymen, and they lived out their lives in New England.

Although there was a religious twist to the episode—the Commonwealth leaders were Puritans—Goffe, Whalley, and Dixwell can been seen as the first of thousands of political dissidents to seek refuge in America.

The United States' reputation as a haven for dissidents derives directly from the Constitution, which guaranteed the nation's citizens a representative government, due process of law, and the protection of fundamental rights, such as freedom of speech and assembly. Such guarantees were practically unprecedented in the 18th century; they still elude many of the world's people today.

A CONDITIONAL HAVEN

To many people considered troublemakers and radicals in their homelands, like the liberals fleeing the failed European revolutions of 1848, America offered the opportunity to make a new life in a land that valued liberty. To others, like Cuban revolutionary José Martí *(see p 125)*, the United States provided a temporary refuge while they worked to free their homelands from colonial rule or tyrannical governments.

America's welcome to dissidents, however, has not been universally warm. During the French Revolution, there were worries that immigrants would try to overthrow the new republic—worries that led to the restrictive Alien and Sedition Acts of 1798. In the late 19th century, many native-born Americans feared that immigrants would bring with them "un-American" ideologies like anarchism and communism. These fears led to a "Red Scare" after World War I that resulted in the forced deportation of several hundred immigrants. A quarter of a century later, the onset of the Cold War fostered another Red Scare, with similar suspicions.

OPPRESSION VS. FEAR

This chapter differs from Chapter 5, "Freedom from Fear," in that not all the groups profiled here came to the United States in desperate fear of their lives— although some of them, like those who arrived from, say, Guatemala and El Salvador in the 1980s certainly

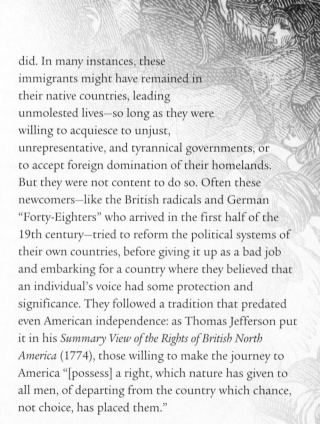

CAN THE CORN LAWS
Britain's hated Corn Laws—which artificially inflated the cost of grain to benefit landowners—were a major target of reformers and radicals between 1815 and 1846. Here, angry citizens demonstrate outside the entrance to the House of Commons.

did. In many instances, these immigrants might have remained in their native countries, leading unmolested lives—so long as they were willing to acquiesce to unjust, unrepresentative, and tyrannical governments, or to accept foreign domination of their homelands. But they were not content to do so. Often these newcomers—like the British radicals and German "Forty-Eighters" who arrived in the first half of the 19th century—tried to reform the political systems of their own countries, before giving it up as a bad job and embarking for a country where they believed that an individual's voice had some protection and significance. They followed a tradition that predated even American independence: as Thomas Jefferson put it in his *Summary View of the Rights of British North America* (1774), those willing to make the journey to America "[possess] a right, which nature has given to all men, of departing from the country which chance, not choice, has placed them."

THE ENLIGHTENMENT

The American traditions of representative government and protection of individual rights—traditions that have attracted countless freedom-seeking immigrants to the United States—are rooted deeply in the Enlightenment, an intellectual movement that flourished in Europe from the late 1600s to the end of the 1700s.

LET THERE BE LIGHT . . .

At the heart of the Enlightenment, or the Age of Reason as it was also called, was the idea that the human condition could be improved through the application of reason and the spread of knowledge. The Enlightenment overlapped, and was influenced by, the rise of modern science: in a sense, the thinkers of the Enlightenment sought to apply the objective methodology of Isaac Newton and other "natural philosophers" to the realm of human affairs.

The ideas of the English philosopher John Locke had a profound effect on the political development of the young United States. In works like *Two Treatises of Government* (1690), he rejected the prevailing view that rulers derived their authority from God, and thus were entitled to unlimited power. Instead, Locke argued that all people possessed fundamental rights to life, liberty, and property, and that it was the government's duty to protect these rights—a concept Thomas Jefferson expressed in the preamble to the Declaration of Independence more than three-quarters of a century

later: "We hold these truths to be self-evident, that all men are created equal, that they are endowed by their Creator with certain unalienable rights, that among these are life, liberty, and the pursuit of happiness."

In essence, Locke contended that the state belonged to its citizens, and not vice versa, so ultimately the consent of the governed was the only proper basis for government—a belief that provided the intellectual timber from which the U.S. Constitution would be framed. This belief also had the effect of legitimizing the expression of dissenting opinions: as the great jurist Oliver Wendell Holmes, Jr., put it in 1905, "[The Constitution] is made for people of fundamentally differing views, and the accident of our finding certain opinions natural and familiar or novel and even shocking ought not to conclude our judgment upon the question whether statutes embodying them conflict with the Constitution of the United States."

Protection from arbitrary authority—the right to trial by jury, for example—was an Enlightenment concern that influenced the Constitution's Bill of

TWO TREATISES OF GOVERNMENT
This is the frontispiece of the original edition of English philosopher John Locke's *Two Treatises of Government*—a work that had a profound influence on the framing of the Constitution.

TRIAL BY JURY
English common law—especially the doctrine of *habeas corpus*, which prevented prisoners from being held indefinitely without charges or prospect of trial—also informed the nascent American legal system.

Rights. Enlightenment political philosophers, including the French legal theorist Montesquieu (his greatest work, *The Spirit of Laws*, is a comparative study of three types of government—republic, monarchy, and despotism—and was influenced by John Locke's theories), also maintained that in an ideal government, power would be structured in such a way that no one branch could dominate the others—an idea that led to the "checks and balances" set out in the Constitution.

Finally, just as Enlightenment philosophy called for the tolerance of different religions, it promoted free speech, on the basis that in a "free market" of ideas, the best would prevail. The French philosopher Voltaire, one of the leading figures of the Enlightenment and a contributor to the *Encyclopédie* (edited by Denis Diderot, the multivolume work championed the skepticism and rationalism of the Enlightenment) summed up this belief in a famous aphorism—"I disapprove of what you say, but I will defend to the death your right to say it."

MEETING OF THE MINDS
Benjamin Franklin (with his son) and Voltaire met for the only time in Paris, 1788. According to John Adams, "The two aged actors upon this great theatre of philosophy and frivolity then embraced."

THE CONSTITUTION

The end of the Revolutionary War in 1783 did not see the new United States emerge as a strong and unified nation. The Articles of Confederation, adopted in 1781, resulted in a weak central government, with each of the former 13 colonies essentially functioning as a more or less independent nation. The political and financial shortcomings of this arrangement were soon evident, especially after Shays's Rebellion, staged in 1786-87 by debt-ridden and frustrated former Continental Army soldiers in Massachusetts. Although brief and nearly bloodless, the episode was a wake-up call to many prominent Americans, and helped lead to the calling of a Constitutional Convention.

From May to September of 1787, 55 delegates, representing every state except Rhode Island, met in Philadelphia to hammer out the framework of a more effective system. The result was the Constitution of the United States, a document that specified a "mixed" national government—one that combined a strong executive (the President) along with a democratically elected legislature (The House of Representatives) and an "upper house" (the Senate, whose members were elected by state legislatures until 1913), as well as a judiciary whose final court of appeal was a national Supreme Court. Each of the states was guaranteed a "republican form of government."

Approved on September 17, 1787, the Constitution was ratified—after much debate—by all the states by May 1790. Together with the Bill of Rights and subsequent amendments, the Constitution remains the fundamental governmental framework of the United States today.

BILL OF RIGHTS
Adopted to mollify those who felt that the Constitution did not explicitly guarantee certain individual and collective rights, the 10 amendments to the Constitution known as the Bill of Rights were ratified on December 15, 1791, during the first U.S. Congress in Federal Hall, New York City.

THOMAS PAINE
1737–1809

Paine was born in Thetford, England. He failed as a corset-maker and as a tax collector, and had two unhappy marriages. At a loose end in London, Paine met Benjamin Franklin, who urged him to immigrate to America.

Arriving in Philadelphia in 1774, Paine found his calling as a journalist. He wrote for the *Pennsylvania Magazine* (including an early denunciation of slavery) and became an ardent Patriot. Early in 1776, he published a pamphlet, *Common Sense*, which argued for independence from Britain and also proclaimed that America should have a government based on the will of the people and equal rights for all. It was a huge success—some 150,000 copies were sold at a time when the total population of the colonies was less than 3 million. Paine followed up with a series of pamphlets, collectively known as *The Crisis*, which aimed to raise the flagging morale of the Patriot forces during the Revolutionary War. After independence was won, Paine returned to England to try to make his fortune as an inventor. He failed again, but the coming of the French Revolution engaged his energies, and he penned *The Rights of Man* in support of the revolutionaries, for which he was elected to the French National Convention.

French Revolutionaries

The French government's decision to enter the Revolutionary War on the Patriot side was very much a case of "my enemy's enemy is my friend"; King Louis XVI and his ministers hoped to weaken France's traditional rival, Britain. The United States could not have won its independence without the help of France, yet that very support helped create the conditions that brought about a revolution that toppled the French monarchy and plunged the nation into chaos. Fear that French "radicalism" would spread to America led to the first restrictions on immigration in United States history.

First migration	1793
Migrated from	**France**
Approx. number in USA	**20,000 (1800)**
Settlement	**Louisiana; New Jersey; Pennsylvania**

The money, arms, and troops France sent to America put a serious drain on the already cash-strapped French treasury, with severe consequences for the nation's shaky economy. In addition, proponents of government reform—including the Marquis de Lafayette, who had fought bravely in the Revolutionary War—drew inspiration from the success of the revolution across the sea.

In 1789, with the financial crisis worsening, the Estates-General (France's representative assembly) met in Versailles, outside Paris. From this meeting emerged a National Assembly, which would soon demand

PLACE DE LA CONCORDE
The largest public square in Paris was renamed the Place de la Revolution, and more than 1,000 people, including the revolutionary leader Robespierre, went to their deaths on a guillotine there.

STORMING THE BASTILLE
The Parisian mob's seizure of the Bastille prison on July 14, 1789—shown here in a later print—is now seen as the spark that set France afire. July 14 is a national holiday in France.

EXECUTION OF LOUIS XVI
An executioner displays the severed head of King Louis XVI on the morning of January 21, 1793. Thousands of spectators cheered "*Vive la Republique!*" at the sight. The device on which the king and so many others died—the guillotine—was invented by Dr. Joseph-Ignace Guillotin as a "humane" method of execution.

ASYLUM IN AMERICA

Antoine Omer Talon was chief justice of the criminal court of France and head of the royal secret service when the revolution broke out in 1789. Having already spent a month in prison, he was smuggled aboard an English ship in a large wine cask. From England he continued to America where, with financial assistance from several sympathetic Americans, he and French exile Louis de Noailles constructed a colony for their fellow countrymen fleeing the guillotine. Called alternately Asylum or Azilum, the Pennsylvania colony opened to French exiles in 1793 and by 1798 had expanded to 50 buildings, including a schoolhouse and a theatre. "La Grande Maison," a two-story log house, was the most impressive building in the colony and meant for Marie Antoinette. In the meantime, it served as Talon's home, as he was general manager of the colony. Unfortunately, the settlement did not last long. The colonists faced animosity from neighboring Americans, as well as mounting monetary problems. While some moved south, many returned to France once Napoleon Bonaparte came to power, and only six families chose to remain in the late 1790s. The French had an impact on the transportation, farming methods and industries of the area, an influence that is still apparent in the names of surrounding villages like Frenchtown and Asylum Township.

® Pennsylvania Historical Museum Commission

reforms like an end to the privileged status of the Church and the abolition of the feudal system. In July of that year, a mob stormed the Bastille prison in Paris, a hated symbol of royal authority.

At first it seemed like the revolution might result in a constitutional monarchy, but the revolution grew more radical as extremist factions jockeyed for power. The king and queen were seized while trying to flee the country in 1791; both were executed in 1793. Revolutionary France was soon at war with much of Europe, including Britain.

REFUGEES OF MANY KINDS

When the revolutionaries turned against the monarchy and the aristocracy, thousands of royalist supporters left France. Many found refuge in Britain and the Netherlands; others came to America, settling in both Spanish-ruled Louisiana and in the United States.

Among them was Charles Maurice de Talleyrand-Périgord. Although he came from an aristocratic background, Talleyrand initially supported the revolution and served in the revolutionary government in its early years. In 1792, when the revolution took a more radical turn, he was denounced by the new National Convention and fled to London. Two years later Talleyrand arrived in Massachusetts, where he

ANGRY REACTION
Pro-French Republicans burn an effigy of U.S. Chief Justice John Jay, chief negotiator of a 1795 treaty with Britain which was denounced by many Americans as (among much else) a betrayal of the nation's ally in the Revolutionary War.

quickly made a fortune in real-estate dealings. He returned to France in 1796 and later served as Napoleon Bonaparte's foreign minister.

In 1793, the radical Jacobin faction took control of the revolutionary government, leading to a "Reign of Terror" that saw the execution of as many as 18,000 people and sent a new wave of refugees abroad. By the time Napoleon Bonaparte came to power in France in 1799, effectively ending the revolution, as many as 20,000 French refugees—royalists and revolutionaries alike—had immigrated to the United States.

Napoleon's final defeat in 1814 led to the arrival of a celebrated refugee—Joseph Bonaparte, Napoleon's older brother and the former king of Spain. The one-time monarch sailed for America with a suitcase full of jewels, which he used to buy a 1,000-acre estate in Bordentown, New Jersey. He lived there for 17 years before returning to Europe.

THE REVOLUTION DIVIDES AMERICA

Many Americans supported the French revolutionaries in the early years of the revolution, although some changed their minds after the execution of the king and queen and the "Reign of Terror" that followed. Generally, the Democratic-Republicans (led by Thomas Jefferson and James Madison) were pro-French, while the Federalists (led by John Adams and Alexander Hamilton) favored neutrality in the conflict between Britain and France—a policy that angered the revolutionary government. When diplomatic efforts to smooth over the rift failed in 1797, war seemed likely.

In addition to the prospect of war, conservative Federalists feared that immigrants from France and other nations would try to foment a bloody revolution in America. Out of this fear came the first piece of Nativist-inspired federal legislation in the United States—the Naturalization Act of 1798. The law raised the residency requirement for citizenship from five to 14 years, barred the immigration of people from nations deemed to be enemies of the United States, and permitted the deportation of foreigners considered "dangerous to the peace and safety of the United States." In addition to these "Alien Acts," as they became known, Congress also passed a Sedition Act that limited freedom of the press and assembly.

In 1800, Thomas Jefferson was elected president, and he ceased enforcement of the Alien and Sedition acts. The brief life of the Alien Acts, however, showed that America's welcoming attitude toward immigrants was conditional rather than absolute.

CITIZEN GENET
1763–1834

The troubled relationship between the young United States and revolutionary France can be told by Edmond-Charles Genet, better known as "Citizen Genet." In 1793, the French National Assembly sent Genet to America to whip up support for the revolutionary cause. Welcomed as a hero at "Democratic clubs," Genet bought four American ships to attack British commerce, despite President George Washington's warning that this would endanger American neutrality. The French government ordered Genet to return, but Genet realized he would likely go to the guillotine. He was allowed to stay in America.

PRESIDENT AND CITIZEN
Genet meets with Washington in this illustration by Howard Pyle. Genet had displeased the President by traveling across America before presenting his credentials.

British Radicals

As it did in France (*see pp 104–105*), the United States' success in establishing a constitutional republic inspired those who sought political reform in Britain. Although Britain escaped the violent revolution that consumed France, political and social radicalism increased in the early 1800s, as rural poverty and the dislocating effects of the Industrial Revolution spread through the nation, spurring immigration to the United States as well as agitation for reform at home.

First migration	**late 1700s**
Migrated from	**England; Scotland**
Approx. number in USA	**1,000 (1806)**
Settlement	**undetermined**

In the run-up to the Revolutionary War, and even after fighting began, there was considerable support for the Patriot cause in Britain. In Parliament, the leaders of the Whig party, including James Wilkes and Edmund Burke, saw a parallel between the struggle of the colonists to assert their rights and their own movement to promote individual liberty in Britain. In a 1774 speech to Parliament opposing the Coercive Acts, which were aimed at punishing the colonists,

GRIM GASHOUSE
The French artist Gustave Doré engraved this view of gashouse workers in Lambeth for his 1872 book *London: A Pilgrimage*. Coal gas provided the city's lighting, but its processing required laborers to work amid noxious and often deadly fumes.

Burke asked his fellow MPs, "How are you to govern a people who think they ought to be free and think they are not?" Other Britons, however, found it difficult to square the colonists' demands for freedom with their acceptance of slavery: the great writer Samuel Johnson observed, "How is it that we hear the loudest yelps for liberty among the drivers of Negroes?"

After the end of the Napoleonic Wars in 1815, a host of social, political, and economic problems beset Britain. Industrialization

WORKING-CLASS HOUSING
Only a few feet of dank alleyway separate terraced houses in Staithes, Yorkshire. Studies in Manchester in the 1840s found as many as 12 people sharing a single room in the city's working-class neighborhoods; a single outdoor "privy" might serve 100 houses.

CHARTIST MEETING

A daguerreotype of the mass meeting of Chartists on Kennington Common, London, on April 10, 1848. The organizers claimed that 300,000 people took part; government officials and the press put the crowd at 20,00–50,000.

put many artisans and craftspeople out of work as machinery replaced human labor; the new mills and factories provided jobs, but working conditions were appalling and wages low. Poverty and suffering were also widespread in the countryside. Before the 1830s, only about 7 percent of England's population had the right to vote in parliamentary elections. As a result, the concerns of poor and working-class people were mostly unrepresented in Parliament.

RADICALISM AND REFORM

In 1819, some 60,000 people gathered at St. Peter's Field near Manchester to hear the political activist Henry Hunt speak in favor of parliamentary reform. Local authorities ordered troops to arrest the meeting's leaders; 11 people died and more than 500 were injured in the resulting violence. Parliament responded to the Peterloo Massacre—as it became known in an ironic reference to the Battle of Waterloo that had ended the Napoleonic Wars four years earlier—and other disturbances by passing acts limiting the publication of radical writings and barring public meetings.

The growth of radicalism, however, ultimately led some of those in power to see the need for some type of reform before outright revolution broke out. In 1832, Parliament passed a Reform Act. The law made parliamentary elections fairer and extended the vote to the middle classes, but even after its passage only about one in five male Britons could vote.

In 1838, a movement for greater democracy—Chartism—arose. The movement took its name from the "People's Charter" drawn up by William Lovett in 1838, in which Lovett and his supporters called on Parliament to give the vote to all British men and undertake other reforms, like annual Parliaments.

Over the next ten years, the Chartists presented petitions to Parliament—including one with 6 million signatures on March 10, 1848 (although this number was disputed)—but Parliament refused to act on them. The more radical Chartists began to imply that they would turn to revolution. In response, authorities broke up Chartist meetings, imprisoned some of the movement's leaders, and deported others to Australia.

A number of frustrated Chartists went to the United States, including a young Scotsman named Allan Pinkerton (*see side panel*). As Chartism faded out, a movement for the reform of Britain's Corn Laws gathered strength. These laws placed heavy tariffs on grain imports, which benefited British landowners, but kept the price of food high and depressed the market for manufactured goods.

The leaders in the campaign to repeal the Corn Laws included Richard Cobden, who traveled through the United States in 1835 and published his observations in an influential pamphlet, *England, Ireland, and America.* The debate over the Corn Laws reached its peak in the mid-1840s after bad harvests in England and the failure of the potato crop in Ireland. Parliament finally repealed the laws in 1846.

Together with his Quaker associate John Bright (who was also a cofounder of the Anti-Corn Law League), Cobden remained an ardent advocate of free trade. Cobden kept close ties with many prominent Americans, especially Charles Sumner, an antislavery senator from Massachusetts. During the Civil War, both Cobden and Bright worked hard to build support for the Union cause in Britain and their letters to Sumner were read to the U.S. Cabinet at President Abraham Lincoln's request.

TOO LATE

This 1820 *Times* article *(right)* advertised a reward for the capture of Arthur Thistlewood, leader of a revolutionary group known as the Spenceans. He tried to escape to America in 1816, but was arrested at the dock before he boarded his ship.

ALLAN PINKERTON
1819–1884

Born in Glasgow, Pinkerton fled to the United States when his Chartist activities led to an arrest warrant. In 1850, he set up the Pinkerton National Detective Agency—the first private detective agency in the world. Pinkerton came up with a catchy motto—"The Eye that Never Sleeps"—thus creating the term "private eye." The agency worked mostly to foil railroad crimes until 1861, when it won nationwide fame by providing security during President Lincoln's inauguration on the eve of the Civil War. During the war, Pinkerton, operating incognito as E. J. Allan, served as intelligence chief for the Union Army.

Pinkerton *(left)*, Abraham Lincoln, and General John McClernand pose for photographer Alexander Gardner at a Union Army camp in October 1862.

German Forty-Eighters

First migration	**1848**
Migrated from	**Germany; Prussia**
Approx. number in USA	**10,000 (1849)**
Settlement	**Missouri; Pennsylvania; Wisconsin**

INDUSTRIAL GERMANY
In 1815, Friedrich Harkort bought a castle in Wetter (shown in this painting by Alfred Rethel) and turned it into a factory to produce steam engines, starting the industrialization of Germany.

THREATS TO THE VIENNA SYSTEM
The Congress of Vienna met to share the spoils of victory over Napoleon. They partitioned Europe as illustrated in the map below. Several countries, however, were shaken by insurrection in 1848.

In 1848, a tide of revolution swept across much of Europe. The revolutionaries' motives varied from country to country, but they were united in their opposition to the status quo and their desire for social and political reforms. In Germany, national unification was also a goal. When the revolutions failed, a brutal crackdown followed, particularly in Germany: many German revolutionaries fled to the United States in the first major influx of political refugees since the French Revolution.

Europe 1815–52

	Small German states
	Areas in revolt against Louis-Napoleon in 1851
♛	Major rebellions and civil wars
	German Confederation
♛	Revolution in 1848–49
-----	Frontiers 1815

BERLIN PLOTTERS
Revolutionaries of all ages and classes meet secretly in a cellar in Berlin—capital of Prussia, the most powerful German state, which was under the rule of the Hohenzollern dynasty.

Napoleon Bonaparte's conquests spread the Enlightenment ideals of the French Revolution across Europe, while those same conquests also awakened a spirit of nationalism in many areas—especially in Germany, which was dominated by France during the Napoleonic era. At the time, however, Germany was not a unified nation. After Napoleon's final defeat in 1815, Europe's monarchs met in Vienna

STREET FIGHTING
A lithograph captioned "The Strange Year of 1848" depicts a revolutionary mob clashing with troops on a Berlin street on March 18, 1848. Eight hours of fighting began when soldiers fired shots, probably accidentally, into a crowd.

to redraw the map of the continent. Out of this Congress of Vienna emerged a German confederation of 39 states. Except for a few self-governing cities, all the German states were ruled by kings or other hereditary rulers.

The next three decades were a difficult time for Germany. In rural areas, a growing population outstripped the available land. Industrialization spread to Germany, but it led to the same social dislocations as it had in Britain (*see pp 106–107*). An emerging middle class, together with students, began to demand political rights and limits on government power in many German states, as well as calling for German unification, but their efforts were mostly frustrated. Then, in the 1840s, a series of crop failures led to rising food prices and shortages—a serious matter in an era when many people in Germany (and the rest of Europe) spent most of their income on food.

REVOLUTION AND REACTION

The spark that set off the explosions of 1848 came in Paris in February, when a popular uprising forced King Louis Philippe from his thrown and led to the establishment of a republic. From France, revolution spread to Austria, Italy, and Germany. In March, after huge demonstrations in Berlin, Prussia's capital, King Frederick William agreed to demands for a constitution and the merger of Prussia with the German Confederation. Similar uprisings swept Bavaria, Saxony, and other states.

In May, representatives from the German states gathered at Frankfurt. In December, this new National Assembly proclaimed the "Basic Rights of the German

People," guaranteeing equality before the law and other rights. In March 1849, the assembly proposed the unification of Germany as a constitutional monarchy.

By this time, however, the forces of reaction had already regained control in Prussia and other states, leading to imprisonment, execution, and exile for thousands of revolutionaries. When Frederick William rejected the crown of a unified Germany, the assembly collapsed and a new wave of repression began. Virtually all the gains made since March 1848 were wiped out.

Some 4,000 of the students, intellectuals, and other Germans who were in the forefront of the revolution elected to go to America rather than remain in a country where, in the words of one German immigrant, "If one appears before an official . . . he must always appear in a bent position with a bent head." These political refugees—dubbed the "Forty-Eighters"—were soon followed by other Germans fleeing poverty and lack of land and opportunity in their homeland in a wave of immigration that continued for decades, and which would profoundly shape the culture of the United States.

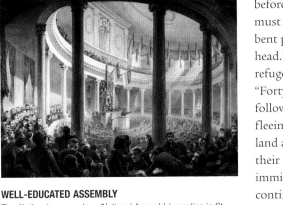

WELL-EDUCATED ASSEMBLY
The *Nationalversammlung* (National Assembly) meeting in St. Paul's Church in Frankfurt. Many of the delegates came from an academic background, leading German wags to dub it the *Gelehrtenparlament* (Parliament of Professors).

> "From the equality of rights springs identity of our highest interests; you cannot subvert your neighbor's rights without striking a dangerous blow at your own."
>
> Carl Schurz

CHILDREN'S GARDEN
This modest building in Watertown, Wisconsin, housed America's first kindergarten, established by Margarethe Meyer Schurz, Carl's wife, in 1856. The kindergarten concept—that young children learn best through activities like crafts and music instead of through rote learning—quickly caught on throughout America.

CARL SCHURZ
1829–1906

The most prominent of the Forty-Eighters, Carl Schurz, was born near Cologne, Prussia, and was a student at the University of Bonn when he was jailed for his participation in the 1848 revolution. He escaped and reached America in 1852, settled in Wisconsin with his wife Margarethe Meyer Schurz, and became a prominent Republican and supporter of Abraham Lincoln. He was a general in the Civil War, after which he served a term as U.S. senator from Missouri and argued for government enforcement of the rights of freed slaves—a position that did not endear him to Presidents Johnson and Grant. In 1872, he led a splinter group of Republicans in forming the Liberal Republican Party, although he ultimately returned to the regular party. Schurz published and edited both German and English newspapers, in which he advocated progressive causes like reform of the federal civil service.

WOMEN'S SUFFRAGE IN AMERICA

Until the mid-1800s, most Americans accepted that suffrage—the right to vote—and other civil rights were restricted to white males. Starting in 1848, however, a number of determined women began actively campaigning for women's suffrage. It took more than 70 years and a Constitutional amendment, however, before all American women were guaranteed the vote.

FIRST STIRRINGS

During the colonial era and for much of the 19th century, American women had the same rights as European women—practically none. In the eyes of the law, women were essentially the property of their husband or nearest male relative. During this era, the idea that women should be able to vote was practically unthinkable. Only New Jersey allowed women to vote in certain circumstances, and this right was taken away in 1807.

In the early 1800s, a movement for women's rights, including suffrage, began to emerge in response to the changing status of American women. Educational opportunities for women increased; women began to make up a significant part of the workforce as industrialization reached the United States; and female intellectuals like Margaret Fuller—inspired in part by European feminists like Mary Wollstonecraft—argued for greater equality between the sexes.

Women were also active in social reform movements, including temperance, immigrant aid, and, especially, abolitionism. Through immigrant-assistance programs, women discovered the ability to impact social inequalities. Numerous women established settlement houses in poor immigrant neighborhoods, providing English lessons, hot lunches, child care, and counseling.

Most historians date the start of the struggle for women's suffrage in the United States to 1848, when Carrie Chapman Catt and Elizabeth Cady Stanton organized a conference at Seneca Falls, New York. Out of this meeting came a wide-ranging "Declaration of Principles" that included legal equality for women and men, as well as suffrage.

INTERNATIONAL COUNCIL OF WOMEN
Founded by Susan B. Anthony and May Wright Sewell, the International Council of Women held its first convention March 25–April 1, 1888, in Washington, D.C. Nine countries sent 49 delegates. The early international conferences were extensively covered by the press, especially the 1899 meeting in which Anthony met Queen Victoria.

NATIONAL WOMAN'S PARTY
Three members of the National Woman's Party, the successor to the Congressional Union, picket the White House in this photo from around 1917. The New York banner commemorates that state's adoption of women's suffrage after a campaign that included the presentation of a petition signed by more than 1 million men and women.

ELIZABETH CADY STANTON
According to Stanton—shown here with one of her seven children—"Woman's discontent increases in exact proportion to her development."

SUSAN B. ANTHONY
In 1979, Anthony's image was chosen for the first dollar coin (*above*), making her the first woman to be depicted on U.S. currency.

MR. PRESIDENT YOU SAY LIBERTY IS TH[E] FUNDAMENTAL DEMAN[D] OF THE HUMAN SPIRI[T]

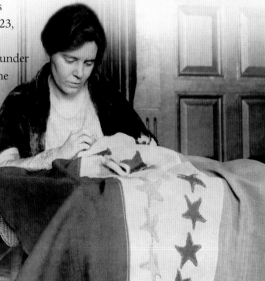

SUFFRAGE OPPOSITION

In the 1910s, several organizations, most notably the National Anti-Suffrage Association, whose headquarters are shown here, formed to fight against votes for women. In a 1914 statement, one group claimed that "an excitable and emotional suffrage"—i.e., women voters—would endanger American democracy.

THE CIVIL WAR AND AFTER

The aftermath of the Civil War split the small movement. In 1869 Congress passed the Fifteenth Amendment, which guaranteed the right to vote to the newly freed slaves, but it applied only to men. The National Woman Suffrage Association (NWSA), led by Stanton and Susan B. Anthony, argued against ratification of the amendment unless it guaranteed women the vote, too. The American Woman Suffrage Association, led by Julia Ward Howe and Lucy Stone, was for ratification. The NWSA was the more radical group, and Anthony was arrested several times for attempting to vote.

The two groups merged in 1890, but the movement for suffrage made painfully slow progress. By 1911, only six states, all of them west of the Mississippi, allowed women to vote.

Around this time, the movement re-energized, inspired both by the Progressive movement in American politics and the Suffragettes fighting vigorously for the vote in Britain. In 1914, Alice Paul, who had worked with the British Suffragette leader Emmeline Pankhurst, formed the Congressional Union for Woman Suffrage. Paul and her associates waged a direct-action campaign, including protests in which activists chained themselves to the gates of the White House. Jailed, some activists went on a hunger strike and were force-fed.

By 1917, women gained the vote in five more states. (Illinois allowed them the vote only in presidential elections.) But suffrage on a national level eluded American women until 1920, when, after a two-year struggle to win ratification, the Nineteenth Amendment to the Constitution became law.

With the right to vote secure, some women's rights activists began to campaign for an Equal Rights Amendment (ERA) to the Constitution. In 1923, the National Woman's Party proposed an amendment stating that "Equality of rights under the law shall not be abridged or denied by the United States or any state on account of sex." Although the proposed amendment passed Congress, it was ultimately not ratified by the required number of states to become law.

ALICE PAUL

Born into a Quaker family in New Jersey in 1885, the charismatic Alice Paul was the guiding force behind the establishment of the National Woman's Party in 1916. She was a mentor to several generations of feminist activists until her death in 1977.

VICTORIA WOODHULL
1838–1927

One of the most unusual feminists in 19th-century America was Victoria Woodhull. Victoria and her sister Tennessee were child performers in the family's traveling "medicine show" before Victoria married at age 15. Divorcing in 1864, Woodhull and her sister moved to New York and set up a stock brokerage with the backing of financier Cornelius Vanderbilt. They ploughed their Wall Street winnings into a weekly newspaper to promote not only women's suffrage, but also free love between men and women—a shocking idea to most Americans at the time. In the 1870s, Woodhull became the first woman to testify for a Congressional Committee (in support of women's suffrage) and to run for president (as candidate of the Equal Rights Party).

An 1872 *Harper's Weekly* cartoon says, "Get thee behind me, Mrs. Satan!"

Austro-Hungarians

First migration	**1820**
Migrated from	**Austria-Hungary**
Approx. number in USA	**4.3 million (1920)**
Settlement	**Midwestern states; Texas; New York**

MOSTAR
Pictured is part of the city of Mostar, the historical capital of the Austro-Hungarian province of Bosnia-Herzegovina, as it looked in 1905, 17 years after it passed from Ottoman to Austro-Hungarian rule. The domed church in the photo was originally a mosque.

JOSEPH PULITZER
1847–1911

Born in Mako, Hungary, Pulitzer came to America in 1864. After serving in the Union Army, he became a reporter at a German-language newspaper in St. Louis, Missouri. By 1878, Pulitzer was publisher of St. Louis's biggest newspaper, the *Post-Dispatch*. In 1883 he moved to New York City and bought the *New York World*; he turned it into a newspaper aimed at a working-class audience, filled with articles exposing corruption along with sensational reporting on crime and scandals. Pulitzer's will endowed the annual awards for excellence in journalism and the arts that bear his name.

Between 1820 and 1920, some 4.3 million people immigrated to the United States from the countries that formed the Austro-Hungarian Empire, most of them after 1867, making the area the fourth-largest source of immigrants to the United States. For many of these immigrants, the desire to escape the repressive policies of the imperial government in Vienna played an important role in their decision to set out for America.

Today, Austria is a small, landlocked nation; from 1867 to 1918, however, the dual monarchy of Austria-Hungary encompassed 250,000 square miles of Central and Eastern Europe, with a population of about 50 million.

An 1867 *Ausgleich* (compromise) united the monarchies of Austria and Hungary and led to the formation of an empire ruled by Emperor Franz Josef of the Hapsburg dynasty. The empire was a patchwork of ethnic groups, including Germans, Croats, Magyars, Romanians, Bosnians, Herzegovinians, Poles, Slovenes, Ruthenians, Serbs, Slovaks, Czechs, and Jews; at least 15 languages were spoken across the empire.

Inevitably, there was religious, ethnic, and cultural tension among these different peoples, and between these groups and the imperial government. Although the empire's 1867 constitution established religious freedom in theory, the Hapsburgs had close ties with the Vatican, so the Roman Catholic Church enjoyed special status—a source of resentment for the empire's Protestant minority, especially in Bohemia (now the Czech Republic), and for the empire's 2 million Jewish subjects. Many Czechs immigrated to the United States in the wake of the *Ausgleich*, settling mostly in the Midwest and in Texas, while tens of thousands of Jews joined in the great wave of Jewish

> "Our republic and its press will rise and fall together."
>
> Joseph Pulitzer

AUSTRO-HUNGARIAN ARMY
All able-bodied males in the Austro-Hungarian Empire were liable to three years' active army service, followed by 10 years on reserve status. In practice, only about 20 percent of all eligible males were called up for service.

Imperial Crest

immigration from Eastern Europe that began around 1880.

In Hungary, the government pursued a policy of "Magyarization" aimed at forcibly assimilating minority groups, particularly the Slovaks of Northeastern Hungary—for example, by forbidding the use of the Slovak language. Although Hungary tried to restrict emigration, large numbers of Slovaks left for America—15,000 in 1884 alone.

For members of minority groups throughout the empire, one of the most hated aspects of life under Hapsburg rule was conscription—forced service—in

IMMIGRANT FARMERS
The great photographer Lewis Hine took this shot of the Katsvans, a Hungarian immigrant family, hoeing beets on a farm near Corunna, Michigan, in 1917. The peak year for immigration from Hungary was 1907, with about 60,000 arrivals.

the army. Many young men fled the imperial territories rather than serve.

Given the rise of nationalism in Europe in the 19th and early 20th centuries, the fact that the Austro-Hungarian Empire lasted for more than 50 years is impressive. The strongest nationalist movement was in the Balkans, where activists in Austrian-ruled Croatia and Bosnia-Herzegovina wanted to unite with the independent nation of Serbia to form a Slavic kingdom. In August 1914, a Bosnian Serb, Gavrilo Princip, assassinated the heir to the throne of Austria-Hungary, Archduke Franz Ferdinand, in the Bosnian capital of Sarajevo. Austria-Hungary declared war on Serbia, with Germany's support; France and Russia declared war on Germany, as did Britain, after German troops invaded neutral Belgium; and World War I began. (Italy, eager to gain Austrian territory, joined the war in 1915).

By the fall of 1918, it was clear that Germany and Austria-Hungary faced defeat. The imperial government granted "self-determination" to the nations under its rule and signed a separate armistice with the Allies on November 4; Emperor Charles (who had succeeded Franz Joseph on his death in 1916) and his family were barred from Austrian territory. Out of the wreckage of the empire came the independent nations of Austria, Hungary, Czechoslovakia, and Yugoslavia. Ethnic conflict in the former empire did not end; more than 70 years later, with the end of the Cold War in 1991, Yugoslavia and its surrounding countries descended into fierce internal conflicts that would again send thousands of refugees to the United States (*see pp 232–233*).

AMERIKA

The mass migration of Europeans had a strong impact upon those left behind. This is evident in the works of two Austro-Hungarian authors, Franz Kafka and Joseph Roth. Born into Jewish families in 1883 and 1894 respectively, the writers experienced a sense of alienation in their native land. While neither traveled to America, it played prominently into their works as a land imbued alternately with opportunity and disenchantment. In Kafka's *Amerika: The Man Who Disappeared* (1927), his portrayal of America is of a fantastical landscape, where the Statue of Liberty greets immigrants with sword held high. Roth presents a more realistic America in *Tarabas: A Guest on Earth* (1934), which he wrote in exile from Nazi Germany. Nicholas Tarabas is a Russian revolutionary banished to New York City, a concrete confinement compared with the farm of his youth. From Europe, Kafka and Roth created their own Americas and through the experiences of their characters, displayed their desires and fears of immigration, a harsh reality for millions.

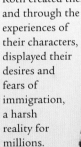

FRANZ KAFKA

AMERIKA

THE MAN WHO DISAPPEARED
The New Translation by Michael Hofmann

Poles

First migration	**1795**
Migrated from	**Poland**
Approx. number in USA	**2,000,000 (1920)**
Settlement	**Chicago, Illinois; Detroit, Michigan; New York City; Pennsylvania**

WAWEL CASTLE
Wawel Castle in Krakow, on the banks of the Vistula River, was the home of Poland's monarchs from the 11th century until the 17th century, when King Sigismund III moved the nation's capital to Warsaw.

From 1795 to 1919, the historic nation of Poland was divided between Germany, Russia, and Austria. Eventually, at least 2 million Poles—motivated both by poverty and by the oppressive policies of their nation's foreign overlords—immigrated to the United States. They settled in both big cities and rural areas.

From the late Middle Ages through the 17th century, Poland was a powerful nation; over centuries its territory grew to include much of Central and Eastern Europe. But by the mid-1700s, the Polish state was in decline—weakened by long wars with Sweden and the Ottoman Turks and infighting. Poland's neighbors—Prussia to the west, Russia to the east, and Austria to the south—wasted no time in exploiting this weakness. In 1772, these three nations engineered the first partition of Poland, which lost roughly half of its population and a third of its land. A joint Russian-Prussian invasion in 1793 put down nationalist resistance. The rebel leaders included Tadeusz Kosciuszko (*see below*). In 1795, Poland ceased to exist as an independent nation; the final partition divided Poland up between Prussia (after 1870, the leading state of Germany), Russia (which set up the Duchy of Warsaw to oversee its Polish territories), and Austria (which ruled the southern region of Galicia—now part of the Ukraine).

FOREIGN DOMINATION

Despite the loss of their independence, the Polish people kept a fierce sense of their own cultural, religious, and national identity. A few Poles immigrated to America as political refugees after the partition of 1795, but the first major Polish immigration came in the mid-1800s—mainly single men seeking their fortunes before returning to Poland. They were known as *za chlebem* (immigrants for bread), but most of them wound up staying in America. Back home, Prussian and Russian rule grew ever more onerous. Russia moved to a policy of "Russification" that led to the barring of the Polish language in

BATTLE FOR INDEPENDENCE
Polish nobleman Tadeusz Kosciuszko leads Polish troops into battle against Russian forces in this painting by Alexander Osipovich Orlovsky. The artist himself served as a volunteer with Kosciuszko's Nationalist forces.

government and education. The situation was similar in German-ruled Poland, where many Poles existed as virtual serfs. And everywhere, most Poles lived in poverty—the former Poland fell behind the rest of Europe in industrialization and agriculture.

INDEPENDENCE AND AFTER

All these factors combined to create a huge increase in emigration from Poland to the United States around the turn of the 20th century. Because Poland was not an independent nation during the great wave of immigration from the 1880s to 1914, it is difficult to differentiate Polish immigration from German,

THE VISTULA TO THE HUDSON

Two young Polish women in traditional dress prepare to leave Ellis Island in this photograph from around 1910—the same year in which a study counted about 900,000 Polish-speaking Americans.

THE PARTITIONS OF POLAND

In the late 18th century, the Russians, the Hapsburgs, and Prussia settled their differences at Poland's expense and removed the country from the map, despite resistance of Polish patriots.

The partitions of Poland and the pogroms 1772–80

- frontier of Poland in 1699

Partition of Poland in 1772
- to Prussia
- to Russian Empire
- to Habsburg Empire

Partition of Poland in 1793
- to Prussia
- to Russian Empire

Partition of Poland in 1795
- to Prussia
- to Russian Empire
- to Habsburg Empire
- frontiers in 1795
- Pale of settlement
- Jewish population > 20,000
- Jewish Population > 40,000
- Settlement forbidding Jewish residency

Russian, and Austro-Hungarian immigration at the time, but probably 2 million Poles came to America in this period. They settled not only in big metropolises like Chicago, New York, and Detroit, but also in rural areas like western Pennsylvania, where many worked as coal miners—the same trade they had plied in Poland's Carpathian Mountains.

Poland finally became an independent nation in 1919, in the wake of World War I, only to be partitioned once again—between the Soviet Union and Nazi Germany—in 1939–1941. After horrible suffering in World War II, Poland regained nominal independence, but the nation was part of the Soviet Bloc. During this period a few refugees managed to reach the United States. With the emergence of the Solidarity movement in the early 1980s, Poland took the lead in the struggle that ultimately led to the downfall of communism in Eastern Europe, although the economic dislocations that followed the end of the Cold War have sparked a new wave of immigration from Poland to America.

COMFORT FOOD

Polish immigrant Julia Balik and her daughter make the Polish staple, pierogies—small pies of dough with fillings like cheese, meat, or potato—at their store in McKees Rocks, Pennsylvania, in this 2002 photograph.

CASIMIR PULASKI
1747–1779

Several foreign-born officers volunteered for the Patriot cause during the Revolutionary War. A Polish count, Casimir Pulaski, made the supreme sacrifice. Benjamin Franklin recommended him to George Washington, and Pulaski arrived at Washington's headquarters in August 1777. Pulaski distinguished himself by leading a cavalry charge during the Battle of Brandywine. Promoted to brigadier general, he took command of a cavalry and light infantry unit—Pulaski's Legion. On October 9, 1779, Pulaski led his troops in a bold attack on the British fort. "While advancing at the head of his men," a historian recounts, "exposed to the most tremendous fire, the intrepid Pulaski received a mortal wound, and fell from his horse."

RADICALISM IN AMERICA

Nationalism was not the only new "-ism" to emerge in 19th-century Europe. In response to the misery and exploitation caused by industrialization, Karl Marx and Friedrich Engels articulated the doctrines of communism, which called on the working class to seize power from those who owned "the means of production," by violent revolution if necessary. Their *Communist Manifesto* appeared in print just as the revolutions of 1848 (*see pp 108–109*) swept Europe. The Russian theorists Peter Kropotkin and Mikhail Bakunin argued for anarchism—the philosophy that all governments were inherently evil and must be destroyed for people to truly be free. More moderate were the socialists, who called for public ownership of major industries and for the establishment of a welfare state.

To many Americans (who tended to lump anarchists, communists, and socialists together), these beliefs represented a danger to free enterprise and democracy. They feared that immigrants would spread the new, radical doctrines in the United States. Real events fueled these fears. In May 1886, a bomb went off in Chicago's Haymarket Square during a rally in support of striking workers, and 15 people were killed. The police arrested eight anarchists, seven of them immigrants from Germany, for the bombing, despite flimsy evidence. In the trial that followed, seven of the defendants were sentenced to death. Four were eventually hanged; one committed suicide in prison. Chicago governor John Peter Altgeld (also a German immigrant) pardoned the remaining defendants, although that action wrecked his political career. Fifteen years after the Haymarket episode, Leon Czolgosz, the son of Polish immigrants, assassinated President William McKinley in Buffalo, New York.

The success of the Bolshevik Revolution in Russia in 1917, coupled with terrorist bombings in New York City and Washington, D.C., led to a post-World War I "Red Scare" that saw thousands of foreign-born radicals arrested in 1919. Hundreds were deported.

AMERICANS IN THE SOVIET UNION

In addition to those deported in the "Red Scare," a handful of Americans—most of them immigrants from Russia or formerly Russian-ruled territories—moved to what was then the Soviet Union following the Bolshevik Revolution. Most notable was the Kuzbas Autonomous Industrial Colony, a coal-mining community in Siberia, organized in part by William "Big Bill" Haywood of the radical Industrial Workers of the World (IWW) labor union. African-American

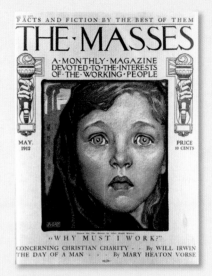

THE MASSES
Published between 1911 and 1918, and edited for most of that time by Max Eastman, *The Masses* published the work of some of the leading left-leaning writers of the day, including Upton Sinclair and John Reed, with illustrations from the likes of John Sloan and Rockwell Kent. The U.S. government shut down the magazine in 1918 for its antiwar stance.

DEADLY EXPLOSION
Although this print shows demonstrators firing on police during the chaos that followed the explosion of the bomb in Haymarket Square, an inquiry found that most of the policemen who suffered gunshot wounds were caught in the crossfire of other officers.

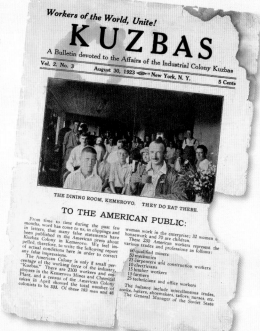

RED ARK

The *USS Buford*, a rusty military transport ship, sailed for Russia with 249 "Red" deportees (and 250 soldiers to guard them) on December 21, 1919. A newspaper described the passengers as "America's Christmas present to Lenine [sic] and Trotzky [sic]."

intellectuals—including singer and actor Paul Robeson and writers Langston Hughes and Claude McKay—also spent time in the country, attracted by the Soviet Union's supposed freedom from racism. The Great Depression of the 1930s—an era when some Americans came to believe that Soviet-style communism offered the only viable alternative to American-style capitalism—brought several hundred American citizens to the Soviet Union, including Walther Reuther, the future head of the United Auto Workers union. Like Emma Goldman, most were quickly disillusioned, and most, like Reuther, managed to return to America. At least 10 of those who did not died in the Soviet Union's concentration camps—the dreaded Gulag—during the Stalinist terror of the late 1930s and 1940s.

The United States and the Soviet Union became allies during World War II, but the coming of the Cold War led to another Red Scare in America, including the investigations of Congress's House Un-American Activities Committee and the anticommunist witch hunts of Senator Joseph McCarthy in the 1950s. While there was indeed considerable Soviet espionage going on in the United States, some of it aided by American citizens, this new Red Scare created a widespread climate of fear in which some émigré academics, like psychoanalyst Erik Erikson (*see p 242*), lost their posts, while some refugee intellectuals, like writer Bertolt Brecht (*see p 271*), chose to leave the United States.

KUZBAS COLONY

Lenin personally approved the creation of the Kuzbas Autonomous Industrial Colony in the hopes that the expertise and experience of American immigrants would upgrade the Soviet Union's mining industry. By 1927, however, most of the American colonists had left.

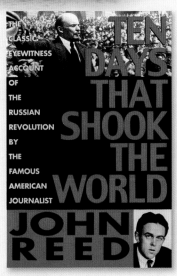

JOHN REED

American journalist John Reed wrote the above classic eyewitness account of the Bolshevik Revolution of October 1917.

Emma Goldman

Emma Goldman was born in Lithuania in 1869 and came to the United States in 1884, bringing with her a commitment to radicalism that was strengthened by her experiences in the textile mills of New England. In 1889, she moved to New York City and became the lover of fellow anarchist Alexander Berkman, who attempted to assassinate industrialist Henry Clay Frick in 1892. Unstinting in her support for Berkman, she wrote and spoke extensively in support of radical causes—including birth control—which earned her a couple of jail sentences.

Goldman achieved nationwide notoriety when presidential assassin Leon Czolgosz claimed that he had been inspired by her writings. The federal government responded by revoking her U.S. citizenship on a technicality in 1908. Undeterred, Goldman launched the influential radical journal *Mother Earth*. Federal investigators seized *Mother Earth*'s subscriber list in 1918 to identify "radicals" for investigation.

When the United States entered World War I in 1917, Goldman spoke out against the war and the government's introduction of conscription. Sentenced to two years for sedition, she was deported in 1919, and wound up aboard the steamship *Buford* (*see above*). Like many American and European radicals, Goldman's hopes that the new Soviet Union would be a paradise for the working class were quickly dashed. Confronted with the reality of Soviet tyranny, she published *My Disillusionment with Russia* in 1923. After fleeing the Soviet Union, Goldman lived in several European nations. She died in Canada in 1940.

CLEARING THE STREETS
Demonstrators in Petrograd (now St. Petersburg), Russia, scatter for cover as troops fire—obeying Czar Nicholas II's order to curb "all the disorders on the streets of the capital"— in February 1917.

Soviet Dissidents

First migration	1917
Migrated from	**former Soviet Union; Estonia; Latvia; Lithuania; Poland; Hungary; Romania Czechoslovakia; Albania; East Germany; Yugoslavia**
Approx. number in USA	**1,080,000 (1991)**
Settlement	**New York; Philadelphia; Chicago; Boston; Cleveland; Pittsburgh; San Francisco**

MOSCOW

The Kremlin *(left)*, or fortified town, seat of the Soviet government until its dissolution in 1991, looms over the Moskva River. The Soviet government made Moscow the nation's capital in 1918 out of fears that Petrograd, which lies close to the borders of several European nations, was too vulnerable to attack.

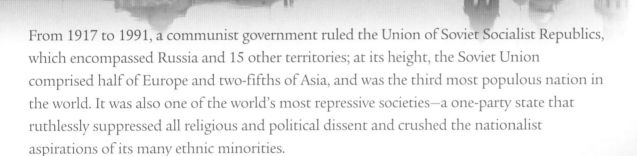

From 1917 to 1991, a communist government ruled the Union of Soviet Socialist Republics, which encompassed Russia and 15 other territories; at its height, the Soviet Union comprised half of Europe and two-fifths of Asia, and was the third most populous nation in the world. It was also one of the world's most repressive societies—a one-party state that ruthlessly suppressed all religious and political dissent and crushed the nationalist aspirations of its many ethnic minorities.

RUSSIAN FAMINE

Two years of brutal civil war followed the Revolution of 1917–18, as the "Red" Bolshevik regime struggled against several "White" armies. The war devastated much of the country, leading to a massive famine that began in early 1921. Some 35 million people—like the children shown here—suffered severe malnutrition, and as many as five million died.

In the spring of 1917, Russia's government, battered in World War I and beset by internal unrest, collapsed. Czar Nicholas II abdicated in March, and a provisional government took over. In October, the Bolshevik (communist) party seized power.

Although many American and European intellectuals greeted the establishment of the Soviet Union as a huge step forward for humankind, the new nation's repressive nature was evident from the beginning. Under the dictatorial rule of Vladimir Lenin, the secret police (the *Cheka*, later known as the NKVD and still later as the KGB) unleashed an ongoing reign of terror against real and perceived opponents of the new regime. Lenin also laid the foundations of the notorious Gulag network of labor and punishment camps.

The aristocracy, the wealthy, the Russian Orthodox clergy, and other "bourgeois elements" were systematically dispossessed and persecuted. Some managed to flee

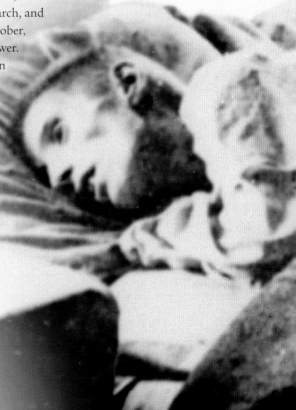

PETROGRAD

A street scene in Petrograd in May 1917, after Lenin arrived in the city from exile in Switzerland. His return was encouraged by the German government, which hoped the Bolsheviks would undermine the Russian war effort.

to Western Europe, but few made it to the United States. Among those who did was Walter Kerensky, who had briefly ruled Russia as head of the provisional government. Kerensky came to America in 1940, later becoming a professor at Stanford University's Hoover Institution. He died in New York in 1970.

The revolution was followed by two years of bloody civil war as the Bolsheviks successfully fought off challenges from the forces of several White (anticommunist) groups. The war, and the famine that followed, claimed perhaps 2 million lives and created 1.5 million refugees, about 30,000 of whom settled in America before the immigration restrictions of the 1920s went into effect. By then, the Soviet Union had effectively sealed its borders. For the rest of its existence, the Soviet Union restricted the movement of its citizens; very few were permitted to travel abroad.

Ironically, one of the leading figures of the revolution, Leon Trotsky, had spent time in the United States as a political refugee. Imprisoned after

> "The end may justify the means as long as there is something that justifies the end."
>
> Leon Trotsky

LEON TROTSKY
Leon Trotsky commanded the Soviet forces in the civil war. His insistence that the Soviets foment revolution around the world, rather than achieving "socialism in one country" added to his conflict with Stalin.

the failed revolution of 1905, Trotsky escaped in 1907. After being expelled from several European countries for his revolutionary activities, he lived in the New York City borough of the Bronx in 1916–17 before returning to Russia. Second only to Lenin in the Bolshevik hierarchy, Trotsky was a rival of Josef Stalin for leadership of the Soviet Union following Lenin's death. Stalin eventually succeeded in exiling Trotsky; he was assassinated in Mexico City in 1940 on Stalin's orders.

Stalin's ruthless drive to destroy his enemies reached into America itself. In 1936, as Stalin launched the "Great Terror" of the late 1930s (*see pp 208–209*), Walter Krivitsky, the chief Soviet intelligence officer in Western Europe, was working undercover in the Netherlands. Realizing that he would likely become a victim of Stalin's purges if he returned to the Soviet Union, Krivitsky escaped to America. He later wrote his

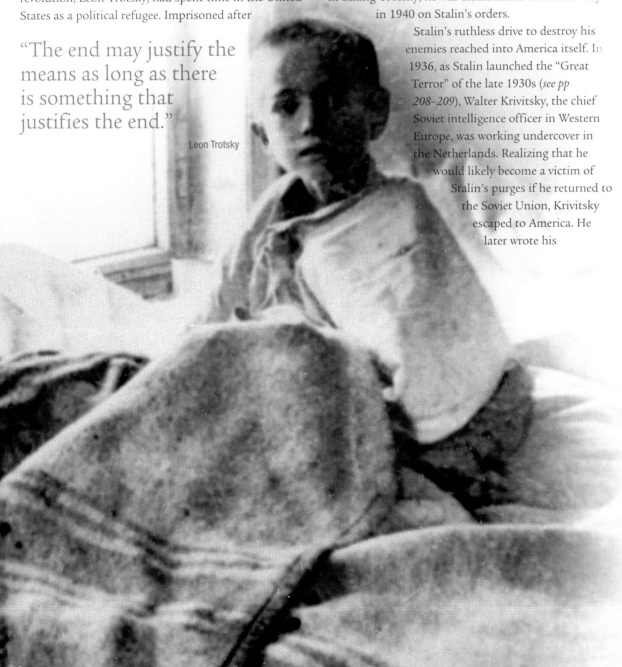

EAGLE OF KIEV
1899–1972

Born into a middle-class family in Kiev, Igor Sikorsky was fascinated with flight from an early age. In 1910, he built and flew his first fixed-winged plane. He followed this up with the amazing *Ilya Mouromets* (named after a Russian folk hero) in 1913. The largest plane built up to that time, it featured four engines and an enclosed cabin.

In March 1919, despairing of opportunities under the Bolsheviks, he immigrated to America and set up a small aircraft company on Long Island. Success came in the 1930s, when Sikorsky's flying boats were adopted by Pan-American Airways for their routes in the Caribbean and Latin America and, at the end of the decade, across the Atlantic and Pacific oceans.

Sikorsky then returned to his first love—helicopters. In September 1939, Sikorsky (who always acted as his own test pilot) climbed into the cockpit of a VS-300 and made the first-ever successful flight.

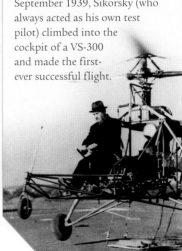

autobiography, *I Was Stalin's Agent*, the last words of which were "I got away safely." This proved premature. On February 10, 1941, Krivitsky was found dead of a gunshot wound in a Washington, D.C. hotel. The murder was never solved but is believed to have been the work of a Soviet agent.

DISPLACED PERSONS AND REFUGEES

The United States and the Soviet Union were allies during World War II, but not long after Germany's surrender in May 1945 did the chill of the Cold War set in. The Soviets oversaw the formation of communist governments in the nations they had occupied in Central and Eastern Europe, including Estonia, Latvia, Lithuania, Poland, Hungary, Czechoslovakia, Romania, and East Germany. Yugoslavia and Albania also came under communist rule, but the dictators in those countries—Josip Broz Tito and Enver Hoxha, respectively—kept independent from Moscow.

The effects of World War II and communist expansion in Europe led to a huge refugee crisis. Congress revised U.S. immigration policy to allow the resettlement of European refugees—or "displaced persons," as they were officially known—in America. The Displaced Persons Act (1948) and subsequent legislation brought about 400,000 people to America. In 1956, Hungary erupted in rebellion against its communist government. After Soviet forces moved in and crushed the uprising, President Dwight

TRAGIC TREK
Fleeing the failed uprising against Soviet domination, Hungarian refugees trudge toward the Austrian border in this 1956 photo. Some 5,000 refugees crossed the border on November 4th alone—the day Soviet tanks rolled into Hungary.

Eisenhower used his executive authority to allow the admission of 35,000 Hungarian refugees. All told, about 750,000 European refugees arrived in the United States from 1945 to 1965.

Fear of communist influence in America, however, led to a second "Red Scare" in the late 1940s and early 1950s. In 1952, Congress passed the McCarran-Walter Act, the first major immigration law since 1924. It liberalized immigration policy in some respects, but it also permitted the deportation of immigrants and naturalized citizens who were found guilty of "subversive activities," and barred the admission of immigrants who were former communists or members of organizations with real or suspected ties to communism. As a result of these provisions (which were finally repealed in 1988), U.S. immigration authorities banned many prominent intellectuals from immigrating to, or even visiting, the United States.

DISSIDENTS, REFUSENIKS, AND *GLASNOST*

In the Soviet Union, executions and imprisonment declined after the death of Josef Stalin in 1953, but subsequent Soviet leaders continued to harass and persecute dissidents. Some were forcibly committed to so-called "mental hospitals." Others were exiled to remote areas within the Soviet Union (like the physicist Andrei Sakharov) or to the West (like writer Aleksandr Solzhenitsyn—*see pp 248–249*).

FREEDOM SUNDAY
Natan Sharansky speaks to a rally of 200,000 American Jews at the Capitol in Washington, D.C. on December 6, 1987. Timed to coincide with a meeting between President Ronald Reagan and General Secretary Gorbachev, the "Freedom Sunday" rally highlighted the plight of the Refuseniks—Soviet Jews forbidden to leave the country. Sharansky, one of the best-known Soviet dissidents, was allowed to immigrate to Israel the previous year, after 11 years in Soviet prisons and labor camps.

DISPLACED NO MORE
The U.S. Army transport ship *General Black* arrives in New York City on October 30, 1948, carrying 813 "displaced persons" from Europe—the first to be admitted to the United States following the passage of the Displaced Persons Act earlier that year.

In the 1970s, the governments of the United States and other Western nations pressed the Soviet Union to halt its persecution of dissidents, especially after the signing of the Helsinki Accords in 1975. In that agreement, the Soviet government pledged to improve its human-rights record, but in fact it rarely honored that commitment.

The 1970s also saw concern in the West over the plight of the Refuseniks—Jews who wished to leave the Soviet Union, but who were refused permission and suffered official persecution for even applying for exit permits. In 1978, the most prominent Refusenik, human-rights activist Natan Sharansky, was imprisoned on charges of spying for the United States. He was finally allowed to emigrate to Israel in 1986.

By then, Mikhail Gorbachev was in power, and his policy of *Glasnost* (openness) made it possible for tens of thousands of Refuseniks to leave the Soviet Union. Most went to Israel, although many eventually immigrated to the United States.

GORBACHEV AND REAGAN

Right: Ronald Reagan and Mikhail Gorbachev sign the Intermediate Nuclear Forces Reduction Treaty, a landmark piece of arms-control legislation on December 8, 1987, two days after "Freedom Sunday." The rapport these two leaders achieved, despite their vast ideological differences, was a key factor in ending decades of fear and mistrust. *Below:* A California license plate celebrates the spirit of the era.

THE FALL OF COMMUNISM

Moscow schoolchildren on a toppled statue of Josef Stalin—one of the many physical symbols of the Soviet regime pulled down as *Glasnost* gave way to the fall of Communism itself—are photographed in September 1991. Three months later, the Soviet Union itself ceased to exist, replaced by the Commonwealth of Independent States (CIS).

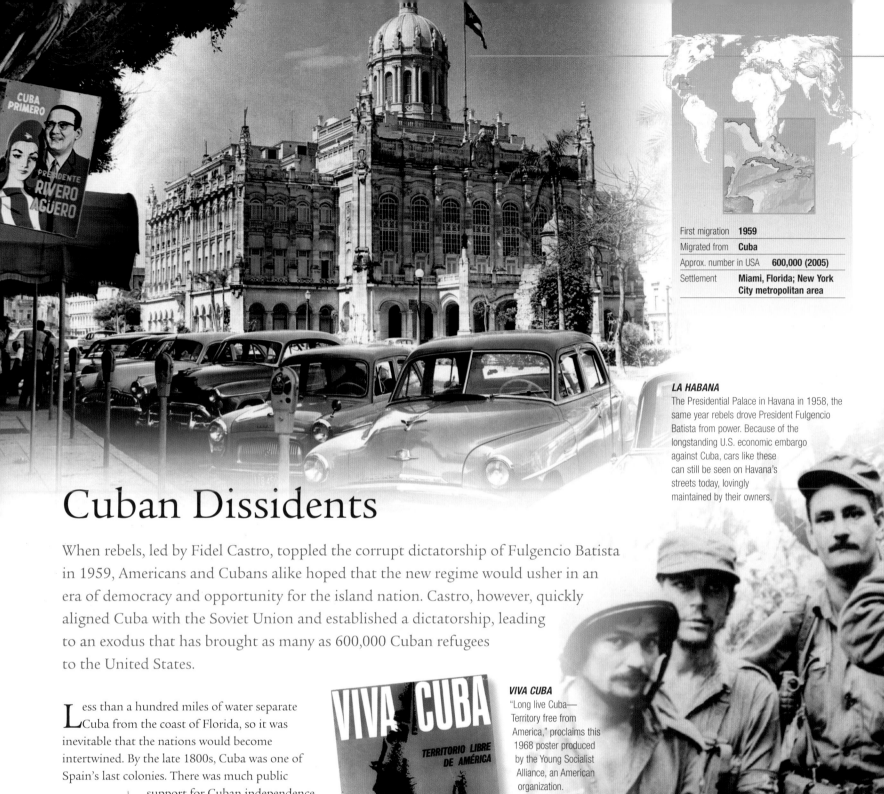

First migration	1959
Migrated from	**Cuba**
Approx. number in USA	**600,000 (2005)**
Settlement	**Miami, Florida; New York City metropolitan area**

LA HABANA
The Presidential Palace in Havana in 1958, the same year rebels drove President Fulgencio Batista from power. Because of the longstanding U.S. economic embargo against Cuba, cars like these can still be seen on Havana's streets today, lovingly maintained by their owners.

Cuban Dissidents

When rebels, led by Fidel Castro, toppled the corrupt dictatorship of Fulgencio Batista in 1959, Americans and Cubans alike hoped that the new regime would usher in an era of democracy and opportunity for the island nation. Castro, however, quickly aligned Cuba with the Soviet Union and established a dictatorship, leading to an exodus that has brought as many as 600,000 Cuban refugees to the United States.

Less than a hundred miles of water separate Cuba from the coast of Florida, so it was inevitable that the nations would become intertwined. By the late 1800s, Cuba was one of Spain's last colonies. There was much public support for Cuban independence in America, and, in the Spanish-American War of 1898, U.S. forces expelled the Spanish. Cuba gained independence, but in many respects the nation became a dependency of the United States, with sugar production and tourism the

VIVA CUBA
"Long live Cuba— Territory free from America," proclaims this 1968 poster produced by the Young Socialist Alliance, an American organization.

mainstays of its economy. From 1933 onward, with the exception of a few years, the Cuban government was in the grip of dictator Fulgencio Batista, and the Cuban people were in the grip of oppression and poverty.

REMEMBER THE *MAINE*
The wreckage of the U.S. battleship *Maine* in Havana Harbor, 1898. The cause of the explosion remains unknown, but accusations that the Spanish were responsible fueled "war fever" in the United States.

FLEEING FIDEL'S REVOLUTION

The U.S. government initially supported the Batista regime, but, by the late 1950s, his repressive policies came to be seen as a liability. A U.S. arms embargo virtually guaranteed the success of Castro's revolutionary movement. But when Castro proclaimed himself a Communist, nationalized American property, and began arresting and executing dissidents, the U.S. government adopted economic sanctions and other measures aimed at weakening Cuba; with some modifications, they continue today.

In the wake of the revolution, 200,000 Cubans fled to America, many of them educated, middle-class professionals who feared persecution. Most settled in and around Miami, Florida. Castro reacted by restricting immigration, but he relaxed this policy in 1965.

Another 360,000 Cubans came to America between 1965–73, before Castro again halted immigration. The U.S. government financially assisted the resettlement of many of these refugees. By the

TO THE RESCUE
A *Hermanos al Rescate* (Brothers to the Rescue) plane patrols the waters between Cuba and Florida in search of refugees in distress. The group assisted an estimated 4,000 people in the 1990s.

1970s, South Florida had a thriving Cuban-American community, many of whom were politically conservative and devoted to the cause of freeing Cuba from Castro's rule.

MARIEL AND THE *BOLSEROS*

In April 1980, Castro announced that any Cuban who wanted to leave the country could do so by way of the port of Mariel. Between April and October, when Castro closed the port, Cuban-Americans brought 125,000 people to Florida from Mariel, many aboard small craft.

The Marielitos differed from earlier Cuban immigrants in that many were unskilled workers. (The assertion that Castro used the Mariel boatlift to empty out Cuban prisons, however, is untrue; only 2 percent of the Mariel refugees were considered criminals under U.S. law.)

Cubans continued to flee to America, many of them in ramshackle boats and rafts. An unknown number of these *bolseros* (raft people) died in the attempt. Before 1994, Cubans who reached Florida were allowed to stay, but that year the Clinton administration changed its policy in order to discourage the *bolseros*. Over the next decade, *bolseros* intercepted by the Coast Guard were sent to camps at the U.S. Naval Base at Guantanamo Bay, Cuba. This shift in policy created debate in America, as did the case of Elián González, a young Cuban boy who survived the sinking of a refugee craft in 1999. In 2000, the Supreme Court ordered Elián returned to his father in Cuba, over the protests of family members in Miami.

As of this writing, Castro remains in power in Cuba, and U.S. policy toward that nation—and those who wish to emigrate—remains controversial.

CASTRO
Fidel Castro (*fourth from left*) and other Cuban revolutionaries at a secret base in June 1957. The group includes Fidel's brother Raul (*kneeling*), who became Cuba's Defense Minister.

JOSÉ MARTÍ
1853–1895

Considered Cuba's greatest patriot, Martí was born in Havana and first made his mark as a painter, journalist, and scholar; he published studies of American authors like Whitman and Emerson, as well as perceptive examinations of the relationship between the United States and Latin America. He was also an ardent supporter of Cuban independence, something that landed him first in prison and then in internal exile on Cuba's Isla de Pinos—ironically, later the site of a prison for dissidents under Castro. After being expelled to Spain, Martí came to New York City in 1880 and rallied support for the independence movement among Cuban immigrant communities in that city and in Tampa and Key West in Florida. In 1895, he led an exile force ashore in Cuba, but was killed by Spanish troops at Dos Rios.

CARNIVAL
Revelers dance down Miami's *Calle de Ocho* (8th Street), the main thoroughfare of the city's "Little Havana" neighborhood. Miami is now home to the largest Cuban population outside the island itself.

BOLSEROS AT SEA
Cuban refugees have used an amazing variety of vessels in their attempts to reach Florida—in this case, in 1994, an inner-tube raft. According to a study by the University of Florida, as many as 16,000 Cubans may have perished in the waters between Cuba and Florida between 1959 and 1994.

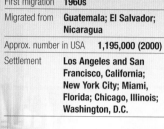

First migration	1960s
Migrated from	Guatemala; El Salvador; Nicaragua
Approx. number in USA	1,195,000 (2000)
Settlement	Los Angeles and San Francisco, California; New York City; Miami, Florida; Chicago, Illinois; Washington, D.C.

SAN SALVADOR
The streets of San Salvador are still plagued by violence in the 2000s, although gang warfare has largely replaced the political conflict of the 1970s and 1980s. In 2004, the city had the highest murder rate in Latin America.

Central American Dissidents

The 1970s and 1980s were a time of turmoil in Central America. In Guatemala and El Salvador, right-wing governments battled left-wing insurgencies, while in Nicaragua, communist Sandinista guerillas overthrew the pro-U.S. regime of Anastasio Somoza in 1979. These conflicts led thousands of refugees to attempt the perilous journey to *El Norte*—the United States—but those who managed to reach America found their status uncertain.

Several Central American nations had a long history of poverty, inequality, and dictatorial governments by the mid-20th century. Six years after a CIA-backed coup overthrew President Jacobo Arbenz Guzmán in 1954, a civil war began in Guatemala that lasted for 36 years, leaving more than 200,000 Guatemalans dead, most of them Mayan Native Americans who make up the majority of the country's population, and creating at least a million refugees. Most of these refugees went to Mexico, but during the 1980s—the bloodiest period of the war—as many as 150,000 may have crossed into the United States.

Guatemala's neighbor, El Salvador, was also consumed by a bitter civil war—from 1980 to 1992—that pitted government forces against the leftist Farabundo Martí National Liberation Front (FMNL). During those years between 300,000 and 500,000 Salvadorans entered America.

GUATEMALAN REFUGEES
Scenes from the Quetzal Edzna camp for Guatemalan refugees, Campeche, Mexico, in 1989–90. As many as 200,000 Guatemalans may have fled into Mexico in the early 1980s; 10 years later, about 40,000 still remained in the camp, which is administered by the United Nations and the Mexican government.

AN UNFRIENDLY RECEPTION

In 1980, Congress passed a new Refugee Act that created the Federal Refugee Resettlement Program and gave priority to refugees from communist nations, so refugees from repressive right-wing regimes like those in El Salvador and Guatemala faced the possibility of deportation. Many Salvadoran and Guatemalan refugees applied for political asylum, but during the early 1980s only about 2 percent of them were granted asylum status, while hundreds were deported each month. As a result, a grassroots movement to shelter Salvadoran and Guatemalan immigrants sprang up (*see side panel*) in many American communities.

In 1990, a compromise gave "Temporary Protected Status" (TPS) to illegal immigrants from countries suffering from "armed conflict or natural disasters," permitting them to remain in the United States for

ROADSIDE MURDER
The bodies of two young women killed by a right-wing death squad are photographed along a highway in El Salvador in 1980. The same year, Archbishop Oscar Romero, an outspoken supporter of the country's poor and oppressed, was killed while saying Mass in the cathedral at San Salvador.

fixed but renewable periods. The introduction of TPS allowed many Salvadorans and Guatemalans to escape deportation; by then these two nationalities represented about 95 percent of those seeking permanent asylum in America.

In Nicaragua, the situation was very different. After the victory of the communist Sandinistas in 1979, President Jimmy Carter granted "Extended Voluntary Departure" status to Nicaraguans who were already in

RODI ALVARADO

In 1995, fearing for her life, Rodi Alvarado fled her abusive husband. She illegally entered the United States and filed for political asylum. Hers has become a landmark human rights case, for if she is granted asylum, she will be the first woman in America to win a case of precedential value. In 2004, the Department of Homeland Security endorsed granting Rodi Alvarado asylum. As of this writing, the final decision is left to the Board of Immigration Appeals.

"Domestic violence in Guatemala is extremely severe. It is very normal that the husband abuses the wife. I think in our country the man never treats the woman as the wife, but really like property. The wife gets used to the man treating her badly because we don't know that we also have value. I always felt a lot of fear and I did try to look for help. There isn't an organization to help. There is nowhere to turn. Women don't have a single right. I'd arrive at the police station and say, 'I need help. I'm being abused by my husband.' They'd tell me, 'No. Go home. That's very normal. He's your husband so we can't help you.' I went to my family. My mother, the only thing she would say was, 'Be good, sweetheart. Go take care of your husband.' To this day, my mother calls me and asks me to forgive her because she couldn't help me. We reach the limit where we can no longer stand the abuse. And we start to think that only death has the solution. I knew I had to get out. Finally, I made the decision to leave, not knowing where I was going. I didn't have a cent on me. I didn't bring anything, absolutely nothing. I just wanted to escape."

the United States. The classification allowed 20,000 Nicaraguans to remain in the United States indefinitely. The Sandinista-dominated government was opposed by U.S.-supported guerrillas known as *Contras*. It was voted out of power in 1990.

> "In Guatemala, six out of ten women murdered die at the hands of the men they marry."
>
> "Breaking Free: A Woman's Journey"

HOPE FOR THE FUTURE
A mural in San Francisco, California—a city second only to Los Angeles in the percentage of Salvadoran immigrants in its population—celebrates the January 1992 armistice that ended 12 years of civil war.

SANCTUARY

Many Americans felt that their government's policy toward Salvadoran and Guatemalan refugees was unjust, and some were willing to break the law in order to hide refugees at risk of deportation. The result was the Sanctuary Movement—a 20th-century "Underground Railroad" that helped refugees cross the Mexican border. Centered at first around churches and synagogues in the Southwest, the movement protected an unknown but significant number of refugees until the introduction of TPS in 1990. A number of Sanctuary activists were arrested; in the best-known case, a federal jury convicted six Sanctuary workers (including Rev. John Fife, *below*, the movement's cofounder) of harboring illegal aliens, although they did not receive jail sentences.

South American Dissidents

First migration	1970s
Migrated from	**Chile; Argentina**
Approx. number in USA	**169,000 (2000)**
Settlement	**New York City; Miami, Florida; California**

As with El Salvador and Guatemala, the realpolitik of the Cold War influenced U.S. immigration policy toward political refugees from South American countries—particularly in Chile, where a U.S.-sponsored coup in 1973 installed a brutal right-wing (but anticommunist) regime. The coup created thousands of refugees, many of whom sought asylum in the United States, but the administration of President Nixon denied them entry.

SANTIAGO
A 1995 photo of Chile's capital city shows the Plaza de la Constitution in the foreground and the Andes Mountains in the background. Spanish conquistador Pedro de Valdivia founded the city in 1541. Today 5.5 million people reside there.

In 1970, Salvador Allende Gossens was elected president of Chile. An avowed Marxist, Allende nationalized foreign property and industries and began a program of land reform. Allende's actions caused concern in Washington, which feared that Chile would become a launching pad for Soviet and Cuban influence in South America, while American companies with holdings in Chile—especially in the copper industry—protested Allende's policy of nationalization.

Allende's attempts at reform also led to high inflation and widespread shortages, which sparked strikes and protests from both right-wing and left-wing groups in the country. On September 11, 1973, rebels from the army, led by General Augusto Pinochet, launched a coup with the approval of the Nixon administration and the support of the C.I.A. The coup succeeded; under siege in the presidential palace, Allende committed suicide, although some believe he was executed.

The United States was the first nation to recognize the Pinochet government. Despite abundant evidence of American support for Pinochet, Washington steadfastly denied involvement in the coup until 1998, when Secretary of State Colin Powell acknowledged the role the United States played, noting that "it is not a part of U.S. history that we are proud of."

During the coup, thousands of Allende supporters sought refuge in foreign embassies. Those that went to the U.S. Embassy, however, were turned away. After Jimmy Carter took office as president in 1977, he reversed Nixon's policy, even authorizing the airlift of about 600 dissidents directly from Chilean prisons to the United States.

They were a fortunate few. During the 16 years of Pinochet's rule at least 3,000 Chileans died at the hands of the government, many of them after prolonged torture. Thousands more were imprisoned in brutal conditions.

SEPTEMBER 11, 1973
Under cover of a tank, Chilean soldiers advance toward Chile's presidential palace during the 1973 coup. According to the military, Allende killed himself in the palace using a gun presented to him by Fidel Castro.

THE "DIRTY WAR"

Argentina, too, suffered from economic chaos and fighting between left- and right-wing factions. In 1976, the army arrested President Isabel Perón and installed a military government.

For the next seven years, the military conducted a campaign, known as the "Dirty War," aimed at rooting out all opposition. Thousands of people simply vanished into prisons and detention camps. The exact fate of many of these *Desaparecidos* (disappeared ones) remains unknown, because the Argentine government destroyed many of its records in the wake of the disastrous war with Britain over the Falkland Islands in 1982, when Britain lost and regained the islands in 74 days.

MADE IN THE USA?
Protesters picket the New York City office of Chile's national airline in 1974. The United States admitted coup involvement in 1998.

The extent of U.S. involvement in Argentina during these years is debated, but recently declassified documents seem to show that Secretary of State Henry Kissinger encouraged the Argentine government during the Dirty War: in one 1976 conversation, Kissinger told Argentine Admiral César Augusto Guzzetti, "I have an old-fashioned view that friends ought to be supported. What is not understood in the United States is that you have a civil war. We read about human rights problems but not the context. The quicker you succeed, the better."

As in Chile, the crackdown on dissent in Argentina led many Argentines to seek asylum abroad; but—also as in Chile—few managed to get into the United States.

ARIEL DORFMAN
1942–

Born in Argentina, Dorfman spent part of his childhood in New York before his family settled in Chile in 1954. He became a professor at the University of Santiago, a highly regarded writer, and an outspoken supporter of Salvador Allende. Dorfman managed to get to the Argentine Embassy during the coup, from which he witnessed many horrible scenes—including the shooting of a refugee who was trying to scale the embassy's walls. Dorfman was eventually exiled to Paris, and in 1980 he moved to America to teach at Duke University. Many of Dorfman's subsequent novels, plays, and essays deal with the experience of repression and exile. His best-known work, in America at least, is the play *Death and the Maiden*, in which a woman confronts the man she believed tortured her in prison. Dorfman also wrote the screenplay for the 1994 movie. He chronicled his own experiences in a 1998 memoir *Heading South, Looking North: A Bilingual Journey.*

"Why am I in exile? Why do I speak English when I swore I wouldn't? It all has to do with the fact of the coup, and the fact that I was spared."

Ariel Dorfman in *The Progressive*

MOTHERS IN MOURNING
Left: A woman tries to save a boy from arrest by Argentine military police—and perhaps becoming one of the "Disappeared"—in this 1982 photograph. *Above:* For more than two decades, the *Madres de Desaparecidos* (Mothers of the Disappeared) have demonstrated in Buenos Aires' Plaza de Mayo.

4

FREEDOM FROM WANT

America has appeared to people everywhere as a

promised land, a destination of vast possibilities.

From the beginning, most immigrants have come

looking for a better life for themselves and their

families. For some, like the 19th century Norwegians,

America meant opportunity. For others, like the

famine Irish, it meant survival. For Mexicans, it has

been both. America is a country founded and built

by immigrants, a place where they found the

livelihood denied them at home.

"The Golden Door"

CHINATOWN GROCER

A Chinese greengrocer awaits customers at his stand on Division Street in New York's Chinatown, home to the largest concentration of Chinese in the Western Hemisphere. Driven from the West Coast by violence and discrimination, around 200 Chinese immigrants had settled in the neighborhood by 1870. Today, the area, roughly two square miles in size, houses 150,000 to 250,000 residents.

THE GOLDEN DOOR

For every immigrant who came to America fleeing political or religious persecution, thousands more came in hopes of a better quality of life for themselves, for their families, and for their descendants. Still, the distinction between immigrants who came for economic reasons and those who came to live in a free society is a blurry one. For many—perhaps most immigrants—it was a combination of freedoms that drew them to America.

From the perspective of the 21st century, when the majority of Americans live in towns and cities and work at non-agricultural pursuits, it is hard to comprehend what a big role the availability of cheap, or even free, land played in spurring immigration. But for much of human history, status was linked to land ownership. In societies as geographically and culturally distinct as Scandinavia and Japan, owning a plot of land meant that a family had the means to survive and, with luck, prosper. Those without land were often condemned to a precarious existence at the whim of a landlord.

When the great period of immigration began in the 19th century, population growth in both Europe and Asia outstripped the available farmland, displacing millions and sending many to America, where the tide of white settlement was opening up the vast American West.

In 1862, Congress passed the Homestead Act, a generous law that gave 160 acres of federal land to any settler who could successfully farm it for five years. For those who could not homestead, there were still large tracts of affordable land, including the hundreds of millions of acres granted by the federal government to the railroads that were knitting the country together in a web of steel, and which the railroads in turn sold to immigrants.

WORKSHOP OF THE WORLD

The great period of immigration also coincided with America's rise as an industrial power. Fueled by abundant natural resources, industrial output grew from relatively modest beginnings until, around the turn of the 20th century, the United States was the world's leading manufacturing nation. Except during economic downturns, immigrants were always needed to dig the canals, lay the railroad tracks, and work the mills, mines, and factories. Conditions were harsh and wages low, but to most immigrants it was still better than what the "Old Country"

offered, and there was always the hope—often fulfilled—that their children would be able to step up into the middle classes. America's rapidly expanding economy also offered entrepreneurial immigrants the chance to go for the Big Money.

THE HUDDLED MASSES?

"Give me your tired, your poor, your huddled masses yearning to breathe free . . ." Emma Goldman's poem, inscribed at the base of the Statue of Liberty, may be great literature, but it is not an accurate description of most immigrants. The truly tired, poor, and huddled usually did not have the energy or resources to make the journey to America. In many instances it was the ambitious, skilled, and educated who elected to leave their homelands in the hope that those skills would be in greater demand in the United States. This is especially true of many of those who arrived in the post-1965 waves of immigrants. Still, throughout the nation's history, there have been plenty of people who came to America fleeing poverty so desperate that the hope of just making enough money to feed themselves (and to send some to the family back home) was motivation enough—from the Irish victims of the Potato Famine in the 1840s to the Mexicans and other Latin Americans of the 21st century.

FREE LAND
Homesteaders at Lawton, Oklahoma Territory, "prove up" their land claims in 1901. The 1862 Homestead Act allowed those who improved 160 acres of public land to keep it.

"Men and women go to America and come back less deferent, less subservient, less humble."

Donna Gabaccia, Historian

THE AMERICAN LABOR MOVEMENT

The history of organized labor in the United States and the history of immigration are intertwined—often uncomfortably. Although some American union members and labor leaders of the 19th and early 20th centuries were immigrants themselves, many favored restrictions on immigration out of fear that employers would turn to low-wage, non-union immigrant labor, driving unionized workers out of their jobs and erasing the movement's hard-won gains. At the same time, unions that represented skilled workers often refused to admit unskilled immigrant laborers.

UNDER THE HAMMER
An antilabor cartoon from around 1890 depicts the Knights of Labor preparing to crush American industry, using the strike as its weapon. Several major strikes took place during the 1890s.

IWW RALLY
Alexander Berkman addresses a June 1914 International Workers of the World demonstration in New York City's Union Square. The Russian-born Berkman served 14 years in prison for the attempted assassination of a company official.

EARLY LABOR MOVEMENT

As the United States grew into a great industrial power in the years after the Civil War, workers began to band together to win better wages and working conditions through collective actions like strikes and boycotts. The first truly effective national labor organization, the Knights of Labor, was founded in 1869, but its membership was relatively small until Terence Powderly, the son of Irish immigrants, took over as leader in 1879. The Knights admitted both skilled and unskilled workers and welcomed immigrants—unless they were from Asia. The Knights supported exclusion of Chinese immigrants in the 1880s (*see pp 154–155*), as did other labor organizations, including the Workingman's Party in California, which was led by Irish-born Dennis Kearney.

There was little government regulation of industry and no legal protection for collective action by workers; business owners generally regarded unionists as troublemakers who sought to violate the "liberty of contract" between worker and employer, so union-organizing activities and strikes were often met with violence. Native-born critics also accused foreign-born unionists of promoting "un-American" philosophies, like socialism and anarchism. Despite this opposition, the organized labor movement slowly made headway as the 19th century gave way to the 20th, especially through the growth of the relatively moderate American Federation of Labor (AFL) (*see side panel*).

THE INDUSTRIAL WORKERS OF THE WORLD

There was, however, a big division in the American labor movement between craft unions, which represented workers in a particular trade, and industrial unions, which represented workers in an industry. The craft unions were made up mostly of skilled workers, and many of their leaders did not want to unite with industrial unions, whose members were often unskilled workers, many of them immigrants. In 1905, a number of industrial unions, fed up with the lack of recognition by the AFL, broke away to form a new and more radical group—the Industrial Workers of the World (IWW). The goal of the "Wobblies," as they were derisively nicknamed by their opponents, was the

formation of one big union to represent all workers, regardless of where they were born or what kind of work they did.

In addition to native-born figures like William "Big Bill" Haywood and Elizabeth Gurley Flynn, the IWW's leadership included immigrants like Italian-born Carlo Tresca and Arturo Giovannitti, and Joe Hill, born Joel Haaglund in Sweden. A songwriter as well as an activist, Hill wrote several classic labor anthems, including "The Preacher and the Slave" and "Casey Jones, the Union Scab." Also unlike the AFL, the IWW sought to overturn the capitalist system rather than working within it. Most active in the mining and timber industries in the western states, the IWW's radicalism earned it the enmity of state and local governments, as

well as business owners. In 1915, for example, Joe Hill was convicted of murder and executed by a firing squad in Salt Lake City, Utah. The evidence against him was circumstantial, and many historians believe his union activities were the real reason for his execution. The final words of Hill's last telegram to Big Bill Haywood ("Don't waste time in mourning. Organize.") became the IWW's rallying cry. When the IWW opposed America's entry into World War I in 1917, the federal government arrested many of its leaders, and government harassment continued during the Red Scare that followed the war. By the early 1920s, the IWW had faded from the American scene.

THE NEEDLE TRADES

At the turn of the 20th century, New York's garment industry depended on immigrant labor. Three-quarters of the workers in the city's sweatshops—small, overcrowded, and unsafe factories—were immigrant women, mainly Italians or Jews from Eastern Europe. They worked as many as 75 hours a week, for wages as low as $1.50 a week for the youngest laborers.

In November 1909, the International Ladies Garment Workers Union (ILGWU), which had been founded in 1900, called a strike against the major garment manufacturers. In a remarkable show of determination, the workers held fast despite intimidation and harassment from the factory owners, including attacks on picket lines by hired thugs. The "Revolt of the 20,000," as it was

called, finally ended in February 1910 with a settlement that won the workers a reduced work week and other concessions. But some garment manufacturers, including the Triangle Shirtwaist Company, refused to recognize the settlement.

On March 25, 1911, a fire broke out at Triangle's factory, killing 146 workers, almost all of them immigrant women. Most could have escaped, but the sweatshop's doors were locked and the building's inadequate fire escape collapsed. Public indignation over the tragedy led to the passage of health and safety legislation and increased recognition for the ILGWU.

The ILGWU expanded in the 1930s under the leadership of David Dubinsky, who emigrated from Russia in 1911 after escaping from Siberia, where he had been imprisoned for union activities by the Czarist government. Dubinsky also supported the formation of the Congress of Industrial Organizations (CIO), which emerged in 1935 to organize workers unserved by the AFL. (The two groups would eventually merge into the AFL-CIO in the 1950s.)

Like Dubinsky, Lithuanian-born Sidney Hillman also survived imprisonment in Czarist Russia before coming to America. After taking part in a 1910 garment workers' strike in Chicago, Hillman helped found the Amalgamated Clothing Workers of America (ACWA) in 1914 and was the union's president until 1946. He later became a leading figure in the CIO.

TRIANGLE FIRE
Firemen damp the dying flames in the Asch Building, which housed the Triangle Shirtwaist Factory, on the afternoon of March 25, 1911. The fact that the tragedy occurred in the heart of New York City's Greenwich Village compounded public shock and outrage.

LOOK FOR THE UNION LABEL
Around 12,000 members of the International Ladies Garment Workers Union demonstrate in Los Angeles in 1948, a year after Congress passed the Taft-Hartley Act. The law overturned some of labor's gains in the 1930s—for example, outlawing the "closed shop," in which union membership was required of all workers in a particular business.

SAMUEL GOMPERS
1850–1924

Born in London to Jewish parents, Samuel Gompers came to New York City with his family in 1863. He inherited both his father's belief in trade unionism and his trade as a cigar-maker. In the 1870s Gompers took over the Cigar-Makers Union; he became convinced that the nation's many small unions needed to unite within a larger organization and so he helped found the Federation of Organized Trades and Labor Unions (FOTLU) in 1881. Five years later the FOTLU became the American Federation of Labor (AFL). By 1892, the AFL's unions had a membership of more than 1 million. Gompers served as the AFL's leader, for all but one year, from its founding until his death, by which time the AFL was the largest labor organization in America.

First migration	late 1600s
Migrated from	**Britain; Germany; Switzerland**
Approx. number in USA	**300,000 (1776)**
Settlement	**Maryland; Pennsylvania; Virginia; the Carolinas**

Indentured Servants

As many as half of all the settlers who immigrated to the English colonies in North America arrived as indentured servants. These people were bound, or indentured, to work for a master for a period of years to pay for their passage to the colonies. Some indentured servants "bound themselves over" willingly; others had no choice in the matter.

In the countryside of the British Isles, tenant farmers had long raised crops and grazed animals on shared land rented from the local lord. Starting in the 16th century, however, landowners began "enclosing" their properties—dividing them up into individual plots, and often converting cropland to grazing land for sheep to reap profits in the wool trade. Because of Enclosure, many people were thrown off the land. They packed overcrowded cities like London, and joblessness, crime, hunger, and disease all soared. Many poor Britons were eager to immigrate to England's colonies in the West Indies and North America, even if that meant doing several years of hard labor for someone else in order to get there. The need for labor in the tobacco fields of Virginia and Maryland led to the development of the indenture system. A colonial planter or his agent would arrange to pay the passage of an immigrant or group of immigrants, either in advance or upon their arrival in the colonies. (Because the greatest demand was for field hands, most indentured servants were young men.) In return, the servant agreed to serve this master for a fixed period of time—usually three to five years. The master had to provide food, clothing, and tools, and sometimes training in a particular trade. After the indenture was served, the servant received a plot of land of his own.

DIVISION OF COMMON LAND
A modern view of the countryside near St. Ives in Cornwall reveals traces of Enclosure—a process that brought thousands of impoverished rural Britons into the indenture system.

INDENTURED TO WED
A 19th-century print depicts the arrival of about 90 English women at Jamestown, Virginia, in 1619. They were sent by the colony's investors to provide wives for the settlers—a colonist who wanted to wed had to pay 120 pounds of tobacco in return for his bride's passage.

IRISH SERVANTS
By the time this advertisement appeared in 1792, indentured servants had ceased to be a major part of the American labor force.

ON-THE-JOB TRAINING
Some indenture contracts stipulated that the master had to teach the servant a trade, like carpentry or, as shown here, plumbing.

BACON'S REBELLION

In the late 1600s, there was considerable tension in Virginia between former servants living on small land grants and the colony's leading planters, who—the smallholders contended—were keeping the best land for themselves and failing to protect them from Native American raids. In 1676, the smallholders took matters into their own hands and began attacking Native American communities. This unauthorized conflict displeased the colony's governor, William Berkeley, who summoned the smallholders' leader, Nathaniel Bacon, to Jamestown, Virginia's capital. Fearing that Bacon would lead the former servants in open revolt against the colonial government, Berkeley ordered Bacon arrested. Bacon was released when things calmed down, but soon afterward he led a group of current and former servants, and slaves, in attacks on the estates of Berkeley's supporters. "Bacon's Rebellion," as it came to be known, ended when Bacon died of disease in October 1622; most of his followers quickly surrendered.

INDENTURED AND UNWILLING

Rising demand for field hands encouraged some unsavory practices. Sometimes poor, homeless, or just unlucky people were kidnapped from the streets of London and other cities, to be indentured to the highest bidder on arrival in America. Many of those kidnapped were children, especially orphans, and women. English authorities also came to see the colonies' need for labor as a way to get rid of petty criminals, prostitutes, and paupers. Thousands were deported from England to the colonies, and those who did not have money to make a new start on their own (which was most) were forcibly "indented." The usual term of indenture was seven years, and once free, they could return to England.

The indenture system had a serious flaw from the planters'

point of view: the servants' labor was temporary, so new servants were always needed. Planters increasingly turned to another source of imported labor—Africans (*see pp 32–33*). Although the first Africans in the colonies had the status of indentured servants, colonial authorities changed their term of indenture so it had no end, and children born to slaves were the property of the master. (In contrast, children born to white indentured servants were free.) Still, white indentured servants outnumbered slaves into the 18th century.

REDEMPTIONERS

While most of the 300,000 or so indentured servants who arrived in America before the Revolutionary War were from the British Isles, the "Redemptioners," as they were called, came from Germany and Switzerland and settled mostly in Maryland, Pennsylvania, and the Carolinas. Often seeking religious freedom as well as land and opportunity, Redemptioners signed an agreement with a ship's captain to pay back the cost of their passage to the colonies within a specific period of time. If they did not, the captain could sell them to the highest bidder. There were no legal protections for Redemptioners, so many of those purchased were treated as slaves.

see pp 32–33

FREEDOM FOR WOMEN
Moll Flanders

In 1722, the English novelist Daniel Defoe published *The Fortunes and Misfortunes of the Famous Moll Flanders, Etc. Who was born in Newgate, and during a life of continu'd Variety for Threescore Years, besides her Childhood, was Twelve Year a Whore, five times a Wife (whereof once to her own brother), Twelve Year a Thief, Eight Year a Transported Felon in Virginia, at last grew Rich, liv'd Honest and died a Penitent. Written from her own Memorandums.* Defoe's broad scope extends across the ocean to colonial America and the issue of immigration. The heroine, Moll, whose eventful history is depicted in the lengthy title, desperately wants to be comfortably middle class. Unsuccessful, she turns to crime, is caught and convicted, and is deported to America. In Virginia, Moll plans to "plant, settle, and in short, grow rich," and as a plantation owner she is able to achieve her dream of economic and social stability. For Defoe, America presented the possibility of a new life for the transported convict and his novel reads as colonial propaganda for the industrious. Through ingenuity, Moll avoids the servitude that usually accompanied deportation, and through hard work, she grows rich. In addition, she gains respectability and social standing, which in a society of such opportunity was relative to money, not birth.

THE
HISTORY
OF
MOLL FLANDERS.

LONDON:
Printed and Sold by J. HOLLIS,
Shoemaker-Row, Black-Friars.

THOROUGHOOD HOUSE
Built around 1680, Adam Thoroughood's house in Princess Anne County, Virginia, symbolizes its owner's rise from poor servant to prosperous planter. Arriving in 1621 as an indentured servant, Thoroughood owned over 5,000 acres of land by the mid-1630s.

Scotch-Irish, Scots, and Welsh

While the English formed the majority of the colonial American population, settlers also included substantial numbers of people from Celtic regions under English rule, including Scotland, Wales, and Cornwall, while the Scotch-Irish—who immigrated from Scotland to Ireland and then to America—became one of the most significant groups in the colonies and in the young United States.

First migration	early 1700s
Migrated from	Scotland by way of Ireland; Scotland; Wales
Approx. number in USA	2 million (2000)
Settlement	All original 13 colonies; Colorado; Kentucky; Michigan; Tennessee; Wisconsin

Ireland became England's first colony when the Normans invaded in the 12th century, but English rule was relatively weak until King Henry VIII reasserted royal authority in the 16th century. England became a Protestant nation during the Reformation (*see pp 60–61*), but the Irish remained Roman Catholic, and they fiercely resented their English overlords, which led to periodic rebellions. In 1603, after one such rebellion in Ulster (part of which is now Northern Ireland), Queen Elizabeth I seized land and encouraged Protestant English and Scots to settle there. Her successor, James I, continued this policy; so did Oliver Cromwell, head of the English Commonwealth, who put down a rebellion in Ulster in the late 1640s, leading to the seizure of more land from the native Irish. The defeat of another Irish rebellion at the Battle of the Boyne in 1690 further consolidated English rule in Ireland and brought even more Scots into the region. By the end of the 17th century, settlers from the Scottish lowlands formed the majority of the population of Ulster.

Despite being the beneficiaries of Irish territory, many Scottish settlers in Ireland were dissatisfied. Although they were Protestant, most were Presbyterians who resented the dominance of the established Church of England, and economic opportunities in the Ulster "plantations" were not much better than in Scotland, as the English owned most of the land.

Starting in the first decades of the 18th century, thousands of Scots began to sail for England's American colonies. Some came as indentured servants (*see pp 138–139*), but most had enough resources to set out on their own, and they tended to immigrate as families or members of church congregations.

"BUTCHER" CUMBERLAND
British general William Augustus, the Duke of Cumberland, earned his nickname for his brutal methods during the Jacobite uprising of 1745, including the execution of over 100 prisoners.

THE BORDERS
Hayfields in Tweed River Valley in the borderlands between England and Scotland. Political and economic strife on the Scottish side in the 18th and 19th centuries led to immigration to America.

MARCHING SEASON
Wearing their traditional sashes, members of the Orange Order march through Belfast, Northern Ireland, on July 12, 2001, to commemorate King William's victory at the Battle of the Boyne. Northern Ireland remains part of the United Kingdom today.

The Scots-Irish, or Scotch-Irish, as they became known, were, along with the Germans who immigrated around the same time, the first significant group of non-English immigrants to the English colonies. As many as 250,000 Scotch-Irish came to America in the 18th century, and at the time of the Revolutionary War, they formed about 10 percent of the population. They settled in all the colonies, but were most numerous in Pennsylvania. The Scotch-Irish brought their anti-English sentiments with them; most were Patriots during the struggle for independence.

Besides wanting to escape English rule, the Scotch-Irish desired land. With much of the Atlantic Coast already settled, many Scotch-Irish immigrants moved westward into the unsettled, Native American–occupied frontier. This willingness to tame the wilderness, and their determination to drive back the Native Americans, gave the Scotch-Irish a reputation for toughness. They were the original pioneers, playing an important role in the settling of Kentucky, Tennessee, and other states.

In the 2000 census, about 4.3 million Americans reported Scotch-Irish ancestry. Given that the distinctions between English, Scots, and Irish ancestry have become ambiguous by the early 21st century, the actual number is likely higher by an order of magnitude. Demographically, Americans of at least partly Scotch-Irish descent make up a large part of the white population in the South, and a significant percentage of the population everywhere that white Southerners have spread as a result of internal migration, especially the Midwest and the West Coast.

Writer (*Born Fighting: How the Scots-Irish Shaped America*) and former Secretary of the Navy James Webb—himself of Scotch-Irish ancestry—described the group's contributions in a 2004 article: "They tamed the wilderness, building simple log cabins and scraping corn patches in thin soil. And they pressed

onward, creating a way of life that many would come to call, if not American, certainly the defining fabric of the South and the Midwest, as well as the core character of the nation's working class."

SCOTS

There were a few Scots in the English colonies in the 17th century, but major Scottish immigration did not begin until after the 1707 Act of Union, which joined England and Scotland to form Great Britain. Lowland artisans and laborers left Glasgow and elsewhere to be indentured servants in tobacco colonies and New York.

Despite the unification of Scotland and England, many Scots considered the English monarchy to be illegitimate. In the "Glorious Revolution" of 1688, the English Parliament had deposed King James II—of the Scottish Stuart dynasty—fearing that he would re-establish Catholicism in England. The line of succession to the English throne switched from the Stuarts to members of Dutch and, later, German royal families. Supporters of the Stuart line, dubbed "Jacobites," launched two rebellions against England in the first half of the 18th century; the Jacobites were finally defeated in the Battle of Culloden in 1746. In the aftermath, several thousand Jacobite leaders were exiled, some of them to England's American colonies.

Around the same time, the "clearance" of the Scottish Highlands—where most of the population spoke Gaelic, professed Catholicism, and lived in virtually feudal conditions—began. The Highland Clearance was similar to the Enclosure movement in England (*see pp 138–139*). Scottish landowners converted farmland to grazing land, displacing thousands of tenant farmers. This continued well into the 19th century. Some landowners paid their tenants' passage to the United States or Canada; others simply drove them from their homes to fend for themselves.

LAST OF THE CLAN
Thomas Faed's 1865 painting, *The Last of the Clan,* captures the anguish of a family of tenant farmers driven from its home during the Highland Clearances. An eyewitness described an 1814 clearing in Strathnaver: "I saw the townships set on fire. . . Few if any of the families knew where to turn their heads or from whom to get their next meal."

THE GAME OF GOLF
Golf is one of the Scots' most enduring contributions to American culture. While there are records of balls and clubs being imported from Scotland to the colonies as early as 1743, the first golf club in the modern sense, the Saint Andrew's Golf Club, was established in Yonkers, New York, in 1888, by Scots-born John Reid.

ANDREW CARNEGIE
1835–1800

Andrew Carnegie was one of the most influential Scottish immigrants. Born in Dunfermline, Carnegie's father was a weaver who was thrown out of work when steam-powered looms replaced handlooms. Like another Scottish immigrant family, the Pinkertons, the Carnegies were active Chartists (*see pp 106–107*). In 1848, when Andrew was 12, the family joined relatives in Allegheny, Pennsylvania, where the boy went to work in a textile mill and attended night school. At 14, Carnegie became a messenger in the Pennsylvania Railroad's telegraph office. He proved to have an amazing facility with the new technology. His skill, intelligence, and hard work brought him to the attention of the railroad's president, who made him his personal telegrapher. By age 30, he was one of the railroad's top executives.

In the 1870s, Carnegie entered the booming steel industry. By 1889, he virtually controlled steel production in America. Despite his belief in organized labor, his status as an enlightened industrialist was tarnished during a bloody strike at his Homestead, Pennsylvania, plant, in 1892, when guards from the Pinkerton Detective Agency clashed with strikers.

Nine years later, Carnegie sold his steel empire to financier J. P. Morgan for a quarter of a billion dollars. Carnegie then set about giving away his immense fortune. Already committed to philanthropy, he declared in an 1889 magazine article that "[A] man who dies rich dies disgraced," and stated that personal wealth must be put to "the improvement of mankind." In Britain, Canada, and the United States, Carnegie set up foundations to fund universities, public libraries, theaters, scholarship programs, and an institution dedicated to the cause of world peace. Carnegie's endowments continue to benefit humankind.

In 1775, the outbreak of hostilities in the American colonies caused the British government to suspend emigration. When the war ended eight years later, immigration to America resumed, with especially large numbers of Scotch-Irish.

Scottish influence has been profound in many aspects of American life, particularly in education, thanks to the long-standing Scottish respect for literacy and scholarship. This emphasis on education led to the founding of numerous schools and colleges, the latter often established to provide ministers for the Presbyterian Church, most notably Princeton University, which began as the College of New Jersey—the fourth college in the colonies—in 1746. Graduates of Edinburgh University formed the faculty of the first medical school in the present-day United States, in New York City in 1767.

Both the Scotch-Irish and the Scots have been well represented in politics as well. By some accounts, close to half the signers of the Declaration of Independence had some Scottish background. In addition to numerous state governors, Supreme Court justices, and other officials, at least a dozen presidents have claimed Scots or Scotch-Irish ancestry, from Andrew Jackson to Bill Clinton. In the words of President Woodrow Wilson—himself the descendant of Scotch-Irish immigrants—"Every line of strength in American history is a line colored with Scottish blood."

WELSH AND CORNISH

Wales united with England in 1536, and while it was a relatively poor area in comparison with England, it managed to escape social and economic disasters on the scale of the Highland Clearance in Scotland and the Potato Famine in Ireland (*see pp 144–145*). Consequently, the Welsh did not immigrate to the United States at the same rate as the Scots and Irish—though some came as indentured servants in the colonial era.

Welsh immigration rose in the 19th century; about 80,000 Welsh immigrants (mostly men in their 20s) arrived in the United States between roughly 1860 and 1920. Most settled in Pennsylvania, where many became coal miners, while farmers tended to settle in the Upper Midwest, especially Wisconsin. Mining was a traditional trade with the Welsh, and also with people from Cornwall, a Celtic enclave in the west of England. Prized by mine-owners for their skill at hardrock mining, Cornish immigrants found abundant opportunities in Colorado and Michigan.

STARS, STRIPES—AND PLAID
This marcher in New York City's National Tartan Day Parade, held every year in the first week of April, is dressed in his family's tartan. (A tartan is the particular pattern associated with each of the more than 300 Scottish clans.) The holiday commemorates the Declaration of Arbroath, which asserted Scotland's independence, on April 6, 1320.

WORKING IN THE COAL MINE
Miners pose at the entrance to a coal mine in Scranton, Pennsylvania, in this photograph from the turn of the 20th century. The anthracite coal region of Eastern Pennsylvania attracted thousands of miners from Wales, most arriving between 1840 and 1860, attracted by wages that were more than double what they received at home.

First migration	**1845**
Migrated from	**Ireland**
Approx. number in USA	**5.2 million (1975)**
Settlement	**Boston; New York**

Irish

Between 1845 and 1850, a devastating fungus destroyed Ireland's potato crop—the main source of food for much of the nation's population. During these years, starvation and related diseases claimed as many as a million lives, while perhaps twice that number of Irish immigrated—500,000 of them to the United States, where they accounted for more than half of all immigrants in the 1840s.

The conditions that led to the potato famine had been developing for years. In 1800, an Act of Union dissolved the Irish Parliament and united Ireland with Britain, while Parliament passed harsh "Penal Laws" that effectively deprived Catholics—who formed the majority of Ireland's population—of all civil and political rights. Much of the land was owned by English landlords and tilled by tenant farmers who raised crops for export. In the early 1800s, Irish farmers who did own land switched from raising food crops to grazing sheep or cattle because of competition from American agriculture. To survive, the rural Irish turned to the potato—ironically, an import from the Americas. By the 1840s, it is estimated that half the population of Ireland lived mainly on potatoes. In 1845, the fungus, or blight, arrived from Europe. Within a few weeks, the potato harvest turned to black mush. The blight returned in 1846 and 1847. By that time Ireland's rural population was dying by the tens of thousands from hunger and disease.

Little was done to relieve Ireland's suffering. At the height of the famine—the year remembered by the Irish as "Black '47"—Ireland exported 4,000 shiploads of grain to Britain, while the Irish fell dead in rural lanes and city streets. The British eventually

TURNED OUT

Evicted from their cottage—probably by an absentee landlord—this family in Derrybeg, Ireland, faces an uncertain fate. British troops were sometimes used to "turn out" tenant families who could not pay the rent.

COFFIN SHIPS

Most of the famine immigrants came packed in the holds of converted cargo ships. During the transatlantic voyage, British ships were only required to supply 7 lbs. of food per week per passenger. Of the 100,000 Irish who sailed to North America in 1847, an estimated one in five died.

LUCKY JEANIE

The *Jeanie Johnson* sailed between Tralee, Ireland, and North American ports from 1848–55 without a single death. Here, a modern replica of the ship sails into Boston Harbor in July 2003.

W. COLE, No. 8 Ann-st.

GROCERY CART AND HARNESS FOR SA—In good order, and one chestnut horse, 8 years old excellent saddle horse; can be ridden by a lady. Also, young man wanted, from 16 to 18 years of age, able to wi No Irish need apply. CLUFF & TUNIS, No. 270 Wi ington-st., corner of Myrtle-av., Brooklyn.

BILLIARD TABLE FOR SALE—Of Leona manufacture; been used about nine months. Also, tures of a Bar-room. Inquire on the premises. No.

NO IRISH NEED APPLY

A help-wanted advertisement from the *New York Times* in 1854—when Irish immigrants made up more than a quarter of the populace—illustrates the widespread prejudice directed against them. One disillusioned newcomer wrote, "Our position in America is one of shame and poverty."

undertook some relief efforts, and private charities distributed food, but there were simply too many sick and starving people.

By the time the blight finally receded in 1850, between 1.5 and 2 million people—perhaps a quarter of the population—had left Ireland for Britain, Canada, Australia, and America. Most of those who immigrated to America did so aboard the notoriously overcrowded, disease-ridden "coffin ships," which landed their human cargoes at eastern ports, especially New York and Boston. Other Irish immigrants went first to Quebec or Montreal (passage was cheaper aboard British ships on the Canada route) and then set out on foot for the United States.

FIVE POINTS

Geoffrey Clements painted this view of New York City's Five Points neighborhood—named for the points created by the intersection of Park, Worth, and Baxter streets—in the 1840s, when it was home to tens of thousands of newly arrived Irish.

> "For these desperate, homeless people, America was not so much a land of opportunity, as a last resort."
>
> "The Golden Door"

My dear mother and father, who can tell when he sets forth to wander wither he may be driven by the uncertain kerns of destiny or when he may return. Or wither he may ever again behold the scenes of his childhood. From the moment you lose sight of the land you have left, all is vacancy. Many a heart-sickening night have I spent during those ten weeks we were tossed upon the merciless waves of the vast Atlantic. To a person pining under sickness and lashed upon the stormy sea, it would seem as if the sun had forgot its course and as if the law of nature itself had been subverted. As we approached the dock, it was thronged with people. My wandering eye ran along the crowd, but I could see no friend to meet, no eye to recognize me. I looked upon the loneliness of my position. I stepped again upon the land, but I felt I was a stranger in the land.

Setting out from the north of Ireland in 1850, George Ritchie, another victim of the famine, writes home about the despair that often grips those forced to leave, excerpted from "The Golden Door."

NO IRISH NEED APPLY

A small number of Irish had immigrated to America during the colonial era, and several thousand arrived in the early 1800s. The "Famine Irish," however, represented the first major influx of Irish immigration into America, and, because so many arrived in a short time, they were one of the most significant immigrant groups in the nation's history. Yet the newcomers faced discrimination. They were Catholic in an era when most native-born Americans were fiercely opposed to "Papism." Most were uneducated and unskilled, and were thought to be prone to drunkenness and fighting. The hated phrase "No Irish need apply" was often attached to handbills advertising job openings. As a result, the Irish crowded into the poorest neighborhoods, like New York City's Five Points. Over time, however, the Irish established themselves in

their new country by sheer hard work and determination. And while the eastern cities remained home to many of the Famine Irish and their descendants, they also spread throughout the rest of the country. The Irish also proved adept at politics, particularly within the ranks of the Democratic Party; in the decades after the Civil War, Irish-dominated political machines, like New York's Tammany Hall, held power in several cities.

Immigration from Ireland slowed after 1850, but it continued into the 20th century; 4.7 million Irish settled in America between 1820 and 1975. In 2002, more than 34 million Americans considered themselves to be of Irish ancestry, making Irish-Americans the country's second-largest ethnic group.

EMERALD PRIDE

The Michael Collins Pipe Band parades in Denver, Colorado, on St. Patrick's Day, 1999. Honoring Ireland's patron saint, the holiday was first celebrated in America in 1762.

GOLD RUSHES

AMERICAN RIVER
A section of the swift-moving American River, site of the 1848 gold strike, as it looks today. Even before the discovery, growing numbers of American settlers were arriving in California; in June 1846, Americans at Sonoma declared independence from Mexico.

Gold pan   Gold nugget

ALL THAT GLITTERS
In December 1848, President James Polk declared that "The accounts of the abundance of gold in [California] are of such extraordinary character as would scarcely command belief were they not corroborated by . . . officers in the public service."

PANNING FOR GOLD
Gold miners in South Dakota in 1889. Panning for gold was hard, monotonous work: miners would drop several handfuls of earth into a pan, then swirl the pan in the water so that the dirt, gravel, and other materials would wash away, leaving the heavier grains of gold to be collected, and then repeat the process over and over again.

The hope of acquiring quick riches from precious metals has lured people to America from the earliest years of exploration and settlement—from the Spanish, seeking mythical cities of gold in the Southwest to the first "gentleman adventurers" of Jamestown (*see pp 26–27*). In the mid-19th century, the discovery of gold in California sparked a major influx of migrants from both within the United States and from abroad, as would, to a lesser extent, later strikes in Colorado, the Dakota Territory, and Alaska.

United States following the Mexican-American War. A Californian newspaper declared, "The whole country from San Francisco to Los Angeles . . . resounds with the cry of GOLD! GOLD! GOLD! . . . and everything is left neglected but the manufacture of shovels and pickaxes."

It took months for the news to reach the East Coast, and when it did, farmers left their plows, artisans put down their tools, and clerks abandoned their counters to rush to California to strike it rich. Over the next year, tens of thousands of mostly single male "Forty-Niners" (as they were called) arrived in the goldfields. Some came overland; others by ship around South America, a journey that took eight months; still others sailed to the Isthmus of Panama, which separated the Atlantic and Pacific oceans before the opening of the Panama

FORTY-NINERS

On January 24, 1848, on the American River in the foothills of California's Sierra Mountains, carpenter James Marshall noticed unusual rocks in the stream that fed the sawmill he was working on. He showed the rocks to his boss, John Sutter (*see side panel*), who realized they were gold. Marshall and Sutter tried to keep the find a secret, but word soon spread throughout California—which Mexico would soon cede to the

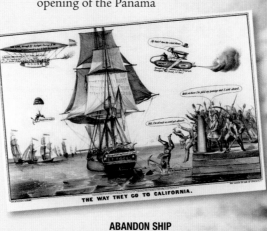

THE WAY THEY GO TO CALIFORNIA.

ABANDON SHIP
Above: An 1849 Currier & Ives lithograph lampoons the eagerness of the Forty-Niners to get to California. *Below:* A photograph from the same year shows ships marooned in San Francisco Bay—their crews having deserted to the goldfields en masse upon arrival.

Canal, then crossed the isthmus by foot or by railroad before boarding ship again for San Francisco. The Forty-Niners also included substantial numbers of foreign fortune hunters, including Mexicans, Peruvians, Chileans, Hawaiians, and Australians.

A few did strike it rich. Most went home disappointed. But many stayed, swelling the non–Native American population of California from around 15,000 in 1848 to around 250,000 in 1852—by which time California had become a state. San Francisco, the gateway to the gold country, was a sleepy port with less than a thousand residents in 1848; by the end of 1849, it was a booming city of 25,000.

At least half of the new settlers in California in 1849 and the following years, however, came to provide goods and services to the gold-seekers, realizing (correctly) that this was a surer way of making money than panning for gold in the streams of the Sierras. These immigrants included Jewish merchants and peddlers like "Big Mike" Goldwater and Bavarian-born Levi Strauss, who arrived in San Francisco in 1853 and later created an iconic American garment—blue jeans—to meet miners' needs for tough trousers.

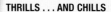

The California Gold Rush also spurred the first significant immigration from Asia to the United States. Between 1849 and 1851, about 25,000 Chinese made their way to what they hoped would be *gam saam* ("gold mountain"). Most, however, found only low-paying work cooking and cleaning for the miners, and the Chinese in California would soon face racial and economic discrimination (*see pp 154–155*).

LATER GOLD RUSHES

The California Gold Rush was the greatest such event in American history, but it was not the last. In 1859, large deposits of gold and silver were found in Colorado. Once again, thousands of fortune hunters poured in.

Similar strikes occurred in Idaho and Montana in the early 1860s. In 1876, gold deposits turned up in the Black Hills of the Dakota Territory—land that the federal government had guaranteed by treaty to the Sioux. The flood of prospectors into the Black Hills led to conflict with the Sioux, including the Battle of Little Bighorn—a rare Native American victory that saw Colonel George Armstrong Custer's 7th Cavalry wiped out. The last great North American gold rushes came at the turn of the 20th century. In 1897, gold was found along the Klondike River in Canada's Yukon Territory—a strike that attracted about 100,000 prospectors. A couple of years later, another lode of gold turned up on U.S. territory near Nome, Alaska. As in the California Gold Rush a half-century before, most of the prospectors who flocked to Nome went home broke, but some stayed; they and their descendants helped make Alaska the 49th state in 1959.

THRILLS . . . AND CHILLS
A poster advertises a theatrical melodrama inspired by the Klondike Gold Rush. That event greatly spurred the growth of Seattle, Washington—the American port city closest to the goldfields.

JOHN SUTTER
1803–1880

John Sutter was born Johann August Suter in Baden, Germany. After traveling around the world, Sutter arrived in California (then ruled by Mexico), took Mexican citizenship, and, in 1840, set up a settlement he named Nuevo Helvetia ("New Switzerland") on a 50,000-acre land grant. Nuevo Helvetia was a mix of commercial enterprise and utopian experiment; he recruited Mexicans, Native Americans, and a handful of Americans and Europeans to work the land, while helping the Americans who were arriving by wagon train. Among Sutter's many enterprises was the sawmill where gold was discovered in 1848. Yet fortune hunters overran his land, and the new U.S. government refused to confirm the status he had enjoyed under Mexican rule. He wound up in conflict with his son, John Sutter, Jr., who wanted to develop Sacramento instead of Nuevo Helvetia. Sutter, Sr. spent the rest of his life lobbying Congress to compensate him for his financial losses. He died just after Congress authorized it.

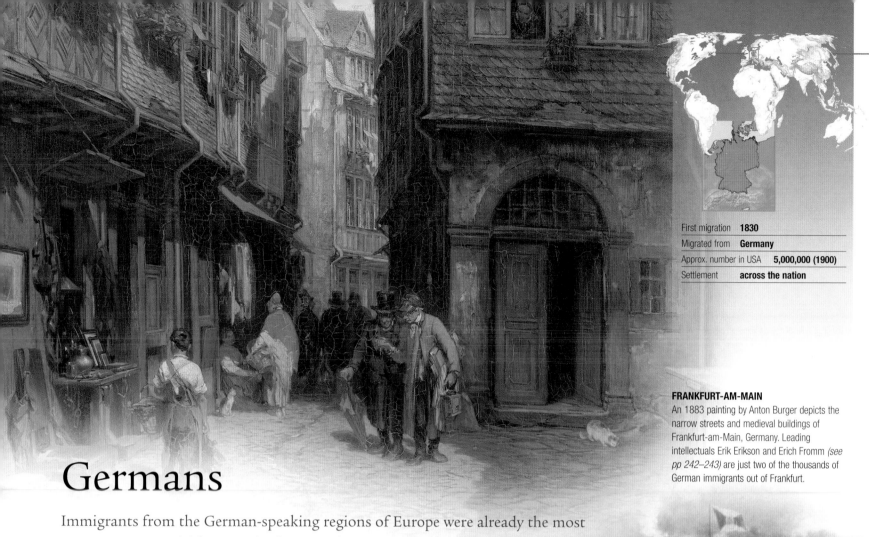

First migration	1830
Migrated from	**Germany**
Approx. number in USA	**5,000,000 (1900)**
Settlement	**across the nation**

FRANKFURT-AM-MAIN
An 1883 painting by Anton Burger depicts the narrow streets and medieval buildings of Frankfurt-am-Main, Germany. Leading intellectuals Erik Erikson and Erich Fromm *(see pp 242–243)* are just two of the thousands of German immigrants out of Frankfurt.

Germans

Immigrants from the German-speaking regions of Europe were already the most numerous non-British group in the United States at the start of the 19th century, but around 1830 a huge wave of immigration from Germany began. All told, five million Germans came to the United States in the 19th century, and today more Americans consider themselves of German ancestry than any other group.

"America, you have it better . . ." So wrote the great German poet Goethe in 1827, when Germany was a loose confederation of kingdoms, principalities, and city-states, united by language and culture, but not much else. Economic conditions varied widely, but in Northern Germany especially, and the early 19th century was a difficult time for most Germans. As in the Scandinavian countries, rapid population growth meant that there was too little land and too many people. Few German farmers owned land, and many had to move from place to place as seasonal laborers.

The arrival of industry brought many people from the countryside to the cities, but German mills and factories—facing competition from British and American industries—could not provide enough decent-paying jobs for the population. In addition to the rural and urban poor, many skilled workers and middle-class professionals were fed up with the lack of opportunity and the denial of political and civil rights in many German states, particularly after the failure of the revolutions of 1848 *(see pp 108–109)*.

About 10,000 Germans—from all areas and social classes—arrived in the United States in the early 1830s, and the number of immigrants rose rapidly as the

READ THE MANUAL
This 1879 guidebook was published to help immigrants planning to settle in Minnesota and the Dakota Territory, which it calls "East Dakota." The territory was divided into the states of North Dakota and South Dakota a decade later; both drew substantial numbers of German immigrants.

FURST BISMARCK
The Hamburg-Amerika line's *Furst Bismarck* steams into New York Harbor. A typical, medium-sized liner of the time, the vessel plied the North Atlantic immigrant route from 1891 until 1904, with each voyage bringing about 700 steerage passengers from Germany to America.

rulers of some German states eased restrictions on emigration. During the peak period from roughly 1860–90, there were only three years in which Germans were not the largest nationality among new arrivals in America. Most were from Northern Germany, but after Germany united under the northern Protestant kingdom of Prussia in 1871, increasing numbers from Bavaria and other mostly Catholic south German states emigrated.

WHERE THEY WENT

Unlike some immigrant groups, the Germans settled widely across the country; by the mid-19th century, there were substantial German enclaves in most major cities, especially Philadelphia, New York, Chicago, and New Orleans. German immigrants were concentrated most heavily in the Great Lakes states and in the Midwest, especially in the "German Triangle" delineated by Milwaukee, Wisconsin; St. Louis, Missouri; and

Cincinnati, Ohio. Since land was the attraction for many German immigrants, they were also well-represented on the frontier, especially the Dakotas (Bismarck, North Dakota's capital, was named for the German statesman), and a sizeable contingent settled in central Texas.

In general, the Germans were accepted by native-born Americans more than other immigrant groups—although, like the Irish, they were the target of Nativist and "Know-Nothing" campaigns in the 1850s. Some Americans, however, were shocked by their attitude toward the Sabbath; in a holdover from Puritan days, many American communities shut down on Sundays, while the Germans used Sunday as a day for sports and relaxation, as well as religious observance. The German fondness for beer also drew criticism from Temperance advocates, as the peak years of German immigration overlapped with the movement to ban alcohol.

GERMANY IN AMERICA

By the turn of the 20th century, Germans formed such a large part of the population that in neighborhoods like Cincinnati's Over-the-Rhine and New York's Kleindeutschland, new immigrants felt right at home with the German-language newspapers, *turnvereins*, and beer gardens. In some communities, public schools offered instruction in German, as well as English. At the same time, elements of German culture became part of American culture: Germans gave their new homeland its iconic foods (the hamburger and the hot dog), the Christmas tree, the kindergarten *(see pp 108–109)*, and a taste for lighter beers *(see side panel)*.

AMERICAN BAVARIA
Nestled in the Cascade Mountains of Washington State, the town of Leavenworth hosts a variety of events celebrating German-American heritage.

TURNVEREIN
German immigrants brought with them the *turnverein*, local gymnastic clubs. The first such club was founded in Cincinnati in 1848. Shown here is the women's "drill team" of the St. Paul, Minnesota, *turnverein* around 1920.

THE BEER KING
1839–1913

In 1857, Adolphus Busch arrived in St. Louis, Missouri, from Hesse, Germany. The last of 21 children born to a purveyor of brewers' supplies, he set up a brewery in 1866 in partnership with his brother-in-law, Eberhard Anheuser. At the time, most American beers were dark hoppy brews derived from British ales. Anheuser-Busch specialized in a lighter, golden fizzier beer produced by the German process of lagering—aging beer in cool conditions. The new style quickly caught on among American beer drinkers, and the brewery also pioneered the pasteurization process, which allowed its product to be shipped around the country without loss to flavor. Busch named the new brew Budweiser, after a village in a German-speaking area of what is now the Czech Republic. By the turn of the 20th century, Anheuser-Busch was America's biggest beer producer.

THE *SLOCUM* DISASTER

The center of German-American life in New York City in the late 19th and early 20th century was the Lower East Side neighborhood known as Kleindeutschland ("Little Germany"). On June 15, 1904, the neighborhood suffered one of the worst tragedies ever to strike an immigrant community. On that day, about 1,300 people—almost all parishioners of St. Mark's Evangelical Lutheran Church—boarded the steamer *General Slocum*, which was to take them to a Long Island park for a Sunday-school picnic. A fire broke out aboard the ship as it steamed up the East River. Instead of immediately putting to shore, the captain decided to speed toward a small island off the Bronx—a move that fanned the flames. Within minutes—and to the horror of onlookers in Manhattan's skyscrapers—the entire ship was on fire. Terrified passengers braved the water to escape the flames, but the *Slocum*'s cork life preservers were so rotten that they were useless, and the lifeboats were wired in place. By the time the flaming wreck beached 20 minutes later, at least 1,000 passengers—most of them women and children—had burned or drowned. The tragedy tore the heart out of Kleindeutschland; almost everyone in the neighborhood had friends and relatives among the victims.

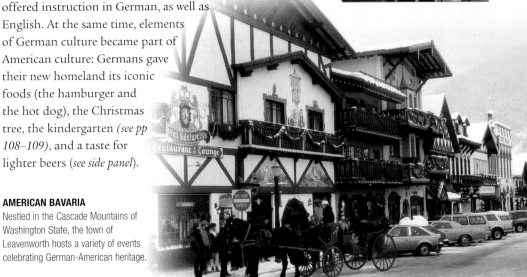

Scandinavians

Scandinavian Vikings were the first Europeans to reach North America more than a thousand years ago, and Sweden was among the first nations to plant a colony in what is now the United States, but major immigration from the Scandinavian nations—Sweden, Denmark, Norway, Finland, and Iceland—did not begin in earnest until the mid-19th century, when a desperate land hunger brought the first of more than 1 million Scandinavians to the United States.

First migration	**1850**
Migrated from	**Denmark; Finland; Iceland; Norway; Sweden**
Approx. number in USA	**1.5 million (1924)**
Settlement	**Great Lake states; Upper Midwest; Pacific Northwest; New York; Pennsylvania; Utah**

The largest and most powerful of the Scandinavian nations in its 17th- and early 18th-century heyday, Sweden was a country in crisis by the mid-1800s. Between 1750–1850, the nation's population doubled, outstripping the available farmland and leading to periodic famines, especially in coastal areas where good land was scarce and the growing season was short.

A few Swedes had come to America in the first half of the 19th century, and many sent back reports about the availability of land across the ocean. Besides these "America Letters," European steamship lines and American railroads, eager to profit from the emigrant trade, circulated brochures throughout Sweden. Early Swedish immigrants were realistic about the challenges they faced in their adopted homeland, including the difficulties of farming in the tough terrain of the upper Midwest. In 1850, an immigrant farmer told a visiting writer from Sweden: "None who are not accustomed to hard, agricultural labor ought to become farmers in this country. No one who is in any other way well off in his native land ought to come hither."

RUGGED LAND
Pictured below is a lake outside Stora Blasjon, Sweden, close to the Norwegian border. Less than 10 percent of Sweden's land is suitable for farming, and the growing season is short—only 120 days in the northern part of the country.

WATER MINING
Swedish peasants mine iron ore from the bottom of a frozen lake in this 19th-century woodcut. Slight economic activities like water mining were vital because of Scandinavia's short growing season.

Around 1860, the Swedish government relaxed restrictions on emigration. Over the next 20 years, at least 150,000 Swedes immigrated to America, mostly as families. Some settled in cities, especially Chicago and New York, but most pursued their dream of land ownership by moving to Wisconsin, Minnesota, and the Dakotas, where the climate and landscape were similar, in many respects, to their homeland.

A smaller wave of immigration from Sweden began around 1890, but most of these immigrants were single men and women who sought factory jobs or work as servants in cities,

> For the comfort of the faint-hearted I can, therefore, declare with truth that here, as in Norway, there are laws, government, and authorities. But everything is designed to maintain the natural freedom and equality of men. In regard to the former, every one is free to engage in whatever honorable occupation he wishes, and to go wherever he wishes without having to produce a passport, and without being detained by customs officials. Only the real criminal is threatened with punishment by the law. In writings the sole purpose of which seems to be to find something in America which can be criticized, I have read that the American is faithless, deceitful, hard-hearted, and so forth. I will not deny that such folk are to be found in America, as well as in other places, and that the stranger can never be too careful; but it has been my experience that the American as a general rule is easier to get along with than the Norwegian, more accommodating, more obliging, more reliable in all things. The oldest Norwegian immigrants have assured me of the same thing. Since it is so easy to support oneself honorably, thieving and burglary are almost unknown.
>
> Excerpted from *Ole Rynning's True Account of America*, published by the Norwegian-American Historical Association in 1926.

rather than land for farming; many of these immigrants settled in the Pacific Northwest, particularly in Seattle, Washington.

NORWEGIANS

In Norway, which was politically united with Sweden from 1814–1905, economic conditions were worse for the mostly rural population: during the 19th century, on a percentage basis, Norway sent more people to America than any other nation except Ireland. As many as 1 million Norwegians immigrated between the early 1800s and 1924.

The first Norwegian immigrants were motivated more by religious than economic considerations. In the 18th century, a handful of Norwegian Moravians (*see pp 78–79*) joined their mainly German co-religionists in Pennsylvania. In 1825, six Norwegian families who dissented from Norway's state-run Lutheran Church sailed for

> ## "America fever was the name Norwegians gave to the spreading enthusiasm for emigration."
>
> Todd Nichols, Historian

America aboard the sloop *Restaurationen*, a vessel that has passed into history as the "Norwegian Mayflower." With the help of local Quakers, the "sloopers"—as these immigrants became known—settled in upstate New York.

The social and political freedoms of the United States were also a factor in Norwegian immigration. In the words of a contemporary historian, "The fact that the U.S. was a republic where the people held regular elections to place political officials in power was appealing to many people in Norway. The possibility of voting rights was quite appealing to many Norwegian men and women."

Like their Swedish neighbors, prospective Norwegian immigrants were inspired by "America Letters," by marketing materials from steamship and railroad companies, and by visits from neighbors who had prospered in America. In 1871, a Norwegian who subsequently immigrated noted that a villager visiting from Minnesota "infected half the population in that district with what was called the America fever . . . No more amusement of any kind, only brooding on how to get away to America. It was like a desperate case of homesickness reversed."

TRUE ACCOUNT OF AMERICA
Published in Norway in 1838, this book promises a "True Account of America for the Enlightenment and Benefit of the Peasant and the Common Man, Written by a Norwegian who arrived there in the month of June 1837."

SODBUSTERS
Norwegian immigrant Beret Olesdater Hagebak poses outside her sod hut in Lac Qui Parle, Minnesota, in 1896. On the Western plains and prairies, sod replaced wood as a building

JACOB RIIS'S PHOTOGRAPHY

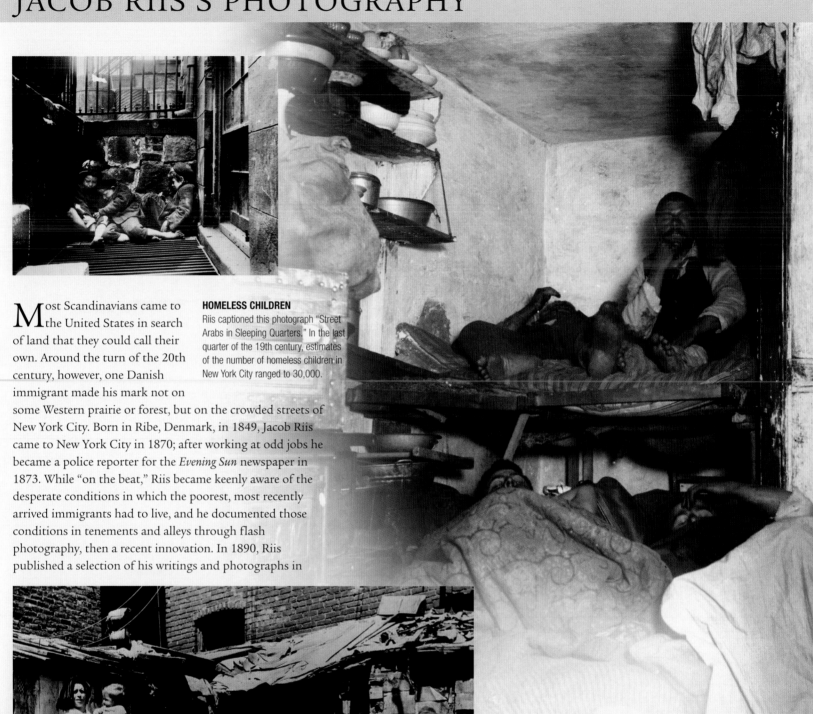

HOMELESS CHILDREN
Riis captioned this photograph "Street Arabs in Sleeping Quarters." In the last quarter of the 19th century, estimates of the number of homeless children in New York City ranged to 30,000.

Most Scandinavians came to the United States in search of land that they could call their own. Around the turn of the 20th century, however, one Danish immigrant made his mark not on some Western prairie or forest, but on the crowded streets of New York City. Born in Ribe, Denmark, in 1849, Jacob Riis came to New York City in 1870; after working at odd jobs he became a police reporter for the *Evening Sun* newspaper in 1873. While "on the beat," Riis became keenly aware of the desperate conditions in which the poorest, most recently arrived immigrants had to live, and he documented those conditions in tenements and alleys through flash photography, then a recent innovation. In 1890, Riis published a selection of his writings and photographs in

book form. *How the Other Half Lives* was an instant hit of muckraking journalism, and it sparked a major public outcry. Future president Theodore Roosevelt, then New York's police commissioner, famously wrote to Riis: "I have read your book, and I have come to help." The book inspired legislation aimed at bettering tenement conditions. Riis wrote several other books, including his autobiography, *The Making of an American*, before his death in 1914. In later years, some critics accused Riis of having exploited his photographic subjects for dramatic purposes, but he remains one of America's pioneering photojournalists and a matchless chronicler of the immigrant experience.

The Norwegians settled in the rural Midwest, though substantial numbers put down roots in cities. As with the Swedes, Norwegian immigration in the 1890s—by which time much of the free or cheap land in the west had already been claimed—shifted to young single men and women rather than families.

DANES AND ICELANDERS

With a milder climate, a smaller population, and more productive agriculture, Denmark sent fewer immigrants to America. Before 1860, most Danish immigrants were converts to Mormonism (*see pp 70–71*). At least 20,000 Danish Mormons settled in America before 1900, most in Utah. Between 1860 and 1920, perhaps 300,000 Danes immigrated, mostly for economic reasons. The Danes tended to settle in urban areas, with the exception of Iowa, which became home to a substantial Danish farming population.

Denmark ruled the North Atlantic island of Iceland from the 15th century until 1944. In the 19th century, Iceland suffered the same problems of population growth and land scarcity that plagued Sweden and Norway. By 1900, about 100,000 Icelanders had immigrated to America, most settling within Scandinavian communities in the upper Midwest.

FINNS

While Finland has cultural and religious ties to the Scandinavian countries, the nation was ruled by Russia from the early 18th century until 1919, and the Finnish people speak a language that is very different from the other Scandinavian tongues. Small numbers of Finns—usually listed as Swedes or Russians in the records of the time—were present in the colonies, starting in the New Netherlands in the 17th century. They made a major contribution to America with the log cabin (*see p 31*), a form of shelter developed in Finland's harsh landscape that proved well suited to the American frontier.

From 1900 to 1924, about 200,000 Finns immigrated to America, motivated both by the hope for a better life and the desire to escape Russian domination. The Great Lakes states, especially Michigan—where many Finns found work both in automobile plants and in mines—remains the heartland of *Suomi* (Finnish) America.

SOLVANG
Far above: The town of Solvang (from the Danish words for "sunny fields") in California was founded in 1911 by Danish-Americans who had originally settled in the Midwest. *Above:* The town's annual "Danish Days" festival includes traditional costumes, foods, and folk dancing.

A NICKEL A NIGHT
Immigrant lodgers in a Bayard Street "flophouse," where five cents bought a spot on the floor. Those who could not afford even this accommodation were allowed to sleep in police-station basements, but this practice ended in 1896.

CITY SHACKS
Far left: Too poor to even afford the rent for a room, an Italian immigrant family makes do in an improvised courtyard shack.

First migration | 1848
Migrated from | China
Approx. number in USA | 1.5 million (2000)
Settlement | Boston; New York City; San Francisco; Los Angeles; Chicago; Houston; Seattle; Washington, D.C.

FUJIAN
Old dwellings in Yondin in the Fujian, or Fukien, Province on the southeastern coast. The majority of pre-World War II Chinese immigrants came from Fujian, Guangdong (Canton), and Zhejiang.

Chinese

People from China were the first Asian immigrants to the United States, starting in the mid-19th century. Although, for most, dreams of economic betterment dissolved in the face of popular prejudice and official discrimination, exemplified by Congress's Chinese Exclusion Act of 1882. Nevertheless, the Chinese came to prosper in the United States through sheer determination.

TAKING IT ON THE CHIN
A cartoon by Edward Keller, captioned "First Blow Against the Chinese," depicts the violence directed against Chinese immigrants in 1870s San Francisco by the Workingmen's Party.

OPIUM STEREOTYPE
Nativist prejudice focused on the alleged predilection of the Chinese to opium addiction—while the practice certainly existed, it was wildly exaggerated in anti-Chinese propaganda. Opium import was, in fact, forced upon the Chinese during the commercial treaties with the United States and Europe.

Despite its vast size and venerable heritage, China was a nation in decline in the early 19th century. A rapidly growing population—400 million people by 1850—outstripped agricultural production, while the nation's rulers, the Qing dynasty, were weakened by corruption and by a rebellion at the turn of the 19th century. Starting in 1839, the European powers and the United States inflicted a series of humiliating commercial treaties on the Qing government.

China already had a long tradition of emigration—a tradition that planted communities of overseas Chinese from Indochina to South America. There were practically no Chinese in America, however, until news of the California Gold Rush (see pp 146–147) brought up to 25,000 immigrants—almost all of them from Guangdong (Canton)—to California.

The Chinese found themselves unwelcome as miners and took what jobs they could as cooks, laundrymen, or laborers. Many later found work on the Central Pacific and other railroads (see pp 162–163). By 1870, there were about 60,000 Chinese in the United States, three-quarters of them in California, the rest in New York and a few other cities. They were largely men and, since most were unable to make enough money to bring over their families, they lived a lonely existence.

EXCLUSION AND ACCEPTANCE

The Chinese were also subject to intense prejudice. This was due partly to simple racism, and partly to economics. California's economy suffered a downturn in the 1870s, and many working-class Californians feared that the Chinese—who were willing to work for low wages—would take their jobs. The completion of the Transcontinental Railroad, which threw thousands of Chinese immigrants out of work, compounded the problem. Agitators played on these fears, whipping up public sentiment against "coolie labor." California and other states passed discriminatory laws, including one that forbade the Chinese from testifying against whites in court. Mob attacks on Chinese homes and businesses became commonplace.

And yet the Chinese-Americans showed resilience. They formed self-sufficient enclaves—known as "Chinatowns"—in cities from San Francisco to Boston, and established a tradition of communal self-help that remains a hallmark of Chinese-American society today.

In 1882, Congress banned further immigration from China completely. The Chinese Exclusion Act, however, had certain loopholes—allowing, for example,

ON DISPLAY
A shopkeeper in San Francisco's Chinatown sells eggs, vegetables, and spices in this 1898 photo. Coming from a highly entrepreneurial culture, many Chinese immigrants—then and now—aimed to own their own businesses, many of which are found in major U.S. cities' Chinatowns.

ANGEL ISLAND

Poem on a barrack wall

From 1910–40, Angel Island in San Francisco Bay was the port of entry for immigrants arriving from Pacific routes. Over a million people were processed at the station, including 175,000 Chinese and 150,000 Japanese. Often called the "Ellis Island of the West," Angel Island went by a more candid name within the Immigration Service—"The Guardian of the Western Gate"—since Angel Island was intended to control the flow of Asian immigrants into America. Although Chinese immigration was restricted, U.S. law granted citizenship to anyone who could prove his father was a citizen. Because most of the birth and citizenship records in San Francisco were destroyed in the 1906 earthquake and fire, some immigrants (who came to be known as "paper sons" and "paper daughters") bought false documents that identified them as the children of American citizens. On average, these immigrants spent two to three weeks at the station, allowed outside the barracks only for meals, extensive interrogations, and supervised recreation. The rest of their time was passed in confinement, waiting. Today, the frustration of the experience at Angel Island can be witnessed in over 100 poems etched by the detainees upon the barrack walls.

students and merchants to enter the country. These immigrants often brought with them "paper sons" or "paper daughters" who, although unrelated, posed as family members. In this way, the Chinese population in America managed to grow; and, while the Chinese Exclusion Act of 1882 also forbade immigrant Chinese from seeking naturalization, children born in America were automatically citizens.

In 1943, with the United States and China allies in the war against Japan, Congress struck down the exclusion law. A new wave of Chinese immigrants arrived after the immigration reforms of the mid-1960s. In contrast to the mainly Cantonese immigrants who had come earlier, the new immigrants included people from Taiwan and Hong Kong. More than 330,000 Chinese arrived between 1976–86, the fourth largest immigrant group during that period.

CHINESE NEW YEAR
Members of the Wah Lum Kung-Fu Athletic Association of Boston participate in the 25th annual Dragon Boat Festival on June 13, 2004. Boston's Chinatown is not as large as New York City's, which has grown into the largest Chinese-American enclave in the United States. The Chinese New Year is celebrated in every Chinatown across America.

TERRACED PADDIES
The beauty of this photograph of a girl harvesting rice near Longji in the Guangxi Zhuang Autonomous Region belies the fact that much of China's population lives in rural poverty. In 2003, the average per-capita income for rural residents in Guangxi was 2,095 yuan (about US $250), about a third of urban workers' salaries.

ORGANIZED CRIME

SHORT TAILS GANG

Jacob Riis (*see pp 152–153*) photographed members of the Short Tails gang—seen in their hideout beneath the docks around Corlear's Hook in New York City—around 1890. Along with rival gangs like the Swamp Angels and the Daybreak Boys, they terrorized the Manhattan waterfront for decades.

country; in one historian's words, they "managed the opening of businesses, made funeral arrangements, and mediated disputes, among other responsibilities." But the Chinese associations also included a criminal component, the tongs. In the late 19th century, warfare between two competing tongs, the Hip Sing and the On Leong, plagued New York City's Chinatown for years.

Since the colonial era, the vast majority of immigrants to America have been law-abiding people seeking to make an honest living. Human nature being what it is, however, other immigrants brought outlaw traditions with them, which—mixed with homegrown elements—led to the rise of organized crime in America.

AMERICAN GANGLAND

In the 19th century, many young immigrant men joined local gangs—which often combined social and political functions with petty crime—sometimes in response to the hostility immigrant communities faced. In New York City, for example, Irish gangs like the Whyos, the Dead Rabbits, and the Plug Uglies fought epic battles with Nativist gangs, episodes chronicled in Herbert Asbury's 1928 book *The Gangs of New York* and later brought to the movie screen by Martin Scorsese.

Chinese immigrants brought with them a tradition of social and benevolent associations that played an important role in Chinatowns across the

"OUR THING"

The most famous imported criminal organization, by far, are the groups known collectively as the Mafia, *La Cosa Nostra* ("our thing," roughly, in Italian), or the Mob.

The American Mafia has its origins in secret societies from mainland Italy and Sicily like the Camorra and the so-called "Black Hand." The term "Mafia" was first heard in 1891, when several Italian immigrants in New Orleans were suspected of assassinating the city's police chief; a mob of angry locals lynched 11 of the suspects. In another episode that won national attention, Detective Joseph Petrosino of the New York Police Department (himself an Italian immigrant) was murdered in Palermo, Sicily, in 1909, while investigating Mafia activities.

The early Mafiosos specialized in murder for hire, blackmail, and intimidating local merchants into paying for "protection." The arrival of Prohibition in 1920 handed the Mafia, as well as gangs from other immigrant groups, a golden opportunity for expansion. Within a few years, organized crime dominated the manufacture, transportation, and sale of illegal alcohol in major cities, especially New York City and Chicago.

In the latter city, Al Capone, the Brooklyn-born son of immigrants from Naples, took over the bootlegging racket by

SPILLED SUDS

Prohibition agents dump bootleg beer into a sewer. The Eighteenth Amendment's ban on the sale and manufacture of alcohol was a "noble experiment" to supporters, but the law was difficult to enforce—there were never more than about 2,800 agents for the entire country.

UNLUCKY VALENTINE'S DAY

"Only Capone kills like that!" exclaimed George "Bugs" Moran upon learning that seven men, most of them members of his gang, lay dead in a Clark Street, Chicago, garage. They were cut down with Thompson submachine guns.

COOL CUSTOMER
Charles "Lucky" Luciano poses for a mug-shot photo in 1936. In the words of crime writer Edna Buchanan, "He downsized, he restructured and he used Standard & Poor's as much as Smith & Wesson to change forever the face of organized crime."

intimidating those whom he could and killing the rest, abetted by a corrupt city government and police force. The high (or low) point of Capone's career was the St. Valentine's Day Massacre of 1929, in which his submachine-gun-wielding henchmen slayed seven members of a rival gang in a South Side garage. Ironically, Capone was finally brought down not by criminal prosecution, but by a conviction of tax evasion in 1931.

LUCIANO, LANSKY & CO.

In addition to the Italian Mafia, Irish and Jewish gangs were also active in bootlegging and related activities. The repeal of Prohibition in 1933 did not halt the growing power of organized crime; the mobsters had already diversified into drugs, gambling, prostitution, and other rackets.

The leading post-Prohibition mobster was Sicilian-born Charles "Lucky" Luciano, who survived the gang wars of the 1920s largely due to his alliance with Jewish gangsters like Bugsy Siegel and Meyer Lansky. As with Al Capone before him, Luciano was nabbed not for serious crime but for pimping, and sent to prison. When World War II started, however, Luciano was recruited by U.S. Naval Intelligence to keep the peace on New York's waterfront, which was controlled by the Mob. When Allied forces prepared to invade Sicily, Luciano also agreed to help the Allies by using his influence against the Italians and their German overlords. As a result of this deal, he was released from prison and deported to Italy in 1946. He later helped his old pal Meyer Lansky turn Cuba into a Mob fiefdom before a heart attack felled him in 1962.

The Mafia's power began to decline in the 1960s when informers violated *omerta*, the legendary "code of silence." Furthermore, the passage of the federal Racketeer Influenced and Corrupt Organizations Act of 1970,

a.ka. the RICO Statute, undercut the Mafia by giving police and prosecutors wider powers. The extent of the Mafia today is debated, but it is certainly a shadow of its former self.

THE NEW MOBS

Just like Prohibition, the federal government's "War on Drugs" (proclaimed during the Nixon Administration and pursued ever since) provided opportunities to a new wave of gangsters—from West Indian *ganja* smugglers to Latin American *narcotraficantes*—whose influence reaches into American immigrant communities. In addition, the collapse of the Soviet Union and the fall of communism in Eastern Europe brought the Russian and Albanian mobs to America.

Like their 19th-century predecessors, newer immigrant groups have both brought criminal societies with them (like the Hong Kong Chinese Triads) and established new ones (like the Mexican-American Latin Kings gang).

FROM RUSSIA . . . WITH CRIME
FBI agents arrest two alleged Russian mobsters for extortion in 1995. Involved in activities from drug smuggling to money laundering, the "Mafiya" has a reputation for brutality; a New York City policeman reportedly said, "They'll shoot you just to see if the gun works."

THROWING SIGNS
Historically, many gangs have blurred the line between criminal activity and promoting cultural pride—like the Puerto Rican gang *Las Netas*, members of whom are shown here displaying recognition signs during the Puerto Rican Day Parade in New York City in 2000.

Japanese

First migration	**1880s**
Migrated from	**Japan**
Approx. number in USA	**350,000 (2005)**
Settlement	**California; New York City; Honolulu, Hawaii; Chicago, Illinois; Seattle, Washington**

From 1693, the island nation of Japan existed in almost complete isolation from the rest of the world until, in 1853, U.S. warships forcibly opened Japan to trade. Fearing that their nation would wind up a colony of the Western powers unless it modernized itself, Japanese leaders brought the Emperor Meiji to power in 1868 and began a program of industrialization. Within decades, Japan's feudal social system was largely overturned, throwing many peasants off the land.

Starting in the mid-1880s, between 300,000 and 400,000 Japanese immigrated to Hawaii (an independent nation until its annexation by the United States in 1898). Most were contract laborers, working the islands' sugarcane plantations, often under brutal conditions. Nevertheless, the Japanese community in Hawaii thrived, and eventually Hawaiians of Japanese ancestry formed the majority in the islands.

Immigration to the American mainland began in large numbers around 1900, with some Japanese coming from Hawaii and others directly from Japan. Like the Chinese before them, these first immigrants were mainly single men. Settling largely in

MOUNT FUJI
At more than 12,000 feet, *Fujiyama* (Mount Fuji) is not only Japan's highest mountain; it is also considered a sacred symbol of the nation itself. *Sakura* (the blossoms of the cherry tree) can be seen in the foreground; they also have great cultural significance for the Japanese.

JAPANTOWN
A traditional *tori* (gateway) leads into Peace Plaza in Nihonmachi—San Francisco's Japantown, today home to about 12,000 residents of Japanese birth or descent. It is one of only three distinct Nihonmachis in the United States; the others are in San Jose and Los Angeles.

PAPERS, PLEASE
California Congressman John Raker (*second from right*) examines the entry visas of a group of Japanese "picture brides" at Angel Island, in San Francisco Bay, in July 1920.

WORKERS' HOUSING
The crude shacks at left housed Japanese contract laborers at a Hilo, Hawaii, plantation. Laborers were recruited in Japan (often with the active participation of Japanese authorities) for service of up to five years.

INTERNMENT

A wave of anti-Japanese hysteria gripped the United States in the aftermath of Japan's attack on the U.S. fleet at Pearl Harbor, Hawaii, on December 7, 1941, and Japanese-Americans were not spared. In February 1942, President Franklin Roosevelt signed Executive Order 9066, authorizing the relocation of Japanese-Americans—regardless of their citizenship status—from the West Coast, for reasons of "military necessity." More than 120,000 Japanese-Americans had to leave behind their homes, farms, and businesses and report for internment in inland camps, most of which were located in bleak, harsh areas like Tule Lake and Manzanar in northern California. They would spend the next two years behind barbed wire in crude, overcrowded barracks. In protest, more than 5,000 Japanese-Americans resigned their U.S. citizenship. At the same time, many Japanese-American men volunteered for military service; the 442nd Regimental Combat Team, made up of soldiers from both Hawaii and the internment camps, became the U.S. Army's most decorated unit. (Ironically, there was no relocation of Japanese-Americans in Hawaii itself; there were simply too many.) In 1944, the internees were released to try to rebuild their lives. Former internees received some compensation for property losses in the 1960s, but it was not until the late 1980s that the U.S. government formally apologized and authorized restitution payments.

FORLORN FLAG
This photo by Dorothea Lange captures the harsh environment at the Manzanar relocation camp in the high desert east of Los Angeles.

California, Oregon, and Washington State, they worked mostly as agricultural laborers, but over time, many were able to purchase farms of their own.

Again like the Chinese, the Japanese faced hostility and discrimination. Besides fear of competition for jobs, the very success of some of the Japanese immigrants, especially in agriculture, caused resentment. In 1913, California passed the Alien Land Law, which prohibited Japanese (and Chinese) from owning land in that state because they were not eligible for U.S. citizenship, although many Japanese immigrants found ways to circumvent the prohibition.

By that time, immigration from Japan was already restricted, due to a series of protocols between the Japanese and U.S. governments between 1906 and 1908, collectively known as the "Gentlemen's Agreement." The agreements did permit immigration by wives and children of immigrants already in the United States, so, in a manner similar to the Chinese-American system of "paper children," many Japanese women came to America as "picture brides." By the time the immigration restrictions of the 1920s kicked in, about 100,000 Japanese lived on the U.S. mainland. During World War II, however, both the *Issei* (Japanese immigrants) and the *Nissei* (their American-born offspring) were victims of one of the worst violations of civil rights in American history (*see panel*).

Japanese-Americans are the third largest Asian-American community, following Filipino-Americans and Chinese-Americans. The largest Japanese-American communities are in California, Hawaii, Oregon, and Washington. Each year, some 7,000 new Japanese immigrants enter the United States.

BUILDING THE RAILROADS

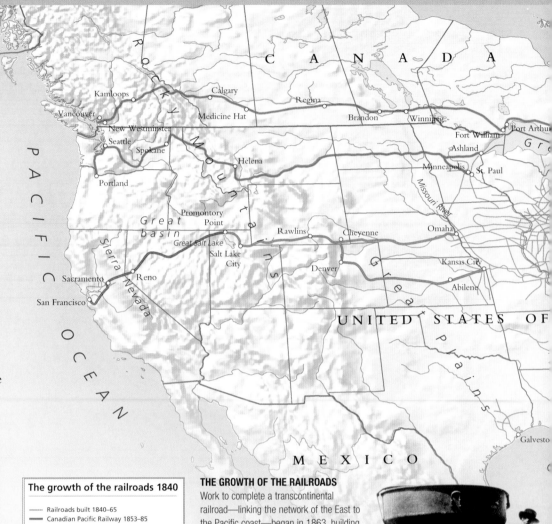

The 19th-century railroad boom in the United States had a profound effect both on internal settlement and on immigration. First, railroads provided easy access to the interior of the country; many immigrants now settled inland instead of staying in the East Coast cities. Second, the federal government subsidized railroad companies with huge land grants, and those companies in turn actively recruited immigrants in Europe to buy homesteads on these lands. Third, the need for labor to build the railroads brought many immigrants to America—some all the way from China.

ACROSS THE CONTINENT

A railroad that would span the entire United States and link both coasts was first proposed in the 1830s; the project officially began when President Abraham Lincoln signed the Pacific Railroad Bill on July 1, 1862. By that time, rail lines from the East had reached Omaha, Nebraska, but there was a 1,700-mile gap to the nearest railhead in California, at Sacramento.

To bridge this gap, Congress authorized the Central Pacific Railroad to lay track eastward from Sacramento, while the Union Pacific simultaneously worked its way westward.

THROUGH TO THE PACIFIC
This is an early advertising poster distributed by the Union Pacific. In the 1880s, competition for passengers became so intense that travelers could go from various Midwestern cities to California for as little as $1.

The growth of the railroads 1840

——	Railroads built 1840–65
——	Canadian Pacific Railway 1853–85
——	Central Pacific Railroad 1863–69
——	Union Pacific Railroad 1865–69
——	Kansas Pacific Railroad 1870
——	Northern Pacific Railroad 1870-83

THE GROWTH OF THE RAILROADS
Work to complete a transcontinental railroad—linking the network of the East to the Pacific coast—began in 1863, building east from San Francisco, and continued in 1865, building westward from Omaha, Nebraska.

Building the line through the plains, mountains, and deserts of the West was one of the most challenging engineering feats of the 19th century—and it was accomplished largely by human muscle power.

For the Central Pacific, the most daunting task was crossing the Sierra Nevada Mountains—an enterprise that involved tunneling through miles of solid rock and moving millions of tons of earth. This brutal, dangerous, and backbreaking work was done largely by Chinese immigrants wielding hand tools. Some of the Central Pacific's Chinese workers had arrived in California in the wake of the gold rush (*see pp 146–147*); others were recruited as contract laborers in the Chinese region of Guangdong (Canton). Between 10,000 and 20,000 Chinese worked on the Central Pacific, making up at least two-thirds of the line's construction crews. Over 1,000 died in accidents,

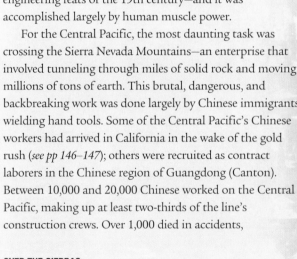

OVER THE SIERRAS
Chinese laborers pose aboard a Central Pacific handcar. They were paid $25 a month, in contrast to white workers, who got $35 plus meals. The Chinese lived in simple dwellings and cooked their own meals, often consisting of fish, dried oysters, fruit, mushrooms, and seaweed.

avalanches, and explosions. (The latter occurred frequently because of the unstable nitroglycerin used to blast tunnels.)

The Union Pacific's work crews also included many other immigrants, especially Irish; in 1866, facing a shortage of workers, the line began signing up laborers in the Irish neighborhoods in the eastern cities. Civil War veterans (both Union and Confederate) and freed slaves joined the Irish as the Union Pacific laid tracks across the Great Plains. The two lines finally met at Promontory Point, Utah, on May 10, 1869. People and goods could now cross the continent in days rather than months; one newspaper proclaimed "the annexation of the United States." Five days later, the first transcontinental train left Omaha on the four-day, four-hour, 40-minute run to San Francisco, featuring a special no-frills "immigrant fare" of $40 (first class was $111, second class, $80).

GREAT NORTHERN RAILWAY
A postcard from the 1950s promotes the Great Northern's service. The introduction of diesel-electric locomotives, like the one shown here, further reduced travel time between Chicago and Seattle.

Central Pacific and other railroads mainly through grants of public land along each route-of-way. By the early 1870s, Washington had given away about 175 million acres of western land to around 30 railroads. The land-grant system was rife with corruption, but it had the happy effect of making millions of acres of inexpensive land available to immigrants—especially from Germany and Scandinavia, where the rail lines maintained a small army of salesmen, and which they flooded with brochures.

Perhaps the most significant of later railroads was the Great Northern Railway, the brainchild of Canadian-born James J. Hill. After building railroads in Canada, Hill conceived a northern route from the Great Lakes to the Pacific, which he built, largely without the government support enjoyed by other American railroads. Completed in 1890, the "Empire Builder," as it was advertised, did much to facilitate Scandinavian, German, Russian, and Ukrainian immigration to the Upper Midwest and Pacific Northwest. Hill later added the St. Paul, the Northern Pacific, and the Chicago, Burlington, and Quincy railroads to his transportation empire.

> "From both east to west, immigrants laid the tracks and built the cities in between."
>
> "The Golden Door"

GOLDEN SPIKE
A rowdy crowd celebrates the driving-in of the ceremonial "golden spike" joining the tracks of the Union Pacific and the Central Pacific at Promontory Point, Utah, on May 10, 1869. Total track mileage was 1,086 for the U.P., 690 for the C.P.

LAND ON THE LINE
The federal government subsidized the construction of the Union and

THE CANALS
Before railroads dominated the 1840s–50s, America underwent a canal-building boom. Many states financed canal projects to link rivers and lakes to inland cities or coastal ports in order to boost commerce. The most important was the Erie Canal in New York State. Completed in 1825, it linked the Great Lakes with the Hudson River, giving the port of New York access to the produce of the West. Immigrant laborers, especially Irish, played a big role in constructing the canals.

Italians

Between around 1880 and 1924, more than 4 million Italians immigrated to the United States, half of them between 1900 and 1910 alone—the majority fleeing grinding rural poverty in Southern Italy and Sicily. World War I slowed Italian immigration and the restrictions of the 1920s largely halted it, but by that time Italian-Americans formed perhaps 10 percent of the country's population. Today, Americans of Italian ancestry are the nation's fifth-largest ethnic group.

First migration	mid-1700s
Migrated from	Italy
Approx. number in USA	473,338 (2000)
Settlement	California; New York; New Orleans, Louisiana; Boston, Massachusetts; Philadelphia, Pennsylvania

In the mid-1700s, some Italians settled in Florida (then Spanish territory), and, from the colonial era to the early 19th century, a handful of Italians came to America; most were from Northern Italy and many were skilled artisans, like the stonemasons Thomas Jefferson brought over to build his Virginia mansion, Monticello—which means "little mountain" in Italian. By 1870, there were about 25,000 Italian immigrants in America, many of them Northern Italian refugees from the wars that accompanied the *Risorgimento*—the struggle for Italian unification and independence from foreign rule. Most settled in New York, New Orleans, and in and around San Francisco, where they laid the foundations of Northern California's renowned wine-making industry.

Unification came in 1861, but it did not equal prosperity. Southern Italy, including Naples and Calabria, along with the island of Sicily, remained among the poorest places in Europe, where landless peasants tried to scratch a living from poor soil, continually exploited by landowners under a system still virtually feudal. Malnutrition and disease were rife; so was violence, given the weakness of the central government and, in some areas, a tradition of banditry.

FARE L'AMERICA

The huge wave of Italian immigration after 1880 was drawn mainly from these impoverished areas, and it was sparked, to a great extent, by a reduction in transatlantic fares by the major steamship lines. As with many immigrant groups, the advance guard was made up mainly of men. Some were bachelors looking to make some money quickly and return to Italy with a nest egg; others were sons or fathers who hoped to send money back home, and to save enough eventually to bring their families over. (Many Italian communities came to depend on money sent home from immigrants, in the same way many Latin American, Caribbean, Asian, and African communities do today.) The initial destination for most was New York: between 1880 and 1920, probably a

WE'RE HERE
A mix of hope and apprehension written on their faces, an Italian mother and her children locate their baggage before landing from Ellis Island in this 1905 photo.

SUN-BAKED LANDSCAPE
A 19th-century painting by Giuseppe de Nittis depicts a farm outside Naples. Poor soil and a semi-feudal social system drove millions of immigrants from Southern Italy and Sicily to seek a better life in America.

MULBERRY STREET
A hand-tinted photograph shows Mulberry Street, the bustling heart of New York City's Little Italy, around 1900. Immigrants coming from a single village in Italy often occupied the same block after arriving in the neighborhood.

SLICE OF HISTORY

Italy has contributed more than its share to America's table. The cheese-and-tomato pie known as pizza has ancient roots in Italy, but it emerged in its modern form in Naples in 1889, when cooks produced pizza Margherita—a combination of mozzarella cheese, tomato sauce, and basil leaves—to celebrate a visit from King Umberto I and his queen, Margherita. (The red, white, and green colors mirrored the Italian flag.) Italian immigrants to Chicago are generally credited with introducing pizza to America, but Lombardi's in New York City—founded in 1905 and still in operation—claims to be America's first pizzeria. Pizza was a mainly urban taste until after World War II.

third of them settled in the city and the surrounding area instead of moving on, although Italian enclaves developed in most American communities of any size.

After leaving Castle Garden or Ellis Island, newcomers were often met by a *padrone*—a man who had arrived earlier, perhaps from the newcomer's village, and who had connections. The *padrone* offered to find him a place to live and a job—in return for a big share of the newcomer's wages. Often the *padrones* were agents of American factories in need of cheap labor. The system was exploitative, but in the words of one historian, "If American officials and the press saw the *padrone* system as evil, to most immigrants it was a necessary evil. The *padrone* looked after them and helped them to adjust in this strange land."

When an Italian left his village or city to cross the Atlantic, he was said to be going to *fare l'America* (going to make America). And many did just that. The arrival

> ## "In America, the poor can talk to anyone."
> Rosa Cavalleri

of the Italians occured at a time when earlier immigrants, particularly the Irish, were starting to move up into the ranks of the middle class, and the Italians took their places as manual laborers. In New York, for example, Italian immigrants (together with African-Americans) made up most of the construction crews that built the city's vast subway system. Others spread out throughout the country working on more far-flung construction projects.

Many Italian immigrants—perhaps as many as half—did go home after a few years, where they were known as *ritornati*. But many of those who stayed succeeded in bringing over their families, and, in the early 1900s, Italian women made up a large part of the workforce in New York's garment industry and in the textile mills of New England. As the Italians put down roots in America, they managed to preserve many of the traditions of their homeland. The local Catholic

FREEDOM FOR WOMEN
Rosa Cavalleri

Like many immigrant women, Rosa Cavalleri escaped the poverty and inequality of Italy for a life of freedom and opportunity in America. Unlike most immigrant women, she left behind a record of her experience. Her memoir, *Rosa: The Life of an Italian Immigrant*, set down by her friend Marie Hall Ets, is one of the few accounts of immigration from a woman's perspective. Forced to follow her abusive husband to America, Rosa was an unwilling immigrant, despite her friend's consolation: "It is wonderful to go to America even if you don't want to go with Santino. You will get smart in America." Rosa became excited upon first seeing New York: "Other poor people, dressed in their best clothes and loaded down with bundles, crowded around. America! The country where everyone could find work! Where wages were so high no one had to go hungry! Where all men were free and equal and where even the poor could own land!" By the time she arrived at her new home, a mining camp in Missouri, Rosa had already witnessed this equality in action. "The ladies wore hats," she observed, "but they were riding the same class with us poor." Rosa was gradually instilled with the confidence of her new home and she fled to Chicago to begin a new life as a cleaning woman in a settlement house. There she discovered her gift for storytelling, stories which have come to represent the experiences of an entire immigrant generation.

A. P. GIANNINI
1870–1949

Born to immigrants from Genoa, Italy, Amadeo Peter Giannini, or "A.P." as he was known, opened a bank in San Francisco's North Beach neighborhood in 1904. The Bank of Italy was set up to meet the needs of the hard-working immigrants pouring into San Francisco. At the time, few working-class Americans had bank accounts, and banks rarely extended credit or made loans to those without major assets. In contrast, the Bank of Italy welcomed small depositors, lent money liberally, and even stayed open late to accommodate customers with a long workday. It was an immediate success.

On April 18, 1906, an earthquake and fire devastated San Francisco. Loading $2 million into a vegetable wagon, Giannini set up an improvised bank in the rubble and began making building loans "on a face and a signature." His generosity played a major role in the rapid rebuilding of the city.

The Bank of Italy expanded throughout California in the 1920s and its lending policies helped develop the state's agricultural and motion-picture industries. In 1930, the bank went nationwide as the Bank of America, for a time the biggest bank in the country.

SAN GENNARO
With the descendants of New York's original Italian immigrants now dispersed to the suburbs and across the country, Little Italy has become a tourist district, but, every September, crowds mob Mulberry Street for the Festival of San Gennaro, Naples' patron saint.

parish was the social center of most communities, and religious festivals—like the San Gennaro festival in New York's Little Italy—remain part of Italian-American life. The Italians brought over a tradition of strong local association, many settling in neighborhoods where streets were populated from a single village in the "Old Country."

Because the majority of arrivals during the great wave of Italian immigration came from a rural background, the challenges of making a living in an urban environment were difficult. Many eked out a living through home-based piecework—knitting garments together, rolling cigars, or assembling artificial flowers, at a small fixed rate for each item.

But not all Italian immigrants put down permanent roots in cities like New York, Boston, and Philadelphia. A significant percentage settled in other

TUNNEL VISION
Italian-American workers shore up a subway tunnel under New York's East River in this 1907 photo. Wages for these laborers ran from $1.50 to $2.00 a day. The new subway system gave residents, including many immigrants, a chance to move out of the crowded Lower East Side.

parts of the country, bringing skills acquired in their homeland—like stonemasonry, wine-making, and fishing—to destinations like New York's Hudson River Valley, Northern California, and the San Francisco Bay area, respectively. And wherever they went, Italian-American workers were determined to fight for their rights. Many were active in the labor movement, including the IWW (see pp 136–137).

Like the Irish who preceded them and the Jews who arrived around the same time, the Italian-Americans had to contend with prejudice and discrimination from both Anglo-Saxon Americans and earlier arrivals

because of their language, religion, and culture. In 1920, two Italian-born radical unionists were arrested for murder in connection with a payroll robbery at a shoe factory in Braintree, Massachusetts. Seven years later, Nicolo Sacco and Bartolomeo Vanzetti died in the electric chair, following a trial that remains controversial. In the opinion of many Americans, then and now, they were condemned more on the basis of their ancestry and their anarchist beliefs than on the evidence, much of which was later discredited.

Even today, Italian-Americans fight a stereotype inspired by the mob-related criminal activities of a handful of their number (*see pp 158–159*). But also like the Irish and the Jews, Italian immigrants and their descendants rapidly rose into the middle and upper classes and made significant contributions in many fields (*see side panels*).

In the 2000 U.S. Census Report, Italian-Americans were found in all 50 states of America, the highest numbers on the East Coast.

ITALIAN TALES

OL' BLUE EYES
"When somebody called me a 'dirty little Guinea' there was only one thing to do—break his head."
Frank Sinatra on his Hoboken upbringing.

FIRST GENERATION DONE GOOD
In the 20th century, three sons of Italian immigrants became, arguably, the best big-city mayor, the best ballplayer, and the best singer of their times, proving that their parents' sacrifices directly affected the New Country's political and cultural arenas.

THE LITTLE FLOWER
Fiorello LaGuardia was born in New York City in 1882, but he spent much of his childhood on remote U.S. Army posts in the waning days of the "Wild West," while his immigrant father worked as a musician. From 1900 to 1906, LaGuardia worked for the State Department in Hungary and in Trieste, Italy, hometown of his Hungarian-Italian Jewish mother. Returning to America, he worked as an interpreter at Ellis Island while putting himself through law school. In 1916, LaGuardia won election to the House of Representatives as a Republican (thanks to his heritage, he was able to make campaign speeches in Yiddish, Italian, and Serbo-Croatian) and was a pilot in World War I. He was elected mayor of New York City in 1933, remaining in office for three terms and leading the city through the challenges of the Depression and World War II. LaGuardia was immensely popular, thanks both to his honest and nonpartisan administration and to his unflagging energy and his ebullient personality. During World War II, he simultaneously served as mayor and as head of the national civil-defense program.

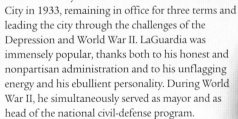

JOLTIN' JOE
Son of an immigrant father who fished the waters off San Francisco, Joe DiMaggio played for the San Francisco Seals before being called up to the majors by the New York Yankees in 1936. (Baseball was a family thing—Joe's brothers

YANKEE CLIPPER
With a single to left field during a game against the Washington Senators on June 29, 1941, Joe DiMaggio shatters George Sisler's 1922 record for hitting safely in 42 consecutive games.

Vincent and Dom would also have major-league careers.) DiMaggio was soon nicknamed "the Sultan of Swat" for his hitting and "the Yankee Clipper" for his baserunning—and he was an outstanding fielder, too. His bat helped propel the Yankees to a World Series victory over the New York Giants in his first season, and he led the American League in home runs the following year. The greatest feat of his career came in 1941, when he hit safely in 56 consecutive games—a record that remains unbroken more than 60 years later. Known as "Dago" to his teammates, DiMaggio accepted the moniker not as a malicious slur, but as a sign of the ignorance of the times.

THE CHAIRMAN OF THE BOARD
The prototype of the modern pop star, Francis Albert Sinatra was born in Hoboken, New Jersey, in 1915. After stints as a crooner with big bands, Sinatra went solo in the early 1940s and quickly astonished everyone with his hypnotic effect on his audience. His career faltered later in the decade, but he reinvented himself both as a serious actor (winning an Oscar in 1953) and as a musician, releasing a series of landmark records for Columbia. As the 1950s turned to the 1960s, Sinatra was the epitome of cool as leader of the hard-partying "Rat Pack" that careened around Hollywood and Las Vegas. Throughout his long career, Sinatra came in for criticism for his sometimes stormy personal life, his hot temper, and his alleged ties to the Mafia.

READING THE NEWS
Mayor LaGuardia reads the papers (including the cartoons) to the people of New York City during the newspaper delivery drivers' strike of 1945—now commemorated by radio station WNYC's Fiorello LaGuardia Recording Studio.

LAND RUSHES

The Homestead Act of 1862 (*see pp 134–135*) opened up vast tracts of the American West to agricultural settlement, as did the federal government's land grants to railroads (*see pp 162–163*). In the years following the Civil War, however, cattle ranchers, sheepherders, and farmers rapidly occupied much of this land. By the late 1880s, the federal government faced increasing pressure to open up the lands it had set aside for the Native Americans to white settlement.

THE TRAIL OF TEARS

In the 1830s, Washington bowed to demands from Southern politicians to remove the Native Americans of the so-called Five Civilized Nations—the Cherokees, Chickasaws, Choctaws, Creeks, and Seminoles—from their homelands to an "Indian Territory" west of the Mississippi River, an area bounded by the present-day states of Kansas, Arkansas, Texas, and Missouri. The U.S. Army forcibly herded these Native Americans westward on what would become known as the "Trail of Tears"; of the Cherokee alone, 4,000 people—a

quarter of the nation's population—died of hunger, exposure, and disease along the way. The Five Civilized Tribes were followed by other Native American nations. By 1860, there were about 60,000 Native Americans in the region. "Indian Territory" was supposed to remain closed to white settlement forever, but the federal government reneged on its pledge. During the Civil War, most of the Native American nations, sided with the Confederacy; in retaliation, the government seized much of the territory in 1866 and declared it to be "unassigned land."

BOOMERS AND SOONERS

In the 1870s, railroad executives, real-estate speculators, and would-be settlers—collectively known as "Boomers"—lobbied the government to allow non–Native Americans into the unassigned land. In the

TRAIL OF TEARS
Robert Lindneux's 1942 painting captures the hardship and anguish of the Cherokee "removal." Although the U.S. Supreme Court ruled the removal illegal in 1832, President Andrew Jackson ordered the U.S. Army to forcibly escort the Cherokee to "Indian Territory."

THE RACE IS ON
At precisely noon on April 22, 1889, buglers signaled the st of the rush. An eyewitness wrote: "The rush from the line w so impetuous that by the time the first railway train arrived from the north at 25 minutes past twelve o'clock, only a few of the hundreds of boomers were anywhere to be seen."

GUSHER

Photographer Dick Man captioned this 1905 view of Cleveland, Oklahoma, "The City of Oil Derricks." An oil strike in July 1904 turned the small community into a boomtown in just a few months.

SOONERS

Troops escort Sooners out of "Indian Territory" in this *Harper's Weekly* cover illustration. In fact, there were too few soldiers to patrol the territory effectively in the months before the 1889 rush, so many of those who jumped the gun were able to gain title to their premature claims.

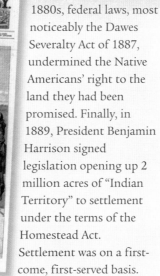

1880s, federal laws, most noticeably the Dawes Severalty Act of 1887, undermined the Native Americans' right to the land they had been promised. Finally, in 1889, President Benjamin Harrison signed legislation opening up 2 million acres of "Indian Territory" to settlement under the terms of the Homestead Act. Settlement was on a first-come, first-served basis.

At noon on April 22 of that year, some 50,000 Boomers—including ex-slaves and recently arrived immigrants—raced into the territory aboard trains, on horseback, and on foot—even on bicycle. A reporter described the scene: "The people went out like flies out of a sugar cask, and in five minutes a square mile of the prairie was spotted with squatters looking like flies on a sticky paper . . . we passed populous towns, built in an hour . . . we had seen the sight of the century." Within a couple of days, the Boomers had claimed every acre of the available land. The following year, Congress organized the area as the Oklahoma Territory.

Many of the 1889 Boomers, however, found that others had snuck in before April 22 and staked out land claims in advance of the official opening. These "Sooners," as they were called, gave the future state of Oklahoma its nickname—the "Sooner State."

TERRITORY TO STATE

Over the next 22 years, the federal government took possession of most of the remaining Native American lands, and there were subsequent land rushes in 1891, 1893, 1901, and 1911, although none matched the drama of 1889. In the final land rushes, the government instituted a lottery system to avoid the chaos and lawlessness that characterized the 1889 rush. By the time

the 1911 land rush took place, Oklahoma had already been admitted to the Union as a state, and the motivation for most Boomers was not land for farming, but for oil prospecting. Oil was found in Oklahoma around the same time it became a state in 1907: the discovery enriched some of the Native Americans who had managed to hold onto their land, and it also attracted fortune-hunting immigrants from overseas.

A THANKLESS JOB

While the image of an unstoppable tide of white settlement swamping Native American lands is engrained in the popular imagination—with good reason—the federal government made occasional efforts to protect areas reserved for Native Americans from trespassing prospectors and settlers. Although many of the federal officials charged with looking after the Native Americans' interests were often corrupt or incompetent, other "Indian agents" worked hard to keep whites out of Native American lands and to protect Native Americans from attack by settlers. An angry settler murdered one such agent, Robert Neighbors, in 1859 after he escorted Native Americans to safety from a white mob in Texas. The U.S. Army, too, not only fought Native Americans, but also occasionally stepped in to guard their reservations from land- or gold-hungry whites.

APACHE AGENT

"Indian Agent" V. E. Stottler poses with an Apache woman at the Mescalero Agency in New Mexico, 1898. It was the policy of the Bureau of Indian Affairs (BIA) to pressure Native Americans to assimilate, for example, by banning tribal language and dress, and forcibly sending children to BIA-run boarding schools.

First migration	**1848**
Migrated from	**Mexico**
Approx. number in USA	**9 million (2000)**
Settlement	**California; Texas; Arizona; Ilinois; New York**

CHIAPAS CHURCH
The town church of San Cristóbal de las Casas in the Southern Mexican state of Chiapas. Rapid population growth and widespread poverty in the rural region has fueled political unrest and spurred immigration to the United States in recent years.

Mexicans

The United States and Mexico share both a long border and an uncomfortably intertwined history. Large-scale Mexican immigration to the United States began early in the 20th century, and, from 1965 onward, Mexicans have formed the single largest immigrant group in America. This massive movement of people continues to have profound—and controversial—significance for both nations.

INDEPENDENCE DAY
A celebration in Mexico City's *zócalo* (main square) commemorates Mexico's Independence Day, September 16, the day in 1810 when Miguel Hidalgo, a parish priest in the town of Dolores, called for the country to free itself from Spanish rule.

The history of modern Mexico begins in 1519, when the Spanish conquistador Hernan Cortés landed in Mexico and began a campaign that toppled the Aztec Empire. Over the next three centuries, Spanish settlers and native Mexicans intermarried to form the *mestizo* (mixed race) population that remains the majority in Mexico today. A revolt against Spanish rule began in 1810, and in 1821 the nation won its independence from Spain.

The new Mexican Republic offered land to American immigrants in an effort to settle its sparsely populated northern states, including Texas. In the 1830s, differences between the mostly American settlers in Texas and the government in Mexico City flared into war. Texas achieved independence in 1836 and was annexed by the United States nine years later.

An old Mexican saying—"Pity poor Mexico, so far from God and so close to the United States"—sums up U.S.-Mexican relations following the annexation. President James Polk used border disputes as a pretense to declare war in 1846, and in the conflict that followed, the United States seized almost a fifth of Mexico's territory, including California, Arizona, New Mexico, and parts of several other future U.S. states. Only about 100,00 Mexicans lived in these areas at this time; they became U.S. citizens in the

treaty that ended the war. Over the next six decades, several thousand Mexicans crossed the border to work as agricultural laborers and cowboys. During this period, Mexico successfully defended against a French invasion, but the nation remained poor, and its rural *mestizo* and Indian populations were exploited by the ruling *peninsulares* (Mexicans of Spanish ancestry).

From around 1910–20, Mexico was consumed by revolution and civil war—a period that also saw U.S. military interventions between 1914 and 1917. In response to the poverty and unrest in their homeland, many Mexicans crossed the Rio Grande into the United States. Exact numbers do not exist given the porous nature of the border, but, between 1910 and 1930, at least a half-million Mexicans arrived to look for work in Texas, California, and the Southwestern states.

THE REVOLVING DOOR

During these years, U.S. immigration policy toward Mexico followed a "revolving door" model: in periods of prosperity, like the 1920s and during World War II, when Mexican labor was needed, state and federal authorities tended to turn a blind eye toward Mexican immigration, but during the Depression of the 1930s, many Mexicans—as well as their American-born children—were forcibly deported to preserve jobs for European-Americans.

ACROSS THE BORDER
The border post at International Bridge—now known as The Bridge of the Americas—linking El Paso, Texas, with Juárez, Mexico, as seen in 1937—when the Great Depression made Mexican immigrants unwelcome in America.

VIVA VILLA
Mexican rebel leader Francisco "Pancho" Villa's 1916 raid on Columbus, New Mexico—which left 16 Americans dead—caused U.S. President Woodrow Wilson to send 12,000 troops, under General John J. Pershing, into Mexico.

THE ZOOT SUIT RIOTS

In 1942, ethnic tensions combined with wartime paranoia in Los Angeles to spark an episode known as the Zoot Suit Riots. By that time, the city's Mexican-American population had grown to about 250,000, most living in *barrios* (neighborhoods) that had little involvement with the greater city. Many young Mexican-Americans resented this state of virtual segregation. Thanks to the wartime economic boom, they had good jobs for the first time, and they spent their money on dancing, socializing, and flashy clothes—including the "zoot suit."

The "zoot suiters"—also known derisively as *pachucos* (punks)—were much resented by the city's white residents and by sailors and other servicemen based nearby. As historian Eduardo Pagan described the situation in a 2001 PBS documentary, from the zoot suiters' perspective, "[E]verything around you told you you're not one of us. You're not American. And because you're not American, because you're not white, you're supposed to remain in your neighborhoods. You can't go to our clubs. You can't go to our restaurants. You can't go to our movies."

Non-Mexican Angelenos associated young Mexican-American men with gang crime, while military personnel felt they should have traded their zoot suits for uniforms. (In fact, Mexican-Americans volunteered in large numbers after Pearl Harbor.) In August 1942, a young Mexican-American man was murdered at a party. The Los Angeles police rounded up some 600 suspects—most of them zoot suiters. This incident and the trial that followed stoked already high tensions. On May 31, 1943, sailors and civilians began attacking zoot suiters (and African-Americans and Filipinos) on the streets. For more than a week, violence raged across the city. It was the worst episode of ethnic violence in Los Angeles until the Watts Riots in 1965.

ZOOT SUIT RIOTS
Sailors armed with lead pipes look for Mexican-American youths to attack on the streets of Los Angeles during the Zoot Suit Riots of June 1943. The violence stopped only after military authorities barred off-duty servicemen from the city. Afterward, the city council banned the wearing of zoot suits.

BRACEROS AND BORDER-CROSSERS

During World War II, many American farm workers enlisted in the armed forces, creating a desperate need for agricultural labor. In response, the U.S. and Mexican governments began the Bracero program (the name comes from the Spanish for "hired hand"), which allowed Mexicans to enter the United States legally to work on American farms. The program was extended after the war; by the time it ended in 1964, some 4 million Mexicans had come to America. But while it was successful for American farmers, the program's benefits for the *braceros* remains controversial; critics contend that many *braceros* were overworked, underpaid, and forced to live in substandard conditions, often in violation of their contracts.

A continuing need for farm and domestic labor in Texas and California spurred further Mexican immigration, both legal and illegal, in the decades after World War II. By the 1970s, some 60,000 Mexicans

BRACEROS

Mexican *braceros* harvest chile peppers on a California farm in this photograph from 1964—the year the controversial cross-border program ended. One U.S. Labor Department official described the system as "legalized slavery." Many former *braceros*, however, were unable to find work in their homeland and recrossed the border as illegal immigrants.

Cesar Chavez *(right)* breaks bread with Senator Robert F. Kennedy.

CESAR CHAVEZ
1927–1993

Born to Mexican immigrant parents in Yuma, Arizona, Chavez personally experienced the prejudice, mistreatment, and backbreaking work that migrant agricultural workers endured. In the early 1960s, inspired by the Civil Rights movement and its philosophy of nonviolence, he took the lead in founding the National Farm Workers Association, later the United Farm Workers (UFW). The organization scored several victories in the mid-1960s, and Chavez won national attention in 1968 when he undertook a 25-day hunger strike. In the 1970s and 1980s, he spearheaded boycotts of grapes and lettuce to protest both the exploitation of workers and the use of harmful pesticides—although the UFW's organizing efforts were hampered by competition from the nation's largest union, the AFL-CIO (the two unions eventually agreed to a peace pact). Chavez was also instrumental in securing the passage of California's Agricultural Labor Relations Act, although the law was, at best, only partly successful in bettering the lot of the state's migrant farm workers. Faithful to *la Causa* (the Cause) to the end, Chavez received a posthumous Presidential Medal of Freedom the year following his death.

POROUS BORDER

Clutching their children, two Mexican women wade across the Rio Grande in 1983. Known as the *Rio Bravo del Norte* in Mexico, the river forms the border between Mexico and Texas; shallow along much of its length, the waterway is a small barrier to illegal immigration.

MANUEL

Manuel is from Boca de Rivera, Mexico. He illegally crosses the border into the United States whenever his family runs out of money and he needs to find work.

"I've made the trip across the border maybe 15, 20 times. The reason that I had to leave my house, my country, my family, is because in Mexico life is very difficult. It's hard to get a job down here. And if you get a job, it's not enough pay and you can't survive. In the U.S. there are better opportunities. Nobody else knows how it feels when you have to leave your family. But, there's no option. I've got no choice. Once I get to the border I scope things out. The first chance I get, I'll try to cross. It is a game, like cat and mouse. Sometimes you get lucky and you don't get caught. Sometimes you get caught and it's pretty bad. But all you got to do is try again and again until you make it. The desert is very tough, very dangerous. You can get bitten by snakes. There are robberies. And sometimes you get killed. One of the main reasons that I don't want to take my family with me is because I know how risky it is . . . I go to Chicago and once I get a job, I work as hard as I can to send money to my family. When I come back home from the United States, I say, I hope this was my last time. But I have to go again. Things are very bad here in Mexico."

"As long as there is poverty on one side of the border, and prosperity on the other, Mexicans will continue to cross to the United States."

"The Golden Door"

entered the United States legally every year; Mexicans constituted one in six immigrants to America between 1960 and 1990. But these numbers were dwarfed by illegal immigration. In the 1980s alone, the overworked and under-resourced U.S. Border Patrol turned back an average of 1 million illegal Mexican immigrants each year. Unlike immigrants from Europe, Asia, Africa, and the Caribbean, Mexicans only had to cross a river to get into the United States. Yet, over the decades, an unknown number have died of exposure in the southwestern deserts, and many more continue to be exploited by the professional smugglers (coyotes) who facilitate their passage.

Still, illegal or legal, Mexican immigrants do the hard, low-paying jobs that other Americans are increasingly unwilling to do, and they have been a major part of the workforce, not only in California, Texas, and the Southwest, but in parts of the Midwest and in cities like Chicago and New York, since the start of the 20th century.

LA RAZA IN AMERICA

In the 1960s and 1970s, a distinctive and assertive Mexican-American cultural consciousness—*La Raza* or "the Race"—gathered strength. Figures like cultural leader Ernesto Galarza and labor organizer Cesar Chavez (*see side panel*) achieved national prominence. During these same years, a resurgence of Nativist sentiment focused on illegal immigrants from Mexico. Partly in response, the Immigration Reform Act of 1986 established harsh penalties for employers of illegal immigrants, while offering amnesty to Mexicans who had lived in America since 1982. Some Americans believed the passage of the North American Free Trade Agreement (NAFTA) in 1993 would slow illegal immigration by stimulating Mexico's economy, but the jury is still out, and the collapse of the Mexican *peso* in 1994–95 proved to be a further spur to immigration. The sheer number of Mexican immigrants and their descendants in America continues to have a major impact on American society, in everything from food to economics to music, and Spanish-speaking Americans—the majority of whom are of Mexican ancestry—are poised to become the nation's "majority minority" in the future.

DEPORTEE

As a deported illegal Mexican immigrant passes through the border checkpoint at Mexicali, on the Mexico-California border, a volunteer hands out an invitation to stay at a shelter in the town. The number of deportations has increased recently due to the general tightening of border security following the 9/11 attacks.

First migration	1900
Migrated from	**Puerto Rico; Jamaica; Dominican Republic**
Approx. number in USA	**3 million (2005)**
Settlement	**Florida; New Jersey; New York**

Caribbeans

Thanks to their close proximity, the islands of the Caribbean and the United States share an interconnected history, but there was relatively little immigration from the Caribbean until fairly recently. Over the last half-century or so, however, the three islands of the Dominican Republic, Jamaica, and Puerto Rico—the first two, independent nations, the third a U.S. commonwealth—have collectively sent at least 2.5 million immigrants to the United States.

OLD SAN JUAN
A view of the La Perla *barrio* (neighborhood) in San Juan, Puerto Rico's capital and largest city, in the 1980s. The seaside *barrio* is generally considered the city's poorest district.

SUGAR ISLAND
Laborers harvest sugarcane in this photo from 1939. During the 1930s, the U.S. government tried to reform Puerto Rico's virtually single-crop economy, with only limited success.

In 1898, Puerto Rico became a U.S. territory following the Spanish-American War; Puerto Ricans received American citizenship in 1917, and, in 1952, the island became a self-governing commonwealth within the United States. Until the mid-20th century, the economy was agricultural and dominated by mainland companies. Sugarcane was the main crop—from 1900 to 1940, some three-quarters of the population depended on sugar cultivation for their living.

There was little movement of people to the mainland until the late 1940s, when Operation Bootstrap—a program aimed at bringing industry and modernization to the island—began during the charismatic governorship of Luis Muñoz Marin. Mainland and foreign investment led to an economic shift away from agriculture and helped to raise living standards, but the program also had the paradoxical result of spurring emigration from Puerto Rico. Between about 1945 and the turn of the 21st century, at least 1 million Puerto Ricans moved to America in search of higher wages than they could earn at home. Most came to New York City; because they can move freely between Puerto Rico and the mainland, Puerto Ricans are sometimes called "people of two islands," the islands being Puerto Rico and Manhattan.

In the 1940s and 1950s, many Puerto Ricans found work in New York's garment industry, where they replaced the largely Jewish and Italian workforce. However, with the decline of the city's garment industry in recent decades, Puerto Rican immigrants have had to find work elsewhere.

JAMAICANS

The combination of slave labor and sugar made Jamaica one of the world's most coveted pieces of real estate from the 16th to the 19th centuries; the island was disputed constantly by the European powers, eventually coming under British control. With the end of slavery in the British Empire in 1838 and a shift in sugar production to other locations, Jamaica's economy began a long decline. Jamaica became an independent nation in 1962.

TO MARKET
Jamaicans carry bananas to market around 1900, the year the island first exported the fruit overseas; they were grown on both small farms and large plantations. As in Puerto Rico, sugar was the mainstay of Jamaica's economy until other crops were introduced.

From around 1900 to 1930, several thousand Jamaicans came to the United States in search of opportunity, including Marcus Garvey (*see side panel*) and the parents of Colin Powell, who would serve as Chairman of the United States Joint Chiefs of Staff (1989–93) and Secretary of State (2001–04).

Over the next few decades, most Jamaican emigrants chose to go to Britain, but after that nation tightened its immigration policies in 1967, many came to America. By 2002, there were more than 736,000 Americans of Jamaican birth or ancestry.

Besides poverty, political unrest and high crime in Jamaican cities like Kingston led growing numbers of Jamaicans to decide to immigrate in the 1960s and 1970s, among them many educated professionals. Starting in the 1980s, Jamaican agricultural workers began arriving in Florida and other southern states. In recent years, women—often nurses and health- and child-care workers—have made up an increasing percentage of Jamaican immigrants. While the search for work has led Jamaicans to settle across the country, New York City remains the center of the Jamaican-American community—more than 6 percent of the city's population was Jamaican-born in 2002.

THE SMALLER ISLANDS

Growing numbers of immigrants from several smaller Caribbean island nations have come to America in recent years, most notably Barbados, the Bahamas, and Trinidad and Tobago—all former British colonies with English-speaking populations. In the 2000 census, about 165,000 U.S. residents claimed Trinidadian or Tobagian ancestry; the figures for Barbadian and Bahamian ancestry were about 54,000 and 32,000, respectively, and more than 230,000 people claimed West Indian or British West Indian ancestry.

The main motivation for these Caribbean immigrants is economic. Although these island nations are generally better off than their larger neighbors, lack of opportunity and professional advancement at home have inspired many skilled and educated islanders to emigrate. The destination for most are the cities of the East Coast, especially New York City and Miami.

The smaller islands have brought big figures to the American cultural scene, among them acclaimed poet Derek Walcott and historian and political activist C. L. R. James.

KINGSTON TOWN
A soldier patrols the Hannah Town neighborhood of Kingston, Jamaica, in December 2002. Street violence—both drug-related and politically motivated—has plagued Jamaica's capital. In 1980, about 800 Jamaicans died in clashes between supporters of rival political parties.

MARCUS GARVEY
1887–1940

A legendary and influential figure among people of African descent both in America and around the world, Marcus Garvey was born in Jamaica. He came to New York City to expand his Universal Negro Improvement Association (UNIA), an organization that eventually enrolled 2 million members. Garvey urged economic self-sufficiency for African-American communities. He also contended that black people would always be aliens in white-dominated nations and urged his followers to plan for a return to Africa. Garvey was a brilliant orator and organizer, but his mismanagement of the organization's finances led to a conviction on mail-fraud charges. He was deported to Jamaica in 1927 and died in London in near obscurity.

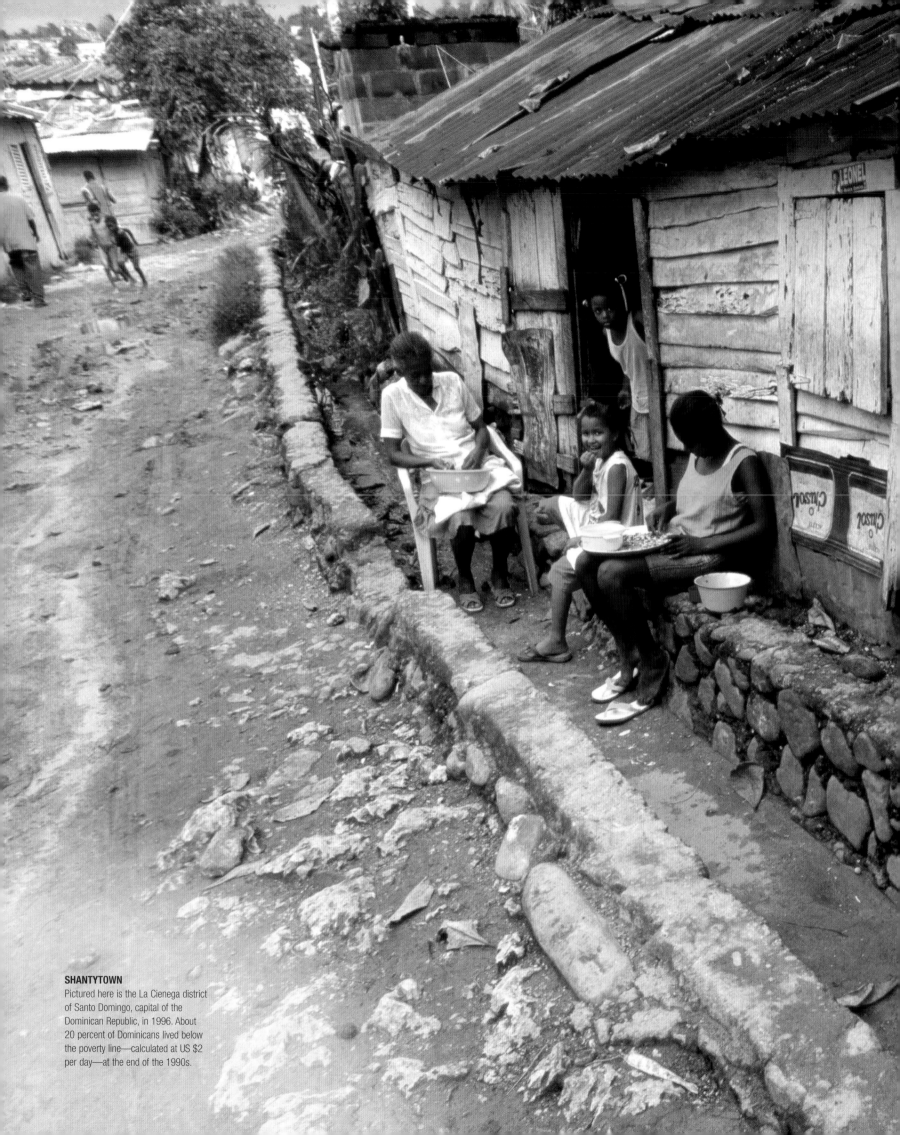

SHANTYTOWN
Pictured here is the La Cienega district of Santo Domingo, capital of the Dominican Republic, in 1996. About 20 percent of Dominicans lived below the poverty line—calculated at US $2 per day—at the end of the 1990s.

FACE OF ANGUISH
A Dominican woman cries after being arrested by Puerto Rican police for entering the commonwealth illegally in 2004. She and her companions had set out from the Dominican Republic in two small wooden boats.

DOMINICANS

The Dominican Republic shares the island of Hispaniola with Haiti (*see pp 222–223*), and like its neighbor, the country's history has been marked by periods of violence and dictatorship that contributed to widespread poverty among its people.

In 1822, as Spanish colonies throughout the Americas threw off colonial rule, rebels declared independence, in what is now the Dominican Republic, as the State of Spanish Haiti. The new nation was short-lived. Haitian troops invaded and stayed for 22 years. The Haitians ended slavery in the area, but their domination weakened an economy that the Spanish had never developed in more than 250 years of rule.

In the 1830s, a group of patriots led by Juan Pablo Darte formed to oppose Haitian rule. Their cause was helped by civil war in Haiti itself. Haitian troops withdrew in 1842, and two years later an independent Dominican Republic came into being. Independence brought neither prosperity nor democracy. With a few exceptions, for the next 60 years the new nation was ruled by a succession of dictators who lined their pockets at the expense of an impoverished populace. (In an interesting historical "what if?" some prominent Americans, including President Ulysses S. Grant, favored making the Dominican Republic a U.S. protectorate, or annexing it outright. An annexation treaty failed in the Senate by a single vote.)

By the early 20th century, the Dominican Republic was in a state of near-anarchy; the United States took over the republic's finances from 1905 to 1941 and, from 1916 to 1924, U.S. forces occupied the country.

VIVA LA REPUBLICA
A reveler salutes spectators during New York City's Dominican Day Parade in 1999. An annual event since 1981, the parade marks the August 16, 1863 assertion of independence by Dominican patriots during a period of Spanish re-occupation.

In 1930, Rafael Trujillo became dictator. He brought stability to the Dominican Republic, but his rule was brutally repressive; he also banned immigration from the republic. Trujillo was assassinated in 1961, setting off more political chaos. In 1965, revolution broke out. The United States sent in troops, ostensibly to protect American and European citizens, but mainly out of fear the country would wind up in the Communist camp, as Cuba had a few years earlier. The troops withdrew the next year after the U.S.-backed candidate, Joaquín Balaguer, won the presidential election.

The country's economy improved somewhat over the next decade, but poverty and corruption remained endemic. These conditions led to a huge wave of immigration to America from the early 1960s. By 2000, there were just over 1 million Dominicans in America, about half of whom had arrived between 1990 and 2000 alone. The early 1990s—when the country's economy suffered a downturn—saw thousands of Dominicans attempting to reach Puerto Rico by boat across the 75-mile Mona Passage; as with Haitian and Cuban boat people, many died in the attempt.

This migration continues today, although at a lower rate. Dominicans are now the fourth-largest Latin-American immigrant group in America, after Mexicans, Puerto Ricans, and Cubans. More than 80 percent of Dominicans live in just three states—New York, New Jersey, and Florida—and they have become one of the most significant immigrant groups in New York City, poised to overtake Puerto Ricans as the city's largest Latin-American community in a few years.

The Dominican community in America faces many of the same problems as earlier arrivals. Many are unskilled and uneducated; the unemployment rate for Dominican-Americans was about twice that of the national rate in 2000, while a 1999 study found that their per-capita income was roughly half that of the national average. On the other hand, high-school and college graduation rates for first-generation Dominican-Americans have risen; also, as with earlier arrivals, education is proving a path to a better life.

First migration	**1875**
Migrated from	**Bangladesh; Egypt; India; Iraq; Jordan; Lebanon; Pakistan; Palestine; Syria**
Approx. number in USA	**5 million (2005)**
Settlement	**Chicago; Detroit; Los Angeles; New York City; Washington, D.C.**

South Asians and Middle Easterners

Immigration to the United States from the Middle East and the Indian subcontinent is a fairly recent development, but one that is rapidly changing the demographics of America. These countries include a diverse mix of religions and ethnic groups and vary widely in form of government and level of economic development, but throughout the region the desire for opportunity in America inspires immigrants.

The Ottoman (Turkish) Empire ruled the Middle East from the 17th century until the end of World War I. While Western Europe and the Americas grew in wealth and power in the 19th century, the Ottoman-ruled lands remained relatively isolated.

The first significant group of immigrants from the Middle East were Christians from Syria and Lebanon—mostly young men—who arrived in America after about 1875. Many came in response to the decline of two of the area's traditional industries—wine-making and silk cultivation. Like many of the first German-Jewish immigrants (*see pp 80–83*), they tended to work as traveling peddlers in the South and West. The more successful were able to open stores; by the turn of the 21st century, there was a small but thriving Syrian enclave in New York City's Lower East Side.

PUNJAB
A horse-drawn cart carries Punjabi farmers past a field mined by the Indian Army in January 2002. The 20,000-square-mile region was divided between India and Pakistan after the end of British rule in 1947, leading to border clashes.

DAMASCUS TO MANHATTAN
Syrian children pose in New York City around 1900. Among the Middle Eastern immigrants who settled in the city was the poet Khalil Gibran, who arrived from Lebanon in 1912. Gibran wrote in both Arabic and English.

Around the same time, families arrived from "Greater Syria," which then included Palestine and Jordan, including many Muslims. Like immigrants from Europe, they were attracted by reports about life in America and by the marketing efforts of steamship lines. Many found work in the textile mills of New England, or in the automobile plants of Detroit—the Detroit metropolitan area had the largest concentration of Arab-Americans in 2004.

The immigration reforms of the 1920s largely halted immigration from the Middle East. When it revived again after 1965, the former Ottoman lands were independent, but mostly undemocratic. Oil brought wealth to some Arab states, but poverty was still widespread. Jews and Christians in mainly Muslim nations felt endangered by the rise of Islamist sentiment following the establishment

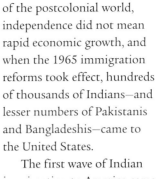

MUSLIMS FOR BUSH
Muhammad Ali Hasan, founder of Muslims for Bush, poses beside a picture of the President at a booth during the 2004 annual convention of the Islamic Society of North America. More than 40 percent of American Muslims voted for George W. Bush in 2000 but Muslim support for Bush declined greatly in the 2004 election.

of the postcolonial world, independence did not mean rapid economic growth, and when the 1965 immigration reforms took effect, hundreds of thousands of Indians—and lesser numbers of Pakistanis and Bangladeshis—came to the United States.

The first wave of Indian immigration to America came around the turn of the 20th century. Up to 10,000 men, mostly Sikhs, immigrated from the overpopulated Punjab region to the West Coast, where they worked as farmhands and railroad and factory workers. They faced the same legal discrimination and Nativist hostility as the Chinese (*see pp 154–155*), and they were also kept out by the 1920s restrictions. Legislation in 1946 (*see side panel*) and 1952 eased these restrictions, and, by 1965, around 6,500 Indians had settled in America.

Partly because Indian immigrants grasped the significance of the switch to the "family preference" system of admissions (*see p 55*), and partly because of American demand for skilled workers and professionals, the rate of Indian immigration more than doubled between 1990 and 2000. Today, the Indian-American population is about 1.7 million, making them the nation's third-largest Asian group, after Chinese-Americans and Filipino-Americans. Indian-Americans have high educational attainments—one-third of adults hold at least a BA degree—and Indian-American engineers and entrepreneurs play a big role in the ongoing digital revolution.

The rate of immigration from Pakistan and Bangladesh has been slower, with about 229,000 and 117,000 in the United States, respectively, in 2002.

J. J. SINGH
BIRTH DATE UNKNOWN

In 1923 the U.S. Supreme Court decided that, like Chinese and Japanese immigrants, Indian immigrants were "aliens ineligible to citizenship." The ruling was resented by America's small Indian community, and, in 1938, the India League of America formed to oppose it and to fight for Indian rights. The first president was Sardar Jagjit (J. J.) Singh, a Sikh immigrant who ran a prosperous import business in New York City. Singh enlisted the help of Henry Luce, publisher of *Time* magazine, and his wife, Republican Congresswoman Clare Booth Luce, who joined with Democrat Emanuel Celler to sponsor a bill permitting Indians to seek citizenship and to set a quota for Indian immigration. In 1946, President Truman signed the Luce-Celler Act into law (*as pictured above*), granting naturalization rights to Filipinos (*see pp 182–183*) and Asian Indians.

WORKING ON THE RAILROAD
A track crew of Hindus are photographed during construction of the Pacific & Eastern Railroad in Oregon around 1909. Immigrants of Indian descent were often referred to as "Hindus," regardless of their actual religion. Between 1899 and 1913, approximately 7,000 "Hindus" came to the United States to work as unskilled laborers in the Pacific region.

of Israel. For these reasons, many Middle Easterns immigrated since 1965 for both religious and economic reasons, including Coptic Christians from Egypt and Chaldean Christians and Jews from Iraq.

It is difficult to establish precise numbers, but there are probably 3 million Arab-Americans today, the majority of them Christians, although Muslim Arabs are the fastest-growing segment. Most live in urban areas, with the highest concentrations in Los Angeles, Detroit, New York, Chicago, and Washington, D.C.

THE INDIAN SUBCONTINENT

In 1947 Britain's empire on the Indian subcontinent became the independent nations of India, Pakistan, and Bangladesh (originally East Pakistan). As in much

FABRIC STORE
A Chicago shopkeeper helps a customer pick fabric for a sari, the traditional draped garment worn by Hindu women and some Sikh and Muslim women.

Filipinos

A nation of more than 7,000 islands, the Philippines came under Spanish rule in the 16th century. Spain ceded the islands to the United States in 1898 as one of the spoils of the Spanish-American War. In effect, the Philippines became America's first major overseas colony—and one which would ultimately be a major source of emigrants to America.

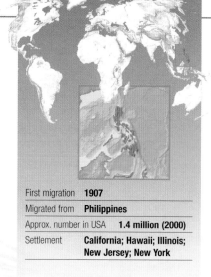

First migration	**1907**
Migrated from	**Philippines**
Approx. number in USA	**1.4 million (2000)**
Settlement	**California; Hawaii; Illinois; New Jersey; New York**

The acquisition was controversial. Many prominent Americans, including industrialist Andrew Carnegie (*see p 142*), protested that the United States was following in the imperialist footsteps of Britain and other European nations. Nevertheless, President William McKinley decided the United States had a mission to "civilize and Christianize" the Filipinos, ignoring the fact that most Filipinos had been Roman Catholics for centuries. Anti-Spanish Filipino rebels, who had expected independence rather than recolonization, began an insurgency against U.S. forces on the islands. The result was a brutal campaign of "pacification" that claimed the lives of about 200,000 Filipinos, most of them civilians. The insurgency was mostly crushed by 1902, but resistance to American rule continued for years on some islands.

Because the Philippines were a U.S. territory, Filipinos were not subject to the same immigration restrictions as other Asian groups. After the "Gentlemen's Agreement" halted Japanese immigration in 1906–07, Filipinos began to move to Hawaii to work on the islands' sugar plantations.

DUMP DWELLERS
Squatters living in *barung-barong*—improvised shanties—in the Payatas refuse dump on the outskirts of Manila. By some accounts, this dump and others are home to as many as 300,000 of the city's poorest inhabitants.

THE PHILIPPINE SCOUTS

For many immigrants from the Philippines, the U.S. military provided entry into America. In 1901, the U.S. Army began recruiting Filipinos into special units that became known as the Philippine Scouts. Officially considered part of the U.S. Army, the Scouts formed a major part of the Philippine defense forces during the years of American rule and in World War II. Besides the Scouts, between 200,000–300,000 Filipinos fought alongside U.S. forces during World War II. Tens of thousands died in the unsuccessful campaign against the Japanese invaders in 1941–42, in brutal conditions in Japanese prison camps, and in guerrilla fighting during the Japanese occupation. In 1944, the U.S. government gave veterans' benefits and eligibility for U.S. citizenship to Filipinos fighting under the stars and stripes. In 1946, however, Congress reneged on that promise with the passage of the Rescission Act, which stated that most Filipino veterans "shall not be deemed to be or to have been [in] service in the . . . national forces of the United States." The law has been bitterly resented ever since both by Filipino veterans who immigrated to America (about 13,000 of whom were still alive in the early 2000s) and by those who remained on the islands. In the 1990s and 2000s, several bills were introduced in Congress in an effort to reverse the Rescission Act; none had passed as of early 2005.

THE PHILIPPINE INSURRECTION
American troops man a defensive position during the Philippine Insurrection, as the 1898–1902 conflict was called in America. Little-remembered in the United States today, the Philippine conflict was the country's biggest military operation between the Civil War and World War I.

There were about 100,000 Filipinos in Hawaii by 1930; today, Hawaiians of Filipino ancestry are one of the state's major ethnic groups. Fewer Filipinos settled on the mainland's west coast and in Alaska during these years, mostly as agricultural laborers.

FILIPINO-AMERICANS

In 1934, Congress passed the Tydings-McDuffie Act, which made the Philippines a commonwealth and set 1946 as the date for independence. The act put Filipino immigrants in a bind; once considered U.S. citizens, they were now ineligible for citizenship, and a tiny quota (50 per year) was set for new immigrants.

Japanese forces occupied the Philippines from 1941 until 1944–45, when the United States recaptured the islands. On July 4, 1946, the Philippines became an independent nation. That same year, the Luce-Celler Act (*see p 181*) made Filipinos in America eligible for citizenship, although immigration was still restricted. Those restrictions were eased a bit by the McCarran-Walter Act of 1952, but the major wave of Filipino immigration began after the 1965 Immigration Act.

The Philippines has long suffered from low economic growth, especially

THE PEOPLE POWER MOVEMENT
A demonstrator slashes a poster of President Ferdinand Marcos during the People Power Movement uprising of February 1986 that ended Marcos's 21 years of rule.

PINOY PRIDE
Dancers in traditional dress celebrate their *Pinoy* (Filipino) heritage at the 1994 Philippine Independence Day Parade in New York City, officially celebrated on June 12th.

during Ferdinand Marcos's corrupt presidency, which lasted from 1965 to 1986. Economic woes and political unrest continued after his ouster. As a result, more than 1.4 million Filipinos immigrated to America by 2000, with more than 400,000 coming between 1990 and 2000 alone—making them, by some accounts, the second-largest immigrant group (after Mexicans) in America today.

Almost half of all Filipino immigrants live in California and about 25 percent of the remainder live in Hawaii, New York, New Jersey, and Illinois. Nursing draws many Filipinos to America, where they can earn up to 20 times more than they do at home. By 2004, so many had immigrated that the head of the Philippine Nurses Association warned of a shortage back home.

Koreans

Korea's traditional name, *Chosin*, means "Land of the Morning Calm," but the nation's recent history has been marked by war and turbulence. After division into two states at the end of World War II, North Korea and South Korea fought a devastating war in 1950–53, a conflict followed by many years of low economic growth and political unrest—conditions that combined to send more than 1 million South Koreans to America.

The Korean Peninsula was largely isolated from the rest of the world until the 1870s, when its more powerful neighbor, Japan, forced the rulers of "the hermit kingdom" to sign trade treaties with several nations, including the United States. After victories in wars against its rivals—China and Russia—for control of Korea, Japan ruled Korea as a colony until 1945. In that year, following Japan's defeat in World War II, the peninsula was divided into North Korea, a communist state ruled by Kim Il-Sung with the support of Russia and, after 1949, the People's Republic of China; and South Korea, ruled by Syngman Rhee with the support of the United States.

In June 1950, North Korea invaded the South. Two days after the invasion, the United Nations condemned North Korea's aggression and called for the use of force. Eventually, 15 nations would send troops, but the main contributors were the United States (about 1.5 million Americans served in Korea between 1950–53) and South Korea's own army. Within weeks, the North Koreans had overwhelmed both the ROK (Republic of Korea) forces and the American troops who had been rushed from Japan to help them. By late July, the North Koreans—driving tens of thousands of refugees before them—occupied the entire peninsula except for a pocket around the southern port of Pusan.

On September 25th, U.N. forces recaptured Seoul and soon drove the invaders back into North Korea and then northward toward the Yalu River, the border

First migration	1903
Migrated from	**South Korea**
Approx. number in USA	**1.1 million (2000)**
Settlement	**California; Hawaii; New Jersey; New York**

A CALM SCENE
A Korean farmer prepares a rice paddy for planting with an ox-drawn plow. Until the 1960s, most Koreans made their living from the land; that number has dropped to about 25 percent in recent years.

HEARTRENDING SIGHT
An orphaned Korean child in the ruins of Inchon, South Korea, in October 1950, after United Nations forces recaptured the city from North Korean troops following a daring amphibious assault and ferocious street fighting.

MEETING OF THE PRESIDENTS
South Korean President Park Chung Hee stands with U.S. President Lyndon B. Johnson on May 1, 1965. Fourteen years later Park was assassinated by the head of the nation's intelligence agency.

between North Korea and the People's Republic of China. In an abrupt reversal of fortune, China sent hundreds of thousands of "volunteers" into North Korea, forcing U.N. troops to retreat. Eventually, the front line stabilized around the 38th Parallel and the conflict turned into a bloody stalemate. Peace talks began in the summer of 1951, but an armistice was not signed until June 1953, leaving the peninsula divided as before. (The main sticking point was the return of prisoners-of-war; many North Korean troops did not want to return to their homeland.) Even 50 years after the conflict's end, there were still 37,000 U.S. troops in Korea, helping ROK forces guard the DMZ (Demilitarized Zone) dividing the two Koreas.

The war devastated both Koreas. An estimated 2.5 million Koreans died in the conflict, two-thirds of them civilians. Initially, it seemed like South Korea was the worse off, as the North retained much of the peninsula's industry and good agricultural land. While North Korea degenerated into a police state and an economic backwater under the paranoid leadership of Kim Il-Sung and his son and successor, Kim Jong-Il, South Korea staged a major recovery—but one fraught with political and social conflict.

South Korea's struggle to rebuild was overshadowed by political problems. The nation was nominally democratic, but its American-educated president, Syngman Rhee, ruled as an autocrat before resigning in the face of widespread protests in 1960. Park Chung Hee ruled South Korea from 1963 until his assassination in 1979. The country's economy revived under Park, but his repressive rule met with strikes and protests. In 1987, South Korea adopted a new, more democratic constitution. By that time, South Korea had gone from being a mostly agricultural nation to a major Asian economic power.

KOREANS IN AMERICA

The first Korean immigrants to the United States were about 7,000 young men who came to Hawaii in 1903–1904 as laborers on the islands' sugarcane plantations. Soon afterward, the "Gentlemen's Agreement" between Japan and the United States (*see pp 160–161*) also restricted immigration from Korea—in part to encourage the migration of laborers from the Philippines, now a U.S. colony, to Hawaii. About 1,000

Korean laborers later moved to the mainland, where many were joined by "picture brides" from their homeland.

After the exclusionary acts of the 1920s, there was little immigration from Korea, except for a handful of students and refugees and, starting in the 1950s, the wives of U.S. servicemen who had married Korean women in South Korea or Japan. Americans also adopted about 100,000 South Korean war orphans.

Korean immigration rose in the early 1960s, when special legislation gave work permits to South Korean doctors and nurses. Thanks to the 1965 reforms, which came about the same time that the South Korean government eased restrictions on emigration, a big wave of immigration began in 1968. By 1980, about 350,000 Koreans had settled in America, rising to 800,000 in 1990 and 1.1 million in the early 21st century. Today, 90 percent of Korean-Americans are post-1965 arrivals or their children.

The biggest concentration of Korean-Americans is in Southern California, where nearly a third live, with the next highest concentration in New York and New Jersey. Many Korean-Americans own stores in urban areas, and their emphasis on education gives their children high representation in the professions, of which there are several Korean-American associations.

WE CAN GET ALONG
Waving Korean flags, Korean-American marchers appeal for cross-community healing after the 1992 L.A. riots. Many Korean-Americans contended that their businesses were targets of violence in the mostly African-American South Central area.

DEFENSIVE ACTION
Rifles at the ready, two Korean-American men guard a store from looters during the L.A. riots. According to some sources, about 2,000 Korean-owned businesses—mostly small grocery stores—were damaged or destroyed in six days of violence.

CHANG-RAE LEE
1965–

Born in Seoul, Lee grew up in New York. Educated at Yale and the University of Oregon, he worked on Wall Street before publishing his first novel, *Native Speaker*, in 1995. An exploration of what it means to be part of two distinct cultures, cast in the form of a mystery involving a Korean-American investigator, *Native Speaker* won an American Book Award and the Hemingway Foundation/PEN Award. Lee followed up with *A Gesture Life*, which also touched on the theme of identity, as well as the complex relationship between the Japanese and Korean peoples. Lee's third novel, *Aloft*, a suburban character study, was published in 2004. Widely acclaimed by critics as one of America's best young writers, Lee also teaches at New York City's Hunter College.

Post-*Glasnost* Immigrants

First migration	1989
Migrated from	former Soviet Union, former Yugoslavia, Poland former Czechoslovakia, Hungary, Romania
Approx. number in USA	1.9 million (2000)
Settlement	New York; California; New Jersey; Chicago, Illinois; Detroit, Michigan; Boston, Massachusetts

The Soviet Union and its satellite nations in Central and Eastern Europe greatly restricted the movements of their citizens, so immigration to the United States from those countries was minimal until the end of the Cold War in 1989–91. The fall of communism in Europe brought freedom to millions, but at a heavy price in economic dislocation and social problems, prompting a wave of immigration—much of it illegal—to America.

The transition from a planned, centralized economy to a free-market system was not an easy one for much of the Soviet Bloc. In fact, the new markets were rarely free; often, formerly state-run enterprises were simply taken over as monopolies by corrupt "oligarchs," many of them members of the former Communist hierarchy. People who had counted on jobs for life now found themselves out of work. Inflation set in as currency reforms began. Crime rates rose. For example, the collapse of Yugoslavia wreaked havoc on the economies of its former component countries; in 2003, unemployment in Bosnia stood at 40 percent.

It is difficult to establish exact figures, but in the years around the turn of the 21st century, at least 2 million people left their formerly communist homelands in search of work. Most went to Western Europe; an unknown number managed to come to America legally. By some estimates there were as many as 200,000 illegal immigrants from the Czech Republic alone in the United States as of 2004.

Eastern Europe has now become a source of low-wage, unskilled labor in American service industries. Unscrupulous contractors operating out of the United States recruit many of these workers in their homelands. The process usually starts when a prospective immigrant answers an ad in a local newspaper or on the Internet promising high-paying jobs in America. After arriving on a student or tourist visa (holders of which are not permitted to work), the contractor sets the new arrival

BIRTH OF SOLIDARITY
Shipyard workers in Gdansk, Poland, walk off the job in August 1980. The strike helped establish Solidarity, a trade union independent of the communist government, which is now seen as the first rip in the Iron Curtain.

POST-SOVIET SCAVENGERS
Homeless Muscovites pick through dumped garbage for food on a winter day in this 2003 photo. Moscow's homeless population that year was estimated at 100,000 out of about 9 million total population.

GET IN LINE
Romanians line up outside a government shop in a Bucharest suburb in November 1989. Just a few weeks later, a popular uprising deposed the nation's dictator Nicolae Ceausescu; on Christmas Day, he was executed along with his wife on charges of genocide and illegal gathering of wealth.

THE COLLAPSE OF COMMUNISM
By the 1970s, it was clear that Communist economic policies were failing the nations of Eastern Europe. By the 1980s, most of the Eastern Bloc was bankrupt. Mikhail Gorbachev abandoned the satellite states in an attempt to save the economy of the USSR.

The collapse of Communism in Eastern Europe

- Soviet Union to 1991
- Soviet-dominated Eastern Europe to 1989
- German Democratic Republic (GDR), united with Federal Republic of Germany 1990
- Czechoslovakia to Dec 1992
- Yugoslavia to 1991
- other Communist state before 1991
- 1990 date of first free election

SERGEY BRIN
1973–

Born in Moscow, Sergey Brin came to the United States to study computer science. While in graduate school at California's Stanford University, Brin teamed up with a fellow student to create Google, a search engine to locate information on the Internet. Following its 1998 debut, Google went on to become the most successful search engine by far (even becoming a verb) and before the company's stock went public in 2004, Brin was estimated to be worth close to $1 billion. The 2004 introduction of Gmail, a Google-based email service, along with new features like Froogle (online shopping) and Google Print (an online book-publishing service), further extended the company's online presence.

Larry Page and Sergey Brin *(right)*, cofounders of the Google empire.

up with a job—at much lower wages than promised, and with the contractor taking a big cut of the earnings. As illegal immigrants, they have no recourse to legal action and are sometime, in worse situations than what they left behind.

In recent years, there have been charges that some U.S. companies have known that their contractors were providing illegal-immigrant labor. In 2001, two managers at Tyson Foods pled guilty to knowingly contracting illegal workers. And in a nationwide sting operation in October 2003, federal officials arrested about 250 illegal-immigrant cleaning-crew workers, including many Eastern Europeans, at Wal-Mart stores in 21 states. Authorities later charged that the retailer's executives knew about their contractors' hiring practices. In March 2005, Wal-Mart settled the case by agreeing to pay an $11 million fine, with its contractors paying an additional $4 million. In the words of Michael J. Garcia, Assistant Secretary for U.S. Immigration and Customs Enforcement, "This case breaks new ground not only because this is a record dollar amount for a civil immigration settlement, but because this settlement requires Wal-Mart to create an internal program to ensure future compliance with immigration laws by Wal-Mart contractors and by Wal-Mart itself."

The end of the Cold War also spurred legal immigration from formerly communist nations like Poland, the Czech and Slovak republics, Hungary, and Romania. Many were able to immigrate through the provisions of the Immigration Act of 1990, which permitted increased admission of people with skills needed by American businesses. Like the South Asians in California's Silicon Valley, Eastern European immigrants are highly represented in technical fields like software engineering (*see side panel*).

THE SERVICE INDUSTRY

Until the years after World War II, manufacturing made up the largest segment of the American economy. In periods of prosperity, semi-skilled and even unskilled workers—native-born and immigrant alike—could usually count on making a living wage in a factory or plant. Since about 1950 on, however, there has been a major shift away from manufacturing toward the so-called service industries like retail, hospitality, and food service. Because wages in the service industries are typically lower, this shift has slowed the economic progress of many recently arrived immigrant groups. At the same time, American industries have aggressively "outsourced" many operations overseas to cut labor costs. Because certain types of work can be done anywhere in the world, thanks to the Internet and other new technologies, American companies are making use of overseas workers—especially in India and Eastern Europe—to handle functions like software programming and customer service. Some think this may lead to a drop in immigration from those regions.

STICKING WITH THE UNION
Members of American labor unions demonstrate against outsourcing at a March 2004 rally in Washington, D. C., as part of a "Show Us the Jobs" campaign cosponsored by the AFL-CIO, which includes more than 13 million of America's workers.

5

FREEDOM FROM FEAR

As of 2005, 20 million people, nearly one out of every 300, cannot go home. They are refugees: victims of war or revolution, targets of an ethnic or religious genocide. In the aftermath of World War II, U.S. immigration policy first granted refugees special status, acknowledging a distinction between immigrants seeking economic betterment and those fleeing violence or persecution. Since then, 4 million refugees have come to America in search of safety.

PLEDGE OF ALLEGIANCE
Vietnamese-American students recite the Pledge of Allegiance in the Little Saigon district of Westminster, California, in Orange County. In the decade following the 1975 fall of Saigon, more than 1 million South Vietnamese have fled from the communist rule of the Socialist Republic of Vietnam. Orange County became home to the largest concentration of Vietnamese refugees in America.

A CENTURY OF GENOCIDE

Chapters 2 and 3 of this book tell the story of the millions of people who came to America to live in a democratic society or to worship freely. For many other immigrants, however, especially in recent decades, getting to America was literally a matter of life or death. Some had the misfortune to be members of a minority race, religion, or ethnic group facing persecution—or even extermination—at the hands of the majority. Others belonged to the "wrong" political party, or social class, or backed the losing side in war.

Some historians have dubbed the 20th century "the century of genocide." From World War I through the end of the Cold War, tens of millions of people were murdered because they happened to belong to a particular ethnic or religious group, as in the Armenian massacres (*see pp 196–197*), or because they stood in the way of totalitarian programs of "social engineering," as in the Soviet Terror famine of the early 1930s (*see pp 208–209*).

RED PARADE
Troops loyal to the new Bolshevik (communist) regime march through the streets of Moscow in this photo from around 1917.

In most of these episodes, the circumstances were such that escape to the United States was simply not an option for the victims. The Holocaust (*see pp 200–205*) is an exception. Although the extent of the Nazi program of extermination was not fully known in the West until it was well underway, *Judenrein* ("cleansing" Germany of Jews) was an explicit goal of the Nazis from the time that Hitler gained power in 1933. Despite ongoing evidence of the Nazi's intentions, like 1938's *Kristallnacht* (*see pp 200–201*), the U.S. government refused to significantly increase the admission of Jewish refugees before World War II broke out, and by the time the United States finally made an effort to prevent the deportation of Jews to the Nazi death camps, it was too late to save more than a handful. The issues surrounding the American response to the Holocaust are complex, but the failure to do more to prevent the deaths of millions of Jews and other victims of the Nazis still haunts America's conscience.

COLD WAR REALITIES

The Cold War led to the linkage of American foreign policy and refugee policy. From 1945 to 1980—and even afterward, to a certain extent—the United States gave priority to refugees fleeing from communist regimes. The 1953 Refugee Relief Act, for example, authorized the admission of more than 200,000 refugees mostly from communist countries, over and above the immigration quotas already in force, while later special legislation allowed people from specific groups—like Hungarians escaping the failed 1956 revolt against Soviet domination—into the United States. With the exception of Cubans (*see pp 124–125*), however, it was difficult for people living in communist countries to take advantage of this policy. In the mid–1970s, the United States faced a major refugee crisis when communist governments seized power in Vietnam, Laos, and Cambodia. People from these nations who had fought with or otherwise aided the United States in its long war against communism in Southeast Asia now faced persecution by their new rulers. In response, the U.S. government authorized the admission of 130,000 Southeast Asian refugees immediately and, between 1975 and 1985, another 700,000 people—about 75 percent of them from Vietnam—were resettled in America.

REFUGEES

Over the last 90 years or so, the emergence of totalitarian regimes and the growth of ethnic and religious strife in many parts of the world—from Sudan in Africa (*see pp 230–231*) to the republics of the former Yugoslavia (*see pp 232–233*)—created a new category of immigrant: the refugee.

PERMANENT RESIDENT CARD
NAME CRITTENDEN, LEE W.
INS A# 022-345-679
Birthdate 10/04/49 Category P26 Sex M
Country of Birth Canada
CARD EXPIRES 11/01/94
Resident Since 11/01/97

C1USA0223456791EAC9730050225<<
4910040M9411014CAN<<<<<<<<<<<<8
CRITTENDEN<<LEE<W<<<<<<<<<<<<<<

REFUGEE POLICY

With the passage of the U.S. Refugee Act of 1980, Congress sought to reform the refugee-admission system by granting refugee or asylum status upon the basis of humanitarian considerations, irregardless of U.S. foreign policy. The act offered safety to those who could demonstrate "a well-founded fear of persecution on account of race, religion, nationality, membership in a particular social group, or political opinion."

Under the act's provisions, a person granted refugee or asylum status could apply for Lawful Permanent Resident status after a year in America, and if he or she met certain qualifications, proceed through the Naturalization process to citizenship. (For the purposes of the law, a refugee is someone who applies for admission to the United States *before* reaching American soil, while an asylum-seeker applies for refugee status while *in* the United States—like someone on a student visa who fears returning to her home country because of a change in government while she was studying in America.) Another act, passed in 1990, gave Temporary Protected Status (TPS) to people fleeing "emergency situations" in their homelands.

The 1980 and 1990 acts were an admirable effort to level the playing field, but they also led to an ongoing debate about the precise definition of "refugee." The 1980 act distinguished between refugees and "economic migrants"— people whose primary motivation in immigrating was to find work and a better quality of life. Critics of this policy have pointed out that in many countries, poverty is so deeply intertwined with government repression or anarchic conditions that would-be immigrants did not necessarily have to be members of a particular religious or ethnic minority or belong to a particular political party to have a "well-founded fear of persecution." This was especially true for the Haitians who attempted to reach America by boat during the 1990s and 2000s (*see pp 222–223*).

Concerns over rising illegal immigration led Congress to pass the U.S. Illegal Immigration Reform and Immigrant Responsibility Act in 1996. The new law required immigrants to demonstrate a "credible fear" of persecution before crossing the U.S. border; if they could not do so in the judgment of immigration officials, they were liable to be placed in detention facilities, creating a Catch-22 situation—they were detained because they could not prove a "credible fear," but they could not gather the documentation to prove that fear while in detention.

Criticism of flaws in U.S. refugee policy has to be balanced against the fact the United States today admits more refugees than any other nation. About 1.3 million refugees came to America legally between 1987 and 2000, and the U.S. Citizenship and Immigration Services (the post-9/11 successor to the Immigration and Naturalization Service) has a 2005 admission quota of 70,000.

WORLDWIDE REFUGEE CAMPS

Few refugees come to the United States directly from their home countries: most are admitted from refugee camps in third countries, which are sustained by aid from international agencies and host nations— which are usually poor nations themselves. As of 2003–04, an estimated 14 million people lived in refugee camps and other shelters, with the largest percentage in Africa. Many refugees spend years or even decades in these camps—15,000 Hmong, for example, spent 10 years in Thailand's Wat Tham Krabok facility before they began to be admitted to the United States in 2004.

UPGRADED GREEN CARD
In 1998, the U.S. Immigration and Naturalization Service announced a revamp of the Permanent Resident Card (*above*) issued to legal immigrants. Known as a "Green Card," although it has not been that color for years, the new version was intended to be more resistant to counterfeiting than its predecessor by incorporating high-tech elements like an optical memory stripe.

PASSING THE TIME
Illegal immigrant detainees shoot pool at the Oakdale, Louisiana, Federal Detention Center in 1986. In the words of one detainee: "In some ways, being detained is worse than being a convicted felon. At least if you're convicted of a crime, you know how long you're being held for."

Those refugees lucky enough to gain admission to the United States are usually penniless, so charitable and religious organizations in America play a major role in financing their transportation and resettlement costs. Those who remain in the camps often endure overcrowded and unhealthy conditions; with refugees unable to work and usually cut off from friends and family, life in refugee camps is an emotional, as well as a physical, ordeal.

Incidents of so-called "warehousing" of refugees has led refugee-advocacy organizations to call on the United States and other Western nations both to increase the pace of admissions and to provide more assistance in repatriating refugees to their homelands when it is safe to do so.

CHECKPOINT CHOKE POINT
The immediate tightening of U.S. borders after the 9/11 attacks led to long waits at border crossing points—like the one shown here at San Ysidro, California, on September 19, 2001. The U.S. Customs and Border Protection is now a division of the Department of Homeland Security.

REFUGEE TRAIN
Overseen by Red Cross workers, Hutu refugees from Rwanda are evacuated from a refugee camp in Zaire by train in 1997, after an overcrowding accident killed 91 refugees.

First migration	1755
Migrated from	**Canada; France**
Approx. number in USA	**3,000 (1788)**
Settlement	**Louisiana**

Acadians

In the mid-18th century, the Acadians—French settlers in what are now Canada's Maritime Provinces—were victims of the struggle between the British and French empires for dominance in North America. Forced from their homeland, they dispersed throughout America, Europe, and the Caribbean; some found a haven in Louisiana, where they formed the basis of the state's distinctive Cajun community.

BAY OF FUNDY
The Bay of Fundy as viewed from Fundy National Park in New Brunswick, Canada. The shores of the bay are the historic heartland of the Acadians, and Acadians still represent about a third of the province's population.

In 1604, a French aristocrat, Isaac de Razilly, led 300 colonists—mostly tenant farmers from the Poitou and Angevin regions—to the island of Saint Croix off the coast of present-day New Brunswick. The following year the colony moved to Port Royal on the Bay of Fundy, which separates New Brunswick from Nova Scotia. Over the next century, settlement spread out along the shores of the bay, which became known as L'Acadie, and the settlers became known as Acadians. (The origins of the name "Acadia" are debated; it may derive from a Native American place name, or from an old French name for "the place of codfish," among other theories.)

The Acadian settlements were self-sufficient, tightly knit communities. The people farmed and fished, got along with the local Miqmac Native Americans, and traded with the English colonies to the south. In 1713, however, Acadia came under British rule as a result of the Treaty of Utrecht, which ended the war of the Spanish Succession—one of the 17th- and 18th-century conflicts between European powers. Four decades later, with another war on the horizon, British authorities demanded that the Acadians take an oath of loyalty to the British crown. The Acadian leaders refused, but offered to pledge neutrality in any conflict between Britain and France.

LE GRAND DÉRANGEMENT

Unfortunately, neutrality was not good enough for Charles Lawrence, Nova Scotia's governor. In July 1755, the colony's governing council announced a campaign to eliminate the Acadian population, which numbered between 10,000–13,000. British troops burned some 6,000

TREATY OF UTRECHT
The actual 1713 Treaty of Utrecht and a commemorative medal. Signed by Britain, the Netherlands, France, and Spain, the treaty put the Acadian homeland under British rule.

LAISSEZ LE BON TEMPS ROULER!

The original Acadians brought French folk music with them, and developed it into a lively, syncopated form of dance music originally based around the Jew's harp and the fiddle. In Louisiana, Acadian musicians gradually brought the accordion (introduced by German settlers) into the lineup to create the now-traditional Cajun style of music and two-step dance. The first commercial recording of a Cajun song—*Allons à Lafayette*, performed by the husband-and-wife duo Joe and Cléoma Falcon—appeared in 1928, and the style influenced the development of modern country music through the songs of, among others, Hank Williams, Sr.

BROTHER MUSICIANS
Legendary Cajun musicians Linus and Ophie Romero work up a tune at their usual venue—under the Evangeline Oak in St. Martinville, Louisiana, along the Bayou Teche.

"Bending above, and resting its dome on the walls of the forest. They who dwell there have named it the Eden of Louisiana!"

Henry Wadsworth Longfellow's *Evangeline*

THE GREAT EXPULSION
A 19th-century print depicts troops forcing Acadians from their homes in 1755. A dispatch to colonial newspapers stated that "We are now upon a great and noble Scheme of sending the neutral French out of this Province . . ." Much of the land was taken by settlers from New England.

Acadian houses and farms, and rounded up their inhabitants for shipment to several of the English colonies to the south, while several thousand Acadians sought refuge among the Native Americans or in French-ruled Quebec. An unknown but significant number of Acadians died, many of them aboard the ships that carried them south. The Acadians would remember this episode as *Le Grand*

LONGFELLOW'S *EVANGELINE*
In 1847, Henry Wadsworth Longfellow—one of the most popular American writers of the day—published *Evangeline*, inspired by the saga of the Acadians. The story of a young Acadian woman's quest to reunite with her lover, from whom she had become separated during the Great Expulsion, the poem inspired the sculpture at right.

EVANGELINE,

A

TALE OF ACADIE.

BY

HENRY WADSWORTH LONGFELLOW.

BOSTON:
WILLIAM D. TICKNOR & COMPANY.
1847.

Dérangement—"The Great Expulsion." The colonies, however, did not want the Acadians: their French origins and language and Roman Catholic religion made them suspect. Most were driven out of one colony after another; Virginia re-deported its quota to England and France.

ACADIANS TO CAJUNS

Starting in 1764, several hundred Acadian refugees arrived in Spanish-ruled Louisiana. The governor welcomed them and gave them land to settle on along Bayou Teche and Bayou Lafourche between Baton Rouge and New Orleans. The major wave of Acadian settlement came in 1785, when seven shiploads of Acadians arrived in Louisiana from France, carrying about 1,600 people in all—survivors of the Great Expulsion and their descendants. In the bayou country, they recreated the kind of settlements they had known in their homeland on the Bay of Fundy. The Acadians—who became known as Cajans or Cajuns—preserved their language and heritage while absorbing elements from their African-American and Anglo-American neighbors, producing a distinctive culture that has influenced American cooking, literature, and music (*see panel above*). Today there are about a million Americans of Cajun heritage, most living in southern Louisiana in the 22-parish area officially known as Acadia.

JAMBALAYA
Louisiana Cajuns took the Spanish rice-and-ham dish known as *paella*—brought to the region by Spanish settlers—and turned it into jambalaya by adding shrimp or crawfish.

First migration	1890s
Migrated from	**Armenia**
Approx. number in USA	**1 million (2005)**
Settlement	**California; Detroit, Michigan; Massachusetts**

ANATOLIA
Pictured above is a 10th-century church in eastern Anatolia, part of the historic homeland of the Armenian people. Over the next century, the area came under the domination of the Seljuk Turkish Empire.

Armenians

Many historians consider the fate of the Armenians during World War I to be the first European genocide of the 20th century. While the Turkish persecution of the Armenians remains controversial, it led to an influx of up to 100,000 Armenians to America. Today, about half of the nation's million or so Armenian-Americans live in California.

Armenia was the first nation to adopt Christianity as a state religion, in about 300CE. In the 16th century, Western Armenia became part of the Turkish Ottoman Empire, and known as Anatolia. For several centuries, the Armenians in Anatolia lived relatively peacefully with their Turkish and Kurdish neighbors. The mid-1890s, however, saw repeated attacks on Armenian communities by Turks and Kurds, and, in

ARMENIAN ORPHANS
In 1918, the part of Armenia in Russian territory declared independence; two years later, Soviet and Turkish forces invaded the region, causing yet more suffering for Armenians. Here, children—many orphaned in recent fighting—await rations from a relief agency in the town of Marash in 1920.

SAFETY ON SHIP
Armenians clamber aboard a French warship off the coast of Syria in this photo from October 1915. They were probably survivors of the brutal forced deportation from their Anatolian homeland.

1896, thousands of Armenians were killed in Istanbul after Armenian activists seized the Ottoman Bank. The number of Armenians killed in the 1894–96 disturbances—and the level of Ottoman government involvement—are still debated, but the deaths may have run into the hundreds of thousands.

THE HORRORS OF 1915

In 1914, Turkey entered World War I on the side of Germany and Austria against the Allies, and conscripted all Armenian men into the army or into labor units; many of them died of mistreatment or were executed. Then, in 1915, the Turkish government ordered the deportation of the entire Armenian population of Anatolia, who were forced to set out on foot through the desert for the Ottoman provinces of Syria and Mesopotamia (modern Iraq). Hundreds of thousands died of thirst, starvation, exposure, and disease, or from attacks by Turkish and Kurdish mobs. Others were massacred by the Turks while resisting deportation. Death estimates range to 1.5 million.

ARMENIANS IN AMERICA

The disturbances of the 1890s sparked the first wave of Armenian refugee immigration; between 10,000 and 15,000 arrived by 1900. Another 70,000–100,000 immigrated after 1915, before the 1924 immigration

NEAR EAST RELIEF
In September 1915 organizations in America banded together to form the American Committee for Relief in the Near East, later chartered by Congress as Near East Relief. Over the next 15 years, they raised more than $110 million in aid for both the survivors of the genocide and the victims of ongoing unrest in the region.

WEAVING FOR RELIEF
In this 1919 photo, Armenian-Americans in Chicago present a public display of rug weaving—a traditional Armenian craft—to raise funds for food shipments to their homeland.

restrictions. Many immigrants settled in New England, particularly in Worcester, Massachusetts, and the greater Boston area. The Armenians found work in mills and factories, and they brought with them entrepreneurship and fine craftwork (*see panel, below*). Others went to work in the car plants of Detroit, while Armenian farmers helped turn California's San Fernando Valley into an agricultural powerhouse.

Post-World War II Armenian immigrants came mostly from Eastern Armenia, which became part of the Soviet Union in 1922. Some were admitted as Displaced Persons; another 14,000 came after the USSR eased restrictions in the 1970s.

CYMBAL SUCCESS

The Zildjian family has been making cymbals since 1623, when the Ottoman Sultan conveyed the name Zildjian (Armenian for "cymbalsmith") on Avedis I, the dynasty's patriarch. The first Zildjian to arrive in America came in 1909; 20 years later, the firm moved from Turkey to Norwell, Massachusetts, with Avedis Zildjian III as its head. The rising popularity of jazz gave the cymbal a new significance, and ever since, Zildjian cymbals have been the instrument of choice for drummers and percussionists.

Russian Jews

Anti-Semitism has been an ugly reality in Europe from the time the Roman Empire adopted Christianity in the 4th century CE. For a millennium and a half, Jews were always segregated, usually discriminated against in law and custom, and occasionally massacred by their Christian neighbors. By the 19th century, Jews had gained a degree of tolerance in some countries, but, in the last decades of the century, a deadly resurgence of violent anti-Semitism began in the Russian Empire, sparking mass immigration to America.

First migration	**1881**
Migrated from	**Russia**
Approx. number in USA	**2 million (1920s)**
Settlement	**New York City; Los Angeles and San Francisco, California; Chicago, Illinois; Boston, Massachusetts; Philadelphia, Pennsylvania; Miami, Florida; Atlanta, Georgia**

The word pogrom literally means "riot" in Russian. Commonly, the term describes the semi-official persecution of Jews in the Russian Empire that began in the early 1880s and continued until the fall of the Czarist government in 1917, and even afterward.

The pogroms fed on the long-standing antipathy many Russian Orthodox Christians felt toward a people whom they believed to be responsible for the murder of Jesus Christ. (To be fair, the same attitude was shared by other Christian groups: the Roman Catholic Church did not officially repudiate the doctrine of Jewish guilt until 1965.)

In addition, pernicious folktales helped create the atmosphere that led to the pogroms. Many Russians believed in the infamous Blood Libel, which held that Jews kidnapped and sacrificed Christian children in their rituals. These beliefs were stimulated by a rise in anti-Semitic propaganda in the 1870s, including faked accounts of Jewish leaders plotting to subjugate Christians and rule the world. These writings were the precursors of the notorious *Protocols of the Elders of Zion*, a forgery that continues to inflame anti-Semitism around the world a century after its 1905 publication.

Finally, the pogroms took place because there was no government counterbalance to anti-Semitic activity. While Czars Alexander III and Nicholas II never officially condoned the pogroms, they stayed silent.

The episode that galvanized the first wave of pogroms was the assassination of Czar Alexander II in 1881. Although only one of the assassin's associates was Jewish, the idea that Alexander II was the victim of a Jewish conspiracy inflamed anti-Semitism in the Pale of Settlement—the area in which most of Russia's Jews had been segregated since the 1790s (*see pp 80–83*). In more than 200 communities in the Pale, especially in

PROSKUROV POGROM
Victims and survivors of the February 1919 pogrom against the Jews of Proskurov, Ukraine, during the civil war that followed the Russian Revolution. Some 1,500 Jews were murdered.

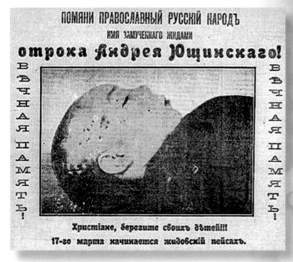

ANTI-SEMITIC PROPAGANDA
During the Beilis trial *(see opposite)*, these anti-Semitic fliers (typical anti-Semitic propaganda) were distributed in Kiev warning non-Jewish parents to watch over their children during the Passover holiday.

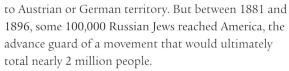

RUSSIAN COSSACKS
A people who lived north of the Black and Caspian seas, the Cossacks received a certain amount of autonomy from the Czarist government in return for military service.

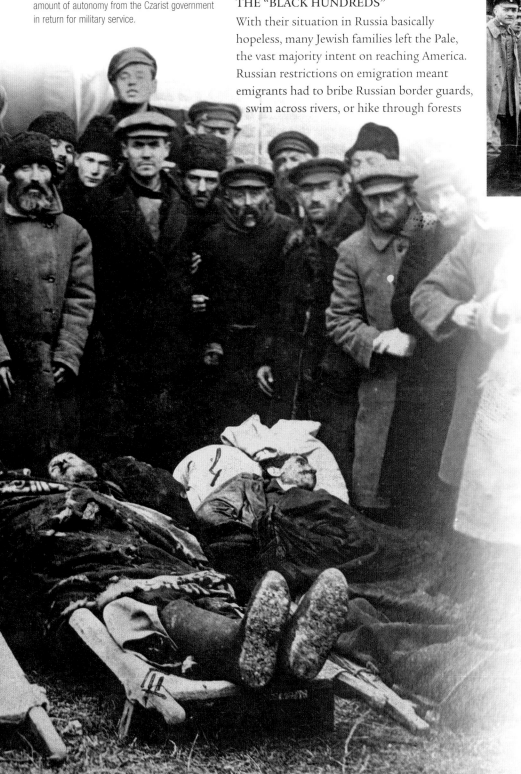

the Ukraine and Crimea, Christians attacked their Jewish neighbors with murder, rape, arson, and looting. Many of the attackers were Cossacks, members of a warlike people loyal to the new czar, Alexander III, a reactionary devoted to "Autocracy, Orthodoxy, and [Russian] Nationalism." In May 1882, Alexander proclaimed the "Temporary Edicts," also known as the "May Laws," which barred Jews from education and politics and greatly restricted Jewish freedom of movement and business activities.

THE "BLACK HUNDREDS"

With their situation in Russia basically hopeless, many Jewish families left the Pale, the vast majority intent on reaching America. Russian restrictions on emigration meant emigrants had to bribe Russian border guards, swim across rivers, or hike through forests

to Austrian or German territory. But between 1881 and 1896, some 100,000 Russian Jews reached America, the advance guard of a movement that would ultimately total nearly 2 million people.

In April 1903, in Kishinev, Bessarabia (now Chisinau, Moldova), a Christian boy was found murdered. The real culprit was a relative, but in an episode that caught the attention of the world, local people killed around 50 Jews, wounded hundreds more, and drove thousands from their homes. Soldiers and police stood by as the attacks happened. This episode, and another that ocurred in the same town two years later, futher spurred Jewish emigration. To

TEMPORARY SAFETY
Jewish refugees in a Russian town around 1912. The previous year, a Jew named Mendel Beilis had been put on trial for murdering a Christian boy, further inflaming anti-Semitic feeling across Russia; international protests led to the charges being dropped in 1913.

many, getting to America now seemed a matter of life and death. The aftermath of Kishinev saw the rise of the "Black Hundreds," paramilitary legions of peasants, nobles, Orthodox clergy, and other anti-Semites who made life intolerable for Jews.

The Bolshevik Revolution of 1917 (*see pp 120–121*) did not end the suffering of Russia's Jews. Many of them had supported the Bolsheviks, so when anti-Bolshevik forces seized Jewish communities, they often slaughtered all the inhabitants.

THE NEW JERUSALEM?
To some Americans, the influx of Jewish immigrants from the Russian Empire was an unwelcome development. In this political cartoon from the 1890s, a stream of Jewish immigrants arrives in New York City, while native-born New Yorkers move out.

Holocaust Jews

With the establishment of Adolph Hitler's Nazi regime in Germany in 1933, a chain of events were set into motion that would culminate in the Holocaust—a term that comes from the Hebrew for "burnt offering." Up to 6 million Jews died during the Holocaust—an almost incomprehensible tragedy that remains, by any standard, the low point of Western civilization. More than 60 years after the end of the Holocaust, people still debate whether the United States could have saved more of its victims by liberalizing immigration policies.

First migration	**1938**
Migrated from	**The Greater German Reich**
Approx. number in USA	**300,000 (1940s)**
Settlement	**New York City, Miami, Los Angeles, Philadelphia, Chicago, San Francisco, Boston, Washington, D.C.**

Born in Linz, Austria, in 1889, Adolph Hitler lived as a failed artist on the streets and in homeless shelters in Vienna until World War I, when he joined the Bavarian Army, serving with distinction. After Germany's defeat, he became an activist in the German National Socialist Peoples Party (NASDP)—the Nazis.

As in Russia, (*see pp 198–199*) anti-Semitism in Germany had ancient religious and cultural roots, but the Nazis took anti-Jewish sentiment to a new level. Nazi ideology drew on the pseudoscience of eugenics to label the Jews as "subhumans," racially inferior to "Aryan" peoples like the Germans. The Nazis also denounced Jewish influence in the post-World War I Weimar Republic government in Germany, and they took advantage of the fact that Jewish activists were prominent in left-wing movements across Europe to condemn "Jewish Bolshevism." Finally, the Nazis attacked the Jews as a rootless, cosmopolitan people who stood outside Germany's traditional *Kultur*.

As early as 1924, in his autobiography *Mein Kampf* (My Struggle), written while in prison for leading a failed coup against the German government, Hitler advocated the ruthless suppression of the Jews. Few Western leaders took notice; Hitler and his small group of followers did not seem

like much of a threat. The worldwide economic depression that began in 1929 hit Germany hard, however, and to many Germans, the Nazis seemed to offer a road to recovery. In 1932, they won nearly 40 percent of the popular vote in elections for Germany's parliament, the Reichstag. Hitler became chancellor in 1933, and through a combination of force, legal trickery, and the democratic process he seized absolute power as *Führer* (leader), sweeping away the last vestiges of democracy in Germany.

THE NUREMBERG LAWS AND *KRISTALLNACHT*

The Nazis wasted little time in establishing their anti-Semitic ideology as official policy. In 1935, the Reichstag passed the Nuremberg Laws, which deprived German Jews of their citizenship and forbade them from government employment, education, and most professions, while Nazi activists—with the approval of the party leadership—led boycotts of Jewish businesses and violently harassed Jews. Three years later came *Kristallnacht* (The Night of Broken Glass). In October 1938, the German

THE *FÜHRER*
Adolph Hitler leads a procession of Nazi officers and officials at the 1938 party conference at Nuremberg. Hitler's virulent anti-Semitism was evident in speeches and writings from as early as 1920, when the Nazis were a tiny group; few people outside Germany, however, took his rabid ideology seriously until it was too late.

MEIN KAMPF
U.S. Army General George S. Patton presented this "deluxe edition" of Hitler's autobiography to the Huntington Library in San Marino, California, after his troops captured it in 1945.

government forcibly deported 17,000 Jews to Poland. When a German Jew in Paris shot a German diplomat in retaliation, the Nazis launched a preplanned attack on the Jews. Mobs raided virtually every synagogue in Germany; thousands of Jewish homes and businesses were looted or destroyed; and 30,000 Jews were shipped to the new concentration camps, like Dachau in Southern Germany. Perhaps 200,000 Jewish refugees managed to flee abroad after *Kristallnacht*—but many were unwelcome anywhere, including America.

In September 1939, Germany invaded Poland, beginning World War II. The conflict brought millions of Jews across Europe under Nazi rule, from the Baltic States to Greece (*see map at right*). In June 1941 Germany invaded its erstwhile ally, the Soviet Union; as the German army advanced, *Einsatzgruppen* (special units), of a total of 3,000 men, followed in its wake, executing tens of thousands of Jews, sometimes with the help of local people.

THE GREATER GERMAN REICH

The Nazi empire included countries absorbed before the war, countries allied with or controlled by Germany, occupied nations of Western Europe, and vast areas of Eastern Europe. The Nazis set up around 15,000 concentration camps; most of the deaths of the Holocaust took place in about 40 main camps.

The Greater German Reich 1942

Greater German Reich
Areas occupied by Germany and Finland
Italy and areas occupied by Italy
Axis satellites
Allied territories
neutral states

Organization of persecution
▽ concentration camp
◈ extermination camp
■ site of mass killing
✪ ghetto
800 number of Jews killed

THE "FINAL SOLUTION"

In November 1942, Nazi leaders met in the Berlin suburb of Wannsee, where they officially endorsed the *Endlösung der Judenfrage*—the "Final Solution"—the deliberate extermination of the Jewish people. Most of the Jews in the territory conquered by Germany had already been herded into urban ghettos. Now they were shipped to a network of concentration camps (*see map above*). The strongest were worked to death in the service of the German Reich. The rest were slaughtered immediately in gas chambers—their remains cremated in massive ovens— in camps like the huge Auschwitz-Birkenau compound in Poland, where at least 1 million people died in 1942–44.

The Jews were not the only victims. The camps also claimed several million others whom the Nazis considered *untermenschen* (subhuman), including Romany (Gypsy) people, homosexuals and other "social deviants," Poles, and Russians, as well as dissidents and resistance fighters from all of the German-occupied nations and territories.

KRISTALLNACHT

Far right: Firefighters put out a fire set by Nazis on November 9, 1938, at Berlin's largest synagogue.
Near right: A Nazi decree of September 1941 forced all Jews in Germany and its occupied territories to wear a yellow star, labeled with the word *Jude* (Jew), on their outer clothing.

THE NUREMBERG RALLY
From 1933 through 1938, Germany's Nazi Party held a huge annual meeting in the Bavarian city of Nuremberg; here, German troops listen to a speech by Hitler at the 1936 rally. Following Nazi Germany's defeat in World War II, the same city was the scene of the war-crimes trial that condemned 11 leading Nazis to death.

THE "FINAL SOLUTION"

Poised at the edge of a mass grave, a Ukrainian Jew awaits a bullet in the head from a member of a German *Einsatzgruppe*. The Nazis started using gas when shooting proved inefficient.

By the time Germany surrendered in May 1945, between 5 and 6 million Jews were dead—about two-thirds of Europe's Jewish population, and over a third of all the Jews in the world.

AMERICAN RESPONSE

Jews hoping to escape by immigrating to America were mostly disappointed. The 1924 law set the quota for German immigrants at 25,000 per year, and despite efforts by American Jewish organizations, the government refused to make exceptions. This was partly because in an America mired in the Great Depression, public opinion was largely

BUCHENWALD SURVIVORS

Emaciated survivors of the Buchenwald concentration camp after their liberation by U.S. troops in April 1945. One of the men in the photo is future Nobel Prize-winning author Elie Wiesel.

"30,000 Jews were sent to concentration camps. For frightened Jews all across Europe, there was only one escape—immigration."

"The Earth is the Lord's"

VOYAGE OF THE *ST. LOUIS*

Nothing sums up the plight of Europe's Jewish refugees in the run-up to World War II better than the 1939 voyage of the Hamburg-Amerika Line steamship *St. Louis*. The liner sailed from Germany to Cuba in May of that year; all but a handful of its 937 passengers were Jews who had bought permits from the Cuban government that would allow them to land and await eventual admission to the United States. When the *St. Louis* arrived in Havana, however, the Cuban government refused to honor all but a handful of the landing permits. Pressure from the U.S. government would have certainly forced Cuba to reverse its decision, but the State Department refused to get involved, and when the *St. Louis* attempted to enter American waters, the U.S. Coast Guard turned the ship away. The *St. Louis* eventually docked in Antwerp, Belgium, in June. Jewish relief agencies managed to broker a deal in which Britain accepted 287 of the 900 or so Jews as refugees; France, Belgium, and the Netherlands took the rest in roughly equal numbers. Unfortunately, Germany overran the latter three nations during World War II, and it is estimated that as many as half the *St. Louis*'s passengers perished in the Holocaust.

against increased immigration of any kind, but it was also because of anti-Semitism in the government. In July 1938, the only two countries in a position to accept large numbers of refugees—the United States and Great Britain, which governed Palestine—still refused to do so. In 1940, a bill authorizing the admission of 20,000 Jewish refugee children did not pass Congress.

In the summer of 1942, the U.S. State Department received reliable reports of the Nazis' plan for a "Final Solution." Many Americans, however, believed that the reports were exaggerated: the idea that the Nazis would attempt to exterminate an entire people seemed incomprehensible. Others sounded the alarm, including journalist Edward R. Murrow, who broadcast in December 1943: "Millions of human beings, most of them Jews, are being gathered up with ruthless efficiency and murdered . . ."

"THE TEST OF CIVILIZATION"

In 1943–44, escapees from the ghettos and death camps confirmed Murrow's story. In January 1944, Secretary of the Treasury Henry Morgenthau, Jr., submitted a paper titled "Report On the Acquiescence of This

D'VORAH SPIRA

D'vorah Spira, a Polish Jew, fled with her family when the Nazis arrived. After the Holocaust she immigrated to America and joined the Hasidic community in Brooklyn.

"We were Polish patriots. We were there for thousands of years and it was our country. We felt that as long as we could live there and have bread on our table, we would continue with the way of our living. We still hoped. You know, people live on hope. However, as soon as the Nazis came in, we knew that we were finished. They were so organized. I escaped to Hungary. The Hungarian government would grant asylum for non-Jewish Poles, so we lived as Polish gentiles. I learned the Hail Mary because sometimes they tested if you were Jewish or not. But they didn't ask me. I was blond, I had long braids, and I looked very Polish. One of my sisters and my youngest two brothers survived. The rest perished. My five brothers and sisters, my father, mother, and my two grandfathers were killed. My brother was 22 years old and he went to Auschwitz. He was strong, he was young, and he did not survive.

"[My two brothers] were very underdeveloped from growing up in the war and needed a lot of medical attention. The great doctors, and the only medical attention that could help them, were in America. So the first anniversary of the finish of the war we arrived in America, the 8th of May, 1946. I had a very favorable opinion of America, aside from its politics. The American knows tolerance and knows that other people have a right to live. They were charitable, they were giving, it's a land of opportunity, and you could be whoever you are. I didn't want to lose the faith and the tradition of our people and I felt that we would have every opportunity here. It's land of liberty. There's still no country to compare to America."

NEVER FORGET . . . NEVER AGAIN
This memorial to the Jews of Berlin who perished in the Holocaust stands on the site of the city's oldest Jewish cemetary, which was deliberately desecrated by the Nazi regime in 1942. In America, the United States Holocaust Memorial Museum in Washington, D.C., which opened in 1993, preserves the memory of this horrible chapter in history.

THE LUCKY FEW
Jewish refugees disembark from the U.S. Army transport *Henry Gibbins* at Hoboken, New Jersey, on August 4, 1944, en route to a facility in Fort Ontario, New York. Journalist I. F. Stone called the admission of a mere 1,000 refugees "a kind of token payment to decency . . ."

Government in the Murder of the Jews" to President Franklin Roosevelt. In response, Roosevelt signed an executive order to establish the War Refugees Board, which saved about 200,000 Jews by removing them from Nazi-held areas and by creating safe havens.

Sixty years after the full horror of the Holocaust became known, most historians believe that the American response was at best inadequate and at worst indifferent. In 1979, Vice President Walter Mondale stated that the Western nations, including America, had "failed the test of civilization." Despite the difficulties, however, about 85,000 Jewish refugees made it to America in the late 1930s, and during the war a few thousand escaped to neutral countries, from which they came to America. After the war, about 85,000 Holocaust survivors were admitted to the United States under Displaced Person legislation.

THE MANHATTAN PROJECT

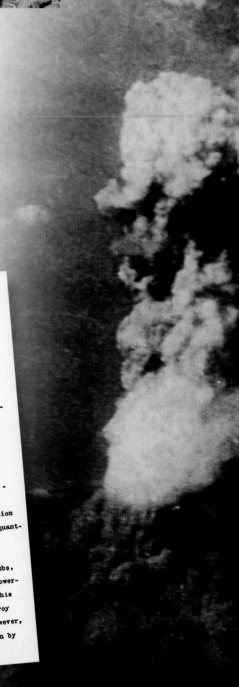

The rise of Fascism in Italy and Nazism in Germany led to a "brain drain" from Europe in the 1930s, as scientists—many of them Jews—immigrated to the United States to take up posts at American laboratories and universities. Many of these scientists participated in the Manhattan Project—the effort to create an American atomic bomb.

A VISIT TO EINSTEIN

On a muggy day in August 1939, Eugene Wigner and Leo Szilard drove out from New York City to Long Island. Wigner and Szilard were both physicists and both Hungarian Jews who had left German universities after the Nazis rose to power. The old friend they were visiting was another refugee from Nazism, and the most famous scientist in the world—Albert Einstein.

Wigner and Szilard told Einstein that along with another Hungarian-Jewish refugee scientist, Edward Teller, they had received disturbing news from colleagues still in Europe: Germany had halted exports of uranium from Czechoslovakia, which it had occupied the year before. To the refugee scientists, the news was evidence that Germany was stepping up its efforts to produce a fantastically destructive device—an atomic bomb.

The idea of such a terrible weapon in the hands of the Nazis was unthinkable to Szilard, Wigner, Teller, and other refugee scientists who had experienced Nazism firsthand. Wigner and Szilard convinced Einstein to leverage his fame by signing a letter to President Franklin Roosevelt warning that "extremely powerful bombs of a new type . . . may be constructed" by Germany. (In fact, the German atomic program never made serious progress.)

The president responded by authorizing a small research program in 1940. In September 1942, with the United States now in World War II, the program expanded into a massive effort to

build an American atomic weapon, an enterprise code-named the Manhattan Project and directed by General Leslie Groves and scientist J. Robert Oppenheimer. In December of that year, another refugee scientist, Enrico Fermi—an Italian physicist with a Jewish wife—oversaw the world's first nuclear chain reaction at the University of Chicago. That event confirmed that it was possible to release huge quantities of energy through a process known as atomic fission.

LOS ALAMOS
A contemporary view of the Los Alamos National Laboratory. More than 60 years after its founding during the Manhattan Project, Los Alamos remains one of the nation's foremost centers for scientific research.

THE LETTER
Einstein *(left)* was a pacifist, and he remained ambivalent about the role he played in the creation of the atomic bomb for the rest of his life—saying, for example, "Since I do not foresee that atomic energy is to be a great boon for a long time, I have to say that for the present it is a menace. Perhaps it is well that it should be. It may intimidate the human race into bringing order into its international affairs . . ."

Albert Einstein
Old Grove Rd.
Nassau Point
Peconic, Long Island

August 2nd, 1939

F.D. Roosevelt,
President of the United States,
White House
Washington, D.C.

Sir:

Some recent work by E.Fermi and L. Szilard, which has been communicated to me in manuscript, leads me to expect that the element uranium may be turned into a new and important source of energy in the immediate future. Certain aspects of the situation which has arisen seem to call for watchfulness and, if necessary, quick action on the part of the Administration. I believe therefore that it is my duty to bring to your attention the following facts and recommendations:

In the course of the last four months it has been made probable - through the work of Joliot in France as well as Fermi and Szilard in America - that it may become possible to set up a nuclear chain reaction in a large mass of uranium,by which vast amounts of power and large quantities of new radium-like elements would be generated. Now it appears almost certain that this could be achieved in the immediate future.

This new phenomenon would also lead to the construction of bombs, and it is conceivable - though much less certain - that extremely powerful bombs of a new type may thus be constructed. A single bomb of this type, carried by boat and exploded in a port, might very well destroy the whole port together with some of the surrounding territory. However, such bombs might very well prove to be too heavy for transportation by air.

A FLASH IN THE DESERT

The Manhattan Project's greatest physical challenge was creating enough fissionable material from uranium to make bombs. To save time, the project's scientists, engineers, and technicians simultaneously pursued two different techniques for producing these elements—electromagnetic separation and gaseous diffusion—at two separate facilities, one at Hanford, Washington, and one at Oak Ridge, Tennessee. Constructing and maintaining both facilities was a massive undertaking; ultimately, the Manhattan Project would employ 125,000 people, involve over 30 research sites, and run through a $2 billion budget. And it all had to be kept secret.

Secrecy was the reason that a former boys' boarding school at remote Los Alamos, New

SCIENTIST AND GENERAL
J. Robert Oppenheimer and General Leslie Groves at the Alamogordo test site after the first nuclear blast. Watching the awesome explosion, Oppenheimer thought of words from a Hindu scripture, the *Bhagavad-Gita*: "Now I am become death, the destroyer of worlds." Groves was just happy to see that it worked.

HIROSHIMA
The distinctive "mushroom cloud" of an atomic detonation rises 30,000 feet into the air over Hiroshima at 8:16 a.m., August 6, 1945. The copilot of the B-29 bomber *Enola Gay*, which delivered the bomb, wrote in his logbook at the sight: "My God, what have we done?"

TRINITY TEST SITE
Scientists watch as the world's first atomic bomb is hoisted into place at the test site near Alamogordo. The explosion vaporized the entire 100-foot tower except for small pieces of concrete and steel at its base.

Mexico, was chosen as the project's scientific headquarters in 1943. Over the next two years, hundreds of American, British, Canadian, and European scientists moved to Los Alamos to work on the bomb, including several who had earlier fled Nazi Germany and Fascist Italy for America, including German-born Hans Bethe and James Franck and Italian-born Emilio Segrè.

At 5:30 a.m. on July 16, the world entered the atomic age with the successful test of "Trinity," a bomb equivalent to between 15,000 and 20,000 tons of conventional explosives at nearby Alamogordo, New Mexico. After Germany's surrender in May 1945, Japan was the target for the new weapon. Some of the Los Alamos scientists, led by James Franck, urged the U.S. government to demonstrate the bomb on an unpopulated area, but President Harry Truman authorized the bombing of Japanese cities. On August 6, "Little Boy" was dropped on Hiroshima; "Fat Man" fell on Nagasaki three days later. Together the two blasts killed at least 100,000 people. Japan surrendered on August 14, ending World War II.

Critics believe that the United States had ulterior motives in bombing Japan—especially impressing the Soviet Union. Still, the number of military and civilian deaths in an invasion of Japan would have been far higher than the death toll from the bombs themselves.

ENRICO FERMI
1901–1954

Born in Rome, Enrico Fermi became a professor of physics at the University of Rome in 1927. In 1938, his experiments won him the Nobel Prize for Physics. Rather than return to Mussolini's Italy from the award ceremony in Sweden, Fermi fled with his family to the United States. Fermi was working at the University of Chicago when, on Dec. 2, 1942, he oversaw the first controlled nuclear chain reaction, which proved that an atomic bomb was a practical proposition. News was transmitted to the Manhattan Project's leaders in a coded message: "The Italian navigator has successfully landed in the New World." Fermi became a U.S. citizen in 1944 and later headed the University of Chicago's Institute of Nuclear Studies.

COTTON COLLECTIVE
Farm laborers harvest cotton on a collective farm in the Uzbek Soviet Socialist Republican (now Uzbekistan) in Central Asia in 1979.

Soviets

During the murderous reign of dictator Josef Stalin, who ruled the Soviet Union from about 1929 until 1953, the numbers of Soviet citizens killed and imprisoned rose into the tens of millions. Escape to America was not an option, and in a sad chapter of post-World War II history, the United States actually delivered large numbers of Soviet refugees back to their home country to face an awful fate.

In 1928, Stalin introduced the first "Five-Year Plan," a program aimed at modernizing Soviet industry. To pay for imported machinery and to feed industrial workers, the government forced the nation's peasants off the small plots of land they had gained after the revolution and onto vast collective farms, where most of the harvest was earmarked for export or for redistribution in the cities. Most peasants bitterly resented collectivization, often burning crops and slaughtering livestock rather than turning them over to the government.

In response, Stalin announced the "liquidation of the kulaks as a class." The kulaks (from the Russian word for "tight-fisted") were so-called "rich peasants"

whom Stalin blamed for the resistance to collectivization, although most of these people were not rich but simply slightly more prosperous than their neighbors. In 1930-31, some 1.8 million kulaks were deported to labor settlements in Siberia and other remote regions; at least 500,000 were killed or died en route, and more would die of hunger, exposure, and overwork in the years ahead.

Collectivization resulted in a human tragedy whose death toll certainly approached—and may have exceeded—that of the Holocaust (*see pp 200–205*). In 1932-33, famine swept the Ukraine (then a Soviet republic) and Western Russia as special Communist Party troops seized all the grain they could find,

PLANNED ECONOMY
"With honor, we will fulfill and fulfill again Stalin's new Five Year Plan," reads the caption on this 1946 propaganda postcard. The Soviets were on the 13th plan when the government collapsed in 1990–91.

AGRICULTURAL FACTORY
A *kolkhoz* (collective farm) is photographed in the early 1930s. Stalin envisioned the farms as "grain factories . . . organized on a modern scientific basis"; in fact, Soviet grain production was 67.6 million tons in 1934—against 73.3 million tons in 1928, before collectivization.

RAOUL WALLENBERG
1912–1947

RAOUL WALLENBERG
1912–1947

In July 1944, Raoul Wallenberg arrived in Budapest, Hungary. Scion of one of neutral Sweden's wealthiest families—and a graduate of the University of Michigan—Wallenberg was given a diplomatic post at the Swedish legation, but his real job was to save as many Jews as possible from deportation to the Nazi death camps. With support from the Swedish government and the U.S. War Refugee Board (*see p 205*), Wallenberg issued thousands of Jews with protective passports and set up a network of safe houses. By the time Soviet forces took Budapest, Wallenberg had rescued about 100,000 Jews, at great personal risk. In January 1945, Wallenberg visited Soviet military headquarters, where he was apparently arrested on charges of spying for the United States. Over the next 20 years there were reports that he had been sighted alive in Soviet prisons or labor camps, but it now seems likely he died in Soviet custody in 1947. In 1981, he was made an honorary citizen of the United States—one of only six foreigners to have the honor.

leaving the region's peasants to starve. Historians estimate that between 5 and 7 million people perished during those years. Amazingly, there was little outcry in the West. As with the Holocaust, some refused to believe that state-sponsored murder on such a scale was possible, while a number of left-wing American and European intellectuals chose to ignore reports of widespread starvation, or even defended it as a regrettable but necessary by-product of the Soviet drive to build a "worker's paradise."

In the late 1930s, Stalin consolidated his power by purging many of his old revolutionary colleagues, usually after staged trials for imaginary crimes. The purges accelerated into a period of terror in which at least a million people were executed by the NKVD (the Soviet secret police, headed by Nikolai Yezhov after September 1936) and millions more vanished into the vast network of forced-labor camps known as the Gulag system (which later became notorious as a place for political prisoners and as a mechanism for repressing political opposition to the Soviet state).

FAMINE ORPHAN
This parentless child begs on the streets of Kiev, during the 1922–23 famine.

The reasons for the period of widespread purges, now known as "the Great Terror," are still not completely clear. Some Western historians believe that Stalin created the terror in order to force the population to carry out his intensive modernization program, or to fragment society to preclude dissent, or simply out of brutal paranoia. Whatever the causes, the purges, in the end, weakened the Soviet state rather than strengthened it.

Only a few thousand Soviet citizens managed to immigrate to the United States during the grim 1930s. Yet in order to make it there, they usually had to escape to Western Europe by bribing border guards or otherwise slipping across the frontier. Capture meant death or being sent to the camps.

NO TOMBSTONE UNTURNED
Members of the Soviet Youth League search a graveyard for hidden grain in 1930. The government used troops and members of Communist Party organizations in the drive for collectivization.

FORCED RETURN

Although the Soviet and German governments had secret links since the 1920s, the Nazis and the Soviets were publicly enemies. In August 1939, the two governments stunned the world by signing a nonaggression pact. Secret protocols divided Eastern Europe between the two nations; the Soviets occupied the Baltic states of Estonia, Latvia, and Lithuania and part of Romania, and two weeks after Germany invaded Poland, the USSR invaded Eastern Poland.

Having ignored warnings from Western leaders and his own spies, Stalin was taken by surprise when Germany invaded the Soviet Union in June 1941. The result was a titanic struggle that ended in victory for the Red Army, but at a cost of at least 20 million Soviet lives. Even as the Soviet Union was fighting for its very existence, Stalin found the resources to punish various ethnic minorities whom he suspected of disloyalty. Ethnic Germans from the Volga region, Muslim Chechens and Ingush, and other groups were deported to Central Asia and Siberia. Hundreds of thousands died in the process.

The end of the war left several million Soviet citizens behind British and American lines in Western Europe. Some, captured during the war, had survived horrific conditions in German prisoner-of-war camps.

THE LAST GULAG

The camps of the Gulag (the name is an acronym for the Russian words for "Chief Administration of Corrective Labor Camps") housed about 100,000 prisoners at the end of the 1920s and 5 million, or more, by the mid-1930s. Inadequate rations, overwork, and the harsh climate (many camps were located above the Arctic Circle) led to an average annual death rate of around 10 percent; the usual sentence for political crimes, 30 years, was effectively a death sentence. The actual number of people sent to the camps—and how many died—will probably never be known. Some camps remained in operation after the fall of the Soviet Union—including the Perm-35 camp, shown above.

> "If the opposition (citizen) disarms, well and good. If it refuses to disarm, we shall disarm it ourselves."
>
> Josef Stalin

Others had fought with the German armed forces either as volunteers or conscripts. Stalin demanded that the Western Allies repatriate all the Soviet citizens under their control. In fact, few wished to return to Soviet territory. They knew that Stalin considered all Soviets who had "allowed" themselves to be captured to be traitors, and that they faced execution or imprisonment upon their return. In addition, many of the ex-POWs and displaced persons were Balts, Ukrainians, and members of other groups who had no desire to return to homelands ruled by Moscow.

Ultimately, U.S. and British authorities repatriated some 2 million Soviets, sometimes at gunpoint. Most met the fate they had dreaded. Repatriation reached into the United States: some 5,000 Soviet nationals in American POW camps were shipped back to Europe and into Soviet custody.

In a tragic episode in August 1945, 154 prisoners at Fort Dix, New Jersey, rioted when the time came for repatriation, attempting to fight off guards with table legs and knives and forks. Nine prisoners and three guards were injured; three prisoners committed suicide. Despite national headlines after the riot, the remaining prisoners were sent to the Soviet occupation zone in East Germany. Their fate remains unknown.

Of the Soviet citizens who escaped repatriation in 1945, some were able to immigrate to America as "Displaced Persons," including 20,000 ethnic Russians. In 1952, the Soviet government tightened its already restrictive immigration policies; henceforth, any Soviet citizen who escaped to the West was officially a "non-person," and the family members they left behind were subject to persecution and imprisonment. This harsh policy was implemented until the détente of the 1970s, when a series of treaties eased tensions between the Soviet Union and the United States.

NON-AGGRESSION PACT

Josef Stalin (*third from left*) with Soviet Foreign Minister Vyacheslav Molotov *(right)* and German Foreign Minister Joachim von Ribbentrop *(left)* at the signing of the Soviet-German Non-Aggression Pact, in Moscow, August 23, 1939. Less than two years later the two nations would be locked in a war of annihilation.

YURI ORLOV
1924–

Internationally, the distinguished physicist Yuri Orlov is as celebrated for his human rights activism as he is for his scientific achievements. This was not the case in his native Soviet Union. During his childhood in the 1930s, Orlov witnessed the destruction of his home village by Stalinist collectivization. He was first persecuted for his human-rights activities in 1956, when he was fired from the Moscow Institute of Theoretical and Experimental Physics and sent to the Soviet satellite of Armenia, where he worked on particle acceleration. He eventually returned to Moscow and, in 1976, he founded the Moscow Helsinki Watch Group to monitor Soviet compliance with the Helsinki Accords, signed the year before. As chairman of the group, he was arrested in 1977. Detained incommunicado for 15 months he was finally charged with "anti-Soviet agitation and propaganda." He received the maximum sentence: seven years hard labor and five years internal exile. Although scientists and human-rights activists around the world worked for his release, it was not until 1986 that he was freed from Siberian exile. Stripped of his Soviet citizenship, he was deported to the United States in an exchange for a Soviet spy. As a senior scientist at Cornell University, Orlov continues to promote humanitarian causes and, in 1995, he won the Nicholson Medal for Humanitarian Service.

Vietnamese

The Vietnam War was the longest war in American history, and the most divisive conflict on the home front since the Civil War. In the aftermath of America's long and ultimately futile struggle to keep South Vietnam from communist domination, close to a half-million Vietnamese came to the United States as refugees between 1975 and 1986, making them the second-largest immigrant group during this period.

First migration	**1975**
Migrated from	**Vietnam**
Approx. number in USA	**988,000 (2000)**
Settlement	**California; Texas; Seattle, Washington; Boston, Massachusetts; Washington, D.C.**

Vietnamese history can be seen as a succession of struggles for independence from foreign rule. From 111BCE to 939CE, China ruled what is now Vietnam, although the Vietnamese continually rebelled against their Chinese overlords. From 944CE until the late 18th century, Vietnam was beset by conflict between competing dynasties and occasional periods of Chinese occupation.

In 1802, Vietnam was again united and independent under the Nguyen dynasty, but, in 1858, French forces seized the city of Da Nang. Over the next

HO CHI MINH
The future president of North Vietnam in a photo from around 1945, when his Vietminh guerrillas fought alongside American operatives against Indochina's Japanese occupiers. As a young man, Ho traveled the world as a ship's cook and seaman and is known to have visited New York City and Boston.

SAMPANS
Watercraft on the Huong River near the city of Hue. The capital of the Nguyen dynasty, which ruled much of Vietnam from the 1600s until the French period, Hue was the scene of an epic battle between U.S. Marines and North Vietnamese troops in the 1968 Tet Offensive.

HANOI

Civilians follow Vietminh troops in a suburb of Hanoi in October 1954. The city became the capital of the Democratic Republic of Vietnam, a.k.a. North Vietnam, after the July 1954 Geneva Accords divided Vietnam into two states.

DIEN BIEN PHU

France's troops in Indochina included indigenous forces—like the Vietnamese soldiers photographed here, on patrol near Dien Bien Phu, the French military base near the Laos border, in January 1954—as well as troops from France and the nation's African colonies.

two decades, the French consolidated their hold over Vietnam, and, by the turn of the 20th century, they added Laos and Cambodia to their Indochinese empire. The French developed Indochina's economy, but the Vietnamese resented French domination as they had China's.

When Nazi Germany defeated France in 1940, control of Indochina passed to Japan, Germany's Asian ally. Many Vietnamese resisted the Japanese occupiers in hopes of securing independence following an Allied victory. After Japan's surrender in 1945, however, the French attempted to reassert their rule over Indochina, sparking a conflict that would last for 30 years and claim millions of lives.

THE 10,000 DAY WAR

American military involvement in Vietnam began during World War II, when teams from the Office of Strategic Services (the predecessor to the CIA) supplied weapons and advisers to guerillas fighting the Japanese occupiers. The most prominent guerrillas leader was Ho Chi Minh. Born Nguyen Ai

THE TET OFFENSIVE

The ruins of Cholon, Saigon's Chinese neighborhood, after heavy fighting during the Tet Offensive in 1968. Many members of Vietnam's ethnic Chinese minority fled the country after the final North Vietnamese victory in April 1975; however, Cholon still contains a large portion of Vietnam's Chinese.

Quoc in 1890, Ho claimed to have an independent, democratic Vietnam as his goal, but he was also a Moscow-trained Communist agent who had helped found the Vietnamese Communist Party before World War II.

With the return of French rule, Ho and his followers, the Vietminh, launched an anti-French insurgency that dragged on for eight years. The United States—committed to the containment of communism around the world as the chill of the Cold War set in—supported the French; by the early 1950s, America was picking up 80 percent of the tab for France's war in Vietnam.

In 1954, the Vietminh captured a major French force at its base at Dien Bien Phu. The French government had had enough. The United Nations brokered a deal that called for Vietnam to be divided into two states: the Democratic Republic of Vietnam, ruled by Ho's communists, and U.S.-backed South Vietnam. Elections would be held in 1956 to decide on a unified Vietnamese government.

With American approval, South Vietnam refused to hold the elections. In 1959, a new insurgency began in South Vietnam, with North Vietnamese-backed rebels, the Vietcong, fighting against an increasingly corrupt and repressive South Vietnamese regime.

The United States provided military advisers, weapons, and other aid to South Vietnamese forces, but Vietcong attacks increased. In August 1964, after a mysterious attack on two U.S. warships by North Vietnamese vessels, Congress passed the Gulf of Tonkin Resolution, which gave President Lyndon Johnson the power to wage an undeclared war in Vietnam. Soon afterward, the United States began a

bombing campaign against North Vietnam that would last seven years. In April 1965, the first regular U.S. troops landed in South Vietnam. By 1969 there were over 500,000 U.S. military personnel in the country.

For the U.S. military, Vietnam was a frustrating conflict. American forces had mobility and firepower on their side, but their commanders chose to fight a guerrilla war with conventional tactics, including large-scale "search and destroy" missions that proved ineffective against an elusive enemy.

In February 1968, the North Vietnamese and Vietcong launched a countrywide offensive during Tet, the Vietnamese New Year holiday. In military terms, the Tet Offensive was a communist defeat. In public-relations terms, however, Tet was a communist victory; it showed that America was fighting a war it could not win, and it fueled growing antiwar sentiment at home.

President Johnson's successor, Richard Nixon, introduced a policy of "Vietnamization"—the gradual withdrawal of U.S. forces, while turning the war effort

OUT OF THE RUNNING
Lyndon Johnson's presidency was partly a casualty of the Vietnam War; in March 1968, after the Tet Offensive, he surprised the nation by announcing he would not run for re-election.

THE FALL OF SAIGON
A North Vietnamese tank smashes through a gate in Saigon as the city falls in April 1975. Aircraft brought a few thousand of America's South Vietnamese allies to safety aboard ships offshore; thousands more were abandoned to a harsh fate.

over to the South Vietnamese. In 1973, the Paris Peace Accords led to the full withdrawal of U.S. forces. By then, over 58,000 Americans had died in Vietnam.

The accords did not bring peace. The North Vietnamese invaded the South in 1974; in April 1975, they captured the South Vietnamese capital, Saigon, and united the country under communist rule.

THE BOAT PEOPLE

Perhaps 10 million South Vietnamese became refugees during and after the final North Vietnamese offensives. Many were members of the South Vietnamese armed forces and their families, or officials of the South Vietnamese government. All feared retribution from the new communist regime for having cooperated with the Americans. Others were members of Vietnam's ethnic Chinese minority; mainly merchants or owners of small businesses, the Chinese feared repression under Vietnam's new rulers. (The Chinese gained

OPERATION BABYLIFT

During the war, U.S. servicemen fathered many children with Vietnamese women—estimates range from 15,000 to 400,000. (In addition, hundreds of thousands of other Vietnamese children had been orphaned by the war.) As the North Vietnamese closed in on Saigon there was much concern in the United States over their fate. In the spring of 1975, the United States began "Operation Babylift," an effort to bring as many of these children as possible to America and other countries, chiefly Australia and Canada. Military and civilian aircraft brought between 2,000 and 3,000 children out of South Vietnam before its conquest by North Vietnam. (Tragically, the first Babylift aircraft crashed on takeoff, killing more than 300 children, half of them infants.) In 1987, Congress passed the Amerasian Homecoming Act, which authorized further resettlement of the offspring of Americans in Vietnam; the legislation brought another 75,000 Vietnamese to the United States.

another impetus to immigrate after Vietnam and China went to war in 1979.) Still others were Catholics or Buddhists fearing persecution under the officially atheist government. All fears were justified. After the fall of Saigon (renamed Ho Chi Minh City, after the North Vietnamese ruler, who had died in 1969), the new government imprisoned about 1 million South Vietnamese in "re-education camps." Many spent years in brutal conditions, and thousands were executed.

In response, about 1.1 million South Vietnamese fled the country after 1975. Getting out, however, was not easy. Vietnam is located on a peninsula, and the nations on its border, Laos and Cambodia (*see pp 216–219*), were now also under communist rule, so most refugees had no choice but to set out aboard rickety, overcrowded boats by way of the South China Sea or the Gulf of Thailand. The lucky ones reached Thailand, Malaysia, Hong Kong, and Indonesia, then wound up languishing for years in refugee camps.

BOAT PEOPLE
Having been driven out of Malaysian waters, a boatload of Vietnamese refugees seeks sanctuary in Indonesia's Anambas Islands in this photograph from August 1979.

VIETNAMESE IN AMERICA

Some Vietnamese refugees were resettled in Australia, Canada, and Europe, but for most, the destination was America. After the fall of Saigon, the U.S. government authorized the admission of 130,000 Vietnamese. When the plight of the boat people attracted worldwide attention in the late 1970s, President Jimmy Carter used executive authority to raise the number of Vietnamese accepted from refugee camps to 14,000 a month. Although people continued to flee Vietnam into the mid-1990s, nearly all later boat people have been regarded as economic, not political, refugees.

Because many Vietnamese refugees were military officers, government officials, and businesspeople, many have prospered in the United States.

LEARNING THE ROPES
A bilingual volunteer gives recently arrived Vietnamese immigrants a tour of a supermarket in a Washington, D.C. suburb in the early 1990s as part of an outreach program. About 40 percent of Vietnamese immigrants chose to make California their home, and more than 100,000 settled in Texas; today, these two states account for more than half of the United States' Vietnamese-born population, which numbers about 1 million in total.

Laotians and Cambodians

First migration	1975
Migrated from	**Laos; Cambodia**
Approx number in USA	**341,000 (2000)**
Settlement	**California; Massachusetts**

The war in Vietnam was part of a larger conflict against communist influence in Southeast Asia—a conflict that involved Laos and Cambodia, the nations on Vietnam's western border that were also once part of French Indochina. As with Vietnam, these nations fell under communist rule in 1975, precipitating a wave of refugees to the United States; in Cambodia, the communist takeover led to death and suffering on a monumental scale.

Most of present-day Laos was ruled by Siam (now Thailand) until the French added the landlocked territory to its Indochinese empire at the turn of the 20th century. France gave Laos partial independence in 1949 and full independence in 1953. The same 1954 agreement that divided Vietnam into two states recognized the communist Pathet Lao movement as the government in Laos's northern region, with the Royal Laotian Government (RLG) ruling the rest of the country. After an attempt at coalition government, civil war broke out between the Pathet Lao and the RLG in the late 1950s, and the United States sent aid and advisers to help the latter. In 1961, a 14-nation conference in Geneva led to a cease-fire, but by 1963 the Pathet Lao, bolstered by supplies and troops from North Vietnam, controlled most of the north and east of Laos.

Laos's geographical position made it inevitable that the country would be drawn into the conflict in Vietnam. The nation's mountainous eastern region sheltered the Ho Chi Minh Trail—the route used by the North Vietnamese to infiltrate troops and supplies into South Vietnam. After America stepped up its presence in Vietnam, the U.S. Air Force began bombing the trail, while the U.S. military and CIA recruited Laotians—many of them ethnic minorities like the Hmong (*see pp 220-221*)—to fight the communists.

In May 1975, after the fall of Saigon, the Pathet Lao captured the capital, Vientiane, although anticommunist guerrillas continued fighting in parts of the country for several years. Motivated by the same fears that led South Vietnamese refugees to take to the

SUPPLY LINE
Porters tote supplies across a rope bridge along the Ho Chi Minh Trail in this undated photo by North Vietnamese photographer Trong Thanh. The Ho Chi Minh Trail was actually a network of trails running 1,200 miles from North Vietnam through Laos and Cambodia and into South Vietnam.

ANGKOR WAT
King Suryavarman II of the Khmers, a dynasty that once ruled much of Southeast Asia, built the magnificent temple complex at Angkor Wat in Northwest Cambodia in the 12th century.

REFUGEE CHILDREN
Laotian children line up for the daily milk ration at Nong Khai Refugee Camp in Thailand, one of 21 refugee facilities set up along the Laos-Thailand border in the late 1970s and early 1980s.

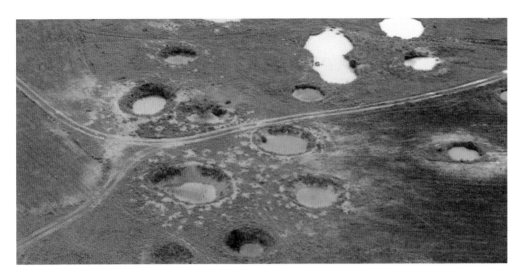

THE LEGACY OF CONFLICT
Bomb craters still dot the landscape of Laos. U.S. aircraft dropped about a million cluster bombs on Laos during the Vietnam War. These bombs released smaller bomblets, a third of which failed to explode initially, and more than 10,000 people have been killed or injured in accidental detonations.

ASSISTANCE PROGRAMS
Many Laotian and Cambodian refugees had never seen a motor vehicle or used an electrical appliance before reaching America. In this photograph, Laotians in Marin County, California, receive instruction in how to use an American bathroom.

sea, hundreds of thousands of Laotians crossed the Mekong River to refugee camps in Thailand over the next decade. From there, about 200,000 were resettled in the United States.

LAOTIANS IN AMERICA

In the late 1970s, the U.S. government began to accept large numbers of Laotians, employing nongovernmental voluntary agencies to find homes and American sponsors for the newcomers. Of these sponsors, 60 percent were families, 25 percent were churches and other organized groups, and the rest were individuals. A second wave of refugees relied heavily on relatives already in America who could be sponsors.

While many Vietnamese refugees were skilled, urban, and educated people, the Laotian refugees were mostly rural people from a society that was still largely agrarian and premodern, making life in America a difficult adjustment for some. In 1982 and 1986, the U.S. government set up assistance programs to provide education and job placement and otherwise help the Laotians make the transition to American society. Laotians frequently work in hazardous, low-income jobs, and 44 percent of the working population is employed in the low-skilled job sector as operators, fabricators, and laborers. One third of all Laotians in the United States live in poverty and receive public-assistance income.

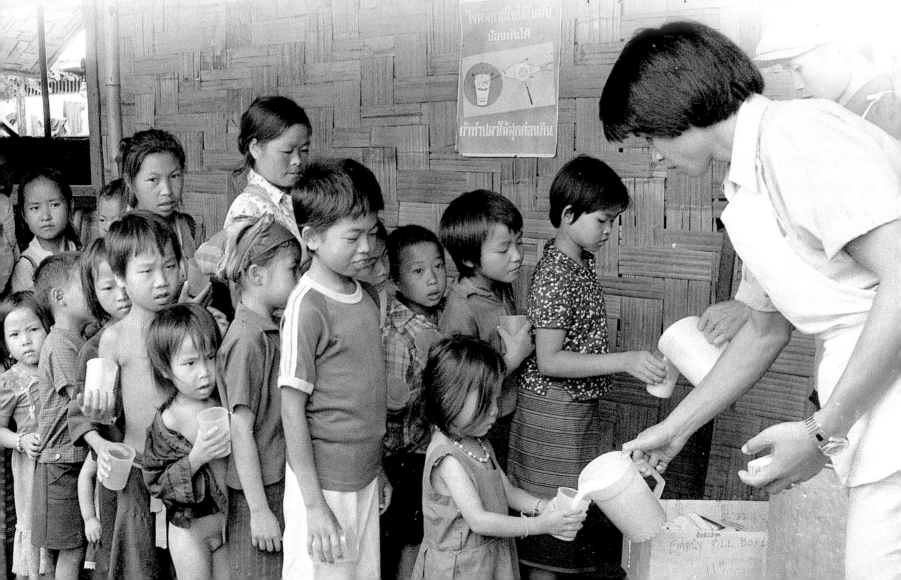

CAMBODIANS

Modern Cambodia has its origins in the kingdom of the Khmers, which flourished in 800–1400CE and at one time ruled much of Indochina. After a long decline, however, Cambodia came under domination by Siam and, in the 1800s, France. Cambodia gained its independence in 1953, and, from 1955 to 1970, the nation was ruled by a member of the Cambodian royal family, Norodom Sihanouk. He tried to keep Cambodia neutral in the conflicts raging in Vietnam and Laos—despite pressure from the U.S. government, because North Vietnam used Cambodian territory as a base for its war effort in Vietnam.

In 1969, the United States began a secret four-year air war in Cambodia, and, in 1970, U.S. and South Vietnamese forces briefly invaded the country. By that time a coup had ousted Sihanouk, and a communist guerrilla army, the Khmer Rouge, intensified its war against the central government.

TUOL SLENG

Photos of the victims of Pol Pot *(right)* line the walls at the Tuol Sleng Museum in Phnom Penh *(above)*. Tuol Sleng (the name translates as "hill of the poison tree") was one of the Khmer Rouge regime's most infamous prisons; of the estimated 20,000 people imprisoned there, only seven emerged alive. It is now a museum.

DITH PRAN
1942–

Dith Pran covered the fighting in Cambodia as a journalist in the early 1970s. When the nation's capital, Phnom Penh, fell to the Khmer Rouge in April 1975, Pran and his American colleague, *New York Times* reporter Sydney Schanberg, decided to stay in the city. Narrowly escaping execution, Pran and Schanberg found shelter in the French Embassy, but while Schanberg was able to leave the

President Ronald Reagan meets with Dith Pran in May 1985. In the same year, the United Nations High Commissioner for Refugees appointed Pran a Goodwill Ambassador.

country, Pran was arrested by the Khmer Rouge and sent to a labor camp, where he managed to survive four years under brutal conditions. He finally escaped to Thailand in 1979. Fifty of his relatives—every family member except his sister—perished under Khmer Rouge rule. Meanwhile, Schanberg had published *The Killing Fields*, an account of the Cambodian genocide (later made into a movie), which won a Pulitzer Prize in 1976; Schanberg dedicated the award to Pran, not knowing whether his colleague was alive. From Thailand, Pran emigrated to America, where he now runs the Dith Pran Holocaust Awareness Project, dedicated to raising public awareness of the Cambodian genocide and to helping refugees worldwide.

In April 1975, the Khmer Rouge gained control of the country. What followed was one of the worst genocides of the 20th century. Under the leadership of Pol Pot, the Khmer Rouge attempted to turn Cambodia (which they renamed Kampuchea) into a purely agrarian, communist society. Towns and cities were depopulated, their residents forced into the countryside or into labor camps; education, religion, money, and private property were abolished. Over the next few years, as many as 1 million Cambodians—one-third of the entire population—died as a result of Khmer Rouge rule. Finally, in 1979, Vietnam invaded Cambodia, which it occupied until 1989.

CAMBODIANS IN AMERICA

Only about 13,000 Cambodians managed to escape the "killing fields" and reach the United States between 1975 and 1979, most by way of refugee camps in Thailand. The number of Cambodian refugees rose rapidly after the Vietnamese overthrow of the Khmer Rouge: between 1980 and the early 1990s, about 147,000 Cambodians were admitted into the United States as refugees. Today, Cambodian-Americans are overwhelmingly concentrated in two states: California, home to about 100,000, mostly in the Los Angeles area; and Massachusetts, home to about 30,000, mostly in and around Boston.

THE "KILLING FIELDS"
Hands bound behind their backs, the corpses of executed Cambodians molder in an open field. About 20 percent of those who died during the Khmer Rouge years were executed outright; the remainder perished of starvation, disease, and hardship. Under the Khmer Rouge's bizarre ideology, mere literacy was enough to merit execution.

YEAR OF THE DRAGON
Dancers in Long Beach, California, celebrate *Chaul Chnam Thmey*—the Cambodian Lunar New Year— in April 2000. The traditional holiday spans three days (April 13–15), but many Cambodian-Americans now adjust both the dates and the duration to fit the Western-style weekend.

Hmong

During the Vietnam War, the United States recruited members of Southeast Asia's ethnic minorities as allies against the communists. In Laos, the Hmong people aided America in a mostly secret war; with the American withdrawal from Southeast Asia, the Hmong were left to face the wrath of the nation's communist rulers, although many would ultimately find refuge in the United States.

First migration	1976
Migrated from	Laos
Approx. number in USA	275,000 (2005)
Settlement	California; Minnesota; Wisconsin

The origins of the Hmong—also known as the Miao or Meo—can be traced back to Southwest China around 4,000 years ago. In the early 19th century, under persecution from China's Manchu rulers, many Hmong migrated southward, establishing communities in what are now the nations of Laos, Myanmar (Burma), Thailand, and Vietnam. Settling mostly in mountainous areas, they preserved distinct customs and traditions in their adopted homelands; unlike most Southeast Asians, for example, they followed a shamanistic religion, embracing a belief in powerful spirits, rather than adopting Confucianism or Buddhism. Wherever they settled, the Hmong subsisted through small-scale farming, with extended families typically living under the same roof. Although all Hmong share a certain common culture, there are actually about 80 distinct Hmong groups, set apart from one another by differences in dress and dialect.

The first significant contact between the Hmong and the U.S. military came in the early 1960s, when Laos—which at the time had a Hmong population of about 300,000—was in the midst of a civil war between communist and royalist factions (*see pp 216–217*). Details of this early contact remain murky, but most sources state that CIA agents persuaded Vang Pao, an anticommunist Hmong leader, to raise a force of warriors to fight against both the indigenous communist Pathet Lao guerrillas and the North Vietnamese, who were using Laos as a staging and supply area for their war against South Vietnam. The Hmong fighters were trained by several hundred Green Berets of the U.S. Army's Special Forces and supplied by Air America, the CIA's private airline. Hmong forces also protected radar stations that guided U.S. Air Force B-52s to Laotian targets in a secret bombing campaign. By 1970, at least 40,000 Hmong fighters were directly involved in America's clandestine war in Laos.

HMONG IN AMERICA

Although close bonds had formed between American military personnel in Laos and their Hmong allies, the U.S. government at first

SECRET WARRIORS
Right: Vang Pao, leader of the U.S.-allied Hmong forces from 1961 to 1973. He fled to America with his family following the communist victory in 1975, where he settled in California and remains an active figure in the American Hmong community. *Above:* Hmong pilots flew these T-28 aircraft, carrying bombs, from a secret base at Long Cheng, Laos.

distanced itself from the Hmong as it tried to disengage from Southeast Asia in the early 1970s. When the Pathet Lao took control of the country in 1975, only a handful of Hmong were flown to safety, despite promises that the United States would protect them in the event of a communist victory. Some Hmong escaped into Thailand. Others continued to fight the Pathet Lao. Hmong fighters, and their families who stayed in Laos faced swift and terrible revenge from the country's new rulers. Many were sent to re-education camps, and the communists may have even used poison gas against Hmong villages.

As more and more Hmong arrived in Thai refugee camps, the U.S. government finally owned up to its responsibilities to its former allies. Between 1976 and around 1990, some 100,000 Hmong were admitted to the United States as refugees; current estimates of the Hmong-American population range from 250,000 to 300,000.

Two states—Minnesota and Wisconsin—are home to most Hmong in America, who were initially placed by local church-based

PEOPLE OF THE MOUNTAINS
Hmong women and children are photographed in a village along the Mekong River in Laos's Luang Prabang province. Most Hmong villages consist of 20 or so houses, each home to an *ib tsev neeg*—an extended family, usually including several generations.

BAN NAPHO
Hmong refugees at Ban Napho Refugee Camp in Thailand, 1996. Three years later, the camp was the scene of rioting when Hmong refugees resisted forced repatriation to Laos; in recent years, Hmong organizations in America have protested conditions in Ban Napho.

refugee-relief groups. By 2000, as many as 70,000 Hmong had settled in the Twin Cities of Minneapolis-St. Paul, Minnesota, and their suburbs, with another 50,000 in Wisconsin; in some cities there, like Sheboygan, Hmong made up more than 10 percent of the population by the turn of the 21st century. California also has a large Hmong community, with over 25,000 in Fresno alone.

Life in America has been a challenge for the Hmong. Even more than other Laotian immigrants, they came from an agrarian, pre-industrial society, which, until the mid-20th century, did not have a currency or a written language. Most Hmong had never seen a car before arriving in the United States.

The landscape of the Upper Midwest, so dissimilar from that of their homeland, has added to feelings of dislocation and isolation for many Hmong immigrants. So has America's individualistic, media-saturated popular culture, which is also very different from the intensely traditional and family-based Hmong society; sociologists report deep divisions between American-born Hmong and their Laotian-born parents and grandparents.

Despite tensions between the Hmong and their native-born neighbors, and among the Hmong themselves, they have succeeded in establishing themselves as one of America's most distinctive immigrant groups, adding an element of diversity to many homogenous Midwestern communities, and blending their own traditions—especially embroidery and other sewing techniques, a specialty of Hmong women—into the American cultural mosaic.

THE WISCONSIN HMONG VETERANS
The state government of Wisconsin declared May 14, 2003, Lao-Hmong Appreciation Day in honor of "their heroic contributions on behalf of the United States during the Vietnam War." Here, Hmong veterans attend a ceremony at the state Capitol in Madison.

PORT-AU-PRINCE
Fishing boats moored in the harbor at Port-au-Prince, Haiti's capital and largest city. Precise population figures are had to come by, but the city now has a population of at least 1 million.

Haitians

The Caribbean nation of Haiti has long been the poorest country in the Western Hemisphere. A combination of grinding poverty and a despotic and brutal political culture has led more than 400,000 Haitians to immigrate to the United States—both legally and illegally—in the last three decades. In recent years, American policy toward Haitian immigration has become controversial, with some charging that the U.S. government makes a distinction between political refugees and economic migrants that is basically meaningless.

WYCLEF JEAN
1972–

Born Nelust Wyclef Jean in Croix-des-Bouquets, Haiti, Jean came to America with his family at age nine, living in Brooklyn and then in New Jersey. In the late 1980s, Jean joined with his cousin Samuel Prakazrel Michel (better known as Pras) and Lauryn Hill to form a rap group, the Tranzlator Crew. The group later changed its name to the Fugees, from a slang term for Haitian immigrants. The Fugees released their first album in 1993 but the group did not hit it big until 1996's *The Score*, which blended jazz, reggae, and R&B, and sold more than 6 million copies. After *The Score*, the trio split, with Jean achieving success as both as a solo artist and a producer. Jean is also a prominent activist and advocate for Haiti and the Haitians; in 2004, he founded Yéle Haiti to raise funds for development projects and community initiatives.

Haiti comprises the western third of the island of Hispaniola, which it now shares with the Dominican Republic. At the end of the 17th century, Haiti, then known as Saint-Domingue, came under French rule. The population, made up mostly of the descendants of slaves brought from Africa, rose up against their masters in 1791, winning independence from France in 1804 and making Haiti the second independent republic in the Western Hemisphere after America. Yet a series of dictators ruled the nation, and by the early 1900s, Haiti was in a state of anarchy.

In 1915, U.S. Marines occupied Haiti. They built schools, hospitals, and roads, improved public health and sanitation, and trained an indigenous *gendarmerie* to deal with the Caico bandits who terrified the countryside. After the Americans withdrew in 1934, however, civil society in Haiti broke down.

In 1957, François Duvalier, known as "Papa Doc," was elected president. Seven years later, he declared himself President for Life—a position he kept by way of the *Tontons Macouts*, a secret police force that tortured and murdered any real or suspected opponent. After his death in 1971, Papa Doc was succeeded by his 19-year-old son, Jean-Claude, "Baby Doc," who continued his father's murderous policies.

Baby Doc's succession crushed any hopes of political or economic reform, so thousands of Haitians fled to the United States. This wave of Haitian immigrants consisted of educated, middle-class professionals who could afford to fly to American by commercial airliner, and most settled in New York City.

INTO THE SEA

In the 1970s, Haiti's economy deteriorated to the point where the poorest Haitians were willing to take their chances aboard small boats or rafts in an effort to reach America, some 700 miles away. By the early 1980s around 1,000 refugees a month were washing up on Florida's shores or being rescued at sea; as with the Cuban *bolseros* (see pp 124–127) an unknown number died en route.

DEADLY DYNASTY

François "Papa Doc" Duvalier makes his acceptance speech upon being elected president of Haiti in 1957. Under his rule and that of his son and successor, Jean-Claude "Baby Doc" Duvalier, any dissent was met with repression.

BOAT PEOPLE
Refugees intercepted in the Windward Passage between Haiti and Florida await transportation to the detention camp at the Guantanamo Bay U.S. Naval Station in Cuba.

Most of these new immigrants were unskilled and uneducated; the jobless rate among Haitian immigrants in southern Florida was about 33 percent during the 1980s and 1990s.

In 1986, a coup ousted Baby Doc Duvalier, ushering in a period of violence that drove even more Haitians to flee. In 1990, the first elections in decades won Jean-Bertrand Aristide the presidency, but Haiti's military rulers forced Aristide out of the country. A U.S. military intervention restored Aristide to power in 1994, but he failed to bring stability to Haiti, and thousands continue to flee each year.

In the 1990s, the United States established a controversial policy toward Haitian refugees: those caught ashore or interdicted by the Coast Guard at sea were taken into custody and either deported back to Haiti immediately or detained, sometimes for many months, at the U.S. Naval Base at Guantanamo, to await repatriation. Refugee-rights activists and others have criticized this policy as unfair, contrasting the treatment of Cuban refugees with that of Haitians: Cubans who reached America were typically allowed to stay and apply for asylum. Critics have also charged that U.S. policy violated Article 33 of the 1951 United Nations Convention on refugees, which proclaims that no "state shall expel or return a refugee in any manner . . . where his life or freedom would be threatened."

Government officials contended that most Haitians fleeing to America were economic migrants who did not meet the "well-founded fear of persecution" criteria for admission as refugees under U.S. immigration law. Proponents of reform argue that conditions in Haiti are so dire, because of political violence and turmoil, that many Haitians indeed fear for their lives.

RACIST REFUGEE POLICY?
Together with members of the Congressional Black Caucus (CBC), Haitian-Americans protest near the U.S. Capitol on October 30, 1997. According to the CBC's chair, Rep. Maxine Waters (D-CA), "Haitian refugees who barely managed to escape brutal political and economic hardships were subjected to the highest degree of political hypocrisy and racism."

DEATH IN THE STREETS
A victim of the violence that wracked Haiti in 1994—which pitted supporters of the exiled President Jean-Bertrand Aristide against the military government—lies dead in Port-au-Prince. Many such murders were the work of the so-called *attachés*—civilian "enforcers" working for the police.

U.S. COAST GUARD

2¹2533

Africans

The transition from colonial rule to independence has not been an easy one for many African nations. The continent has few functioning democracies: many countries have been racked for decades by ethnic strife, the corrupt actions of brutal dictators, stagnant (or worse) economies, and deadly famines. Increasing numbers of Africans have sought refuge in the United States, although—as with refugees from Latin America and the Caribbean—some charge that U.S. immigration policy toward Africa is unfair.

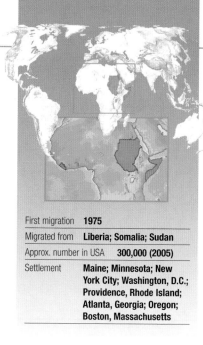

First migration	1975
Migrated from	**Liberia; Somalia; Sudan**
Approx. number in USA	**300,000 (2005)**
Settlement	**Maine; Minnesota; New York City; Washington, D.C.; Providence, Rhode Island; Atlanta, Georgia; Oregon; Boston, Massachusetts**

In recent years, the situation in much of Africa has grown even worse. In 1994, for example, the majority Hutu people in Rwanda rose up against the minority Tutsi, leaving as many as 800,000 people dead and creating 2 million refugees. In Sudan, Africa's largest country, government-backed Arab militias launched a campaign of ethnic cleansing in the Darfur region in 2003—something U.S. Congress declared tantamount to genocide—creating another massive refugee crisis.

The Refugee Act of 1980 opened the way for increased numbers of political refugees and asylum-seekers from African nations. According to the U.S. State Department, 138,000 Africans were admitted to America between 1980 and 2003. Despite this influx, some Americans—including members of the Congressional Black Caucus—argue that U.S. policy toward African refugees has elements of bias, because regional ceilings for admission of African refugees have not been

CAMEL CONVOY
Goatherds lead their charges through the desert toward a watering hole in the western Sudanese region of Darfur.

LIBERIAN NATIONAL COMMEMORATION

Young Liberian women celebrate July 26, Independence Day. After seizing power in 1980, Sgt. Samuel K. Doe added a new holiday: April 12 became National Redemption Day to mark the coup in which he deposed President Torbert.

met. The slowdown in refugee admissions since the 9/11 attacks has led to a further decline.

LIBERIANS

One of the most troubled nations on the continent, Liberia, on the western coast of Africa, has a unique connection to the United States—it was founded in 1822 as a colony for freed American slaves. Although that scheme was mostly unsuccessful, the Americo-Liberians—descendants of the freed slaves—controlled the nation's government and economy for many decades, even though they represented only a small minority of its population. This changed when a 1980 military coup brought Samuel K. Doe, an indigenous Liberian, to power, but he was deposed in 1990 and seven years of civil war followed. The government stabilized somewhat in 1997, but an even more brutal internal conflict began in 1999; over the next four years, thousands of Liberians died, and tens of thousands became refugees. U.N. peacekeepers arrived in 2003 and America accepted 7,000 Liberian refugees as part of a 2004 resettlement program.

SOMALIANS

Italy and Britain colonized the East African region that is now Somalia in the 19th century. After World War II, Italian Somaliland and British Somaliland gained independence from their respective colonial rulers, and a united Somalia emerged in 1960. The new country, however, was beset by poverty and occasional conflicts with the neighboring nations of Ethiopia, Djibouti, and Kenya. In 1969, General Mohamed Siad Barre took control of the government, ruling as a dictator until he was overthrown in a coup in 1991. Afterward, various factions fought for power in the capital, Mogadishu, and the outlying parts of the country, while up to 400,000 Somalis died of war-related starvation.

With Somalia in chaos, supplies of food and other aid sent by relief organizations were routinely looted. In response, a U.N. peacekeeping force, including a U.S. contingent, arrived in Somalia in 1992. The following

MISSION TO MOGADISHU

Two U.S. Humvees and a tank escort a food convoy on its way through the Somali capital, Mogadishu, during the 1992–94 United Nations intervention. The U.S. military dubbed its mission "Operation Restore Hope."

year, 18 American troops were killed in Mogadishu while trying to capture an associate of Mohammed Farah Aidid, the country's most notorious warlord. U.S. troops were withdrawn in 1994. A decade later, Somalia, still plagued by unrest and hunger, is reliant on foreign aid.

From 1991 to the early 2000s, between 800,000 and 1 million Somali refugees fled the starvation and warfare in their homeland for camps in Djibouti, Kenya, Ethiopia, Burundi, and Yemen. The United States admitted almost 30,000 Somalis as refugees by 1999, many of whom were resettled in Maine and Minnesota, and, since 1991, Somalis in the United

FRAGILE PEACE

Cartridge cases carpet a street in Monrovia, Liberia's capital. During the street fighting in the summer of 1993, at least 1,000 people died. With U.N. support, a peacekeeping force managed to restore order.

HASSAN BILITY
BIRTH YEAR UNKNOWN

Critical of Charles Taylor's administration and the deteriorating human rights situation, Liberian journalist Hassan Bility's work for the weekly *The Analyst* resulted in a six-month imprisonment in 2002. Questioned by President Taylor himself, Bility was accused of collaborating with rebels and declared a prisoner of war. Held incommunicado without trial, some supporters feared he had died as a result of torture. His treatment was internationally condemned, and a campaign for his freedom eventually led to his release. He lives in exile in America with his family.

RUSHING THE TRUCK
Desperate to get out of the path of the National Patriotic Front of Liberia (NPFL)'s soldiers as they advance toward Monrovia, people from the city of Paynesville pack into a truck in this photograph taken on August 5, 1990.

States have been granted Temporary Protected Status (TPS). As is the case with refugees from several predominantly Islamic nations, however, admission of Somalis slowed after the 9/11 attacks.

In 2003, the U.S. State Department announced a special admission of up to 13,000 Somali Bantus, members of an ethnic group that has long suffered persecution, including enslavement, in Somalia. With the aid of private charities and church groups, the Bantus will be resettled in 50 communities across the United States.

SOMALI IMMIGRANTS
Two 10-year-old Somali immigrant girls chat before their class begins at the Highland Avenue Elementary School in Columbus, Ohio, in this June 1999 photograph.

BAIDOA
Somali women and children in a refugee camp outside Baidoa, Somalia, about 120 miles from Mogadishu. In the late 1990s, fighting in the area led to the withdrawal of most humanitarian workers and blocked food supplies, leading to starvation and disease in the Baidoa camps.

SUDANESE

Sudan, Africa's largest nation in terms of land mass, was jointly ruled by Egypt and Britain until it gained independence in 1956. For centuries, there have been deep divisions between the northern two-thirds of the country, where the population is

VICTIM OF FAMINE
With the distended stomach characteristic of extreme malnutrition—and an empty food bowl on his head—a Dinka child arrives at a famine-relief station in Thiet, Sudan. The Dinka are one of 19 different ethnic groups in Sudan, who collectively speak more than 100 languages.

JANJAWEED
Members of a Janjaweed militia pull into the market in the town of Mistiria, Darfur, in October 2004. This particular unit styled itself as "The Quick and the Horrible." Musa Hilal, alleged mastermind of the Janjaweed's operations, uses the town as his base.

largely Arab in ethnicity and Muslim in religion, and the southern region, where most of the people are African Christians or animists. These divisions widened after independence, as successive governments in Khartoum, Sudan's capital, sought to impose Islamic law over the whole country, sparking rebellions in the south. From 1983 to 2002, an estimated two million Sudanese died in what amounted to a 20-year civil war.

A 2002 cease-fire between the national government and southern rebel groups briefly held out hopes of an end to Sudan's long nightmare. In 2003, however, the government launched a campaign against so-called "insurgents" in the state of Darfur on Sudan's western border with Chad. Observers have charged that the Sudanese government is arming and aiding Arab militias, the Janjaweeds, in depredations against civilians that include burning homes and villages, destroying crops and livestock, and outright murder. At least 100,000 people have fled from Darfur into Chad, and in 2004 the U.S. Agency for International Development warned that hundreds of thousands of Sudanese, mostly women and children, were at risk of death from starvation and disease unless the Sudanese government halted the Janjaweeds and allowed increased humanitarian aid into Darfur. Evidence of ethnic cleansing in Darfur has led to fears that a humanitarian tragedy on the scale seen in Rwanda in 1994 may be possible.

In addition to giving $62 million (in 2004) to aid the Sudanese refugees in Chad, the United States admitted about 20,000 Sudanese as refugees between the early 1980s and the early 2000s; as the Darfur crisis widened in 2004, refugee advocates have called for another increase in admissions.

BOY SOLDIERS
In Sudan, as in war-torn countries across Africa, boys as young as eight fight and die. Here, boy soldiers of the Sudan People's Liberation Army (SPLA) wait to turn in their weapons in 2001; they were demobilized under the auspices of the United Nations Children's Fund.

THE "LOST BOYS"

In 1987, a remarkable exodus began in Southern Sudan. Some 17,000 young men and boys left their war-torn villages and walked through 1,000 miles of desert, hoping to find refuge in Ethiopia. Most were orphans, and the older boys feared conscription into the various military groups fighting in the civil war. They faced incredible hardships along the way, but those who lived to reach Ethiopia—itself in the midst of civil war— found themselves unwelcome. Thousands were forced back into Sudan at gunpoint, although some managed to reach the Kakuma refugee camp in Kenya, where they remained for years. When news of their plight reached the United States, a number of churches and other organizations sponsored the admission of many of the survivors. Ultimately, more than 3,000 of the "Lost Boys" were resettled in communities across America (*as pictured below*). In 2001, John Deng James—who was only five years old when he left his village—told an interviewer that, "In the United States, you determine who you are, and now I have a vision of my future. I can go to school, I can work, and I can do what I want. . . You have to live where you feel happy. . . I cannot go to Sudan unless there's peace."

Balkan Refugees

First migration	1989
Migrated from	former Yugoslavia
Approx. number in USA	116,000 (2005)
Settlement	New York; St. Louis, Missouri; Milwaukee, Wisconsin; Detroit, Michigan; Chicago, Illinois

SARAJEVO
A 1982 view of Sarajevo showing the White Minaret—the remains of a mosque destroyed by Austrian troops in the 17th century. The Archduke Ferdinand's July 1914 assassination in the city started World War I; 80 years later, it was the center of a struggle between Serbs and Bosnians.

Home to a volatile mix of ethnic and religious groups, Europe's Balkan Peninsula has long been a region whose very name is synonymous with war. After World War I, much of the area united as Yugoslavia, and after World War II, a communist government suppressed conflict between the nation's peoples. But when communist control fell apart at the end of the 1980s, it touched off a series of wars that collectively killed between 200,000 and 300,000 people and made 2 million others refugees. At least 116,000 found permanent shelter in the United States, usually settling where previous Balkan immigrants lived.

By the end of the 14th century, the Ottoman Turks had conquered most of the Balkans, and over centuries of Ottoman rule some of the empire's Christian Slavs converted to Islam, giving regions like Albania and Bosnia large Muslim populations. With the rise of nationalist feeling in the 19th century, the subject peoples of the Balkans rebelled against Ottoman rule. Greece won independence in 1829, and over the next 80 years so did Bulgaria, Montenegro, and Serbia. By 1908, the Ottomans held only Albania and Macedonia, and those were lost in the Balkan Wars of 1912–13. Each of the new nations that resulted from the defeats contained minorities from other nations—a situation that made ongoing internal conflicts inevitable.

After World War I, Serbia and Montenegro joined the former Austro-Hungarian (*see pp 112–113*) territories of Bosnia-Herzegovina, Croatia, Dalmatia, and Slovenia to form a new country, Yugoslavia (the Kingdom of South Slavs), under the rule of the Serbian royal family, who dominated the government.

NAZDROVYE
Despite this 1955 show of friendship with Soviet Premier Nikita Khrushchev at the reception given for the Russian Delegation to Belgrade, Yugoslav President Josip Broz Tito was determined to implement his own brand of communism in Yugoslavia and to stay out of Moscow's orbit.

VUKOVAR
Along with Sarajevo, the Croatian city of Vukovar was the target of heavy shelling from the Yugoslav Army and paramilitary units; an estimated 800,000 bombs and mortar rounds fell on the city during a 86-day siege in 1991, leaving most of it in ruins.

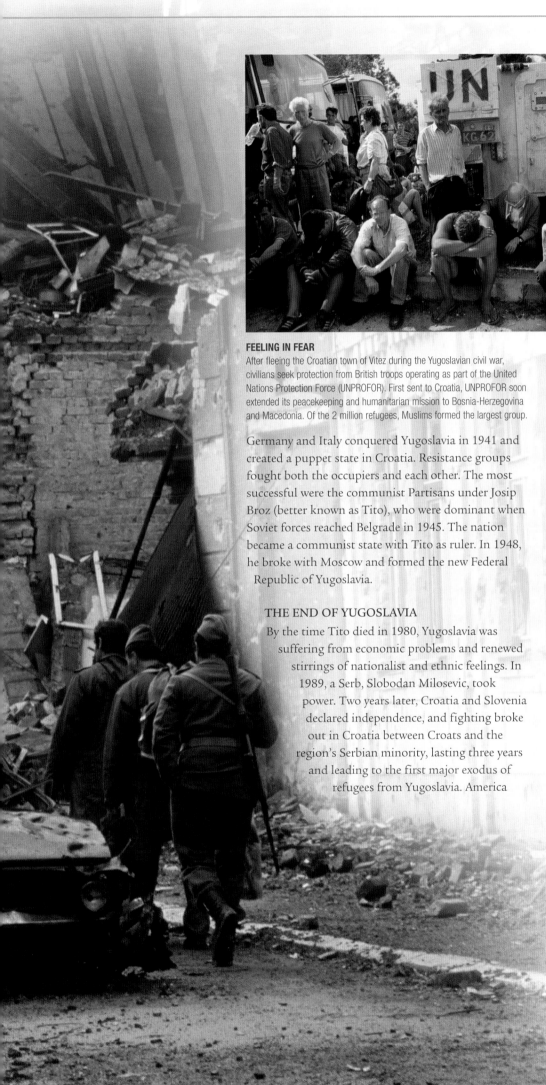

FEELING IN FEAR
After fleeing the Croatian town of Vitez during the Yugoslavian civil war, civilians seek protection from British troops operating as part of the United Nations Protection Force (UNPROFOR). First sent to Croatia, UNPROFOR soon extended its peacekeeping and humanitarian mission to Bosnia-Herzegovina and Macedonia. Of the 2 million refugees, Muslims formed the largest group.

Germany and Italy conquered Yugoslavia in 1941 and created a puppet state in Croatia. Resistance groups fought both the occupiers and each other. The most successful were the communist Partisans under Josip Broz (better known as Tito), who were dominant when Soviet forces reached Belgrade in 1945. The nation became a communist state with Tito as ruler. In 1948, he broke with Moscow and formed the new Federal Republic of Yugoslavia.

THE END OF YUGOSLAVIA

By the time Tito died in 1980, Yugoslavia was suffering from economic problems and renewed stirrings of nationalist and ethnic feelings. In 1989, a Serb, Slobodan Milosevic, took power. Two years later, Croatia and Slovenia declared independence, and fighting broke out in Croatia between Croats and the region's Serbian minority, lasting three years and leading to the first major exodus of refugees from Yugoslavia. America

admitted more than 8,000. Around the same time, Serbs in Bosnia began fighting with their Muslim neighbors and with Bosnian Croats. With the support of federal troops, Serb militias embarked on an ethnic-cleansing campaign, burning villages, besieging cities, and killing thousands.

Representatives of Bosnia, Croatia, and Serbia agreed to a peace settlement at Dayton, Ohio, in 1995. The Bosnian crisis produced more than 800,000 refugees; America granted Permanent Resident Status to about 92,000. By this time, federal Yugoslavia consisted of Serbia and Montenegro, but people in danger of persecution by the Milosevic regime lived in both republics; about 16,000 found shelter in America.

The last major refugee crisis came in Kosovo, a province in Southern Serbia populated mostly by people of Albanian descent. In 1997, the Kosovo Liberation Army (KLA) began a guerrilla campaign for independence. Federal forces occupied about two-thirds of the province in 1998, driving an estimated 350,000 Kosovars into Macedonia and Albania. In May 1999, the United States announced it would admit up to 20,000 Kosovar refugees; about 14,000 came to America before a NATO bombing campaign forced the Yugoslav government to the negotiating table.

By the early 2000s, an uneasy peace took hold in most of the former Yugoslavia, reducing the number of refugees. Those who did arrive in America chose to settle where earlier immigrants from their homelands did. In addition to the human toll of the conflicts, the fighting wreaked havoc on the economies of the former Yugoslav republics, leading to a rise in illegal immigration into the United States (*see pp 186–187*).

SALUTE TO THE FALLEN
Ethnic Albanian fighters of the Kosovo Liberation Army (KLA) raise their rifles in tribute to fallen comrades in August 1999. According to a 2000 report by the U.N. Undersecretary-General for Humanitarian Affairs, the Serb-dominated Yugoslav government conducted "a rampage of killing, burning, looting, forced expulsion, violence, vendetta, and terror" in Kosovo.

6

FREEDOM TO CREATE

Creative spirits have come to America from all over

the world. Drawn to the possibilities of a free society,

they have flourished in the creative openness

of America. However, the United States has not

always been a destination for creative minds;

not until the 20th century, when writers, artists,

and scientists, persecuted by Fascist regimes in

Germany and Italy, had only one hope: flight. Their

books were burned, their lives threatened—and

America was waiting.

"The Art of Departure"

BALANCHINE AND BARYSHNIKOV
Mikhail Baryshnikov, as Harlequin, dances with the corps de ballet in a 1978 New York City Ballet production of *Harlequinade*, choreographed by George Balanchine. Feeling artistically limited under the close monitor of the Communist government, both Balanchine and Baryshnikov defected from the Soviet Union, in 1933 and 1974 respectively.

THE ART OF DEPARTURE

Well into the 20th century, the United States suffered from a sort of cultural inferiority complex. While the nation grew into an industrial power, many Americans felt—with some justification—that it lagged behind Europe in artistic and scientific achievement. Most Europeans, in turn, regarded the United States as a cultural backwater. It would take the contributions of immigrants—many of them fleeing repressive regimes in their homelands—to lift America to global preeminence in the creative fields.

The last decades of the 19th century and the first decades of the 20th century were a time of great innovation in all the arts. Traditional forms gave way to new ones—from cubism in painting to the 12-tone works of composer Arnold Schoenberg (*see pp 264–265*). Sigmund Freud's concept of the subconscious fueled movements like Surrealism, while left-wing ideals increasingly informed the work of European artists and writers, such as Bertolt Brecht (*see p 271*). Meanwhile, the death, destruction, and suffering wrought by World War I led many artists, like George Grosz (*see p 252*), to explore the dark side of the human condition in their work.

The years after the war saw the rise of Fascism in Italy and Nazism in Germany. These regimes sought to control not only their subjects' freedom of action and movement, but their freedom of thought and expression as well. The Nazis suppressed any art that did not conform to their idea of Germanic *Kultur*, and their anti-Semitic ideology put all Jewish artists at risk. After 1933, thousands of artists, writers, musicians, academics, scientists, actors, directors, and designers fled Germany and the countries that came under its domination. Many of these refugees had trouble winning admission to America because of the restrictive immigration laws of the time and anti-immigrant feeling among many Americans.

President Franklin Roosevelt ordered the State Department to issue temporary visas to "those of superior intellectual attainment, of indomitable spirit, experienced in the vigorous support of liberal government, and who are in danger of persecution or death at the hands of autocracy." More than 3,000 people received these visas before the outbreak of World War II put most of Europe under Nazi control. The impact of the refugees from Fascism and Nazism on American intellectual life is incalculable. From scientists like Albert Einstein (*see p 206*) to composers like Kurt Weill (*see pp 266–267*) to writers like Thomas Mann (*see p 246*), they collectively represented the single greatest transfer of talent the world has ever seen.

POSTWAR DEVELOPMENTS

The end of World War II saw the fall of Nazism and Fascism, but the Soviet Union remained a totalitarian state until the introduction of *Glasnost* in the mid-1980s. The Soviet Union's Communist leadership stifled any creative activity that did not adhere to its ideological standards, or which betrayed the slightest hint of dissent. Those who did not toe the party line faced imprisonment, internal exile, or confinement in mental hospitals. The situation was similar in the Soviet Union's satellite nations in Eastern Europe and in other Communist nations, like Cuba.

In the decades of Cold War following World War II, the United States welcomed hundreds of creative refugees from the communist world. Some, like writer Aleksandr Solzhenitsyn (*see pp 248–249*), were exiled by the Soviet government; others, like dancers George Balanchine and Mikhail Baryshnikov (*see pp 268-269*), defected or otherwise managed to escape from their communist homelands.

SOCIAL WORKER
Vasili Neyasov depicted an idealized Soviet "shock worker" in his 1959 painting *A Guy from the Urals*. "Socialist realism" was the only officially approved style in all art forms for much of the Soviet Union's history.

Scientists

The French Revolution (*see pp 104–105*) and the rise of Napoleon Bonaparte spurred the immigration of two great scientific figures in the early years of the American republic. Joseph Priestley—already celebrated as the codiscoverer of oxygen—came to America from England in 1794 to escape persecution for his support of the revolutionary government in France; nine years later, young John James Audubon—who would become the most renowned natural-history artist of his time—emigrated from France to escape conscription into Napoleon's army.

CORSICAN CONQUEROR
Napoleon Bonaparte, emperor of France, watches his troops in action against Russian and Prussian forces in battle at Lutzen, Germany, in 1813. The prospect of conscription into Napoleon's armies was one reason John James Audubon immigrated to America.

JOSEPH PRIESTLEY

Joseph Priestley was born near Leeds, England, in 1733. Like many early scientists, Priestley, who became a minister in 1755, was deeply religious, although unorthodox in his beliefs. He was as famous for his writings on religion and politics as for his scientific work.

Priestley was educated at an academy for Dissenters in Daventry and while teaching at Warrington Academy in the 1760s, he met Benjamin Franklin, who encouraged the electrical experiments that won Priestley admission to the Royal Society in 1766.

In a series of experiments in 1774, Priestley helped establish the modern science of chemistry by discovering that heating mercuric oxide produced a gas, later named oxygen. Priestley continued his chemical work into the 1790s, while keeping up a steady flow of books and pamphlets on his libertarian views on religion, politics, and government. When a conservative backlash swept Britain as the French Revolution grew more radical, his writings were

ELEGANT INSTRUMENT
Priestley *(below)* used the compound microscope at left in his experiments. The instrument, which incorporates two convex lenses, was built by James Martin in London in 1767.

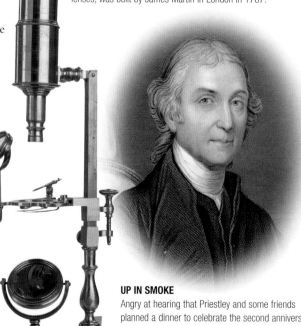

UP IN SMOKE
Angry at hearing that Priestley and some friends planned a dinner to celebrate the second anniversary of the storming of the Bastille (*see pp 104–105*), a mob sacks the radical scientist's house and laboratory on July 14, 1791.

denounced as seditious by the government. In 1791, a mob destroyed his house and laboratory in Birmingham. Priestley and his family moved to London, but the harassment continued. Over the next few years, three of his sons moved to America, and, in 1794, Priestley decided to join them.

Settling in Northumberland, Pennsylvania, Priestley became a friend of Thomas Jefferson, who described the scientist as "one of the few lives precious to mankind." Shortly before his death in 1804, Priestley made a speech to Philadelphia's American Philosophical Society, in which he stated: "Having been obliged to leave a country which has been long distinguished by discoveries in science, I think myself happy by my reception in another which is following its example, and which already affords a prospect of its arriving at equal eminence."

JOHN JAMES AUDUBON

John James Audubon was born in Saint-Domingue (now Haiti) in 1785, the illegitimate son of a French sea captain and his mistress. His father took him and his half sister with him when he returned to France. The young Audubon developed a deep interest in natural history, especially birds, and became a talented artist, studying with the painter Jacques-Louis David.

Audubon's father sent him to America in 1803, to escape being drafted into Napoleon's armies and to look after some property in Pennsylvania. There he conducted America's first bird-banding: by tying string to the legs of a local species, he realized that the birds returned to the same places to nest each year.

In 1819, Audubon traveled the Mississippi River Valley, shooting birds with small-gauge buckshot to preserve their features, and portraying them in their natural habitat. To support his art, Audubon worked as a taxidermist, portrait painter, and teacher.

By 1824, Audubon had assembled a remarkable portfolio. A British engraver, Robert Havell, turned over 400 of Audubon's life-size drawings into color plates and published them in four volumes as *The Birds of America*. The volumes were immediately recognized on both sides of the Atlantic as a masterpiece of both art and natural history. The success of the book allowed Audubon to continue traveling in his quest to draw all of North America's avian species.

AMERICAN BIRDMAN
Above: Audubon with two of the tools of his trade—shotgun and dog.

> "A true conservationist is a man who knows that the world is not given by his fathers, but borrowed from his children."
>
> John James Audubon

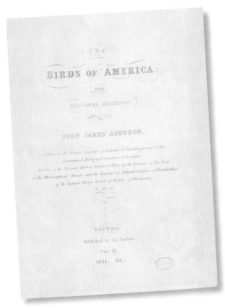

AMERICAN BIRDMAN
The title page of the second volume of *The Birds of America*. The volumes were known as the Double Elephant Portfolio, after the oversize paper needed for the life-size artworks. The great French scientist George Cuvier praised the work as "the most magnificent monument [ever] raised to ornithology."

GRAY KINGBIRD
Audubon's depiction of the Gray Kingbird, the Gray Tyrant, from the original edition of *The Birds of America*. Audubon's portraits included not only the bird itself, but the flora of its habitat.

THE SPACE RACE

The American effort to build an atomic bomb (*see pp 206–207*) would have been impossible without the brainpower of immigrant scientists. The same is true of another great American technical feat—the first manned landing on the moon. There was a big difference, however, between the immigrant scientists who worked on the Manhattan Project and those who helped launch America's space program: the former fled a Nazi-dominated Europe to freedom in the United States, while the latter worked for the German war effort.

VON BRAUN AND THE V-2

While Nazi Germany failed to make real progress toward an atomic bomb, German scientists and engineers did develop a number of highly advanced weapons during World War II, including the first operational jet aircraft, the V-1 flying bomb, and most importantly, the V-2 rocket—the ancestor of both modern military missiles and the rockets that sent U.S. satellites and astronauts into space during the heyday of the "Space Race" between the United States and the Soviet Union.

The V-2 was largely the brainchild of Werner von Braun. Born into an aristocratic German family in 1912, he became passionately committed to

VON BRAUN'S ROCKET
Von Braun with a model of a V-2 missile. Originally the A-4, the missile was renamed V-2 by Nazi Germany's propaganda ministry; the "V" stood for "Vengeance Weapon."

making space travel a reality. Braun began conducting experiments with liquid-fueled rockets after graduating from Berlin's Technical Institute. His experiments won him financial support from the German Army, which was investigating the military potential of rockets. During World War II, with vast resources at his disposal, von Braun and his chief engineer, Walter Dornberger, oversaw the development of the V-2, a 50-foot-long, liquid oxygen-fueled missile, carrying 1,600 pounds of explosives 50 miles into the earth's atmosphere on the way to its target. They were ready to launch by September 1944.

OPERATION PAPERCLIP

Both the United States and the Soviet Union coveted Germany's rocket technology, and both nations grabbed German scientists and rocket parts in the last days of WWII. To avoid being captured by the advancing Soviets, von Braun led his team westward from their base at Peenemünde on Germany's Baltic coast. They surrendered to U.S. forces in early May 1945. A few months later, von Braun and about 100 of his colleagues—considered "wards of the army"—arrived at Fort Bliss, Texas, before moving to the army's facility at White

SOVIET FIRES EARTH SATELLITE INTO SPACE; IT IS CIRCLING THE GLOBE AT 18,000 M. P. H.; SPHERE TRACKED IN 4 CROSSINGS OVER U.S.

SHOCK AND AWE
The success of Sputnik in 1957 unnerved an America that had been confident that it was far ahead of the Soviets in all aspects of science and technology, and led to increased government funding for research and education.

SUCCESS
Explorer 1 launches on January 31, 1958, four months after Sputnik's launch. The first American satellite to be put into orbit, Explorer 1 was carried by a Jupiter-C rocket—which had been developed to test guided missile components—from Cape Canaveral in Florida.

PAPERCLIPPED
Von Braun (*seventh from right in the first row*) and his team at Fort Bliss, Texas, in 1947. Seven years later, the first group of Operation Paperclip technicians and scientists became naturalized U.S. citizens.

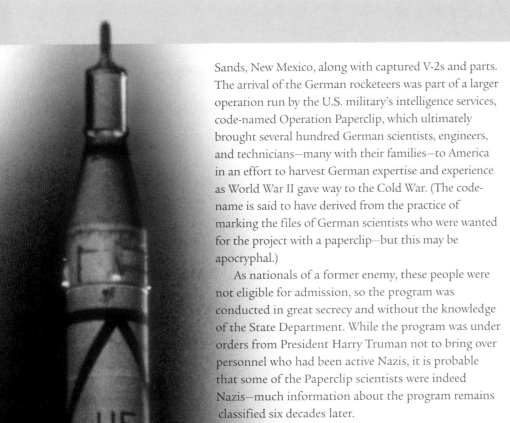

Sands, New Mexico, along with captured V-2s and parts. The arrival of the German rocketeers was part of a larger operation run by the U.S. military's intelligence services, code-named Operation Paperclip, which ultimately brought several hundred German scientists, engineers, and technicians—many with their families—to America in an effort to harvest German expertise and experience as World War II gave way to the Cold War. (The code-name is said to have derived from the practice of marking the files of German scientists who were wanted for the project with a paperclip—but this may be apocryphal.)

As nationals of a former enemy, these people were not eligible for admission, so the program was conducted in great secrecy and without the knowledge of the State Department. While the program was under orders from President Harry Truman not to bring over personnel who had been active Nazis, it is probable that some of the Paperclip scientists were indeed Nazis—much information about the program remains classified six decades later.

After two years in a British POW camp, Walter Dornberger was brought to America in 1947 to help start the U.S. Air Force's guided missile program. In 1950, von Braun moved from White Sands to Huntsville, Alabama, to direct the U.S. Army's ballistic missile development, and also to work toward putting a satellite into orbit. The Soviets, however, beat America into space with the October 1957 launch of the Sputnik satellite.

TO THE MOON

The humiliation of Sputnik and the effort to catch up with the Soviets (the first successful U.S. satellite launch, Explorer I, took place in January 1958) focused national attention on von Braun. Given his wartime activities, he would always be a controversial figure. Von Braun steadfastly maintained that while he had worked for the German military, he was merely an apolitical scientist. He had to have been aware, however, that Germany's wartime rocket program was made possible by the forced labor of concentration-camp inmates—and despite his contention that he had created the "[V-2] to open the gates to other worlds, not to seed destruction on earth," the 4,000 V-2s launched from September 1944 until March 1945 killed about 20,000 people in Britain, Belgium, and France. Despite the moral ambiguities, von Braun became a popular figure in America. In addition to his work for the military and the government, he wrote books and articles promoting space exploration and served as a technical adviser for the Walt Disney Corporation.

Following the creation the National Air and Space Administration (NASA) and the acceleration of the Space Race after President John F. Kennedy made a manned mission to the Moon an American goal, von Braun's major achievement was the development of the massive Saturn rocket—the launch vehicle used for all the important space missions of the 1960s, including the Apollo moon landing in August 1969. Von Braun was one of the most important figures in the effort to put the Stars and Stripes on the Moon—using technology he had pioneered under the Nazi swastika. Von Braun remained with NASA until 1972, when he became a consultant to the aerospace industry. He died in 1977 in Alexandria, Virginia.

V-2 TO SATURN V
A 1969 photo shows von Braun with the Saturn V rocket that would soon carry three astronauts to the Moon. *Right:* The multistage Saturn grew out of this design, first sketched by von Braun in 1964.

INNER EXPLORER
Sigmund Freud's *(left)* theories, first articulated in 1900's *The Interpretation of Dreams (above)*, revolutionized the study of human behavior. Freud made one trip to America—in 1909, to lecture at Massachusetts's Clark University—and he did not like the country very much.

ERIKSON'S NATIONAL BOOK AWARD
Erik Erikson accepts the National Book Award for *Gandhi's Truth* in 1970. He gave the cash prize to groups that pursued Gandhi's philosophy.

Psychoanalysts

In 1900, Austrian doctor Sigmund Freud published *The Interpretation of Dreams*. The book, and Freud's subsequent writings, established a new technique of pyschological therapy—psychoanalysis—which sought to uncover subconscious impulses in individual behavior. Controversial at the time, Freud's ideas revolutionized the behavioral sciences. Freud and many of his associates were Jewish; in 1933, Nazi mobs burned Freud's books, and a year later psychoanalysis was banned in Germany. Freud was put under house arrest when Germany annexed Austria in 1938, but he was eventually allowed to go to London. By then, other leading figures in the movement had already fled Nazi persecution for America.

ERIK ERIKSON

Born in Frankfurt, Germany, in 1902, Erik Erikson originally trained as an artist. In 1927, while teaching at a school in Vienna, Austria, he met Anna Freud, daughter of Sigmund Freud and a pioneering psychoanalyst in her own right. After undergoing psychoanalysis with Anna, Erikson himself entered the field. His initial focus was on the impact of society and culture on child development.

Erikson immigrated to America in 1933 when the Nazis came to power in Germany. (Although he was not Jewish, Erikson had been raised by his Jewish stepfather; the experience of growing up in both Jewish and Christian milieus later led Erikson to explore the concept of the "identity crisis"—a term he coined.) He took a position at Harvard Medical School and in his clinical practice was Boston's first child psychoanalyst.

In 1940, after switching to Yale University, Erikson did fieldwork on the Sioux Native American reservations in South Dakota to study further the effects of culture on the social and intellectual development of children. From these studies and additional work at the University of California at Berkeley, Erikson developed his best-known theory: that all individuals pass through eight distinct phases of

personality development—which Erikson called "psychosocial stages"—each of which is centered on a crisis that the person must overcome before moving on to the next stage. His collection of essays in support of this theory, *Childhood and Society*, was published in 1950.

In that same year, however, Erikson ran afoul of the anticommunist paranoia of the era. Refusing to take the loyalty oath to the U.S. government required of Berkeley's faculty, he resigned to work at the Austen Riggs Center in Stockbridge, Massachusetts. He later returned to Harvard, remaining on their faculty until his death.

Erikson combined his psychoanalytical work with his interest in history in several popular studies of historical figures, including *Young Man Luther* (1958) and *Gandhi's Truth on the Origins of Militant Nonviolence* (1969). The sweeping social changes in post-World War II American society also engaged Erikson, and he explored the impact of these changes on individuals in books such as *Identity: Youth and Crisis* (1968). In it, he wonders if "some of our youth would act so openly confused and confusing if they did not know they were supposed to have an identity crisis?"

ERICH FROMM

Like his contemporary and fellow immigrant Erik Erikson, Erich Fromm was deeply interested in how society shapes human behavior. A philosopher as much as a social scientist, Fromm was also a critic of modern consumer society and an advocate of a "new enlightenment," which would balance individual needs against the good of society as a whole.

Fromm was also born in Frankfurt, Germany. After earning his PhD in sociology at Heidelberg University, Fromm switched fields and completed training as a psychoanalyst in 1930. Shortly afterward he set up a clinical practice in Berlin. With the rise of the Nazis, Fromm—a Jew descended from distinguished rabbinical families—left Germany for the United States in 1934 to teach at Columbia University in New York City. He became a U.S. citizen in 1940.

Fromm came to believe that Freud placed too much emphasis on the role instinct plays in human behavior. In Fromm's view, behavior was largely a matter of the individual's learned response to social conditions. These views put Fromm at odds with Freudians who made up most of his colleagues. He stirred up more controversy with his 1941 book, *Escape from Freedom*, in which he advanced the idea that individuals "take refuge" in totalitarian movements, like Nazism, out of fear of the responsibility that accompanies freedom.

THE HUMANIST
Erich Fromm at work. "There is hardly any activity, any enterprise," Fromm wrote, "which is started out with such tremendous hopes and expectations, and yet which fails so regularly, as love." *The Sane Society* and 1956's *The Art of Loving* made Fromm one of America's most important social thinkers.

RESERVATION KIDS
Sioux, or Lakota, children on their South Dakota reservation. Erikson's fieldwork among Native Americans influenced his writings on individual personality development, and on the role of social and cultural influences on that process.

In his most influential work, *The Sane Society* (1955), Fromm argued that both communism and capitalism lead to individual alienation and dehumanization, and he called for a new model for society, combining socialism with individual freedom.

Fromm's ideas had a big influence in the social and intellectual ferment of the 1960s. He was active in many liberal causes, including the civil rights and anti–Vietnam War movements. He taught in Mexico City in his later life, and died in 1980 in Switzerland.

FREEDOM FOR WOMEN
Dr. Ruth Westheimer

Born Karola Ruth Siegel in Frankfurt, Germany, in 1928, Westheimer was sent to school in Switzerland by her mother after *Kristallnacht* (*see pp 200–201*) and her father's subsequent imprisonment by the Nazis. Stranded in Switzerland by the outbreak of World War II in September 1939, the young girl had to support herself by working as a servant. After the war's end, she learned that her parents had died in Auschwitz.

Like many European Jews whose lives had been shattered by the Holocaust, the orphaned teenager hoped to make a new life in Palestine. Westheimer—who was only 4' 7" tall—joined the Haganah, a Jewish defense force, at age 17. (Decades later, she would tell an interviewer that she still remembered how to disassemble a submachine gun.) In 1948, after Palestine became the State of Israel, she was severely wounded by an exploding shell during the first Arab-Israeli War.

Following recovery and marriage to another Israeli soldier, Westheimer moved to Paris, studied at the Sorbonne, had a child, divorced, and moved to New York City, where she earned a degree in sociology while supporting herself and her child by working as a maid. In 1961, she became a U.S. citizen when she married Fred Westheimer. Ruth Westheimer became interested in human sexuality when she took a job at Planned Parenthood while working toward her PhD in education in the 1960s. After studying with the noted sex therapist Dr. Helen Singer-Kaplan at New York Hospital-Cornell Medical Center, Westheimer went into private practice in the 1970s.

In 1980, Westheimer began broadcasting a radio show, *Sexually Speaking*, on a New York station. Despite the fact that the show aired at midnight and lasted only 15 minutes, she developed a devoted following, especially after she began taking phone calls from listeners. Syndication won her a nationwide audience, and her popularity soared with the 1984 debut of her TV show, which ran until 1991. Books (including several best sellers), videos, a website—even a board game—followed, and today Westheimer remains an active and popular media personality.

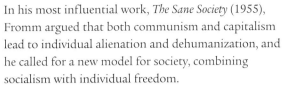

BOOK BURNING
Their arms raised in the party's salute, young Nazis watch as 20,000 "non-Aryan" books go up in flames in Berlin's Operaplaz in May 1933. "What good fortune for governments," Hitler once said, "that the people do not think."

Writers

The free flow of ideas and freedom of expression are anathema to totalitarian regimes of every kind. In the 20th century, the Nazi and Soviet governments and those of their satellite nations imposed rigorous state censorship on all writing and publishing. In Germany, the *Reichskammer* (Reich Chamber) banned and burned books it considered anti-German, subversive, or which were written by Jewish authors. In the Soviet Union, the Union of Soviet Writers, founded in 1932, used a carrot-and-stick approach to control publishing in that country; writers who produced works in the approved "Socialist realism" style were well paid, but those who did not toe the ideological line were denied membership in the union—which, during Stalin's rule, could amount to "a writer's death sentence," in the words of author Yevgeny Zemyatin. Later, dissenting Soviet and Eastern European writers turned to the *samizdat* (self-publishing) system, secretly circulating copies of their manuscripts—usually carbon copies or mimeographs—among like-minded friends and colleagues.

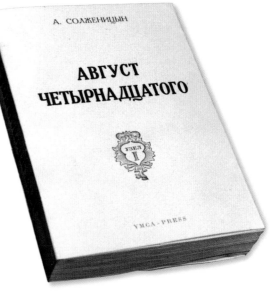

AUGUST 1914
An original Russian edition (1972) of Aleksandr Solzhenitsyn's historical novel *August 1914*, the first in a cycle of works about the origins of the Soviet state. The novel was partly inspired by the experiences of the author's father in the Russian Army during World War I.

THOMAS AND HEINRICH MANN

Born in Lübeck, Germany, Thomas Mann won the 1929 Nobel Prize for Literature for his writings, including the novels *Buddenbrooks* (1900) and *The Magic Mountain* (1924), and the short novel *Death in Venice* (1912). Although his work up to that point showed a certain mistrust of democracy, the failure of the Weimar Republic and the rise of the Nazis led Mann to rethink his philosophy. In 1930, he made a public speech in Berlin, "an Appeal to Reason," warning against the dangers posed by the Nazi Party. His novel, *Mario the Magician*, which attacked Italian Fascism, was published that same year.

HEINRICH MANN
Arriving in America penniless, Heinrich Mann and his wife Nelly depended on his younger brother Thomas, with whom he had a tense relationship.

Mann was on a European lecture tour when Hitler came to power in 1933. Warned not to return by family and friends, he came to the United States in 1938, two years after the Nazi government stripped him of German citizenship. After three years in Princeton, New Jersey, Mann moved to Pacific Palisades, California. He became a U.S. citizen in 1944.

Mann produced some of his finest work during his time America, including *Doktor Faustus* (1947), a metaphoric examination of totalitarianism, and the darkly comic *The Confessions of Felix Krull, Confidence Man* (1954). After 1952, he spent most of his time in Switzerland, where he died in 1955.

Thomas Mann's older brother, Heinrich (born 1871) was also a writer and, like Thomas, Heinrich came to the United States to escape the Nazis. Unlike Thomas, who was essentially conservative in his politics and writing, Heinrich was an ardent leftist who satirized what he saw as the German tendency toward militarism and authoritarianism in several popular novels. In 1940, Heinrich managed to escape from Germany to the Unoccupied Zone in France and then into neutral Spain, ultimately settling in Los Angeles, where he died in 1950. Today, Heinrich is best remembered for his novel *Professor Unrat* (1905), which became the basis for the classic film *The Blue Angel* (1930), starring fellow German immigrant Marlene Dietrich (*see p 277*).

NEWLY ARRIVED
Thomas Mann, his daughter Erika, and his wife Katja Pringsheim Mann, shown here just after landing in New York from the liner *George Washington*.

PUBLIC INTELLECTUAL
Left: German writer Hannah Arendt with a newspaper reporter in an undated photo. *Below:* Surrounded by guards and isolated behind bulletproof glass, Adolph Eichmann speaks during the 1961 trial that Arendt chronicled in her book *Eichmann in Jerusalem.* Arendt's controversial conclusions about Eichmann and the nature of his crimes estranged her from some of her friends in the American intellectual community.

HANNAH ARENDT

Social and political philosopher Hannah Arendt penned perceptive examinations of both the roots of totalitarianism, and its effects—which she experienced personally. Born in 1906 in Hannover, Germany, Arendt first studied at the University of Marburg, where she had a brief but intense intellectual and romantic relationship with Martin Heidegger, a major 20th-century philosopher whose reputation would later be clouded by his Nazi Party membership. Startling many of her fellow intellectuals, after World War II Arendt resumed contact with Heidegger and even tried to help him regain an academic position during de-Nazification in postwar Germany when he was banned from teaching for five years.

Arendt gained her doctorate in 1928 after further studies at the universities of Freiburg and Heidelberg. As a Jew, she was barred from university teaching after the Nazis came to power, and she was imprisoned briefly for aiding Jewish refugees and for compiling

Germany and the Soviet Union, showing how the abandonment of Enlightenment ideals (*see pp 102–103*) led to the development of those murderous regimes.

In the 1950s, Arendt became associated with the group of liberal, but anticommunist, intellectuals centered on the *Partisan Review* magazine, and she joined the faculty of the University of Chicago. In 1961, the *New Yorker* magazine commissioned her to report on the trial of Adolph Eichmann, the Nazi officer who was one of the chief architects of the

> "Only the mob and the elite can be attracted by the momentum of totalitarianism itself. The masses have to be won by propaganda."
>
> Hannah Arendt

evidence of the regime's anti-Semitic activities. In 1933, she fled to Paris, where she continued to work for Jewish refugee organizations and married a fellow German refugee, Heinrich Blücher. When the Germans overran France in 1940, French authorities interned Arendt and her husband in the country's Unoccupied Zone, but they managed to escape to America with the help of Varian Fry (*see side panel*).

In New York City, Arendt learned English and worked as an editor and researcher while writing her first major work, *The Origins of Totalitarianism*, which was published in 1951. The book explored the roots of modern anti-Semitism and traced the rise of Nazi

Holocaust. Eichmann, who fled to Argentina after the war, was captured by Israeli agents in 1960, tried in Jerusalem, and hanged in 1962. Arendt expanded her coverage of the trial into the book *Eichmann in Jerusalem* (1963), in which she argued that rather than being innately sadistic, Eichmann was an unimaginative functionary doing what he perceived to be his job—a condition she famously described as embodying " the banality of evil."

Arendt taught at New York City's New School for Social Research until her death in 1975, publishing several more books, most notably the posthumous *A Life of the Mind* (1978).

SUCCESS AND SCANDAL
Nabokov poring over his beloved butterfly books. In 1964, six years after *Lolita* brought him fame, fortune, and some notoriety, he told an interviewer: "Writing has always been for me a blend of dejection and high spirits, a torture and a pastime."

VLADIMIR NABOKOV

A brilliant writer in both Russian and English, Vladimir Nabokov was born in St. Petersburg in 1899. While still in his teens, Nabokov published two books of poetry and developed a lifelong passion for lepidoptery (the study of butterflies)—he later published a number of important papers on butterflies and discovered several species, including "Nabokov's wood nymph." Although the Nabokovs came from the aristocracy, his father was a liberal politician and journalist who ran afoul of the country's new Communist government. In 1919, the Nabokovs went to England, where he studied at Cambridge University, and then to Germany where Nabokov lived for the next 16 years, publishing novels in Russian while supporting himself as a language teacher, a crossword-puzzle writer, and a boxing instructor. In 1937, he left Germany and moved to Paris. Three years later, after the German conquest of France, Nabokov and his family came to America with a loan from another Russian émigré, the composer Sergei Rachmaninoff *(see pp 262–263)*. Nabokov became a U.S. citizen in 1945.

In America, Nabokov switched to writing in English and taught at several universities, an experience he chronicled in his novel *Pnin* (1957). In 1958, he became a household name following the American publication of *Lolita*. The tale of a middle-aged professor's passion for an underage girl, the controversial novel was banned in some communities, but its commercial success (and that of the movie version, directed by Stanley Kubrick in 1962) bought him the financial independence to pursue both his writing and his butterfly hunting. The novel that many consider his masterpiece, the highly experimental *Pale Fire*, was published in 1962. Nabokov spent most of his later life in Switzerland, where he died in 1977.

ALEKSANDR SOLZHENITSYN

No other writer did as much as Solzhenitsyn to expose the horrific nature of totalitarianism in its Soviet form. Born in 1918 into a Cossack family in Kislovodsk, in the northern Caucasus, Aleksandr Isayevich Solzhenitsyn was studying mathematics and literature when the Germans invaded the Soviet Union in June 1941. He served with distinction as a frontline artillery officer, but he was accused of treason on the basis of letters to a friend in which he had criticized Stalin. Sentenced to eight years imprisonment, Solzhenitsyn's mathematical skills won him four years in a *sharashka*—a scientific and technical research center staffed by prisoners—under comparatively decent conditions. In 1950, however, he was transferred to Ekibastuz, a hard-labor camp for political prisoners in Kazakhstan.

Solzhenitsyn was released in 1953. Because he had been sentenced under Article 58 of Soviet law, which forbade political prisoners to return to European Russia, he remained in Kazakhstan until 1956, when the new Soviet leader, Nikita Khrushchev, repudiated many of Stalin's policies.

In 1958, Solzhenitsyn completed a novel, *One Day In the Life of Ivan Denisovich*, based on his experiences at Ekibastuz. As part of Khrushchev's drive to "de-Stalinize" Soviet society, the government permitted publication of the novel in 1962. It was an immediate sensation both in the West and in Soviet Union: *One Day* was the first book published in the USSR to describe what prisoners endured in the Gulag.

IMMIGRANT WRITINGS

The lure of America; the struggle to adjust to life in a new country; the tug-of-war between the culture of the Old Country and the culture of the new; conflict between immigrant parents and their "Americanized" children—these concerns of immigrants have long been staples of American memoir and fiction.

The greatest memoirist of the Eastern European immigrant experience is Mary Antin, who fled with her family from the Russian pogroms *(see pp 198–199)*. Antin told the story of her journey from the village of Plotzk to Boston and her life in America in *The Promised Land* (1912). Nien Cheng's 1987 memoir, *Life and Death in Shanghai*, is a poignant chronicle of the author's persecution during China's Cultural Revolution of the 1960s and her eventual immigration to America. In *Unto the Sons* (1992), journalist Gay Talese used his own family's history in Italy and America as the basis for a brilliant examination of the

Italian-American experience. These are just a few of the countless memoirs written by immigrants who found both joy and sorrow in a new land.

In fiction, O.E. Rölvaag, who emigrated from Norway in 1886, wrote a three-volume saga of a Norwegian immigrant family; the best-known volume, *Giants In the Earth*, was published in 1927. Native-born writer Willa Cather also wrote of midwestern immigrants in *O Pioneers!* (1913) and *My Antonia* (1918). More recently, Korean-born Chang-rae Lee *(see pp 184–185)* explored the experience of Asian immigrants in *Native Speaker* and *A Gesture Life*, while Julia Alvarez—born in New York City but raised in the Dominican Republic—wrote of assimilation in *How the Garcia Girls Lost their Accents* (1991). Illegal immigration figures heavily in T. Coraghessan Boyle's *The Tortilla Curtain* (1995) and Jonathan Raban's *Waxwings* (2003).

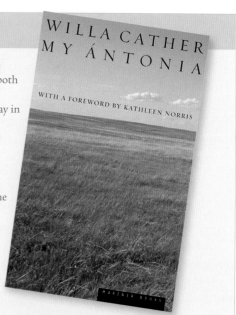

types," in his words—the author worked 12 hours a day on a cycle of historical novels, collectively known as *The Red Wheel*. In 1994, after the fall of the Soviet Union, the 75-year-old Solzhenitsyn returned to his homeland.

JOSEPH BRODSKY

Joseph Brodsky has the distinction of being considered one of the finest poets of the late 20th century in two languages—his native Russian and the English of his adopted homeland, the United States. Born in Leningrad (now St. Petersburg) in 1940, Brodsky left school at an early age but taught himself several languages and read widely while working at odd jobs. His early poems won him the attention of the Leningrad literary community—and that of the Soviet authorities. In 1963, Brodsky was hauled before a judge who asked him how someone without higher education dared to call himself a poet. Brodsky replied that he believed poetry came not from education but from God. This earned him a sentence of five years imprisonment for "social parasitism." In a rare instance of Soviet intellectuals standing up to the regime, several leading writers spoke up in Brodsky's defense, and he was released after serving 18 months. As an officially denounced writer, however, he could publish only a few poems in Russia; most of his work had to be smuggled out for publication in the West.

In 1972, Soviet authorities let Brodsky leave. After some time in Europe he came to America, where he taught at the University of Michigan, later dividing his time mostly between Brooklyn and Massachusetts. Brodsky became a U.S. citizen in 1977, the same year he won the Nobel Prize for Literature. He dedicated himself to making poetry a part of American life, "as ubiquitous," as he put it, "as gas stations, if not as cars themselves." He even suggested placing poetry anthologies next to bibles in hotel rooms. He served as Poet Laureate of the United States in 1991–92.

After Khrushchev's fall from power, Solzhenitsyn ran afoul of the hard-liners who took control. They prevented the publication of his next two novels, although copies circulated in *samizdat* form and were smuggled to the West. Solzhenitsyn won the Nobel Prize for Literature in 1970, but he did not attend the award ceremony in Sweden, out of fear the Soviet authorities would bar him from returning.

Meanwhile, in a great feat of covert scholarship, Solzhenitsyn amassed the material for a three-volume, 1,800-page work, *The Gulag Archipelago*, a history of the camp system from its establishment after the Bolshevik Revolution through the Stalin era. Excerpts were published in France in 1973, and in February 1974, Soviet authorities arrested Solzhenitsyn on charges of treason and expelled him and his family to West Germany. After some time in Switzerland, Solzhenitsyn moved to the rural village of Cavendish, Vermont, which would be his home for the next two decades. Living in a farmhouse on 50 acres of land surrounded by a fence—"to keep away the reporters and the idle

BACK IN THE (FORMER) USSR
Russian President Vladimir Putin meets with Aleksandr Solzhenitsyn at the writer's house outside Moscow in September 2000.

CAPITOL POET
Joseph Brodsky is photographed with the U.S. Capitol in the background following his 1991 appointment as Poet Laureate by the Library of Congress. He died five years later.

ANDRÉ BRETON
1896–1966

After the outbreak of World War II, Nazi persecution of artists, writers, and intellectuals extended into the countries occupied by Germany; among those affected was the French writer André Breton, one of the founders of the surrealist movement. Breton was born in Normandy. While studying medicine, he encountered the writings of Sigmund Freud, whose concept of the subconscious would have a profound effect on the development of surrealism in art and literature. After World War I, Breton became involved in dadaism, a movement, mainly in the visual arts, that rejected traditional forms and styles in favor of a deliberately irrational (and to critics a nonsensical) approach to art.

In 1924 Breton published *The Surrealist Manifesto*, calling for an art that would be "pure psychic automatism." Appearing at a time when World War I had swept away old certainties, Breton's ideas were embraced by intellectuals in art, film, and photography. He was an avowed Marxist who believed art was a means to social change.

Breton left German-occupied France for America in 1941. During his five-year sojourn there, Breton curated an exhibition of surrealist art at Yale University, made radio broadcasts, and published two more manifestos, *The Artistic Genesis and Perspective of Surrealism* (1941) and the *Prolegomena to a Third Manifesto of Surrealism or Not* (1942).

Photojournalists

Photography developed in Europe in the 1830s and 1840s, and the new medium was an immediate sensation in the United States. Americans would prove especially adept at what came to be called photojournalism—using the camera to document current events and, sometimes, to achieve social change—and a number of immigrant photographers made important contributions to the field. During the Civil War, an immigrant from Scotland, Alexander Gardner, assisted the famous photographer Matthew Brady in the field: many of Brady's best-known wartime photographs may in fact have been taken by Gardner or by his fellow assistant, Timothy O'Sullivan, who was probably born in Ireland. Brady's refusal to share credit led Gardner and O'Sullivan to leave his employ, and both went on to produce remarkable photos of the Western frontier. In the 1890s, Danish-born Jacob Riis (*see pp 152–153*) pricked the conscience of a nation with his photos of the immigrant poor in the book *How the Other Half Lives*.

NATURE'S PENCIL
Above: Matthew Brady's mobile "Photographic Outfit" outside Petersburg, Virginia, during the Union Army's siege of the city in 1864.
Below: the Graflex Company's Speed Graphic's combination of ruggedness, portability, and high-quality optics made it the camera of choice for photojournalists.

LIFE MAGAZINE
The golden age of American photojournalism began in 1936 when publisher Henry Luce introduced *Life* magazine, which set out to use the "mind-guided camera" to capture the world as it was. The magazine pioneered the photo-essay, which combined photos and text to tell a self-contained story. One of *Life*'s original staff photographers was German-born Alfred Eisenstadt, who came to America in 1935. (Eisenstadt was Jewish and in danger following the Nazis' rise to power.) A master of the candid shot, Eisenstadt ultimately produced 2,500 photo essays and 90 covers for the magazine. His best-known photo caught a sailor and a young woman kissing in New York's Times Square during the celebration that marked the Allied victory over Japan in World War II.

Life's coverage of the war produced some of the finest photos of the conflict. Many were the work of Hungarian-born Robert Capa. A legendary figure who first won fame for his frontline photos during the Spanish Civil War (1936–39), Capa seemed to court

Life's first issue

LOOKING AT LIFE
Together with its chief competitor, *Look* (published from 1937 to 1971), *Life* magazine was the original venue for photos that have become icons of the American experience—like Alfred Eisenstadt's V-J Day scene *(below)*.

danger—he liked to say, "If your pictures aren't good enough, then you aren't close enough"—and he landed with the first wave of U.S. troops during the invasion of Normandy on D-Day, June 6, 1944. Capa took 106 photos on that deadly morning, but unfortunately a darkroom technician in London destroyed all but 10 of the negatives by drying the film too quickly. The grainy, shaky shots that survived, however, brilliantly conveyed the danger and terror of combat. Capa became a U.S. citizen in 1946; eight years later, he died after stepping on a land mine while covering France's war in Indochina (*see pp 212–213*).

EDWARD STEICHEN

Born in Luxembourg in 1879, Steichen came to America with his family in 1882, settling ultimately in Milwaukee, Wisconsin. He bought his first camera in 1895 and was barely out of his teens when his photographs began to be publicly exhibited. In 1900, he became a naturalized citizen of the United States.

Steichen's precocious work came to the attention of Alfred Stieglitz—America's most famous photographer at the time—and in 1902, Stieglitz, Steichen, and several other photographers established the Photo-Secession Group, a collective that sought to win recognition for photography as an art form rather than simply a recording medium. Steichen's photography in the early 1900s reflected his study of painting—particularly the work of avant-garde artists like Pablo Picasso and Henri Matisse, whose works were exhibited at the Photo-Secession's "291" gallery in New York City, alongside the group's own photos.

During World War I, Steichen served as head of the U.S. Air Corps's Photographic Division. The experience was a revelation. Before the war, he strove to give his photos "painterly" effects by manipulating negatives and prints. The practical wartime photography he had overseen convinced Steichen to change his style to straightforward realism. This approach served him well in the 1920s and 1930s, when he became a successful commercial photographer, running his own studio as well as contributing celebrity portraits and fashion shots to magazines like *Vogue* and *Vanity Fair*.

Although he was 63 years old when the United States entered World War II, Steichen went back into the service; when the Army would not take him, he joined the Navy as head of its Naval Photographic Institute, which chronicled the war in the Pacific. After the war, Steichen became director of the Photography Department at the Museum of Modern Art in New York City. Partly at the urging of his brother-in-law, the poet Carl Sandburg, Steichen curated the most famous photographic exhibition of the 20th century: "The Family of Man." Intended to promote cultural understanding, the exhibition presented 500 photos of people from around the world, winnowed down by Steichen and his staff from more than 2 million submissions. Millions of people saw the exhibit both at the Met, where it opened in 1955, and on its subsequent tours. By the time Steichen died in Connecticut in 1973, after a career that spanned seven decades, he was revered as a towering figure of 20th-century photography.

EDWARD STEICHEN
Lieutenant Commander Edward Steichen surveys the deck of an aircraft carrier in this November 1943 photo. Steichen's photos of the Pacific War appeared at the Metropolitan Museum of Art in an exhibition titled "Power in the Pacific" the following year.

ROBERT CAPA
Robert Capa went ashore on D-Day with the soldiers of the 16th Regiment of the 1st Infantry Division—straight into German machine-gun fire. As he snapped the first of 106 photos, he repeated a sentence from the Spanish Civil War to himself—"*Es una cosa muy seria*" (This is a very serious business).

ART MUST SAVE THE STATE
"Glory to the Victorious People! Glory to the Land of Stalin!" proclaims the caption to this Soviet propaganda poster. Visual imagery like this was an essential element of the cult of personality fostered by Stalin and Hitler.

Visual Artists

The first decades of the 20th century were a time of great ferment and innovation in the arts, as traditional forms and styles gave way to a broad, new movement generally called modernism. After Hitler came to power in 1933, his minister of propaganda set up the *Reichskammer* to control media and the arts in Germany. The Nazis denounced modernist art as decadent, only fit for display in the exhibit *Entartete Kunst* (Degenerate Art). With their freedom of expression stifled (and often in danger for their political views as well) German artists crossed the Atlantic to work—and live—in freedom.

GOEBBELS GESTICULATES
Nazi Propaganda Minister Joseph Goebbels. Hitler summed up the Nazi attitude toward modernist art: "Anyone who sees and paints a sky green and fields blue ought to be sterilized."

RAISING CAIN
George Grosz at work on his painting *Cain, or Hitler in Hell*. In his memoirs, Grosz recalled a nightmare he had in 1932, which ended with a friend advising him to emigrate to America. The dream came true a year later.

GEORGE GROSZ

In the words of one critic, the scathing, satirical drawings and paintings of George Grosz amount to "the most definitive catalog of man's depravity in all history." Grosz was born in Berlin in 1893; according to some sources, his birth name was Georg Gross, but he later changed it after becoming so disillusioned with his homeland that he disliked having a typically German-sounding name. Grosz was a magazine illustrator before joining the German Army shortly before the outbreak of World War I. His experiences in the trenches mentally shattered him and he was discharged in 1915. After two years as a struggling artist in Berlin he was recalled to the army, but he broke down again and spent time in a mental hospital. Grosz took part in the failed left-wing Spartacist uprising in Berlin in 1919 and was arrested, but escaped from detention.

Grosz produced his best-known work in the years after the war, when he was associated with the dadaists (*see p 249*). His stock-in-trade, collected in portfolios including *The Face of the Ruling Class* (1921) and *Ecce Homo* (1922), were vicious caricatures that attacked the social inequities of the Weimar Republic, contrasting images of fat businessmen and venal politicians with those of maimed veterans, prostitutes, and the jobless. This ferocious social criticism did not sit well with the Weimar authorities (who fined him for insulting the army) or, later, with the Nazis, who labeled him "Cultural Bolshevist Number One." Grosz was also briefly a member of the Communist Party in the early 1920s, but left the party after a visit to the Soviet Union revealed the regime's totalitarian nature.

Grosz left Germany in 1933 to take a teaching position at the Art Student's League in New York City. He became a U.S. citizen five years later. In America, Grosz's work grew less vitriolic, and he frequently contributed drawings and cartoons to magazines. With the coming of World War II in 1939, the darker side of his work reemerged, expressed in paintings like *The Survivor* (1944) and *Cain, or Hitler in Hell* (1944). Grosz died in 1959 after returning to his native Berlin.

JOSEF ALBERS

A distinguished artist in a variety of media, Josef Albers was also a teacher, critic, and theoretician whose ideas deeply influenced postwar American art. Born in

Bottrop, Germany, in 1888, Albers studied and taught art before enrolling as a student at the Bauhaus in Weimar in 1920. Founded in 1919, the Bauhaus was a school that taught not only architecture and fine arts, but also industrial design and crafts like metalwork and typography. The modernist aesthetic that developed at the Bauhaus, as well as the school's innovative teaching methods, did much to shape 20th-century art, architecture, and design; the school's faculty included some of the best artists and craftsmen of the era, among them painter Wassily Kandinsky, designer Marcel Breuer, and architects Ludwig Mies van der Rohe and Walter Gropius (*see pp 258–259*). Albers joined the faculty of the Bauhus in 1922, three years before the school moved from Weimar to Dessau. Pressure from the Nazis led to the closing of the

SQUARE DEAL
Josef Albers in his studio, 1972. According to the artist, "As 'gentlemen prefer blondes,' so everyone has a preference for certain colors and prejudices against others. This applies to color combinations as well."

Bauhaus in 1933, and Albers and his wife Anni, a textile artist, moved to the United States that year. With the help of architect and critic Philip Johnson, Albers obtained a position as head of the art department at the newly founded Black Mountain College in North Carolina, a small school with a philosophy of learning similar to that of the Bauhaus. Albers remained there until 1949.

In 1950, Albers began work on his best-known project—*Homage to the Square*, a series of paintings with superimposed squares of color. By restricting form to the simple square, Albers was able to experiment with the relationship of color within an artwork, and with the viewers' perceptions of color. Albers continued the series for the rest of his life, and in 1971, the square paintings received a retrospective at New York's Metropolitan Museum of Art—the museum's first such exhibition featuring a living artist. *Homage to the Square* and other works of this period are credited with inspiring the Color Field and Op Art movements.

Also in 1950, Albers began a decade as head of Yale University's art department. His students included many future luminaries of the art world, including Robert Rauschenberg. In 1963, Albers published *The Interaction of Color*, now considered one of the seminal theoretical works on modern art. He continued to write, paint, and teach until his death in 1976.

HANS HOFMANN

Like Josef Albers, Hans Hofmann is equally significant both for his own body of work and for his influence as a teacher on generations of American artists. Hofmann's paintings—with their dazzling brushwork, geometric forms, and bold color—and his emphasis on improvisation and spontaneity in composition particularly inspired the painters of the abstract expressionist movement (*see pp 256–257*).

Born in Weissenburg, Bavaria, in 1880, Hofmann studied art at Munich before moving to Paris—then the undisputed capital of the visual arts—in 1904. Arriving at a time when the city was in the midst of an amazing explosion of creativity in the visual arts, Hofmann rubbed shoulders with the likes of Henri Matisse and Pablo Picasso and quickly absorbed a variety of styles, from impressionism to pointillism.

World War I broke out while Hofmann was visiting Germany and, unable to return to Paris, he established the Hans Hofmann School of Fine Arts in Munich in 1915. The school flourished for several years, but, by

ILYA AND EMILIA KABAKOV

Before *Glasnost*, Russian artist Ilya Kabakov (*right*) illustrated children's books, mostly by Italian and English authors. After *Glasnost*, he was able to accept invitations for residencies around the world. Since 1989, his wife Emilia has also been his collaborator. They travel from a home base in Long Island, New York.

"In Stalin's time unofficial art was not possible. Soviet art, social realism, was the artistic climate for all life. It was in the propaganda, the children's books, in the schools, in the exhibitions. The Artists' Union spent a huge amount of energy defining evil and working out all kinds of requirements. They controlled the painting, the theme of your subject. I thank Señor Gorbachev because he opened the door and the atmosphere is a little bit fresher. A gallery in Austria sent me an invitation for a residency. Before it would have been absolutely not possible, but it was a new time. Then came an invitation from France. So I started to travel. I always wanted to enter one home—the home of art society where the history of art is being made. It was always in Europe and in the United States. This place is called the Art World—where there are exhibits, where masterpieces are being created where the history of art is running its due course.

"Each [artist] felt as if he lived in a vacuum, in an artistic emptiness. We were denied access to a multitude of forms and all kinds of directions, which testify to the full artistic life. You had to choose whether to ignore the real life around you and live in the world of fantastic, but as we were told, 'correct' artistic expression. Or whether to try to express what was overflowing each of us: that horrible hopeless existence we led all day long, all our lives. This was the basis on which unofficial art as we know it was born. The work and life of the tiny unofficial circle of conceptual artists took place really on the edge of life. The strategy to survive for the Soviet artist is the double life. Only friends come in your studio."

THE PALACE OF PROJECTS
One of the Kabakovs' installations was photographed at its New York City showing on July 1, 2003. The pavilion is constructed of wooden supports and white plastic.

1930, the growing power of the Nazis began making things difficult for Hofmann and his students. In that same year, the University of California at Berkeley invited Hofmann to teach a summer course. He traveled back and forth between Europe and America

Hofmann was in his 60s before his reputation as an artist began to exceed his renown as a brilliant teacher of art. His landscapes and still lifes moved toward abstraction, and he developed a spatter and drip technique that preceded Jackson Pollock's (see p 256)

> "During the Cold War, America opened its doors wide to creative talents fleeing Communism."
>
> "The Art of Departure"

over the next couple of years before deciding, in 1932, to remain in the United States rather than live under Nazi rule. In 1933, Hofmann reconstituted his School of Fine Arts in New York City, with a branch in Provincetown, Massachusetts. He became a citizen of the United States in 1941.

HOFMANN'S HANDS
Hans Hofmann gives physical expression to his theory of how colors "push and pull" on the surface as he ponders a painting in progress, in this photograph from May 1957—the same year he received an important retrospective at New York City's Whitney Museum.

better-known drip pieces. Hofmann's first show in America was at the California Palace of the Legion of Honor, San Francisco. In the mid-1940s, his work came to the attention of the great arts patroness Peggy Guggenheim, who organized his first major exhibition in New York City at her Art of this Century Gallery.

In 1958, Hofmann finally retired from teaching to devote himself to painting full-time. He was widely honored both in the United States and abroad in his last years, with many major exhibitions and retrospectives. He died in 1966.

ABSTRACT EXPRESSIONISM

New York City in the late 1940s saw the emergence of a new style of modern art that captured both the critical and public imagination. Dubbed abstract expressionism, the movement was widely hailed as a uniquely American style—its most famous exponent was the hard-drinking, Wyoming-born Jackson Pollock—but immigrant artists were among its chief influences and practitioners. While some dismissed it as overhyped, puerile nonsense, abstract expressionism dominated modern art well into the 1950s. Some art historians draw a parallel between the rise of the movement and the United States' emergence as a global superpower after World War II: after abstract expressionism, the art world's center of gravity shifted from Paris to New York.

AMERICAN ACTION

Abstract expressionism was not a single style; works ranged from the riotous drip paintings of Jackson Pollock to the cool, colorful squares of Mark Rothko. What these paintings had in common were a rejection of traditional composition, a nonrepresentational approach, and the appearance of being created through a spontaneous or even subconscious process—but even given these parameters, it is impossible to generalize.

The two major influences on abstract expressionism were German-born Hans Hofmann (*see pp 253–255*) and Arshile Gorky, born in Turkey in 1904 of Armenian ancestry. Gorky, who endured the death of his mother and other relatives in the Armenian Genocide (*see pp 196–197*), escaped from Turkey with his sister and arrived in America in 1920. After studying at the Rhode Island School of Design, Gorky moved to New York City in 1925 to teach at the Grand Central School of Design. As a painter, he developed a distinct style in the late 1930s that critics have called "biomorphic"— paintings that combined images of objects like flowers superimposed over fields of radiant color. Just as his work won widespread recognition, however, Gorky suffered a series of personal tragedies and committed suicide in 1948.

Abstract expressionism coalesced in New York's Greenwich Village in 1947, when Jackson Pollock began the first of his "Action Paintings," which he produced by dripping, tossing, or even pouring paint directly from the can onto canvases, often huge ones. Championed by critic Clement Greenberg and collector Peggy Guggenheim, Pollock became the public face of the movement, which included artists such as Robert Motherwell and Helen Frankenthaler, and two immigrant artists, Willem de Kooning and Mark Rothko.

TORMENTED ARTIST
Arshile Gorky's traumatic childhood experiences during the Armenian Genocide contributed to his lifelong battle with depression. He abandoned his birth name because, he believed, Americans would be more receptive to a painter with a Russian-sounding name.

WILLEM DE KOONING

Next to Pollock, the best known of the early abstract expressionists was Willem de Kooning. Born in 1904 in Rotterdam, the Netherlands, de Kooning worked as a commercial artist until 1926, when—fleeing a dull job and a difficult family life—the 22-year-old stowed away on a British freighter bound for New York City. He arrived with no money and spoke only one word of English ("yes"), but managed to support himself by house painting in New Jersey before moving to Manhattan. For the next two decades, de

JACKSON POLLOCK
Pollock is seen using his pouring technique in this photograph. The artist's image as a rough-and-tumble character added to the public appeal of the abstract expressionist movement, but his heavy drinking and womanizing took a toll on his work. Pollock died in a car crash in 1956.

WILLEM DE KOONING
Left: de Kooning mixes paints in his studio. *Woman I,* one in the series of paintings that catapulted de Kooning to fame in the early 1950s. "Art never seems to make me peaceful or pure," he said in 1951. "I do not think of inside or outside—or art in general—as a situation of comfort."

Kooning lived a hand-to-mouth existence while systematically exploring a variety of styles in his paintings. During the Depression, he worked for a year for the Works Projects Administration, but he had to leave the program when administrators discovered he was an illegal alien. He finally gained citizenship by marrying Elaine Fried, a fellow artist, in 1943.

Throughout the 1940s, de Kooning's work became less figurative and more abstract. Public recognition began with his first New York show in 1948, the same year he taught at North Carolina's Black Mountain College. In 1950–1952, de Kooning labored on the painting *Woman I*. While not a totally abstract work like Pollock's drip paintings, its violent imagery and its obvious emotional intensity established de Kooning as one of the country's greatest painters. The female form remained a major theme of de Kooning's paintings through the 1960s, along with land- and waterscapes, before he turned largely to sculpture. De Kooning's later years were marred by Alzheimer's disease, and he died in 1997 in East Hampton, New York.

MARK ROTHKO

In the 1950s, several abstract expressionists moved to a style known as Color-Field Painting, which eschewed the wild slashes and dashes of Action Painting for solid blocks of color. The best known painter in this style was Mark Rothko, born Markus Rothkovich to a Jewish family in Dvinsk, Russia in 1903. In 1913, Rothko immigrated with his family to Portland, Oregon. He described the experience to painter Robert Motherwell: "You don't know what it is to be a Jewish kid dressed in a suit, a Dvinsk not an American, idea of a suit, traveling across America and not able to speak English . . ."

After two years at Yale University and some time traveling around the country, he settled in New York City in 1925. At various times he had planned to be a lawyer, engineer, or labor organizer, but he turned to art, because, in his words, "I wanted to raise painting to the level of poignancy of music and poetry."

Apart from some classes at the city's Art Institute, Rothko had no formal training as an artist, and his early works were relatively realistic. In the 1930s and early 1940s, he began to explore a more expressionist approach. Around 1950, Rothko began creating the paintings that made his reputation—massive, unframed canvases with rectangles of pure color bleeding into one another. He worked in this simultaneously simple and complex style for the rest of his career.

Although his name was often mentioned in the same breath as Pollock and de Kooning, Rothko disliked being labeled as an abstract expressionist. While he had some important commissions in the late 1950s and early 1960s, and an exhibition at the Metropolitan Museum of Art in 1961, Rothko was mainly an "artist's artist" until winning public acclaim in the 1960s for the 14 large, related works that he painted for an interfaith church in Houston, Texas. By then, however, Rothko was in the grip of depression, and he killed himself in his New York studio in 1970.

MARK ROTHKO
Above: Rothko in 1961. *Left:* Rothko's painting *Number Ten* (1950). The Museum of Modern Art passed on the work; two years later, architect Philip Johnson bought the painting and donated it to MOMA.

Architects

American architect and critic Philip Johnson coined the term "International Style" in 1932 to describe the clean-lined, unadorned buildings being designed by Europe's leading architects. Two of the most prominent architects of the style, Ludwig Mies van der Rohe and Walter Gropius, came to the United States after the Nazis closed the Bauhaus *(see p 253)*, an influential German school of design and architecture, in the early 1930s. As both teachers and practicing architects, Mies and Gropius helped establish the International Style as the leading architectural movement from the 1930s to the 1970s.

LUDWIG MIES VAN DER ROHE

Born Maria Ludwig Michael Mies in Aachen, Germany, in 1886, Mies worked in the Berlin office of Peter Behrens. He won widespread fame with his design for the German Pavilion at the 1929 International Exposition in Barcelona, Spain. (Mies also designed the Barcelona chair, now an icon of modern furniture design, for the pavilion's interior.)

A year later, Mies became director of the Bauhaus, which he had to shut down in 1933 after the Nazis—who loathed the school's modernist

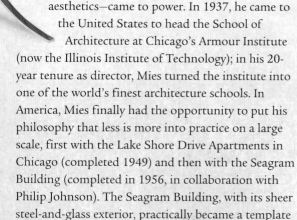

Mies's Barcelona Chairs

aesthetics—came to power. In 1937, he came to the United States to head the School of Architecture at Chicago's Armour Institute (now the Illinois Institute of Technology); in his 20-year tenure as director, Mies turned the institute into one of the world's finest architecture schools. In America, Mies finally had the opportunity to put his philosophy that less is more into practice on a large scale, first with the Lake Shore Drive Apartments in Chicago (completed 1949) and then with the Seagram Building (completed in 1956, in collaboration with Philip Johnson). The Seagram Building, with its sheer steel-and-glass exterior, practically became a template

INTERNATIONAL EXEMPLAR
Ludwig Mies van der Rohe and Philip Johnson's Seagram Building towers 38 stories over New York City's Park Avenue and embodies ideas that Mies *(right)* had articulated 30 years earlier in Germany.

BAUHAUS
The name *Bauhaus* means "house of building" in German. The artisans and teachers of the school—shown below in its Dessau, Germany, location—collectively influenced 20th-century architecture and design more than any other single institution.

for hundreds of structures worldwide. Awarded the Presidential Medal of Freedom in 1963, Mies died in 1969, shortly after the completion of his last major work, the National Gallery in Berlin.

WALTER GROPIUS

Born in Berlin in 1883, Gropius worked in the same firm as Mies, where he became deeply committed to the idea that there had to be a marriage of appearance and utility in the era of the machine and mass production in order to, in his words, "breathe a soul into the dead product of the machine."

His early career was interrupted by service in the German Army in World War I and complicated by a brief, troubled marriage to Alma Schindler Mahler (the widow of composer Gustav Mahler). A major turning point came in 1920, when he took over the newly established Bauhaus. In 1925, the school moved from Weimar to Dessau, into a building Gropius designed. He went into private practice in 1928.

Gropius left Germany in 1934. After several years in England, he came to the United States, accepting a position as chairman of the architecture department at Harvard, which he held until 1952. He designed several houses (including his own) in collaboration with Marcel Breuer, and, in 1946, he joined with several former students to found The Architects' Collaborative (TAC); its finished commissions included campus facilities at Harvard and the U.S. Embassy in Athens, Greece, as well as an uncompleted design for the University of Baghdad. Gropius's last major work, designed in collaboration with Italian-born Pietro Belluschi, was New York City's Pan Am Building (completed 1963; now the MetLife Building).

Ironically, the Pan Am Building created a backlash against the International Style in architecture. Many New Yorkers hated the fact that the building obstructed views up and down Park Avenue and dwarfed Grand Central Station, the Beaux-Arts-style railroad terminal (completed in 1913) at its base. Starting in the 1970s, American postmodern architects, including Canadian-born Frank Gehry and Chinese-born I. M. Pei (see pp 260–261), rejected Mies's dictum that less is more in favor of a more decorative style.

PAN AM BUILDING
At the time of its completion in 1963, the Pan American Building was the largest commercial structure in the world. It even included a helicopter landing pad on its roof.

TWO IMMIGRANT ARCHITECTS
Walter Gropius *(left)* and Pietro Belluschi pore over blueprints of the Pan Am Building. The Italian-born Belluschi designed more than 1,000 buildings in his career, including New York City's Lincoln Center for the Performing Arts.

ELIEL AND EERO SAARINEN

Born in 1873 in Rantasalmi, Finland, Eliel Saarinen was already Finland's foremost architect and the designer of buildings as far afield as Canberra, Australia, when he decided to move his family to the United States in 1923 to take up a teaching position at the University of Michigan. The year before, Eliel won second place in a competition for a design of a new headquarters for the Chicago Tribune newspaper; even though his design was not selected, American architects and critics immediately acclaimed it as a bold step forward in skyscraper design. From the mid-1920s until his death in 1950, Eliel was closely

associated with the Cranbrook Academy of Art in Bloomfield Hills, Michigan, first as president and later as head of the graduate program in architecture. Eliel also collaborated with his son Eero (born in 1910 in Kirkkonummi, Finland), most notably on an expansion of the Smithsonian Institution in Washington, D.C. in the 1940s. Eero went on to become one of America's most highly regarded architects in his own right. In the 1950s and 1960s, Eero designed buildings for General Motors, Yale, the Massachusetts Institute of Technology, and the CBS Corporation; his best-known works are the TWA Terminal at New York's JFK Airport (completed 1962) and the soaring Jefferson National Memorial (better known as the Gateway Arch) in St. Louis, Missouri (designed 1948, completed 1965). As a furniture designer, Eero produced pieces that are considered classics of "mid-century modern" design, including the 1948 womb chair. He died in 1961.

. . . AND SON
Eero Saarinen in 1956 with a model of his design for a new U.S. Embassy building to be built in London's Grosvenor Square. The building was completed six years later.

WEST COAST MODERNISM

While Frank Lloyd Wright was certainly the most celebrated American residential architect of the 20th century, in California, at least, he had to compete for commissions, for a time, with a couple of émigré architects—including a former employee. Vienna-born Richard Neutra (1892–1970) came to the United States in 1929—the first major International Style architect to set up shop in

Richard Neutra

America. In Southern California, Neutra designed sleek homes that took advantage of the mild climate and abundant light by integrating indoor and outdoor living spaces and incorporating expanses of glass. His best-known commissions are the Lovell House in Los Angeles (actually designed before he immigrated, and featured in the 1997 movie *L.A. Confidential*), the Tremaine House in Montecito, and the Kaufmann House (1946) in Palm Springs (commissioned by the same family who got Frank Lloyd Wright to design their famous Pennsylvania home, Fallingwater). Another Austrian-born architect to make his mark was Rudolph Schindler (1887–1953), who came to America in 1914 and found work in Frank Lloyd Wright's office. A few years later, Wright sent him to Los Angeles to oversee construction of Hollyhock House *(below)*. Schindler soon struck out on his own, although he sometimes worked in partnership with Neutra. In part because he liked to build with reinforced concrete—which did not age well—Schindler's work fell into obscurity, but his reputation as a pioneer of "West Coast modernism" revived in the 1980s.

I. M. PEI

Ieoh Ming Pei was born in Canton, China, in 1917, and grew up mostly in Hong Kong and Shanghai. Pei's father, a banker, wanted him to complete his education in England, but Pei chose to go to the University of Pennsylvania in 1935 to study engineering. Pei transferred to the Massachusetts Institute of Technology for architecture.

Unable to return to China after the outbreak of World War II, Pei studied at Harvard University's Graduate School of Design and worked for the National Defense Research Committee. With the war over, Pei taught for a time before becoming chief architect of the New York construction firm Webb and Knapp in 1948. Over the next seven years, he designed several large-scale, urban-renewal projects around the country.

In 1955, Pei formed his own firm, I. M. Pei & Associates, and quickly built his reputation with commissions like the National Center for Atmospheric Research in Boulder, Colorado, the John F. Kennedy Memorial Library at Harvard University, and the John Hancock Tower in Boston. Pei was deeply influenced by the International Style, but he had his own distinct way with geometric forms—like the glass pyramid he designed for the entrance to the Louvre Museum in

TAKING FLIGHT
The swooping curves of Eero Saarinen's TWA Terminal at New York's Idlewild Airport (later John F. Kennedy International Airport) were meant to suggest flight. In the early 2000s, preservationists fought plans by the Port Authority of New York—the agency that owns and maintains the airport—to redevelop the terminal in a way that would have compromised the original design.

GO WEST
Eero Saarinen's design for St. Louis's Gateway Arch won a competition held by the city in 1947, but the actual structure was built between 1961 and 1967. At more than 600 feet in height, it is the tallest monument in the United States.

Paris (1987)—and with materials—using precast concrete frames in the Kips Bay Towers apartment complex in New York City (1963).

In 1974, critic Ada Louise Huxtable wrote that Pei "may very likely be America's best architect." Pei continued to produce outstanding work in the 1980s and 1990s; as of this writing, his most recent major project was the Rock and Roll Hall of Fame and Museum in Cleveland, Ohio (1995).

Musicians

As in all the arts, the beginning of the 20th century was an era of innovation in music, from the development of Arnold Schoenberg's 12-tone style to the politicized musical theater of Kurt Weill and Bertolt Brecht. The Nazis—rigorously opposed to any deviation from their reactionary cultural standards—labeled such music as "degenerate," not only for its modernism, but because many of its practitioners were Jews, or political leftists, or both. This would drive four of the greatest modernist composers to America in the 1930s, while the great Italian conductor Arturo Toscanini, a refugee from Fascism in Italy, brought the joys of traditional classical music to millions of Americans through his radio and television broadcasts.

BRAVO MAESTRO
Many leading Nazi officials were avid fans of classical music—provided it was traditional in form and "Aryan" in origin. Here, Joseph Goebbels, Hermann Goering, and Adolf Hitler *(first row, left to right)* applaud conductor Wilhelm Furtwangler after a performance by the Berlin Philharmonic Orchestra.

The Bolshevik Revolution of 1917 drove two great musical figures—the composer Igor Stravinsky and the composer and pianist Sergei Rachmaninoff—into exile. Both eventually made America their home.

SERGEI RACHMANINOFF

Sergei Rachmaninoff was born into an aristocratic family in Semyonov in 1873. After graduating from the Moscow Conservatory, he composed and performed several piano concertos that were rapturously received, and a symphony that was not. Disappointment over the latter lead to a period of depression, a condition that was to plague him throughout his life. He was acclaimed as a virtuoso concert pianist, however, and

he was able to support himself financially through his performances. In 1909, he toured the United States and premiered his *Piano Concerto No. 3*, considered one of the most technically demanding piano pieces ever composed, with the New York Philharmonic.

Rachmaninoff was in Russia during the Revolution of 1917. Perceiving (correctly) that his aristocratic background would only cause him problems under the new regime, he left for a European concert tour—and never returned to Russia. After some time in Copenhagen, he went to New York in November 1918. He ultimately settled in California, although he visited Europe, particularly Switzerland.

PIANO VIRTUOSO
Sergei Rachmaninoff studies a score in this photograph taken during the 1920s. A strict perfectionist, he was often unhappy with his own performances. Igor Stravinsky described him as "[a] six-and-a-half-foot-tall scowl."

Rachmaninoff never fully adjusted to life in America, and his most creative period as a composer proved to be behind him; however, his American years did see the composition of the orchestral piece *Symphonic Dances* (1940) and the popular posthumous *Rhapsody on a Theme of Paganini* (1954). He died in 1943.

IGOR STRAVINSKY

Stravinsky was born outside St. Petersburg in 1882. Although he came from a musical family, Stravinsky studied law until the composer Nikolai Rimsky-Korsakov urged him to pursue a career in music. Stravinsky first attracted attention with his scores for the Ballets Russes dance company under the direction of the legendary impresario Sergei Diaghilev. *The Firebird* (1910) was a huge success, and Stravinsky's follow-up, *The Rite of Spring*, literally caused a riot at its 1913 premiere in Paris thanks to its wild and avant-garde style.

Stravinsky spent World War I in France and Switzerland. The Bolshevik Revolution of 1917 made him persona non grata in his homeland and the Bolshevik seizure of his family's property forced him to earn a living as a concert pianist for a time. He continued to compose ballet scores and orchestral works while living mostly in France, and his deepening Christian mysticism led to such works as *Symphony of Psalms* (1930). By the 1930s, he was considered one of the greatest contemporary composers. Stravinsky was in the United States delivering a series of lectures when World War II broke out. He became a U.S. citizen in 1945, after settling in Hollywood, where he tried his hand at movie scoring. (He was not very successful, although he would still get his own star on the Hollywood Walk of Fame.)

After a creative crisis in the late 1940s and early 1950s, Stravinsky adopted the 12-tone style pioneered by Arnold Schoenberg (*see pp 264–265*), producing a remarkable series of late-period works and continuing to perform until the late 1960s. He died in New York City in 1971.

ARTURO TOSCANINI

The greatest orchestral conductor of the first half of the 20th century, Arturo Toscanini was born in Parma, Italy, in 1867, the oldest of four children and the only son. Toscanini was originally a cellist, but while touring South America in 1886, the 19-year-old was called on to substitute for an incompetent conductor and astonished orchestra and audience alike by conducting Giuseppe Verdi's opera *Aida* completely from memory. (Toscanini's amazing memory was critical to his success as a conductor; his eyesight was so poor he had difficulty reading a score.)

MODERNIST MASTER
Igor Stravinsky at the podium in 1968, still vigorous at age 86. In 1961, critic François Michel called Stravinsky "the greatest musician of our epoch."

FIREBIRD
A scene from the Royal Ballet Company's 1993 production of Stravinsky's *The Firebird*, one of three ballets he composed for the Ballets Russes in 1910–1913—the others were *Petrushka* and *The Rite of Spring*—which made his worldwide reputation.

"Toscanini believed that you can't make music in good faith, without being free. He believed that music did have a moral purpose."

Harvey Sachs, Toscanini biographer

THE MAESTRO
Arturo Toscanini conducts the NBC Symphony Orchestra in 1944. Toscanini held his musicians to exacting standards: he famously told a trumpeter, "God tells me how the music should sound, but you stand in the way."

Twelve years later, he was appointed resident conductor at Milan's La Scala opera house, where he remained into the 1920s, with stints conducting the New York Philharmonic Orchestra and the New York Metropolitan Opera. Everywhere he conducted, Toscanini won acclaim for his ability to bring out the best in his musicians in brilliantly intense performances of both opera and orchestral works—Wagner, Verdi, and Beethoven were his specialties.

Toscanini was also a tenacious opponent of Fascism and Nazism. A vocal critic of Benito Mussolini, Italy's dictator, he was beaten up by Fascist thugs in 1931 for refusing to include the Fascist Party's anthem in a concert, and he rejected offers to perform in Germany after Hitler took power. In 1936, he made a special point (funding the trip out of his own pocket) of conducting the first performance of the Palestine Orchestra (later the Israeli Philharmonic), which was composed mostly of Jewish refugees.

In 1937, after a period with the New York Philharmonic, Toscanini decided to stay in America. A year later, at the age of 70, he raised his baton over the NBC Symphony Orchestra, which had been created by the National Broadcasting Corporation especially for him. The orchestra's weekly radio broadcasts made him a household name and did much to popularize classical music in the United States. In 1948, the orchestra began performing on television as well. Ill health forced his retirement in 1954, and he died in New York in 1957, a few weeks before turning 90.

ARNOLD SCHOENBERG

Born in Vienna in 1874, Schoenberg was mostly self-taught as a composer. His first works were in the Romantic style of Johannes Brahms and Gustav Mahler (the latter composer was one of his mentors), but around the turn of the 20th century he produced a

THE INNOVATOR
Schoenberg conducts a Federal Music Project/Works Projects Administration (WPA) orchestra in Los Angeles, 1937. Approximately 15,000 musicians were employed during the Federal Music Project's peak in 1936.

series of increasingly unconventional compositions that provoked strong responses—both positive and negative—from critics and audiences.

Before World War I, Schoenberg enjoyed more recognition as a teacher and theorist than as a composer. Among his students were Alban Berg and Anton von Webern, both of whom later became major composers, and he published several influential books on composition and musical theory, most notably, *Harmonialehre* (The Theory of Harmony) in 1911.

After service in the Austrian Army in World War I, Schoenberg began to work in an even more radical style. Throwing out traditional Western ideas of melody and tonality, he developed an entirely new, atonal form of music based on a row of 12 notes in the chromatic scale. Schoenberg began composing his first fully 12-tone work, the *Piano Suite, Opus 25*, in 1921, telling a student that "today I have discovered something that will assure the supremacy of German music for the next hundred years."

The Nazis, however, condemned Schoenberg's work, both for its rejection of musical tradition and for the fact that he was Jewish. After losing his post at the Prussian Academy of Arts in Berlin, Schoenberg came to America in 1933, settling in Los Angeles, where he taught at UCLA from 1936 to 1944. (When he became a U.S. citizen he changed the spelling of his name, which was originally "Schönberg.") Schoenberg's American compositions, mostly in the 12-tone style, include works with Jewish themes, such as the choral work *A Survivor from Warsaw* and the opera *Moses and Aron*, which was left unfinished at his death in 1951. While

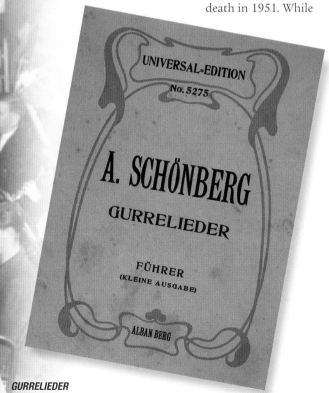

GURRELIEDER
The score for Schoenberg's *Gurrelieder*, a sprawling work for soloists, an orchestra, and an oversized chorus, which he began composing in 1900. Schoenberg was heavily influenced by Wagner, Mahler, and Brahms.

FROM THE NEW WORLD

The premiere of Czech composer Antonín Dvořák's *Symphony No. 9 in E Minor*, better known as the "New World" Symphony, at New York's Carnegie Hall on December 16, 1893, was a defining moment in the nation's cultural history—for the first time, a world-class composer presented an original work, drawn from American themes, on American soil. The symphony was an immediate success and it remains Dvořák's best-remembered work.

Dvořák was born in 1841 in the village of Nelahozeves, in what was then the Austro-Hungarian province of Bohemia and now the Czech Republic. Dvořák showed great musical ability at an early age, but his family's modest means limited his formal training. Dvořák struggled to support himself by teaching and playing the viola while composing his first works, until a government grant eased his financial situation somewhat, and a friendship with the great composer Johannes Brahms brought him his first public recognition.

Dvořák's career took off in the 1870s, largely due to his *Slavonic Dances* (1878), piano duets influenced by the Czech folk music he had heard as a boy in his father's inn. Choral works and symphonies followed, and, in the 1880s, he rose into the top rank of European composers.

In 1892, the National Conservatory of Music in New York City offered Dvořák the substantial sum of $15,000 to serve as its director. He took the job—despite his success, money problems plagued him throughout his life. He was also intrigued by the challenge the position offered: in a letter to a friend, Dvořák wrote

ANTONÍN DVOŘÁK
In the opinion of some critics, the success of Dvořák's New World Symphony led to his other works being unappreciated.

that "the Americans expect great things of me and the main thing is . . . to show them to the promised land and kingdom of a new and independent art, in short, to create a national music. If the small Czech nation can have such musicians, they say, why could not they, too, when their country and people is so immense."

Dvořák's time in America, from September 1892 to May 1895, proved to be among the most fertile of his career after he heard America's homegrown music—from the popular songs of Stephen Foster to Native-American chants to African-American dance music and spirituals. Marrying indigenous music with classical forms and orchestration—as he had done with Czech music—Dvořák's American period produced, besides the New World Symphony, his *"American" String Quartet in F major*, the *B minor Cello Concerto*, and several other works. While based in New York City, Dvořák traveled as far west as Iowa—where he spent the summer of 1893 in the Czech immigrant community of Spillville. After returning to Europe, he continued to compose prolifically until his death in 1904.

Despite the success of Dvořák's music, few American composers of the era followed his lead in incorporating Native-American and African-American chants and spirituals into their compositions. At the time, many critics rejected folk idioms as unsuitable for incorporation in "serious" music.

HALL OF GIANTS
Named for Scots-born industrialist Andrew Carnegie (*see p 142*), who paid for its construction, Carnegie Hall opened in 1891 with a concert conducted by Peter Ilyich Tchaikovsky. It is America's best-known venue for classical music.

the 12-tone style was disparaged by many critics, Schoenberg is recognized as one of the 20th century's most influential and innovative composers.

KURT WEILL

Born in Dessau, Germany, in 1900, Weill first composed traditional symphonies and concerti, but it was the musical plays he produced in collaboration with playwright Bertolt Brecht (*see p 271*)—*The Threepenny Opera* (1928) and the jazzy *The Rise and Fall of the City of Mahagonny*—that first won him fame: the combination of Brecht's satirical words and Weill's jazz-inflected music created a new kind of musical theater. They also enraged the Nazis—the premiere of *Mahagonny* in 1930 in Leipzig, Germany, for example, was disrupted by a staged riot of Nazi thugs, and after Hitler came to power Weill's music was banned in Germany. In danger because of both his music (the composer was branded a "degenerate artist") and his

THE SONGWRITER
Kurt Weill in 1944, at the height of his second career as an American stage composer. Weill's wife, Austrian-born actress and singer Lotte Lenya, performed in many of his works; after his death she kept up an active career (including an Oscar) until her own death in 1981.

Jewish origins (his father was a synagogue cantor), he left Germany in 1933, and, after some time in Paris and London, moved to New York City in 1935.

In America, Weill reinvented himself as a composer of Broadway musicals, collaborating with some of the best writers of the era, including Maxwell Anderson (*Knickerbocker Holiday*, 1938), Moss Hart and Ira Gershwin (*Lady in the Dark*, 1941), and Ogden Nash (*One Touch of Venus*, 1943). Granted U.S. citizenship in 1943, Weill saw the United States as more than a place of refuge. He eagerly embraced the culture of his adopted country and hoped to create a uniquely American musical form that would bridge the gap between opera and the Broadway musical—a concept he put into practice in his "folk opera" *Down in the Valley* (1945) and *Street Scene* (with Elmer Rice and Langston Hughes, 1947). He died of a heart attack in 1950, at the age of 50, after starting work on a musical adaptation of Mark Twain's *Huckleberry Finn* with

POPULAR MUSIC

Latin salsa, Caribbean soca and reggae, Ghanaian soukous, Punjabi bhangra—a spin around the American radio dial in the early 21st century is audible evidence of the impact the most recent waves of immigrants are having on America's popular culture. And while the music of immigrant communities creates the country's growing diversity, foreign-born musicians—particularly from Latin America and the Caribbean—have also enjoyed success on the charts, often by mixing the styles of their native countries with rock or pop elements. In the late 1960s and 1970s, for example, Mexican-born Carlos Santana and his eponymous band mixed West Coast psychedelia with Latin rhythms in a series of brilliant albums. Santana rose to the top of the charts again as a solo artist with 1998's *Supernatural*. Gloria Estefan fled from Cuba with her family as a two-year-old in 1959 because her father—a bodyguard to Fulgencio Batista, the

SUPERNATURAL SANTANA
Carlos Santana (*shown left in concert in 2000*) and his band shot to national fame with a performance at the August 1969 Woodstock Festival. Santana went in a more jazz-oriented direction in the 1970s, before collaborating with, among others, Wyclef Jean and Dave Matthews in the 1990s.

island nation's dictator—was in danger after Fidel Castro overthrew Batista. In 1985, Estefan and her band, Miami Sound Machine, broke big with their first English-language album, *Primitive Love*, a poppy fusion of disco and salsa.

In another example of musical cross-pollination, American rock 'n' roll and rhythm 'n' blues combined with West Indian styles like ska to create reggae, while in New York City in the 1970s, DJs like Jamaican-born Kool Herc introduced the practice of "toasting" over records, which spawned rap.

Of course, all of the distinctive styles of popular music that America has given the world—blues, jazz, country, and rock 'n' roll— have their roots in the cultural traditions of immigrant groups. Settlers from the British Isles in the 17th and 18th centuries brought with them the mournful ballads of their homeland, which formed a cornerstone of modern country music. African-American and European styles blended together in New Orleans around the turn of the 21st century to form jazz—a musical style often called "America's classical music."

MIAMI SOUND MACHINE
Gloria Estefan and the Miami Sound Machine perform at the 2000 Latin Grammy Awards. Cuban influence on American music has been profound, starting with the trumpeter Dizzy Gillespie's "Afro-Cuban" jazz bands.

MACK'S BACK

The playbill for a 1989 revival of Kurt Weill and Bertolt Brecht's *The Threepenny Opera* at Broadway's Lunt-Fontanne Theater. Rock star Sting played the role of Macheath.

Maxwell Anderson. Many later musicians, ranging from Lou Reed and the Doors to Tom Waits and Nick Cave, have recorded Weill's songs or otherwise acknowledged his influence.

BÉLA BARTÓK

Renowned both as an authority on the folk music of Central Europe and as a composer and pianist, Bartók was born in Nagyszentmiklós, Hungary, (now in Romania) in 1881. After studying piano and composition in Budapest, Bartók and his fellow composer Zoltán Kodály began meticulously documenting the native music of the Hungarian peasants, a project that Bartók pursued for many years. He also increasingly incorporated folk themes into his works, including his six piano concertos.

After serving as a sort of musical adviser to Hungary's short-lived Communist government after World War I, Bartók continued to compose and traveled widely as a concert pianist. In the 1930s, he became an outspoken critic of the Nazis in Germany and their right-wing allies in Hungary. By 1940, Hungary's government was under increasing pressure from Germany, and Bartók decided—reluctantly—to leave his homeland for the United States.

Unfortunately, Bartók's experience in America was not as happy as that of many of his fellow refugees from totalitarianism. Despite his European fame, Bartók was not well known in America, and he had to accept a relatively lowly position at New York City's Columbia University, where he transcribed Serbo-Croatian folk songs. Bartók received help from a fellow émigré, Russian-born composer Serge Koussevitzky, who commissioned Bartók to compose a Concerto for Orchestra for the Boston Symphony Orchestra. Unfortunately, Bartók was diagnosed with leukemia. He persevered: one of his doctors later recalled that "he never complained. With high fever up to 102–103° he sat up writing music from his head, composing from memory." Completed in 1943, the concerto is now considered one of his finest works. Bartók finally succumbed to the disease in New York City in 1945.

MULTIMEDIA MAC

A scene from *Mac the Knife,* a 1990 movie adaptation of *The Threepenny Opera.* Brecht and Weill's musical masterpiece included a hit for singer Bobby Darin, whose version of the song "Mac the Knife" topped the pop charts in 1959.

HUNGARIAN SOUL

Left: Béla Bartók in 1927, the year of his first concert tour of the United States. Bartók played more than 600 concerts in 22 countries during his performance career. *Above:* Part of the score for *Cantata Profana* (1930), the composer's only major choral work.

Dancers

Although the nation was a leader in modern dance from the turn of the 20th century onward, the United States had practically no tradition of classical ballet before the arrival of George Balanchine in 1933. "Mr. B" remained the leading figure in American ballet for the next half-century. Like all the arts, ballet—a traditional Russian speciality—was subject to rigid state control in the Soviet Union, and creative frustration led several leading Russian dancers to defect to the West. Some, like Rudolf Nureyev and Natalia Makarova, settled in Europe; for young Mikhail Baryshnikov, America was the destination.

MARIINSKY BALLET

The Mariinsky Ballet of St. Petersburg was first the Imperial Russian Ballet, then the Kirov Ballet (so named in 1935 to honor the murdered Soviet leader), and, from 1991 on, the Mariinsky Ballet. During the Cold War, the company lost three of its best dancers to the West—Rudolf Nureyev to France, Natalia Makarova to England, and Mikhail Baryshnikov to America.

GEORGE BALANCHINE

Born Georgy Melitonovich Balanchivadze in 1904, in St. Petersburg, Russia, Balanchine studied at the Imperial School of Ballet and the St. Petersburg Conservatory of Music. He began choreographing avant-garde ballets that garnered the disapproval of the new Soviet government. Fed up with the lack of artistic freedom in his homeland, Balanchine decided not to return from a 1924–25 tour of Europe. In Paris, he joined the Ballets Russes, and worked with other European ballet companies after the Russes folded in 1929. Balanchine came to the United States in 1933, at the invitation of the arts patron Lincoln Kirstein. The following year, the two organized the School of American Ballet to help fulfill Kirstein's goal of training American dancers in the classical tradition. In 1935, they established a performing company, the American Ballet, which performed in association with New York's Metropolitan Opera, although creative differences between Balanchine and the Met led to the dissolution of the company in 1938.

Balanchine also choreographed for Broadway and the movies; one of his most famous dances was "Slaughter on First Avenue" for the 1936 Richard Rogers & Lorenz Hart musical *On Your Toes*. In 1948, Kirstein and Balanchine established the New York City Ballet, which became, and remains, America's premiere dance troupe. Balanchine served as the company's director and chief choreographer until his death, and he choreographed more than 150 works for the company, including acclaimed productions of *The Nutcracker* (1954) and *Don Quixote* (1965) and numerous performances of the ballets of his fellow Russian émigré Igor Stravinsky (*see p 263*); their association started in the 1920s.

BALANCHINE ON B'WAY

In a publicity photo from 1935, George Balanchine puts dancer Georgia Hiden of the Ziegfeld Follies through the motions backstage.

MIKHAIL BARYSHNIKOV

Born in Latvia of Russian parents in 1948, Baryshnikov showed incredible prowess as a dancer from an early age. While still in his teens, he was the star of Leningrad's (now St. Petersburg) Kirov Ballet, performing in works choreographed especially for him. Increasingly unhappy with life under the Soviet regime—which kept him from dancing in works that did not meet with official approval—Baryshnikov decided to defect to the West while on a tour with the Bolshoi Ballet in 1974.

After the curtain fell on the troupe's final performance in Toronto, Baryshnikov gave the dancers' escort the slip and jumped into a car arranged by sympathizers. After a perod in hiding in Canada, he moved to America to join the American Ballet Theater (ABT). He later said, "I came to this country really not to make money . . . but to be somebody and to spend my life in the most interesting way."

"Misha," as he is nicknamed, performed with the ABT until 1978, when he spent a year with the New York City Ballet before returning to the ABT until 1989. He formed his own touring company in 1990. With his physical presence and brilliant athleticism, Baryshnikov was a crowd-pleaser as well as critical favorite, and his performances did much to popularize ballet in the United States.

In addition to his work in ballet, Baryshnikov has starred in movies including *The Turning Point* (1977), which earned him an Oscar nomination, and *White Nights* (1985); he also held down a dramatic role in a stage version of Franz Kafka's *Metamorphosis* (1989), and made numerous TV appearances, including a guest role in HBO's *Sex and the City*.

MISHA ALOFT
Mikhail Baryshnikov's astonishing physical expression is evident in this photograph from a 1978 rehearsal of Eliot Feld's *Santa Fe Saga* in New York City.

BALANCHINE'S HOMETOWN
In 2003, the New York City Ballet performed at St. Petersburg's Mariinsky Theatre—101 years after George Balanchine's birth in the city. Here, dancers perform *Serenade*—the first ballet he created in the United States, as an exercise for his students in 1934.

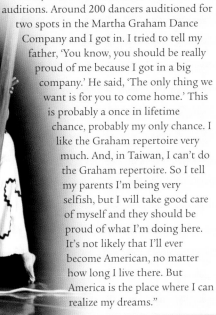

FANG-YI SHEU

Fang-Yi Sheu grew up in a small town not far from Taipei, Taiwan. She is now a principal dancer with the Martha Graham Dance Company in New York.

"I discovered myself in college and decided I wanted to become a professional dancer. My teacher thought I had great potential and encouraged me to come to New York. In Taiwan there's only one professional company. It's definitely not enough for all the dancers. The best and the worst are in New York. I wanted to see what a professional company is like. I wanted to see what a real professional dancer is like. Is it really, really hard? I wanted to see if I could survive. I think quite a lot of dancers want to make their dream come true and come to New York, but the hardest thing is the first step. Do you really have that courage to just pack your suitcase and get the tickets and go? In the beginning I was afraid, but I went with my two suitcases and I started auditions. Around 200 dancers auditioned for two spots in the Martha Graham Dance Company and I got in. I tried to tell my father, 'You know, you should be really proud of me because I got in a big company.' He said, 'The only thing we want is for you to come home.' This is probably a once in lifetime chance, probably my only chance. I like the Graham repertoire very much. And, in Taiwan, I can't do the Graham repertoire. So I tell my parents I'm being very selfish, but I will take good care of myself and they should be proud of what I'm doing here. It's not likely that I'll ever become American, no matter how long I live there. But America is the place where I can realize my dreams."

Theater

Imported plays, often performed by touring companies from England, dominated America's theaters in the country's early years. As the pace of immigration increased, immigrant characters and situations appeared onstage with increasing frequency in the 1870s and 1880s. In the 20th century, the talents of immigrant actors, directors, and playwrights enriched all facets of the American theater.

ASTOR PLACE RIOT

A feud between American and English actors escalated into violence at New York City's Astor Place Theater on May 10, 1849, when a clash between a Nativist mob and troops left more than 20 people dead and 100 injured.

THE MELTING POT

On October 5, 1908, a new play by English writer Israel Zangwill, *The Melting Pot*, opened in Washington, D.C., where it won high praise from no less a figure than President Theodore Roosevelt. The production moved to Chicago and then to Broadway, where it became the hit of the season. The melodrama transposed the plot of Shakespeare's *Romeo*

CRUCIBLE OF NATIONS

The cover of a 1916 edition of Israel Zangwill's play *The Melting Pot* depicts the crucible, in which the "50 barbarian tribes of Europe" would be turned into Americans.

and Juliet to New York City, with the star-crossed lovers now from Russian Jewish and Russian Cossack backgrounds. (In an improbable plot twist, the hero discovers that his lover's father oversaw the pogrom [*see pp 198–199*] that killed his parents.) In the play's climactic moment, the hero proclaims: "Understand that America is God's Crucible, the great Melting-Pot where all the races of Europe are melting and reforming! A fig for your feuds and vendettas! Germans and Frenchmen, Irishmen and Englishmen, Jews and Russians—into the Crucible with you all! God is making the American."

The idea of America as a "crucible of the nations" was not a new one, but the title of Zangwill's play stuck in the popular imagination as a metaphor for the assimilation of immigrants into a common

METHOD MAN

Lee Strasberg as Hyman Roth (a character based on Meyer Lansky, *see pp 158–159*) in the 1974 movie *The Godfather, Part II*. Strasberg learned his craft from immigrant students of the Russian acting coach Konstantin Stanislavski.

American culture. Then and now, however, the melting-pot concept has been controversial. Some critics have charged that it is both unrealistic and unfair to expect immigrants to forsake the language and traditions of their homelands in pursuit of a purely American way of life—especially when there's no consensus on what that way of life actually comprises.

THE YIDDISH THEATER

In the 1890s, Jewish immigrants from Eastern Europe established their own thriving Yiddish-language theater scene on New York City's Lower East Side. By 1918, New York City had over 20 Yiddish theaters. The popularity of the Yiddish theater, in part, was that its original works dealt with issues that its audiences faced in everyday life—like how to reconcile their cultural and religious traditions with the multicultural, materialistic environment of their adopted homeland. Yiddish translations of Shakespeare and Ibsen, along with original plays by writers like Sholem Asch (born in Poland), also provided a welcome artistic diversion from the reality of overwork and overcrowding in the city's streets and tenements.

Stella Adler, daughter of Yiddish actors Sarah and Jacob Adler, became a seasoned Yiddish actor traveling across the country, before studying briefly with Konstantin Stanislavski (*see below*) and establishing the Stella Adler Theater Studio in 1949. Other Jewish immigrants, especially songwriter Irving Berlin (born Israel Baline in Russia), played leading roles in the development of that uniquely American theatrical form—the Broadway musical.

THE METHOD IN AMERICA

The most influential drama teacher of the 20th century was the Russian Konstantin Stanislavski, founder of the Moscow Art Theater, who developed what became known as "the Method"—the idea that actors should inhabit their roles, and draw upon personal emotional memories for inspiration. The chief proponents of Method Acting in America were Lee Strasberg, who was born in what is now the Ukraine, and director Elia Kazan, who was born in Turkey to a Greek family. Kazan was one of the founders of the Actors Studio in New York City in 1947; Strasberg joined a year later. Performers trained by the studio include Anne Bancroft, Patricia Neal, Sidney Poitier, Dustin Hoffman, Al Pacino, and Robert De Niro. Strasberg remained head of the studio until his death in 1982. While best remembered as a teacher, Strasberg acted in several films late in his life.

Kazan won fame directing plays by Arthur Miller and Tennessee Williams and acclaimed films like 1954's *On the*

BERTOLT BRECHT
1898–1956

An unquestionably brilliant and outspokenly Marxist poet and playwright, Bertolt Brecht found refuge from the Nazis in America—but his politics led him to leave the United States as the chill of the Cold War set in. Born in Bavaria, Brecht arrived on the innovative post-World War I theater scene in Berlin and began developing new dramatic forms, like his *Lehrstücke* (teaching plays)—dramas written to indoctrinate the audience in leftist philosophy and intended to be performed outside of conventional theaters. Together with composer Kurt Weill (*see pp 266–267*), Brecht also promoted what he called "Epic Theater," which emphasized narrative over plot. Brecht and Weill's greatest success was the musical play *The Threepenny Opera* (1928), which they followed up with *The Rise and Fall of the City of Mahagonny* (1930), the tale of a cash-obsessed American boomtown.

Brecht's leftist politics and unconventional writings made him a prime target of the Nazis when they came to power. In 1933, he began an odyssey of exile that would take him from Austria to Scandinavia to England, and finally, in 1941, to California. The experience stimulated some of his best work, including the play *Mother Courage and her Children* (1941). In October 1947, the House Committee on Un-American Activities, which was investigating communist influence in Hollywood, questioned Brecht, who declared himself "a guest of this country" and stated (truthfully) that he was not a member of the Communist Party, but the experience convinced him that his political views were making him an unwelcome guest. Returning to Europe, he spent a year in Switzerland before settling in East Berlin. There he continued writing until his death in 1956.

Waterfront—which starred Marlon Brando, perhaps the most famous disciple of the Method—but Kazan's reputation among some of his peers was tarnished because he named names to the House Committee on Un-American Activities (HUAC) during its hearings on communism in Hollywood in the early 1950s. He won an Honorary Oscar for Lifetime Achievement in 1999.

TWO CONTENDERS

Elia Kazan *(left)* and Marlon Brando during the filming of *On the Waterfront*. Kazan's anti-communist testimony caused a rift with his friend and sometime collaborator, playwright Arthur Miller. But, in 1999, Miller defended the Academy of Motion Picture Arts and Science's decision to give Kazan a Lifetime Achievement award.

The Movies

Lights, camera, action: movies are without a doubt America's most important contribution to the popular culture of the entire globe. Around World War I, the American movie industry's center of gravity shifted from New York City and environs, to what was then a sleepy Los Angeles suburb named Hollywood.

Ever since, Hollywood has been synonymous with the movies, and regardless of their birthplace, practically anybody who was, or is, anybody in the film industry—actors, screenwriters, directors, producers, technicians—has spent time there, whether for a few years or for the better portion of their careers. A very partial list of all the foreign-born talents who made their mark in Hollywood includes directors Erich von Stroheim (born in Austria, and also an acclaimed actor); Alfred Hitchcock (born in England); Milos Forman (born in Czechoslovakia); and John Woo (born in China); and actors Rudolph Valentino (born in Italy), Carey Grant (born in England), Sophia Loren (born in Italy), Sean Connery (born in Scotland), and Charlize Theron (born in South Africa).

THE MOGULS

The studios that dominated American moviemaking from the 1920s through the 1960s, were almost entirely the creation of immigrants, most of them Jews from Eastern Europe. Having fled persecution under the Czars, these immigrant entrepreneurs started out with nickelodeons in New York City, expanded into imported European films, and eventually progressed to moviemaking in California. Together they created an indelible image of America in the collective imagination of the world. Although often building on existing American themes, like the Western, the movies of Hollywood's "Golden Age"— 1920s–1950s—established a new American mythos: they portrayed the United States as a country full of energy and opportunity, a land of shining cities and idyllic towns, a place where good always triumphed and the hero always got the girl.

IN LIVING COLOR
A Technicolor movie camera. Developed in the 1920s, the Technicolor process used three separate strips of one-color film (cyan, yellow, and magenta) overlaid on a black-and-white "key."

FROM MINSK TO MGM
Louis B. Mayer—born Eliezer Mayer—is photographed accepting an Academy Award. As head of Metro-Goldwyn-Mayer, he was perhaps the most powerful figure in the movie business from the 1920s through the 1940s.

MOGULS AT THE TRACK
Sam Goldwyn *(left)*, born Schmuel Gelbfisz, and Jack Warner, born Jacob Eichelbaum, relax at the Hollywood Park, home to the Hollywood Turf Club, the horse-racing club that formed under Warner's chairmanship in 1938.

Louis B. Mayer (born in Minsk, Russia) is generally considered the originator of the star system, in which the major box-office draws were contractually tied to the studio. The biggest owner of moviehouses in New England by the end of World War I, he founded two studios in Hollywood, Mayer Pictures and Metro Pictures; in the mid-1920s, they merged with Samuel Goldwyn's (born in Poland) production company to form Metro-Goldwyn-Mayer (MGM), which remained the largest studio for the next three decades. After the merger, Goldwyn remained an influential independent producer. Another merger, which united Adolph Zukor's (born in Hungary) production company and Jesse Lasky's Famous Players Company in 1916, led to the establishment of Paramount Studios.

The four Warner brothers, sons of Polish-Jewish immigrants to Canada, founded their eponymous studio in 1923, and revolutionized the industry with the first successful "talkie," or sound picture, *The Jazz Singer*, four years later. (The movie industry's relative slowness in adopting sound technology stemmed partly from the fact that silent pictures could be understood and enjoyed by speakers of any language— no small thing at a time when American audiences included millions of immigrants.)

William Fox (born in Hungary) founded the company that became Twentieth-Century Fox in 1915, although he went bankrupt in the 1930s. Carl Laemelle (born in Germany) founded Universal Studios in 1915, although, like Fox, he would be ousted from his studio after financial reverses in the 1930s.

The studios began to decline in the 1940s, when federal antitrust rulings forced them to separate production from distribution—that is, they had to sell the theater chains they

COOPER AND CAPRA
Some critics derided Frank Capra's upbeat idealistic movies as "Capracorn," but moviegoers seeking temporary escape from the woes of the Great Depression loved the Sicilian-born director's work—including 1936's *Mr. Deeds Goes to Town*, starring Capra regular Gary Cooper.

owned—and from competition with television. Most survive in some form today as part of the multimedia conglomerates that dominate popular entertainment.

No other film figure advanced the image of America as a land of democracy and decency better than Sicilian-born director Frank Capra. In sentimental comedies like *Mr. Deeds Goes to Town* (1936), *Mr. Smith Goes to Washington* (1939), and *It's A Wonderful Life* (1946), wholesome smalltown values won out over urban cynicism, political corruption, and greed, respectively. During World War II, Capra produced propaganda as the director of a series of documentaries, *Why We Fight*, for the U.S. government.

THE ACTOR

Charlie Chaplin was the best-loved and most popular star of the silent film era, but his politics and his personal life ultimately led to his exile from Hollywood. Born Charles Spencer Chaplin in London's East End in 1889, Chaplin made his stage debut at the age of five. He appeared in his first movie—a Mack

TRAMPING TO AMERICA
With co-star Edna Purviance at his side, Charlie Chaplin takes in the sight of the Statue of Liberty in 1917's *The Immigrant*. Underlying the movie's slapstick comedy was a perceptive tale of the challenges faced by newcomers in getting to America and in adjusting to life in their new country.

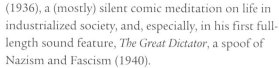

ARTISTS UNITED

While Charlie Chaplin (*third from left*) and director D. W. Griffith look on, Mary Pickford signs the documents establishing United Artists—the first independent movie-production company—on February 5, 1919.

EYE ON FILM

Billy Wilder in the cutting room, in 1951. Wilder often started shooting before scripts were finished. "I have ten commandments," he once said. "The first nine are, thou shalt not bore. The tenth is, thou shalt have right of final cut."

Sennet comedy—while touring America with a music-hall troupe in 1913. Around the same time he perfected the comic persona that would make him legendary—the hapless but ever-optimistic "Little Tramp." Within a few years, Chaplin's short comedies made him one of the most famous and highest-paid movie stars in the world.

Seeking more control over his movies, he joined D. W. Griffith, Douglas Fairbanks, and Mary Pickford in establishing United Artists in 1919. United Artists distributed three of Chaplin's films, most notably *The Gold Rush* (1925), which many critics rank as his best work. Chaplin's liberal politics surfaced in the 1930s, in *Modern Times* (1936), a (mostly) silent comic meditation on life in industrialized society, and, especially, in his first full-length sound feature, *The Great Dictator*, a spoof of Nazism and Fascism (1940).

While his reputation as an artist rose, however, the public's affection for him fell. In the 1920s, many Americans were shocked to learn he had twice been married to teenage girls, though both marriages ended in divorce. (A third marriage, to actress Paulette Goddard, also ended in divorce, in 1942.)

In 1952, Chaplin (who never became a U.S. citizen) traveled to London for the premiere of his autobiographical film *Limelight*, only to learn that immigration authorities planned to bar his return to America. (The action had more to do with his sex life than his politics.) He spent the remainder of his life in Switzerland, making a few more movies and returning to the United States briefly in 1972, to accept—to rapturous applause—a special Academy Award. Queen Elizabeth II knighted him in 1975.

THE DIRECTOR

Born Samuel Wilder in Sucha, in what is now Poland, in 1906, the future Hollywood legend got the nickname "Billy" from his mother, a fan of the Wild West showman "Buffalo Bill" Cody. Wilder began writing scripts for German and French film studios in 1929. After Hitler came to power he moved first to France, and then, in 1934, to Hollywood, where he roomed for a time with another Jewish refugee—Hungarian-born actor Peter Lorre. Wilder's mother, stepfather, and grandmother all died in the Nazis' concentration camps. After knocking around the industry for a few years, Wilder established himself as a screenwriter with *Ninotchka* (1939) and hit it big with the Film Noir classic *Double Indemnity* (1944), which he directed and cowrote with Raymond Chandler. Sometimes working with partners (most notably Charles Brackett and, later, I. A. L. Diamond) and sometimes on his own, Wilder was a triple threat: he wrote, produced, and directed more than 50 movies in his career. He was also remarkable for the range of his work. Wilder was equally adept at terse dramas (1953's *Stalag 17*) and sparkling comedies (1955's *The Seven Year Itch*), and he made movies that centered on subjects that had previously been taboo in the American movie industry, including alcoholism (1945's *The Lost Weekend*) and prostitution (1963's *Irma La Douce*). Perhaps his best film was 1950's *Sunset Boulevard*, which was a brilliant examination of Hollywood itself.

Wilder's career began to decline in the 1960s, and few of his later films were memorable, but when he died in 2002, at 95, he left behind an amazing body of work that had collectively received 20 Academy Award nominations and won four, plus two honorary Oscars.

Hollywood Sirens

Cherchez la (Foreign-born) *Femme Fatale:* American movie audiences tend to like their homegrown starlets to appear on-screen as virtuous and wholesome—something that holds true from Mary Pickford in the 1910s and 1920s, to Doris Day in the 1950s, to Julia Roberts in the 1990s. When it comes to playing sultry temptresses, however, imported actresses usually seem to fit the bill better.

MARLENE DIETRICH

Born in Berlin in 1901, Dietrich began acting on stage in the 1920s. In 1930, she worked with director Josef von Sternberg in Germany's first talkie, *The Blue Angel*; that film established her classic onscreen persona, which was not unlike Greta Garbo's, although Dietrich's languid performances seemed to mask a smoldering intensity rather than a cool reserve. Dietrich exuded a certain androgynous allure—along with Katherine Hepburn, she was one of the first actresses to appear in trousers, onscreen and off. Von Sternberg moved to the United States and convinced Dietrich to join him in Hollywood. In the 1930s, she appeared in classics like *Shanghai Express* (1932), *The Devil Is a Woman* (1935), and *Destry Rides Again* (1939). Dietrich became a U.S. citizen in 1937, but she remained popular in Germany, even with leading Nazis—a sentiment that was not returned. Dietrich loathed the regime, and during World War II, she toured extensively with the United Services Organization (USO), entertaining the troops and earning the admiration of combat soldiers for her willingness to perform right on the front lines: during the Battle of the Bulge one of her shows came under German shellfire. After the war, she acted in a few more films, most notably *Judgment at Nuremberg* (1961), and performed in cabaret before retiring (mostly) in the 1970s. She died in 1992.

GRETA GARBO

Born Greta Gustaffson in Stockholm, Sweden, in 1905, Garbo acted for the Swedish director Mauritz Stiller before MGM lured her to Hollywood in 1925. She starred in several silent films with John Gilbert, who became her offscreen lover as well, and public interest in their relationship helped fuel her early celebrity (so did rumors of bisexuality and her cool aloof demeanor onscreen and off). Gilbert failed to make the transition to talkies, but Garbo did, starring in the film version of Eugene O'Neill's play *Anna Christie* (1930), and scoring big with *Grand Hotel* (1932), in which she uttered what would become her most famous line: "I want to be alone." Garbo's best performances came in the 1930s, including *Anna Karenina* (1935), *Camille* (1936), and *Ninotchka* (1939), a comedy directed by German-born director Ernst Lubitsch, in which she played a prim Soviet official seduced by the sensuality and freedom of the West. Interestingly, Garbo was one of the few Hollywood stars who was even more popular in Europe than in America; some critics believe this is why her career stalled during World War II, when American movies were not available. Whatever the reason, she made only a couple of more movies after the war and lived as a semi-recluse in New York City, until her death in 1990—as if she had chosen her famous remark from *Grand Hotel* as words to live by.

COMRADE GARBO
Garbo tries to resist the capitalist wiles of costar Melvyn Douglas in MGM's *Ninotchka* (1939).

FOR THE BOYS
Marlene Dietrich entertains U.S. troops overseas in 1944. Ernest Hemingway said of her: "If she had nothing more than her voice, she could break your heart."

INGRID BERGMAN

Ingrid Bergman was not a proper Hollywood Siren onscreen; in most of her movies she exhibited an earnest, fresh-scrubbed quality that served as the flip side to the seductive style of her fellow Swedish-American, Greta Garbo. Like Garbo, Bergman was born in Stockholm, in 1915, and became a film star in her native land before moving to America in 1939, to act in the Hollywood version of the Swedish film *Intermezzo*. Bergman followed this up with noted performances in *Casablanca* (1942)—the finest Hollywood film ever made, in the opinion of many critics—*For Whom the Bell Tolls* (1943), and Alfred Hitchcock's *Gaslight* (1945) and *Spellbound* (1946). In the early 1950s, however, a scandalous affair with Italian director Roberto Rossellini led to a messy divorce. Bergman's popularity plummeted and, unable to get roles in Hollywood, she made several films in Europe. She made her American comeback with an Oscar-winning performance in *Anastasia* (1956). In the 1960s and 1970s, Bergman did considerable stage work, but she won another Academy Award for 1974's *Murder on the Orient Express*, and she capped her career with brilliant performances in Swedish director Ingmar Bergman's *Autumn Sonata* (1978), and in the 1982 TV movie *A Woman Called Golda*, in which she portrayed Israeli Prime Minister Golda Meir. She died the same year.

RICK AND ILSA
Humphrey Bogart and Ingrid Bergman in *Casablanca* (1942), a movie directed by Hungarian-born Michael Curtiz and starring other émigré actors Conrad Veidt, Claude Rains, Sydney Greenstreet, and Peter Lorre.

Athletes

Although some of America's favorite spectator sports—baseball, football, and basketball—are more or less native to the United States, and have been little played elsewhere in the world until relatively recently, immigrant athletes and coaches have long made their mark on the nation's playing fields: Norwegian-born Knut Rockne, for example, led Notre Dame University's football team to a 105-12-5 record from 1918 to 1931, and is today revered as the sport's greatest coach.

FORE
Duffers tee off at America's first full-scale golf course—St. Andrews in Yonkers, New York—in 1894. The course, which opened in 1888, grew out of a three-hole course that Scots-born John Reid built near his home.

For immigrant and first-generation children, rooting for local teams and playing sports with their peers has long been a big step toward feeling at home in their new world: a recent study by the University of Illinois's Diversity Research Laboratory determined that participation in school sports not only helped immigrant children adjust more readily to American life, but that their involvement helped their parents do the same. Some immigrant groups brought with them athletic traditions that had not existed in America. For example, the Scots introduced Americans to golf, and the Germans, gymnastics. Today, the growing American interest in soccer—the most popular sport in the rest of the world, where it is known as football—is partly a reflection of the new wave of immigration from Asia, Africa, and Latin America.

TAKE ME OUT TO THE BALL GAME

Baseball, America's "national pastime," has its roots in the English games of cricket and rounders, and in a colonial American game known variously as "base" and "town ball." Cricket was actually a popular sport in early 19th-century America, but it was rapidly overtaken by baseball when the latter's rules began to be systematized. (Some immigrant communities, especially West Indians, keep the sport alive in the United States today.) One convert from cricket to baseball was an English-born journalist named Henry Chadwick. After watching his first baseball game in 1856, he later wrote, "I was struck with the idea that base ball [sic] was just the game for a national sport for Americans, and . . . I came to the conclusion that from this game of ball . . . our people could be lifted into a position of more devotion to physical exercise and healthful outdoor recreation." Chadwick went on to devote much of his life to advancing the new sport in his adopted homeland,

FIGHTING IRISH—AND NORWEGIAN
Norwegian-born Knute Rockne gives a pep talk to Notre Dame's football team at the university's Cartier Field, 1930. "One man practicing sportsmanship," Rockne said, "Is far better than 50 preaching it."

writing several influential instructional books and devising the batting average and the box score. When professional baseball began after the Civil War, one of the first leagues—the short-lived National Association of Professional Base Ball Players (NABPP)—listed seven English-born players and five Irish-born players on its roster, and the number of foreign-born players rose in proportion with the overall increase in immigration over the next few decades.

Wherever Americans went in the world, they brought baseball with them, and in some countries the game put down roots—particularly in Latin America, where American military interventions from the 1890s through the 1930s, often gave locals their first glimpse of the game. The first Latin-American players in the major leagues included Columbian-born Luis Castro (started with the Philadelphia Athletics, 1902); Cuban-born Rafael Almeida and Armando Marsans (started with the Cincinnati Reds, 1911); Mexican-born Mel Almada (started with the Boston Red Sox, 1933); Venezuela-born Alex Carrasquel (started with the Washington Senators, 1939); and Dominican-born Ozzie Virgil (started with the New York Giants, 1956).

The greatest numbers of foreign-born players in the major leagues have come from the Dominican Republic, Cuba, Venezuela, and Mexico (Canada excepted, and if the U.S. commonwealth of Puerto Rico were included on this list, it would rank second). About one-quarter of all major-league players were of Latin-American birth in 2004. These figures should not be taken to imply that Latin-American ballplayers have

had an easy time; they have faced considerable discrimination—especially those with African ancestry, because major-league baseball was segregated by race from the late 19th century until Jackie Robinson broke baseball's color bar in 1947.

Still, Latino ballplayers established themselves through sheer excellence. In recent years, Americans thrilled to the 1998 race between the Chicago Cubs' Dominican-born Sammy Sosa and the St. Louis Cardinals' Mark McGwire to break Roger Maris's record of 61 home runs in a single season. Although McGwire won the duel (70 homers to Sosa's 66), Sosa took the National League's Most Valuable Player Award. In 2004, a trio of Dominican-born players— pitcher Pedro Martinez, left-fielder Manny Ramirez, and first baseman David Ortiz—helped the Boston Red Sox to their first World Series victory in 86 years.

Latin Americans may be the largest immigrant group represented in the major leagues today, but professional baseball includes players from around the world, with Asia increasingly represented, including (as of 2004) the Seattle Mariners's Ichiro Suzuki and the New York Yankees's Hideki Matsui, both from Japan. Tommy Lasorda, manager of the Los Angeles Dodgers from 1976 through 1996 (himself the son of Italian immigrants), summed up contemporary baseball's multicultural quality when he told a reporter, "For starting pitchers we have two Dominicans, one Italian, one Mexican, and one Japanese. In the bullpen we have a Venezuelan, a Mexican, a guy from the United States—and a guy from St. Louis."

ROBERTO CLEMENTE
1934–1972

The first Latin-American player to to be inducted into the Baseball Hall of Fame, Roberto Clemente Walker was born in Puerto Rico. He spent his entire 18-season career with the Pittsburgh Pirates. Clemente was both a fearsome fielder (he won 12 Golden Glove awards) and a four-time National League batting champ, with a lifetime average of .317. He finished his career with exactly 3,000 base hits, the last one scored at his final at-bat in 1972. He endured fans who mocked his accent and sportscasters who insisted, despite his protests, in referring to him as "Bob" or "Robert" Clemente. In 1972, an earthquake hit Managua, Nicaragua. Clemente organized a relief operation and boarded one of the flights delivering supplies. The plane crashed shortly after takeoff.

PLAY IT WELL

For some immigrant parents, a child's passion for American sports was a disrespectful defiance of cultural heritage rather than something to be encouraged. In a famous 1903 letter to Abraham Cahan, the Lithuanian-born editor of New York's *Jewish Daily Forward* newspaper, a father complained, "It makes sense to teach a child to play dominoes or chess, but what is the point of a crazy game like baseball? I want my boy to grow up to be a *mensch* [upright man], not a wild American runner. But he cries his head off." Cahan replied, "Let your boys play baseball and play it well, as long as it does not interfere with their education or get them into bad company. . . Bring them up to be educated, ethical, and decent, but also to be physically strong so they should not feel inferior. . . Let us not so raise the children that they should grow up foreigners in their own birthplace."

STREETBALL
Above: Abraham Cahan. *Right:* A Jacob Riis photo of a stickball game on New York's Lower East Side, *c.* 1910.

ON THE COURT

On December 15, 1891, Canadian-born physical-education teacher James Naismith tossed a ball through a peach basket at a gym at the Young Men's Christian Association school (later Springfield College) in Springfield, Massachusetts. Naismith's intention was to develop an indoor sport that athletes could play during the winter; the result was basketball. (Naismith went on to coach the basketball team at the University of Kansas; he is also credited with inventing the modern football helmet.) More than 100 years later, the team rosters of the National Basketball Association (NBA), America's professional basketball league, included 69 players from 33 countries and territories. Two of the most esteemed, foreign-born players are Hakeem Olajuwon and Yao Ming.

Born Akeem Olajuwon in Lagos, Nigeria, in 1963 (he added the "H" to his first name after converting to Islam), Olajuwon played college hoops at the University of Houston, before joining the Houston Rockets in 1984, as center; in 17 seasons with the team, he helped the Rockets to two NBA championships (1994 and 1995), and garnered the league's Most Valuable Player Award for the 1993–94 season. In 1996, on the occasion of the NBA's 50th anniversary, Olajuwon was named

JAPANESE SUPERSTARS
Hideki Matsui *(front)* of the New York Yankees and Ichiro Suzuki of the Seattle Mariners take batting practice in preparation for the 2003 All-Star Game. They helped the American League to a 7-6 victory over the National League.

one of the top 50 professional players of all time. He retired in 2002, though he continues to hold the NBA record in blocked shots (3,800), and is one of only eight players in NBA history to have racked up over 20,000 points and 12,000 rebounds.

At this writing, Olajuwon's position as center of the Rockets is held by 7′ 5″ Yao Ming, who was born in Shanghai, in 1980. He first came to the world's attention in 2000, as part of the Chinese national team, which also included Wang Zhizhi, who became the first Chinese-born player in the NBA, when the Dallas Mavericks drafted him that same year, and Mongolian-born Menkge Bateer, who was signed by the Denver Nuggets in 2002. (The three seven-footers were nicknamed "the walking Great Wall.") In the 2003–2004 season, Yao ranked seventh in field-goal percentage, 13th in blocked shots per game, and 15th in rebounding average.

The end of the Cold War brought a coterie of hoopsters from the former Soviet Bloc in Eastern Europe, from Vlade Divac (who started in 1989 with the Los Angeles Lakers) to Darko Milicic (a 2003 first-round draft pick for the Detroit Pistons), both from the former Yugoslavia.

ON THE ICE

Ice hockey came to North America with British soldiers who were serving in Canada—where it remains a national passion. In the United States, ice hockey began as a college sport; the first recorded game was in 1895, between Yale and Johns Hopkins universities. In 1917, the professional National Hockey League (NHL) formed in Canada; the first U.S. team, the Boston Bruins, joined in 1924.

For most of the NHL's history, its team rosters were almost completely made up of U.S.- and

THE GOAL IS HEALING

The 1990s saw an influx of illegal Mexican and Central American immigrants to New York City's Long Island suburbs. Lured by the prospect of work in construction and landscaping, these men shared cramped rented accommodations—sometimes as many as 30 living in a single modest house—and they could be seen every day at the roadside, hoping to be picked up by contractors for a day's work "off the books." In the town of Farmingville—where illegal immigrants at one point numbered 1,500 out of 15,000 residents—tensions between some local residents and the newcomers boiled over into violence in 2001. Two immigrant laborers—lured to an empty house on the pretense of a job—were beaten and nearly killed. In the aftermath of the incident, immigrant-rights activist Matilde Parada—herself a refugee from El Salvador—formed an organization called Human Solidarity to heal the divisions between the locals and the newcomers. Realizing that the one thing that united the immigrant community was a love for *futbol* (soccer), she struck a deal: in return for maintaining a local school's soccer field, immigrant teams got to play on it on weekends. It was a small but hopeful step toward resolving a dilemma that resonates in many other contemporary American communities.

FOREIGN HOOPSTERS
Chinese-born Yao Ming (7' 5") of the Houston Rockets covers Yugoslavia-born Vlade Divac (7' 1") of the Sacramento Kings on Divac's home court, March 21, 2004. Divac and his wife have adopted two children orphaned by conflicts in the former Yugoslavia (*see pp 232–233*).

Canadian-born players. That began to change in the 1970s, when Swedish and Finnish players began to be drafted, including Swede Stefan Persson, who was the first European-born player to win a Stanley Cup as a defenseman for the New York Islanders. In the early 1980s, players from the Soviet Bloc defected to play in the NHL, including Victor Nechaev, who played briefly with the Los Angeles Kings in 1982–83.

The end of the Cold War led to a major influx of players from the former Soviet Union and Eastern Europe. By the 2003–2004 season, 236 of the 728 NHL players were European-born, among them 53 Russians, 62 Czechs, and 24 Slovaks.

Martina Navratilova

Martina Navratilova was born in Prague, Czechoslovakia (now the Czech Republic), in 1956. She became the top-ranked women's tennis player there in 1972. Turning pro the next year, she lead Czech teams in international competition; of her first trip to America, she later wrote, "For the first time in my life I was able to see America without the filter of a Communist education, Communist propaganda." She chafed at the restrictions her country's government placed on her; in early 1975, she was ordered to return home during a tournament in Florida, apparently because the authorities feared she might defect. Later that year, aged 18, she did defect, arriving at the New York City office of the Immigration and Naturalization Services after losing in the U.S. Open semifinals. She became a U.S. citizen in 1981.

Navratilova's first years in America were difficult but she roared back to the top in 1978–79, winning back-to-back women's singles at Wimbledon. In the 1980s, she won another six women's singles at Wimbledon, and another in 1990, for a record nine.

In 1986, she returned to Czechoslovakia, playing for the United States in the Federation Cup. Czech fans cheered her; the authorities did not. Navratilova scored her 158th tournament win in 1992, giving her more championship victories than any other player, male or female. She retired in 1994, but returned to the court six years later to play mixed doubles. She took the 2003 mixed doubles at Wimbledon, tying Billie Jean King's record for the most Wimbledon wins, and, at 46, she was the oldest player to have competed at Wimbledon so far.

Navratilova was also one of the first major sports stars to acknowledge being gay, something that took great courage at the time, as it likely cost her millions of dollars in endorsements. Besides her ongoing doubles career, Navratilova remains active as a commentator and a supporter of causes ranging from gay rights to the environment (she has reportedly given more money to charity than any other female sports star.)

RUSSIAN HOCKEY STAR
Sergei Federov of the Anaheim, California, Mighty Ducks became the first Russian-born player in the National Hockey League to score more than 1,000 career points—419 goals, 582 assists—in a February 15, 2004, home game against the Nashville Predators.

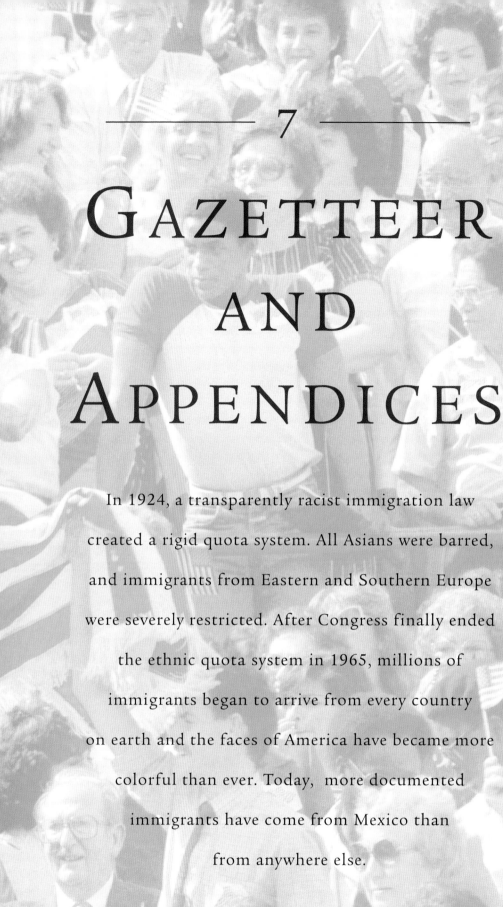

7

GAZETTEER AND APPENDICES

In 1924, a transparently racist immigration law created a rigid quota system. All Asians were barred, and immigrants from Eastern and Southern Europe were severely restricted. After Congress finally ended the ethnic quota system in 1965, millions of immigrants began to arrive from every country on earth and the faces of America have became more colorful than ever. Today, more documented immigrants have come from Mexico than from anywhere else.

"The Golden Door"

PROUD TO BECOME AN AMERICAN
Immigrants, soon to be American citizens, display their patriotism at a naturalization ceremony in Coral Gables, Florida. In addition to fulfilling residency requirements, all naturalization applicants must demonstrate good moral character, attachment to the principles of the Constitution, favorable disposition toward the United States, and knowledge of the English language and American history.

Immigration By State 1990–2000

While this book aims to show the reader why different groups immigrated to America, and from where they came, it is also interesting to see where they have settled upon reaching the United States. The U.S. Census Bureau breaks down American citizens by their race: white, black or African American, American Indian and Alaska Native, Asian, Native Hawaiian and other Pacific Islander, Hispanic or Latino, and any other race or two or more races. The population of each state is broken down by race in the charts below and on the following pages.

During the 1990s, the U.S. immigrant population grew by 11.3 million—faster than any other time in history. In 2003, the Center for Immigration Studies produced a state-by-state report, using information from the U.S. Census Bureau, outlining the top 15 countries from which this growing foreign-born population originated. These state-by-state charts are included below and on the following pages. They show that today's immigrants are more diverse than ever as people are arriving from all parts of the world. However, 60 percent of the total number of foreign-born

residents between 1990 and 2000 are Spanish-speaking Latin Americans; 43 percent from Mexico alone. Yet it is interesting to note that when mass immigration began in the 19th century, Ireland accounted for an even larger portion of the foreign-born population than Mexico does today.

The U.S. Census Bureau uses the term "foreign-born" to refer to anyone who was not a U.S. citizen at birth. This includes naturalized citizens, Lawful Permanent Residents, temporary migrants (such as students), humanitarian migrants (or refugees), and illegal immigrants.

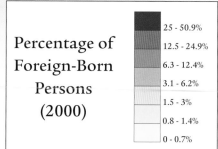

Percentage of Foreign-Born Persons (2000)

- 25 - 50.9%
- 12.5 - 24.9%
- 6.3 - 12.4%
- 3.1 - 6.2%
- 1.5 - 3%
- 0.8 - 1.4%
- 0 - 0.7%

ALABAMA

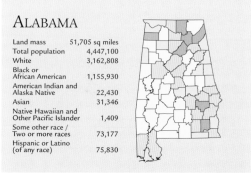

Land mass	51,705 sq miles
Total population	4,447,100
White	3,162,808
Black or African American	1,155,930
American Indian and Alaska Native	22,430
Asian	31,346
Native Hawaiian and Other Pacific Islander	1,409
Some other race / Two or more races	73,177
Hispanic or Latino (of any race)	75,830

	2000	1990	Growth
Total FB Pop.	**88,118**	**42,141**	**45,977**
Mexico	27,103	1,155	25,948
Germany	7,177	5,451	1,726
India	4,589	2,191	2,398
China/HK/Taiwan	4,252	2,573	1,679
Vietnam	3,364	2,283	1,081
Guatemala	3,163	90	3,073
United Kingdom	3,152	2,645	507
Korea	2,884	2,339	545
Canada	2,413	2,425	-12
Former USSR	2,289	190	2,099
Philippines	2,195	1,212	983
Italy	1,738	404	1,334
Nigeria	1,426	639	787
Thailand	1,235	588	647
Kenya	1,048	48	1,000

ALASKA

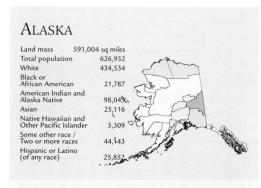

Land mass	591,004 sq miles
Total population	626,932
White	434,534
Black or African American	21,787
American Indian and Alaska Native	98,043
Asian	25,116
Native Hawaiian and Other Pacific Islander	3,309
Some other race / Two or more races	44,143
Hispanic or Latino (of any race)	25,852

	2000	1990	Growth
Total FB Pop.	**33,813**	**22,789**	**11,024**
Philippines	9,555	4,773	4,782
Korea	3,757	2,676	1,081
Mexico	3,106	1,281	1,825
Canada	2,993	2,452	541
Laos	1,788	1,710	78
Former USSR	1,065	127	938
Germany	823	1,668	-845
Vietnam	758	225	533
Thailand	738	318	420
Romania	644	23	621
Japan	623	1,171	-548
Haiti	578	11	567
El Salvador	503	23	480
Panama	481	61	420
Peru	460	130	330

ARIZONA

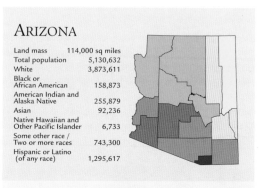

Land mass	114,000 sq miles
Total population	5,130,632
White	3,873,611
Black or African American	158,873
American Indian and Alaska Native	255,879
Asian	92,236
Native Hawaiian and Other Pacific Islander	6,733
Some other race / Two or more races	743,300
Hispanic or Latino (of any race)	1,295,617

	2000	1990	Growth
Total FB Pop.	**649,127**	**274,424**	**374,703**
Mexico	435,001	150,606	284,395
Canada	28,218	15,332	12,886
Germany	15,980	10,928	5,052
United Kingdom	15,615	9,297	6,318
China/HK/Taiwan	11,408	6,152	5,256
Philippines	11,299	4,732	6,567
Vietnam	8,470	4,326	4,144
India	8,457	3,431	5,026
Korea	8,025	4,154	3,871
Former USSR	6,458	1,873	4,585
Guatemala	5,759	1,699	4,060
Former Yugoslavia	5,302	1,252	4,050
Italy	5,139	4,034	1,105
Japan	4,434	2,793	1,641
El Salvador	4,254	1,617	2,637

ARKANSAS

Land mass	53,187 sq miles
Total population	2,673,400
White	2,138,598
Black or African American	418,950
American Indian and Alaska Native	17,808
Asian	20,220
Native Hawaiian and Other Pacific Islander	1,668
Some other race / Two or more races	76,156
Hispanic or Latino (of any race)	86,866

	2000	1990	Growth
Total FB Pop.	**74,054**	**25,005**	**49,049**
Mexico	31,422	2,931	28,491
El Salvador	6,452	246	6,206
Germany	3,405	2,688	717
Vietnam	2,861	1,349	1,512
Marshall Islands	2,604	250	2,354
United Kingdom	2,292	2,002	290
Philippines	2,098	698	1,400
China/HK/Taiwan	1,711	695	1,016
Mongolia	1,516	n/a	1,516
India	1,402	572	830
Former USSR	1,382	134	1,248
Guatemala	1,322	143	1,179
Laos	1,249	1,555	-306
Japan	1,228	745	483
Korea	1,167	538	629

CALIFORNIA

Land mass	158,706 sq miles
Total population	33,871,648
White	20,170,059
Black or African American	2,263,882
American Indian and Alaska Native	333,346
Asian	3,697,513
Native Hawaiian and Other Pacific Islander	116,961
Some other race / Two or more races	7,289,887
Hispanic or Latino (of any race)	10,966,556

	2000	1990	Growth
Total FB Pop.	**8,817,243**	**6,417,052**	**2,400,191**
Mexico	3,889,695	2,434,652	1,455,043
Philippines	670,560	484,277	186,283
China/HK/Taiwan	556,283	382,992	173,291
Vietnam	408,581	267,883	140,698
El Salvador	375,356	279,010	96,346
Korea	269,346	197,000	72,346
Guatemala	205,885	135,284	70,601
India	197,918	85,054	112,864
Former USSR	181,800	84,739	97,061
Iran	160,456	117,184	43,272
Canada	135,135	150,084	-14,949
United Kingdom	131,648	135,995	-4,347
Japan	111,453	97,238	14,215
Germany	92,481	105,413	-12,932
Nicaragua	70,001	6,426	63,575

COLORADO

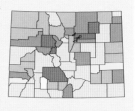

Land mass	104,091 sq miles
Total population	4,301,261
White	3,560,005
Black or African American	165,063
American Indian and Alaska Native	44,241
Asian	95,213
Native Hawaiian and Other Pacific Islander	4,621
Some other race / Two or more races	432,118
Hispanic or Latino (of any race)	735,601

	2000	1990	Growth
Total FB Pop.	**380,841**	**139,890**	**240,951**
Mexico	192,427	32,712	159,715
Germany	20,485	14,358	6,127
Canada	15,415	8,355	7,060
United Kingdom	12,325	7,986	4,339
Vietnam	11,635	5,511	6,124
Korea	11,594	7,431	4,163
Former USSR	10,111	4,467	5,644
India	9,285	1,791	7,494
China/HK/Taiwan	8,586	4,863	3,723
El Salvador	6,054	714	5,340
Japan	5,141	3,423	1,718
Philippines	4,316	3,255	1,061
Italy	3,348	1,776	1,572
Poland	3,290	2,334	956
Laos	3,209	2,082	1,127

CONNECTICUT

Land mass	5,018 sq miles
Total population	3,405,565
White	2,780,355
Black or African American	309,843
American Indian and Alaska Native	9,639
Asian	82,313
Native Hawaiian and Other Pacific Islander	1,366
Some other race / Two or more races	222,049
Hispanic or Latino (of any race)	320,323

	2000	1990	Growth
Total FB Pop.	**375,006**	**277,449**	**97,557**
Poland	29,861	20,916	8,945
Jamaica	28,757	16,328	12,429
Italy	26,443	34,973	-8,530
Canada	20,720	21,987	-1,267
United Kingdom	16,190	16,737	-547
India	15,722	6,956	8,766
Portugal	14,821	14,082	739
Colombia	13,222	5,396	7,826
Mexico	12,994	2,720	10,274
Germany	12,513	13,976	-1,463
China/HK/Taiwan	11,406	5,908	5,498
Former USSR	11,092	8,430	2,662
Brazil	10,726	3,353	7,373
Ecuador	10,127	2,344	7,783
Guatemala	7,414	1,244	6,170

DELAWARE

Land mass	2,044 sq miles
Total population	783,600
White	584,773
Black or African American	150,666
American Indian and Alaska Native	2,731
Asian	16,259
Native Hawaiian and Other Pacific Islander	283
Some other race / Two or more races	28,888
Hispanic or Latino (of any race)	37,277

	2000	1990	Growth
Total FB Pop.	**41,839**	**21,370**	**20,469**
Mexico	8,053	1,019	7,034
India	3,756	1,246	2,510
China/HK/Taiwan	2,809	1,541	1,268
Guatemala	2,792	32	2,760
Germany	2,754	1,470	1,284
United Kingdom	2,070	2,357	-287
Former USSR	1,957	510	1,447
Philippines	1,398	724	674
Haiti	1,368	85	1,283
Korea	1,109	751	358
Bangladesh	1,108	n/a	1,108
Canada	979	932	47
Pakistan	893	183	710
Poland	878	664	214
Italy	862	1,188	-326

DISTRICT OF COLUMBIA

Land mass	69 sq miles
Total population	572,059
White	176,101
Black or African American	343,312
American Indian and Alaska Native	1,713
Asian	15,189
Native Hawaiian and Other Pacific Islander	348
Some other race / Two or more races	73,177
Hispanic or Latino (of any race)	35,396

	2000	1990	Growth
Total FB Pop.	**70,659**	**58,425**	**12,234**
El Salvador	13,214	9,427	3,787
China/HK/Taiwan	2,808	1,911	897
United Kingdom	2,612	2,293	319
Jamaica	2,409	3,045	-636
Dominican Rep.	2,368	1,125	1,243
Ethiopia	2,273	1,769	504
Mexico	2,177	775	1,402
Nigeria	1,815	1,185	630
Guatemala	1,788	1,139	649
Germany	1,580	1,705	-125
France	1,499	1,083	416
Guyana	1,451	1,015	436
Honduras	1,333	216	1,117
Trinidad & Tobago	1,330	1,547	-217
Vietnam	1,330	548	782

FLORIDA

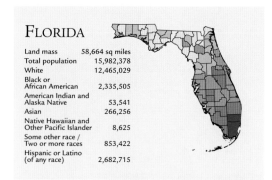

Land mass 58,664 sq miles
Total population 15,982,378
White 12,465,029
Black or African American 2,335,505
American Indian and Alaska Native 53,541
Asian 266,256
Native Hawaiian and Other Pacific Islander 8,625
Some other race / Two or more races 853,422
Hispanic or Latino (of any race) 2,682,715

	2000	1990	Growth
Total FB Pop.	**2,640,882**	**1,656,429**	**984,453**
Cuba	652,660	495,849	156,811
Mexico	189,819	54,414	135,405
Haiti	166,778	81,837	84,941
Colombia	157,307	65,066	92,241
Jamaica	127,591	76,853	50,738
Canada	100,922	76,517	24,405
Nicaragua	98,021	72,017	26,004
United Kingdom	73,029	60,523	12,506
Dominican Rep.	69,449	23,556	45,893
Germany	64,409	55,628	8,781
Honduras	50,599	22,069	28,530
Peru	49,919	22,661	27,258
Venezuela	47,646	14,481	33,165
Philippines	45,642	23,457	22,185
Brazil	43,082	8,682	34,400

GEORGIA

Land mass 58,910 sq miles
Total population 8,186,453
White 5,327,281
Black or African American 2,349,542
American Indian and Alaska Native 21,737
Asian 173,170
Native Hawaiian and Other Pacific Islander 4,246
Some other race / Two or more races 310,477
Hispanic or Latino (of any race) 435,227

	2000	1990	Growth
Total FB Pop.	**573,255**	**172,040**	**401,215**
Mexico	196,011	19,748	176,263
Vietnam	32,811	5,129	27,682
India	25,084	7,600	17,484
Korea	22,624	11,181	11,443
Germany	22,520	13,494	9,026
China/HK/Taiwan	18,605	7,704	10,901
Canada	17,141	7,279	9,862
United Kingdom	15,382	10,572	4,810
El Salvador	13,849	1,453	12,396
Guatemala	12,354	1,043	11,311
Jamaica	11,845	3,454	8,391
Colombia	9,664	2,004	7,660
Philippines	9,524	4,614	4,910
Pakistan	6,563	1,775	4,788
Nigeria	6,492	3,538	2,954

HAWAII

Land mass 6,471 sq miles
Total population 1,211,537
White 294,102
Black or African American 22,003
American Indian and Alaska Native 3,535
Asian 503,868
Native Hawaiian and Other Pacific Islander 113,539
Some other race / Two or more races 274,490
Hispanic or Latino (of any race) 87,699

	2000	1990	Growth
Total FB Pop.	**213,762**	**165,072**	**48,690**
Philippines	104,862	74,957	29,905
China/HK/Taiwan	23,086	16,141	6,945
Japan	19,840	18,389	1,451
Korea	16,450	13,054	3,396
Vietnam	6,551	5,717	834
Micronesia	5,187	902	4,285
Western Samoa	4,810	2,668	2,142
Canada	4,454	4,237	217
Germany	3,995	2,509	1,486
Tonga	3,406	1,776	1,630
United Kingdom	1,622	1,851	-229
Thailand	1,435	1,221	214
Mexico	1,293	1,443	-150
Sweden	1,187	276	911
Marshall Islands	1,151	451	700

IDAHO

Land mass 83,564 sq miles
Total population 1,293,953
White 1,177,304
Black or African American 5,456
American Indian and Alaska Native 17,645
Asian 11,889
Native Hawaiian and Other Pacific Islander 1,308
Some other race / Two or more races 80,351
Hispanic or Latino (of any race) 101,690

	2000	1990	Growth
Total FB Pop.	**65,150**	**28,376**	**36,774**
Mexico	37,204	11,716	25,488
Canada	4,490	3,452	1,038
Former Yugoslavia	2,290	84	2,206
Germany	2,236	1,656	580
Former USSR	1,437	452	985
Philippines	1,419	456	963
China/HK/Taiwan	1,283	920	363
Vietnam	1,282	192	1,090
United Kingdom	1,278	852	426
Sudan	1,136	n/a	1,136
India	1,091	32	1,059
Japan	974	720	254
Switzerland	868	88	780
Korea	806	376	430
Romania	780	64	716

ILLINOIS

Land mass 56,345 sq miles
Total population 12,419,293
White 9,125,471
Black or African American 1,876,875
American Indian and Alaska Native 31,006
Asian 423,603
Native Hawaiian and Other Pacific Islander 4,610
Some other race / Two or more races 957,728
Hispanic or Latino (of any race) 1,530,262

	2000	1990	Growth
Total FB Pop.	**1,531,231**	**939,684**	**591,547**
Mexico	609,068	274,476	334,592
Poland	139,729	83,574	56,155
India	86,242	38,235	48,007
Philippines	67,840	47,370	20,470
Former USSR	56,274	26,982	29,292
China/HK/Taiwan	50,383	29,985	20,398
Korea	37,787	28,818	8,969
Former Yugoslavia	35,258	20,565	14,693
Germany	33,882	41,592	-7,710
Italy	25,259	34,368	-9,109
Guatemala	22,355	11,163	11,192
Pakistan	21,893	7,674	14,219
Canada	20,348	17,094	3,254
United Kingdom	20,329	21,960	-1,631
Greece	17,708	19,920	-2,212

INDIANA

Land mass 36,185 sq miles
Total population 6,080,485
White 5,320,022
Black or African American 510,034
American Indian and Alaska Native 15,815
Asian 59,126
Native Hawaiian and Other Pacific Islander 2,005
Some other race / Two or more races 173,483
Hispanic or Latino (of any race) 214,536

	2000	1990	Growth
Total FB Pop.	**194,992**	**96,909**	**98,083**
Mexico	61,336	10,433	50,903
Germany	11,921	9,221	2,700
Korea	7,997	3,555	4,442
Canada	7,979	5,805	2,174
India	7,753	4,652	3,101
Former USSR	7,584	2,911	4,673
United Kingdom	7,310	6,210	1,100
China/HK/Taiwan	6,977	4,730	2,247
Former Yugoslavia	6,391	3,281	3,110
Philippines	5,647	3,087	2,560
Vietnam	4,099	1,781	2,318
Japan	4,030	3,644	386
Poland	3,832	2,973	859
Honduras	2,892	186	2,706
El Salvador	2,767	240	2,527

IOWA

Land mass	56,275 sq miles	Asian		36,635
Total population	2,926,324	Native Hawaiian and Other Pacific Islander		1,009
White	2,748,640			
Black or African American	61,853	Some other race / Two or more races		69,198
American Indian and Alaska Native	8,989	Hispanic or Latino (of any race)		82,473

	2000	1990	Growth
Total FB Pop.	**85,847**	**44,819**	**41,028**
Mexico	19,987	3,747	16,240
Vietnam	7,770	2,663	5,107
India	5,429	2,221	3,208
Former Yugoslavia	5,395	136	5,259
Korea	5,036	2,436	2,600
Germany	4,373	4,755	-382
Former USSR	4,368	3,747	621
Canada	3,444	2,699	745
China/HK/Taiwan	3,166	2,828	338
El Salvador	2,180	565	1,615
United Kingdom	2,075	2,111	-36
Cambodia	1,985	518	1,467
Laos	1,945	3,095	1,150
Philippines	1,901	849	1,052
Guatemala	1,512	159	1,353

KANSAS

Land mass	82,277 sq miles	Asian		46,806
Total population	2,688,418	Native Hawaiian and Other Pacific Islander		1,313
White	2,313,944			
Black or African American	154,198	Some other race / Two or more races		147,221
American Indian and Alaska Native	24,936	Hispanic or Latino (of any race)		188,252

	2000	1990	Growth
Total FB Pop.	**138,845**	**61,562**	**77,283**
Mexico	64,896	14,760	50,136
Vietnam	8,518	4,397	4,121
Germany	5,915	4,975	940
India	5,479	2,584	2,895
China/HK/Taiwan	4,785	3,100	1,685
Philippines	4,762	1,378	3,384
Canada	4,600	2,529	2,071
Laos	4,284	2,185	2,099
Korea	3,284	2,786	498
United Kingdom	3,028	2,889	139
El Salvador	2,577	452	2,125
Former USSR	2,504	1,430	1,074
Pakistan	1,373	409	964
Japan	1,332	1,272	60
Iran	1,262	651	611

KENTUCKY

		American Indian and Alaska Native		8,616
Land mass	40,409 sq miles	Asian		29,744
Total population	4,041,769	Native Hawaiian and Other Pacific Islander		1,460
White	3,640,889	Some other race / Two or more races		65,066
Black or African American	295,994	Hispanic or Latino (of any race)		59,939

	2000	1990	Growth
Total FB Pop.	**79,796**	**32,559**	**47,237**
Mexico	13,577	803	12,774
Germany	6,707	5,259	1,448
India	5,148	1,351	3,797
United Kingdom	4,435	2,356	2,079
Former Yugoslavia	4,276	148	4,128
Korea	4,040	2,129	1,911
China/HK/Taiwan	3,383	1,496	1,887
Canada	3,284	1,984	1,300
Cuba	3,023	588	2,435
Vietnam	2,724	973	1,751
Japan	2,289	1,552	737
Philippines	1,902	831	1,071
Former USSR	1,775	633	1,142
France	1,141	396	745
Bangladesh	1,127	n/a	1,127

LOUISIANA

Land mass	47,751 sq miles	
Total population	4,468,976	
White	2,856,161	
Black or African American	1,451,944	
American Indian and Alaska Native	25,477	
Asian	54,758	
Native Hawaiian and Other Pacific Islander	1,240	
Some other race / Two or more races	79,396	
Hispanic or Latino (of any race)	107,738	

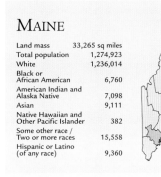

	2000	1990	Growth
Total FB Pop.	**110,708**	**85,425**	**25,283**
Vietnam	16,995	10,884	6,111
Honduras	9,317	7,221	2,096
Mexico	7,394	3,369	4,025
India	6,375	3,483	2,892
Nicaragua	5,918	3,378	2,540
Germany	5,366	4,122	1,244
Cuba	4,811	4,611	200
United Kingdom	4,228	3,438	790
Canada	3,601	2,520	1,081
Philippines	3,570	2,520	1,050
China/HK/Taiwan	3,291	3,729	-438
El Salvador	2,318	1,047	1,271
France	1,927	1,326	601
Nigeria	1,880	798	1,082
Former Yugoslavia	1,630	426	1,204

MAINE

Land mass	33,265 sq miles	
Total population	1,274,923	
White	1,236,014	
Black or African American	6,760	
American Indian and Alaska Native	7,098	
Asian	9,111	
Native Hawaiian and Other Pacific Islander	382	
Some other race / Two or more races	15,558	
Hispanic or Latino (of any race)	9,360	

	2000	1990	Growth
Total FB Pop.	**38,808**	**36,842**	**1,966**
Canada	15,149	18,784	-3,635
Germany	2,714	2,396	318
United Kingdom	2,465	3,109	-644
Former Yugoslavia	2,032	163	1,869
Former USSR	1,968	273	1,695
Cambodia	1,049	417	632
Korea	1,020	313	707
Vietnam	962	577	385
Philippines	919	866	53
Spain	852	106	746
South Africa	679	62	617
Japan	655	492	163
India	655	330	325
Afghanistan	568	36	532
Iran	481	n/a	481

MARYLAND

Land mass	10,460 sq miles	Asian		210,929
Total population	5,296,486	Native Hawaiian and Other Pacific Islander		2,303
White	3,391,308			
Black or African American	1,477,411	Some other race / Two or more races		199,112
American Indian and Alaska Native	15,423	Hispanic or Latino (of any race)		227,916

	2000	1990	Growth
Total FB Pop.	**531,359**	**308,706**	**222,653**
El Salvador	37,980	13,865	24,115
China/HK/Taiwan	34,166	18,277	15,889
Korea	31,254	20,409	10,845
India	28,088	17,547	10,541
Philippines	23,276	12,473	10,803
Former USSR	21,348	8,800	12,548
Jamaica	20,804	11,875	8,929
Mexico	19,797	3,939	15,858
Vietnam	16,159	7,376	8,783
United Kingdom	16,135	12,536	3,599
Germany	15,566	15,881	-315
Nigeria	14,528	5,306	9,222
Trinidad & Tobago	12,466	6,710	5,756
Iran	11,734	7,125	4,609
Guatemala	10,212	3,340	6,872

MASSACHUSETTS

Land mass	8,284 sq miles	
Total population	6,349,097	
White	5,367,286	
Black or African American	343,454	
American Indian and Alaska Native	15,015	
Asian	238,124	
Native Hawaiian and Other Pacific Islander	2,489	
Some other race / Two or more races	382,729	
Hispanic or Latino (of any race)	428,729	

	2000	1990	Growth
Total FB Pop.	**772,653**	**573,040**	**199,613**
Portugal	75,382	72,015	3,367
China/HK/Taiwan	53,495	31,047	22,448
Dominican Rep.	41,551	19,044	22,507
Brazil	38,566	10,830	27,736
Former USSR	38,561	19,026	19,535
Canada	38,043	52,910	-14,867
Haiti	33,640	18,716	14,924
Vietnam	31,805	13,021	18,784
Italy	30,208	38,413	-8,205
India	26,790	11,815	14,975
United Kingdom	25,658	27,217	-1,559
El Salvador	21,103	6,909	14,194
Ireland	17,918	20,764	-2,846
Germany	14,712	13,894	818
Colombia	14,628	6,492	8,136

MICHIGAN

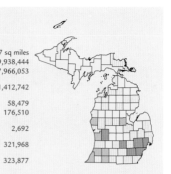

Land mass	58,527 sq miles	
Total population	9,938,444	
White	7,966,053	
Black or African American	1,412,742	
American Indian and Alaska Native	58,479	
Asian	176,510	
Native Hawaiian and Other Pacific Islander	2,692	
Some other race / Two or more races	321,968	
Hispanic or Latino (of any race)	323,877	

	2000	1990	Growth
Total FB Pop.	**526,459**	**352,312**	**174,147**
Mexico	62,289	13,151	49,138
Canada	53,704	53,807	-103
India	39,470	13,013	26,457
Iraq	27,176	13,994	13,182
China/HK/Taiwan	24,307	10,536	13,771
Germany	23,685	23,995	-310
United Kingdom	20,921	24,131	-3,210
Lebanon	17,072	11,041	6,031
Former Yugoslavia	17,017	10,838	6,179
Korea	17,004	8,319	8,685
Italy	16,517	18,475	-1,958
Poland	16,296	19,156	-2,860
Former USSR	15,218	10,567	4,651
Philippines	12,412	9,632	2,780
Vietnam	10,053	5,053	5,000

MINNESOTA

Land mass	84,402 sq miles	
Total population	4,919,479	
White	4,400,282	
Black or African American	171,731	
American Indian and Alaska Native	54,967	
Asian	141,968	
Native Hawaiian and Other Pacific Islander	1,979	
Some other race / Two or more races	148,552	
Hispanic or Latino (of any race)	143,382	

	2000	1990	Growth
Total FB Pop.	**261,030**	**115,097**	**145,933**
Mexico	45,557	3,833	41,724
Laos	26,281	15,153	11,128
Vietnam	13,406	6,776	6,630
Korea	13,312	3,926	9,386
Former USSR	11,826	4,393	7,433
Canada	10,399	10,407	-8
Thailand	10,229	3,666	6,563
India	8,968	2,787	6,181
China/HK/Taiwan	8,487	4,571	3,916
Philippines	8,156	3,410	4,746
Somalia	7,995	n/a	7,995
Germany	5,675	8,075	-2,400
Nigeria	5,523	781	4,742
United Kingdom	4,530	4,730	-200
Ethiopia	4,435	1,082	3,353

MISSISSIPPI

Land mass	47,689 sq miles
Total population	2,844,658
White	1,746,099
Black or African American	1,033,809
American Indian and Alaska Native	11,652
Asian	18,626
Native Hawaiian and Other Pacific Islander	667
Some other race / Two or more races	33,805
Hispanic or Latino (of any race)	39,569

	2000	1990	Growth
Total FB Pop.	**40,134**	**20,997**	**19,137**
Mexico	8,401	729	7,672
Vietnam	3,386	1,995	1,391
Germany	2,631	1,992	639
China/HK/Taiwan	2,481	1,179	1,302
Korea	2,366	747	1,619
United Kingdom	2,229	2,058	171
Canada	1,998	1,356	642
India	1,799	1,374	425
Philippines	1,536	1,113	423
Honduras	1,350	165	1,185
Cuba	1,148	249	899
Thailand	706	153	553
Colombia	695	27	668
Nicaragua	590	81	509
Ireland	516	306	210

MISSOURI

Land mass	69,697 sq miles
Total population	5,595,211
White	4,748,083
Black or African American	629,391
American Indian and Alaska Native	25,076
Asian	61,595
Native Hawaiian and Other Pacific Islander	3,178
Some other race / Two or more races	127,888
Hispanic or Latino (of any race)	118,592

	2000	1990	Growth
Total FB Pop.	**151,108**	**82,769**	**68,339**
Mexico	30,573	4,642	25,931
China/HK/Taiwan	9,476	4,857	4,619
Vietnam	8,164	3,960	4,204
Germany	8,038	8,779	-741
India	7,598	2,664	4,934
Former Yugoslavia	6,858	1,518	5,340
Canada	6,502	4,144	2,358
Philippines	6,296	3,638	2,658
Former USSR	5,549	2,561	2,988
United Kingdom	5,147	5,183	-36
Korea	4,957	3,489	1,468
Italy	2,537	2,673	-136
Iran	2,130	1,307	823
Japan	2,011	2,383	-372
Haiti	2,006	237	1,769

MONTANA

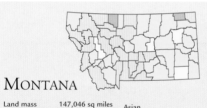

Land mass	147,046 sq miles	Asian	4,691
Total population	902,195	Native Hawaiian and Other Pacific Islander	470
White	817,229		
Black or African American	2,692	Some other race / Two or more races	21,045
American Indian and Alaska Native	56,068	Hispanic or Latino (of any race)	18,081

	2000	1990	Growth
Total FB Pop.	**14,607**	**13,724**	**883**
Canada	5,780	4,009	1,771
United Kingdom	1,248	1,041	207
Germany	798	1,333	-535
El Salvador	571	n/a	571
France	506	116	390
Mexico	505	225	280
Netherlands	483	169	314
Sweden	414	447	-33
Malaysia	413	7	406
Korea	389	326	63
Philippines	344	369	-25
China/HK/Taiwan	252	448	-196
Singapore	252	n/a	252
Poland	230	244	-14
Norway	206	397	-191

NEBRASKA

Land mass	77,355 sq miles
Total population	1,711,263
White	1,533,261
Black or African American	68,541
American Indian and Alaska Native	14,896
Asian	21,931
Native Hawaiian and Other Pacific Islander	836
Some other race / Two or more races	71,798
Hispanic or Latino (of any race)	94,425

	2000	1990	Growth
Total FB Pop.	**75,702**	**26,294**	**49,408**
Mexico	28,996	3,893	25,103
Vietnam	6,076	689	5,387
Germany	3,241	2,431	810
Guatemala	3,217	n/a	3,217
Former USSR	2,963	2,003	960
China/HK/Taiwan	2,710	1,391	1,319
Korea	2,366	920	1,446
India	1,962	1,022	940
El Salvador	1,733	237	1,496
Canada	1,689	982	707
Former Yugoslavia	1,483	109	1,374
United Kingdom	1,462	1,840	-378
Iraq	1,368	38	1,330
Philippines	1,109	890	219
Honduras	812	204	608

NEVADA

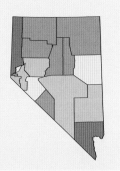

Land mass	110,561 sq miles
Total population	1,998,257
White	1,501,886
Black or African American	135,477
American Indian and Alaska Native	26,420
Asian	90,266
Native Hawaiian and Other Pacific Islander	8,426
Some other race / Two or more races	235,782
Hispanic or Latino (of any race)	393,970

	2000	1990	Growth
Total FB Pop.	**305,573**	**103,962**	**201,611**
Mexico	142,685	32,180	110,505
Philippines	33,046	7,339	25,707
El Salvador	12,243	2,996	9,247
Canada	11,845	6,744	5,101
China/HK/Taiwan	8,845	3,493	5,352
Korea	7,551	3,204	4,347
Cuba	7,206	4,400	2,806
United Kingdom	7,168	5,138	2,030
Germany	6,023	4,654	1,369
Guatemala	5,507	1,069	4,438
Vietnam	4,373	2,836	1,537
Japan	4,316	1,715	2,601
Thailand	2,738	1,606	1,132
Nicaragua	2,644	1,113	1,531
Argentina	2,467	561	1,906

NEW HAMPSHIRE

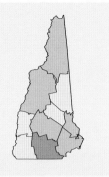

Land mass	9,279 sq miles
Total population	1,235,786
White	1,186,851
Black or African American	9,035
American Indian and Alaska Native	2,964
Asian	15,931
Native Hawaiian and Other Pacific Islander	371
Some other race / Two or more races	20,634
Hispanic or Latino (of any race)	20,489

	2000	1990	Growth
Total FB Pop.	**53,135**	**40,182**	**12,953**
Canada	12,321	12,859	-538
Dominican Rep.	3,454	637	2,817
United Kingdom	3,140	3,851	-711
India	2,973	1,193	1,780
Germany	2,623	2,956	-333
China/HK/Taiwan	2,375	1,042	1,333
Former Yugoslavia	2,262	43	2,219
Colombia	2,232	409	1,823
Brazil	2,057	157	1,900
Korea	1,956	770	1,186
Vietnam	1,329	104	1,225
Greece	1,140	1,275	-135
Philippines	1,071	491	580
Italy	1,055	802	253
Former USSR	1,001	503	498

NEW JERSEY

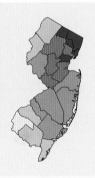

Land mass	7,787 sq miles
Total population	8,414,350
White	6,104,705
Black or African American	1,141,821
American Indian and Alaska Native	19,492
Asian	480,276
Native Hawaiian and Other Pacific Islander	3,329
Some other race / Two or more races	664,727
Hispanic or Latino (of any race)	1,117,191

	2000	1990	Growth
Total FB Pop.	**1,481,157**	**959,127**	**522,030**
India	117,687	52,672	65,015
Dominican Rep.	106,120	35,179	70,941
Colombia	79,902	40,354	39,548
China/HK/Taiwan	71,035	34,328	36,707
Philippines	70,670	38,043	32,627
Mexico	64,614	12,679	51,935
Poland	59,182	39,441	19,741
Italy	58,699	69,449	-10,750
Cuba	52,515	61,280	-8,765
Korea	50,092	27,949	22,143
Former USSR	47,687	23,192	24,495
Peru	43,436	19,911	23,525
Ecuador	43,224	20,186	23,038
Portugal	35,273	34,598	675
Germany	34,154	43,421	-9,267

NEW MEXICO

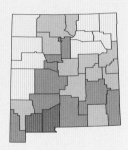

Land mass	121,593 sq miles
Total population	1,819,046
White	1,214,253
Black or African American	34,343
American Indian and Alaska Native	173,483
Asian	19,255
Native Hawaiian and Other Pacific Islander	1,503
Some other race / Two or more races	376,209
Hispanic or Latino (of any race)	765,386

	2000	1990	Growth
Total FB Pop.	**146,347**	**78,669**	**67,678**
Mexico	103,153	48,414	54,739
Canada	4,749	2,334	2,415
Germany	3,971	3,456	515
United Kingdom	3,817	3,171	646
China/HK/Taiwan	2,323	1,110	1,213
Philippines	2,300	891	1,409
India	2,036	789	1,247
Vietnam	1,679	945	734
Switzerland	1,406	114	1,292
Japan	1,388	1,101	287
Guatemala	1,324	852	472
Korea	1,193	1,032	161
Former USSR	1,160	300	860
Italy	1,101	741	360
Former Yugoslavia	1,099	63	1,036

NEW YORK

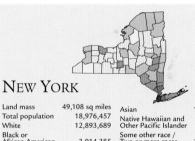

Land mass	49,108 sq miles
Total population	18,976,457
White	12,893,689
Black or African American	3,014,385
American Indian and Alaska Native	82,461
Asian	1,044,976
Native Hawaiian and Other Pacific Islander	8,818
Some other race / Two or more races	1,932,128
Hispanic or Latino (of any race)	2,867,583

	2000	1990	Growth
Total FB Pop.	**3,804,431**	**2,822,756**	**981,675**
Dominican Rep.	415,026	235,790	179,236
China/HK/Taiwan	292,717	188,985	103,732
Former USSR	233,724	103,938	129,786
Jamaica	214,993	143,298	71,695
Mexico	170,386	43,570	126,816
Italy	147,372	189,759	-42,387
Guyana	130,154	76,536	53,618
Ecuador	127,451	65,678	61,773
Haiti	123,737	85,086	38,651
India	117,889	69,129	48,760
Colombia	112,484	83,570	28,914
Poland	97,643	89,136	8,507
Trinidad & Tobago	97,073	63,226	33,847
Korea	91,568	71,389	20,179
Philippines	74,061	49,275	24,786

NORTH CAROLINA

Land mass	52,669 sq miles
Total population	8,049,313
White	5,804,656
Black or African American	1,737,545
American Indian and Alaska Native	99,551
Asian	113,689
Native Hawaiian and Other Pacific Islander	3,983
Some other race / Two or more races	289,889
Hispanic or Latino (of any race)	378,963

	2000	1990	Growth
Total FB Pop.	**436,513**	**115,380**	**321,133**
Mexico	179,236	8,751	170,485
Germany	18,558	11,994	6,564
Vietnam	16,083	3,975	12,108
China/HK/Taiwan	14,777	5,562	9,215
United Kingdom	14,706	8,388	6,318
India	14,343	5,856	8,487
Canada	12,728	6,855	5,873
Korea	11,146	5,304	5,842
El Salvador	10,388	906	9,482
Philippines	7,955	3,492	4,463
Former USSR	6,916	747	6,169
Laos	6,456	1,524	4,932
Honduras	6,320	315	6,005
Guatemala	5,466	270	5,196
Japan	4,773	4,044	729

NORTH DAKOTA

Land mass	70,703 sq miles
Total population	642,200
White	593,181
Black or African American	3,916
American Indian and Alaska Native	31,329
Asian	3,606
Native Hawaiian and Other Pacific Islander	230
Some other race / Two or more races	9,938
Hispanic or Latino (of any race)	7,786

	2000	1990	Growth
Total FB Pop.	**10,933**	**9,510**	**1,423**
Canada	3,253	3,110	143
Somalia	1,268	n/a	1,268
India	1,014	135	879
Vietnam	685	270	415
Kenya	633	n/a	633
Germany	582	830	-248
Former USSR	547	560	-13
Former Yugoslavia	456	n/a	456
China/HK/Taiwan	381	135	246
Iran	380	65	315
Mexico	304	170	134
United Kingdom	254	440	-186
Tonga	184	n/a	184
Italy	178	65	113
Norway	152	555	-403

OHIO

Land mass	41,330 sq miles
Total population	11,353,140
White	9,645,453
Black or African American	1,301,307
American Indian and Alaska Native	24,486
Asian	132,633
Native Hawaiian and Other Pacific Islander	2,749
Some other race / Two or more races	246,512
Hispanic or Latino (of any race)	217,123

	2000	1990	Growth
Total FB Pop.	**339,645**	**255,129**	**84,516**
India	26,072	12,009	14,063
Mexico	23,216	4,293	18,923
Germany	21,566	24,518	-2,952
China/HK/Taiwan	21,161	10,670	10,491
Former USSR	20,834	10,752	10,082
Canada	18,911	15,042	3,869
Former Yugoslavia	15,568	15,257	311
United Kingdom	14,052	18,104	-4,052
Korea	12,164	6,566	5,598
Italy	11,082	18,275	-7,193
Philippines	10,394	6,600	3,794
Vietnam	9,070	3,283	5,787
Japan	8,887	7,248	1,639
Romania	7,711	4,919	2,792
Poland	7,173	8,575	-1,402

OKLAHOMA

Land mass	69,956 sq miles
Total population	3,450,654
White	2,628,434
Black or African American	260,968
American Indian and Alaska Native	273,230
Asian	46,767
Native Hawaiian and Other Pacific Islander	2,372
Some other race / Two or more races	238,883
Hispanic or Latino (of any race)	179,304

	2000	1990	Growth
Total FB Pop.	**133,216**	**63,472**	**69,744**
Mexico	58,145	15,158	42,987
Vietnam	9,562	5,133	4,429
Germany	6,731	5,272	1,459
Canada	5,577	2,352	3,225
China/HK/Taiwan	5,061	2,745	2,316
India	4,860	2,384	2,476
United Kingdom	4,531	3,084	1,447
Guatemala	3,753	279	3,474
Philippines	3,661	1,686	1,975
Korea	3,567	2,712	855
Japan	1,987	1,737	250
Thailand	1,910	689	1,221
Indonesia	1,577	336	1,241
Laos	1,551	856	695
Iran	1,551	1,057	494

OREGON

Land mass	97,073 sq miles
Total population	3,421,399
White	2,961,623
Black or African American	55,662
American Indian and Alaska Native	45,211
Asian	101,350
Native Hawaiian and Other Pacific Islander	7,976
Some other race / Two or more races	249,577
Hispanic or Latino (of any race)	275,314

	2000	1990	Growth
Total FB Pop.	**296,997**	**137,279**	**159,718**
Mexico	117,297	29,705	87,592
Former USSR	17,767	3,710	14,057
Vietnam	17,462	7,295	10,167
Canada	17,185	16,383	802
China/HK/Taiwan	10,692	6,474	4,218
Korea	10,595	5,412	5,183
United Kingdom	10,569	7,192	3,377
Germany	8,930	8,426	504
Philippines	7,782	4,227	3,555
India	6,563	1,989	4,574
Japan	6,124	3,733	2,391
Guatemala	4,656	440	4,216
Romania	4,653	1,422	3,231
El Salvador	2,827	490	2,337
Laos	2,602	2,827	-225

PENNSYLVANIA

Land mass	45,308 sq miles
Total population	12,281,054
White	10,484,203
Black or African American	1,224,612
American Indian and Alaska Native	18,348
Asian	219,813
Native Hawaiian and Other Pacific Islander	3,417
Some other race / Two or more races	330,661
Hispanic or Latino (of any race)	394,088

	2000	1990	Growth
Total FB Pop.	**497,050**	**364,949**	**132,101**
Former USSR	44,998	20,484	24,514
India	38,767	18,013	20,754
Italy	28,752	40,381	-11,629
China/HK/Taiwan	28,287	16,795	11,492
Korea	27,427	16,250	11,177
Mexico	24,306	6,194	18,112
Germany	24,230	27,998	-3,768
Vietnam	23,110	13,029	10,081
United Kingdom	19,648	25,544	-5,896
Philippines	15,199	8,277	6,922
Canada	15,104	12,504	2,600
Poland	11,530	13,637	-2,107
Jamaica	10,036	6,548	3,488
Dominican Rep.	9,078	1,884	7,194
Greece	8,693	8,987	-294

RHODE ISLAND

Land mass	1,212 sq miles
Total population	1,048,319
White	891,191
Black or African American	46,908
American Indian and Alaska Native	5,121
Asian	23,665
Native Hawaiian and Other Pacific Islander	567
Some other race / Two or more races	80,867
Hispanic or Latino (of any race)	90,820

	2000	1990	Growth
Total FB Pop.	**126,046**	**94,357**	**31,689**
Portugal	23,357	23,702	-345
Dominican Rep.	16,172	5,980	10,192
Guatemala	8,390	2,937	5,453
Cape Verde	7,007	3,794	3,213
Colombia	6,372	4,922	1,450
Italy	4,979	5,720	-741
Canada	4,199	5,845	-1,646
United Kingdom	3,760	4,349	-589
Cambodia	3,180	2,376	804
Former USSR	2,807	1,878	929
Poland	2,654	1,363	1,291
Philippines	2,592	1,179	1,413
China/HK/Taiwan	2,455	2,047	408
Germany	2,152	1,661	491
Haiti	2,138	649	1,489

SOUTH CAROLINA

Land mass	31,113 sq miles
Total population	4,012,012
White	2,695,560
Black or African American	1,185,216
American Indian and Alaska Native	13,718
Asian	36,014
Native Hawaiian and Other Pacific Islander	1,628
Some other race / Two or more races	79,876
Hispanic or Latino (of any race)	95,076

	2000	1990	Growth
Total FB Pop.	**116,571**	**47,859**	**68,712**
Mexico	30,524	1,653	28,871
Germany	8,857	6,447	2,410
India	6,597	2,124	4,473
United Kingdom	6,483	4,812	1,671
China/HK/Taiwan	6,211	1,110	5,101
Philippines	6,116	3,084	3,032
Canada	5,683	3,168	2,515
Costa Rica	3,300	162	3,138
Vietnam	3,048	783	2,265
Korea	2,781	1,704	1,077
Colombia	2,762	522	2,240
Guatemala	1,915	195	1,720
Former USSR	1,754	564	1,190
Peru	1,562	120	1,442
Japan	1,417	1,773	-356

SOUTH DAKOTA

Land mass	77,116 sq miles
Total population	754,844
White	669,404
Black or African American	4,685
American Indian and Alaska Native	62,283
Asian	4,378
Native Hawaiian and Other Pacific Islander	261
Some other race / Two or more races	13,833
Hispanic or Latino (of any race)	10,903

	2000	1990	Growth
Total FB Pop.	**14,705**	**7,298**	**7,407**
Ethiopia	2,806	104	2,702
Canada	1,529	980	549
Germany	1,032	574	458
Mexico	857	136	721
Former USSR	813	562	251
Colombia	738	10	728
India	689	97	592
United Kingdom	566	306	260
Philippines	550	247	303
Former Yugoslavia	517	n/a	517
Sudan	467	n/a	467
Korea	454	298	156
Iran	413	58	355
Thailand	395	132	263
El Salvador	394	n/a	394

TENNESSEE

Land mass	42,144 sq miles	Asian	56,662
Total population	5,689,283	Native Hawaiian and Other Pacific Islander	2,205
White	4,563,310	Some other race / Two or more races	119,145
Black or African American	932,809	Hispanic or Latino (of any race)	123,838
American Indian and Alaska Native	15,152		

	2000	1990	Growth
Total FB Pop.	**167,999**	**57,564**	**110,435**
Mexico	51,174	2,019	49,155
Germany	7,999	6,135	1,864
India	7,129	2,961	4,168
Canada	6,918	4,152	2,766
United Kingdom	6,403	4,386	2,017
China/HK/Taiwan	6,124	2,577	3,547
Korea	5,853	2,607	3,246
Philippines	4,186	2,511	1,675
El Salvador	4,092	45	4,047
Japan	4,043	2,940	1,103
Vietnam	3,882	1,542	2,340
Former USSR	3,513	573	2,940
Haiti	3,367	21	3,346
Iraq	2,829	327	2,502
Iran	2,743	1,440	1,303

TEXAS

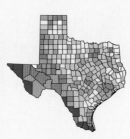

Land mass	266,807 sq miles
Total population	20,851,820
White	14,799,505
Black or African American	2,404,566
American Indian and Alaska Native	118,362
Asian	562,319
Native Hawaiian and Other Pacific Islander	14,434
Some other race / Two or more races	2,952,634
Hispanic or Latino (of any race)	6,669,666

	2000	1990	Growth
Total FB Pop.	**2,885,734**	**1,497,287**	**1,388,447**
Mexico	1,870,787	888,026	982,761
Vietnam	104,356	53,871	50,485
El Salvador	98,247	45,917	52,330
India	78,172	31,953	46,219
China/HK/Taiwan	67,366	38,141	29,225
Philippines	45,665	25,929	19,736
Canada	40,247	21,380	18,867
Germany	40,041	34,398	5,643
Korea	34,469	22,680	11,789
United Kingdom	34,385	27,917	6,468
Honduras	31,430	9,795	21,635
Pakistan	28,714	7,563	21,151
Nigeria	22,421	9,343	13,078
Guatemala	21,540	10,009	11,531
Colombia	18,567	12,426	6,141

UTAH

Land mass	84,899 sq miles
Total population	2,233,169
White	1,992,975
Black or African American	17,657
American Indian and Alaska Native	29,684
Asian	37,108
Native Hawaiian and Other Pacific Islander	15,145
Some other race / Two or more races	140,600
Hispanic or Latino (of any race)	201,559

	2000	1990	Growth
Total FB Pop.	**159,237**	**56,834**	**102,403**
Mexico	64,921	8,365	56,556
Canada	7,196	5,749	1,447
China/HK/Taiwan	6,250	2,648	3,602
Tonga	5,755	1,712	4,043
Germany	5,433	5,995	-562
United Kingdom	5,239	3,677	1,562
Former USSR	4,589	566	4,023
Vietnam	4,524	2,238	2,286
Peru	4,260	568	3,692
Guatemala	3,589	275	3,314
Philippines	3,581	1,149	2,432
El Salvador	3,449	331	3,118
Netherlands	2,928	2,077	851
Former Yugoslavia	2,423	96	2,327
Korea	2,379	1,233	1,146

VERMONT

Land mass 9,614 sq miles
Total population 608,827
White 589,208
Black or
African American 3,063
American Indian and
Alaska Native 2,420
Asian 5,217
Native Hawaiian and
Other Pacific Islander 141
Some other race /
Two or more races 8,778
Hispanic or Latino
(of any race) 5,504

	2000	1990	Growth
Total FB Pop.	25,629	17,271	8,358
Canada	8,146	6,612	1,534
United Kingdom	3,218	1,443	1,775
Former Yugoslavia	2,554	26	2,528
Vietnam	1,852	125	1,727
China/HK/Taiwan	1,382	505	877
Germany	1,278	1,608	-330
Japan	716	231	485
Korea	599	203	396
India	443	214	229
Ecuador	417	n/a	417
France	365	292	73
Marshall Islands	347	n/a	347
Austria	287	250	37
Former Czech.	287	67	220
Argentina	260	10	250

VIRGINIA

Land mass 40,767 sq miles
Total population 7,078,515
White 5,120,110
Black or
African American 1,390,293
American Indian and
Alaska Native 21,172
Asian 261,025
Native Hawaiian and
Other Pacific Islander 3,946
Some other race /
Two or more races 281,969
Hispanic or Latino
(of any race) 329,540

	2000	1990	Growth
Total FB Pop.	584,982	307,506	277,476
El Salvador	55,293	21,003	34,290
Korea	39,346	23,385	15,961
Philippines	36,548	22,416	14,132
Mexico	35,210	7,905	27,305
Vietnam	31,479	19,485	11,994
India	29,665	11,682	17,983
China/HK/Taiwan	23,522	12,327	11,195
Germany	21,148	16,536	4,612
United Kingdom	21,049	16,494	4,555
Peru	16,661	4,350	12,311
Pakistan	15,950	4,404	11,546
Guatemala	15,095	3,567	11,528
Bolivia	13,316	5,478	7,838
Canada	13,067	9,303	3,764
Iran	10,979	8,325	2,654

WASHINGTON

Land mass 68,138 sq miles
Total population 5,894,121
White 4,821,823
Black or
African American 190,267
American Indian and
Alaska Native 93,301
Asian 322,335
Native Hawaiian and
Other Pacific Islander 23,953
Some other race /
Two or more races 442,442
Hispanic or Latino
(of any race) 441,509

	2000	1990	Growth
Total FB Pop.	614,524	317,337	297,187
Mexico	149,281	44,493	104,788
Canada	48,666	43,893	4,773
Philippines	46,382	27,621	18,761
Former USSR	43,846	4,878	38,968
Vietnam	41,636	16,224	25,412
Korea	36,811	20,784	16,027
China/HK/Taiwan	35,876	18,432	17,444
Germany	19,405	19,251	154
United Kingdom	17,219	16,638	581
Cambodia	17,160	7,878	9,282
India	15,500	3,711	11,789
Japan	14,912	12,726	2,186
Thailand	8,419	3,549	4,870
Laos	5,891	5,112	779
Poland	5,637	2,415	3,222

WEST VIRGINIA

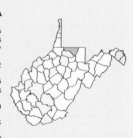

Land mass 24,231 sq miles
Total population 1,808,344
White 1,718,777
Black or
African American 57,232
American Indian and
Alaska Native 3,606
Asian 9,434
Native Hawaiian and
Other Pacific Islander 400
Some other race /
Two or more races 18,895
Hispanic or Latino
(of any race) 12,279

	2000	1990	Growth
Total FB Pop.	17,189	15,891	1,298
Germany	1,749	1,530	219
China/HK/Taiwan	1,695	1,026	669
India	1,621	1,333	288
Philippines	1,531	955	576
Mexico	1,204	154	1,050
Canada	1,002	954	48
Italy	948	1,401	-453
Korea	929	509	420
Pakistan	747	383	364
United Kingdom	638	1,644	-1,006
Japan	610	519	91
Greece	474	215	259
Lebanon	474	303	171
Spain	438	291	147
Bulgaria	420	94	326

WISCONSIN

Land mass 56,153 sq miles
Total population 5,363,675
White 4,769,857
Black or
African American 304,460
American Indian and
Alaska Native 47,228
Asian 88,763
Native Hawaiian and
Other Pacific Islander 1,630
Some other race /
Two or more races 151,737
Hispanic or Latino
(of any race) 192,921

	2000	1990	Growth
Total FB Pop.	190,731	116,749	73,982
Mexico	57,638	9,990	47,648
Laos	15,762	12,183	3,579
Germany	11,881	16,226	-4,345
China/HK/Taiwan	7,716	4,071	3,645
India	7,688	2,531	5,157
Canada	7,429	5,467	1,962
Former USSR	6,583	4,940	1,643
Korea	6,365	2,811	3,554
Thailand	6,205	3,364	2,841
United Kingdom	5,355	5,384	-29
Vietnam	5,013	1,976	3,037
Philippines	4,591	2,458	2,133
Poland	3,950	4,992	-1,042
Italy	3,244	3,956	-712
Japan	2,681	1,542	1,139

WYOMING

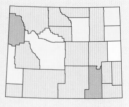

Land mass 97,809 sq miles
Total population 493,782
White 454,670
Black or
African American 3,722
American Indian and
Alaska Native 11,133
Asian 2,771
Native Hawaiian and
Other Pacific Islander 302
Some other race /
Two or more races 21,184
Hispanic or Latino
(of any race) 31,669

	2000	1990	Growth
Total FB Pop.	10,577	8,423	2,154
Mexico	4,785	2,139	2,646
Canada	1,529	968	561
Germany	706	1,008	-302
United Kingdom	522	1,108	-586
France	521	119	402
Argentina	409	n/a	409
Japan	387	219	168
South Africa	372	48	324
Sweden	205	53	152
Australia	187	34	153
India	149	39	110
Brazil	135	n/a	135
Philippines	131	90	41
Portugal	130	99	31
Papua New Guinea	130	n/a	130

Appendices

SUGGESTED READING

(*Please also see p 248.*)

Archdeacon, Thomas J. *Becoming American: An Ethnic History.* New York: Free Press, 1984.

Benton, Barbara. *Ellis Island: A Pictorial History.* New York: Facts on File, 1987.

Brownstone, David M., and Irene M. Franck and Douglass Brownstone (Eds.) *Island of Hope, Island of Tears: The Story of Those Who Entered the New World through Ellis Island In Their Own Words.* Metro Books, 2002.

Conover, Ted. *Coyotes: A Journey Through the Secret World of America's Illegal Aliens.* New York: Vintage, 1978.

Daniels, Roger. *Coming to America: A History of Immigration and Ethnicity in American Life.* HarperPerennial, 1991.

Daniels, Roger. *Guarding the Golden Door: American Immigration Policy and Immigrants since 1882.* New York: Hill and Wang, 2004.

Dinnerstein, Leonard and Roger L. Nichols and David M. Reimers (Eds.) *Natives and Strangers: A Multicultural History of Americans.* New York: Oxford University Press, 2003.

Fischer, David Hackett. *Albion's Seed: Four British Folkways in America.* New York: Oxford University Press, 1991.

Foner, Nancy. *From Ellis Island to JFK: New York's Two Great Waves of Immigration.* New Haven: Yale University Press, 2002.

Gonzalez, Juan. *Harvest of Empire: A History of Latinos in America.* New York: Penguin Books, 2001.

Grunberger, Michael W., and Hasia R. Diner. *From Haven to Home: 350 Years of Jewish Life in America.* New York: George Braziller, 2004.

Handlin, Oscar. *The Uprooted: The Epic Story of the Great Migrations That Made the American People.* Philadelphia: University of Pennsylvania Press, 2002.

Jacoby, Tamar (Ed.) *Reinventing the Melting Pot: The New Immigrants and What it Means to Be American.* New York: Basic Books, 2004.

Miller, Kerby A. *Emigrants and Exiles: Ireland and the Irish Exodus to North America.* New York: Oxford University Press, 1988.

Moreno, Barry. *Encyclopedia of Ellis Island.* Westport, CT: Greenwood Press, 2004.

Portes, Alejandro and Ruben G. Rumbault. *Immigrant America: A Portrait.* Berkeley: University of California Press, 1996.

Takaki, Ronald. *Strangers from a Different Shore: A History of Asian Americans.* New York: Little Brown, 1989.

Tanner, Helen Hornbeck. *The Settling of North America: Atlas of the Great Migrations from the Ice Age to the Present.* New York: MacMillan, 1995.

The Editors of Time-Life Books. *Immigrants: The New Americans.* Alexandria, VA: Time-Life Books, 1999.

Webb, James. *Born Fighting: How the Scots-Irish Shaped America.* New York: Broadway Books, 2004.

WEBSITES

HOW THEY CAME

Ellis Island
http://www.ellisisland.org/

Angel Island
http://www.aiisf.org/

Finding ancestors on ships' passenger lists
http://www.theshipslist.com/

MIGRATION PATTERNS

Migrations
http://www.ucalgary.ca/applied_hist ory/tutor/migrations/

The role of religion in settling America
http://www.loc.gov/exhibits/religion /rel01-2.html

GENEALOGY

The Church of Jesus Christ of Latter-day Saints (the Mormons)
http://www.familysearch.org/

The USGenWeb Project provides Web sites for genealogical research in every county and every state of the United States
http://www.usgenweb.com/

INDIVIDUAL GROUPS

Chinese immigrants on Angel Island
http://www.angel-island.com/

Chinese immigrants on Gold Mountain
http://www.apa.si.edu/ongoldmoun tain/

Jewish Immigration
http://www.loc.gov/exhibits/havent ohome/
Specifically from 1820 to 1924

Latino Stories
http://americanhistory.si.edu/onthe move/themes/story_51_2.html

Muslim Immigration
http://usinfo.state.gov/products/pu bs/muslimlife/immigrat.htm

PHOTOGRAPHS & OBJECTS

New York Public Library Digital Gallery
http://digitalgallery.nypl.org/nypldi gital/dgkeysearchresult.cfm?keywor d=col_id%3A165&so=title

Library of Congress
http://lcweb2.loc.gov/ammem/brow se/ListSome.php?category=Immigra tion,+American%20Expansion

The Golden Door: Immigration Images from the Keystone-Mast Collection (UCR/California Museum of Photography)
http://photo.ucr.edu/projects/immi gration/

OVERALL

The New Americans
http://www.pbs.org/independentlen s/newamericans/

Library of Congress
http://lcweb2.loc.gov/learn/features /immig/immigration_set1.html

US Citizenship and Immigration Services
http://uscis.gov/graphics/aboutus/h istory/index.htm

CURRENT INFO

Center for Immigration Studies
http://www.cis.org/

Index

Note: Page numbers in *italics* refer to illustrations or photographs.

Credits

Every effort has been made to trace copyright holders. DK Publishing apologizes for any unintentional omissions, and would be pleased, if any such case should arise, to add an appropriate acknowledgment in future editions.

Courtesy of Mahnaz Afkhami and family: 96tl, 96lc, 96bl

AKG Images: 104cr

Alamy: © Arcaid 260bl; © Black Star 132-133;

Photo by Steve and Gil Amiaga: 255c

© Amnesty International: 227cr

Andes Press Agency: 131tr

AP Wideworld: 16tc, 41bl, 46tr, 46bl, 71br, 79b, 83br, 84tc, 84b, 85tr, 85bc, 85br, 88tl, 92bl, 92bc, 93tr, 93b, 94bc, 96br, 98-99, 110br, 114bc, 121b, 122bl, 123b, 124tl, 130bl, 134-135, 144br, 145br, 149cr, 155b, 159cr, 166tl, 167br, 170bl, 172tr, 175tr, 175br, 178l, 181tl, 182cl, 185br, 192tr, 192bl, 193b, 201br, 205cr, 207tr, 207c, 209cr, 213tl, 213tr, 213tc, 214bl, 217b, 217t, 219br, 221tl, 221br, 223cr, 222bl, 230tr, 230b, 231tr, 231br, 232tl, 233br, 246bc, 247br, 249tl, 249c, 255tr, 258c, 266tc, 266bl, 278br, 282-283

Denise Applewhite: 185tr

Argonne National Laboratory: 206bc

Art Resource: Bildarchiv Preussischer Kulturbesitz / Art Resource, NY 148tl; Erich Lessing/Art Resource, NY 63br; The New York Public Library/Art Resource NY 52br; Snark/Art Resource, NY 106bl; Digital Image (c) The Museum of Modern Art/Licensed by SCALA / Art Resource, NY 257bc

© Michelle Baxter: 82tl, 165tl

Bridgeman Art Library: Cane Cutters in Jamaica, c.1880 (albumen print photo), Private Collection, Michael Graham-Stewart 32bc; Martin Luther (1483-1556) burning the Papal Bull in 1520 (engraving), English School, (19th century) / Private Collection, Ken Welsh 54-55; The Harkort Factory at Burg Wetter, c.1834 (oil on canvas), Rethel, Alfred (1816-59) / Private Collection, Lauros / Giraudon 108tl; The Battle Between the Russians and Kosciuszko Forces in 1801 (w/c on paper), Orlowski, Alexander (Alexandr Osipovich Orlovsky)(1777-1832)/Muzeum Narodowe, Warsaw, Poland 114bl; Portrait of William Augustus (1721-65) Duke of Cumberland (oil on canvas), Morier, David (c.1705-70) / Private Collection, Philip Mould, Historical Portraits Ltd, London, UK 140bl; The Treaty of Utrecht, 11th April 1713 (pen & ink on paper), French School, (18th century) / Archives du Ministere des Affaires Etrangeres, Paris, France, Archives Charmet 194bl

Bruderhof Communities: 77cr

California Historical Society, FN-15982: 154br

George Catlin Buffalo Chase, a Surround by the Hidatsa 1832-1833 oil on canvas 24x29 inches Smithsonian American Art Museum Gift of Mrs. Joseph Harrison, Jr. © 2005 Smithsonian Institution: 17br

Chicago Historical Society, ICHi-03806: 165cr

The City of New York Seal is used with permission of the Department of Citywide Administrative Services of the City of New York: 30tr

Corbis: 2-3, 9. 20bl, 25cl, 29br, 38tc, 50-51. 62bl, 87br, 88bl, 92tl, 96bc, 104tl, 116tr, 117br, 121tr, 150tl, 204tr, 208cr, 209tc, 211bl, 218bl, 220br, 238bl, 242-243bc, 246c, 247tl, 262br, 277tr; Lynsey Addario 170tl; Lucien Aignerl 206bl; O. Alamany & E. Vicens 196tl; Paul Almasy 227tc; Mark Avery/Orange County Register 69br; Annie Griffiths Belt 56-57, 77tl, 80bl, ; Adrian Arbib 231tl; Archivo Iconografico, S.A. 61tr, 61br, 164tl, 265bcl, 267br; Austrian Archives 112tl, 113cl, 259-259b; Tony Arruza 174tl, 222tl; Marc Asnin 84tl; J.L. Atlan 186tl; BBC 267bc; Bettmann 7tr, 22bl, 24cr, 25tr, 26tr, 28bl, 30tl, 36tc, 36c, 37tr, 41br, 46bl, 51tc, 64br, 65br, 67tr, 69bl, 68-69, 74tl, 82bl, 95tl, 100-101, 103tl, 103br, 112bl, 115l, 155br, 118-119, 120bl, 121br, 123tr, 124bl, 125cr, 125bl, 129tl, 130tl, 136tr, 136br, 137tr, 137bc, 143, 146-147bc, 147br, 149bl, 150tr, 153br, 158tl, 158bl, 158-159c, 160c, 162bl, 164bl, 164-165bc, 168b, 171bl, 171br, 172tl. 180bc, 181tr, 184b, 190-191, 196bl, 196-196bc, 197tr, 198-199bc, 199br, 202-203, 204bl, 206tl, 207br, 209br, 213br, 218t, 218br, 220bl, 222bc, 232bl, 242tl, 242cr, 244-245, 247tr, 260tr, 260cr, 261r, 262tl, 265tr, 268bl, 269tc, 271tr, 272tl, 276tl, 277bl, 282-283; Bernard Bisson 186bl, David Butow 185cr, 188-189; CinemaPhoto 273cr; Geoffrey Clements 145tr; Stephanie Colasanti 80br; Keith Dannemiller 173bc; Howard Davies 128-129b; Francoise de Mulder 214-215bc; Leonard de Selva 104bl; Macduff Everton 130tl; John Farmar 24bl; Najlah Feanny 126-127; Kevin Fleming 70-71c, 77br; Owen Franken 211tr; Marc Garanger 208tl; Raymond Gehman 19b, 25b; Bill Gentile 51tr; eerle Geo 88br; Lowell Georgia 146tl; Philippe Giraud/Good Look 114tl; Michael Gore 184tl; Philip Gould 155tr, 195tl, 195tr; Farrell Grehan 139br, 140tl; Antoine Gyori 232-233c; Robert Holmes 152tl, 160bl; Angelo Hornak 257tl; Jeremy Horner 176-177; Dave G. Houser 95br, 131br; Hulton-Deutsch Collection 124tl, 179tl, 209cl, 212c, 252c; Robbie Jack 263br; Bryson John 167tr; Wolfgang Kaehler 120tl; David Keaton 86tl, Brooks Kraft 76b; Bob Krist 166br; Kim Kulish 187cr; Lake County Museum 163tr; Jacques Langevin 122tr; Danny Lehman 172br; Julie Lemberger 269bc; Andrew Lichtenstein 159br; Massimo Listri 78tl; Ludovic Maisant 62tl; The Mariners' Museum 4-5; Francis G. Mayer 68bl; Joe McDonald 76tl; Minnesota Historical Society 148bl, 149tc, 151br; Kevin R. Morris 216tl; Museum of the City of New York 46tr; Jehad Nga 226c; P.PERRIN 210; Jacques Pavlovsky 215tr; Carl & Ann Purcell 128tl; Jose Fuste Raga 160tl; Steve Raymer 213b, 268tl; Roger Ressmeyer 217c; Patrick Robert 228-229, 233tr; Charles E. Rotkin 259tr; Bob Rowan 155tc; Michael T. Sedam 149br; Sean Sexton Collection 144tl; SCHWARZ SHAUL 96tc; S.I.N. 266cr; Lee Snider/Photo Images 21c, 28tl, 68tc, 163br; Joseph Sohm; ChromoSohm Inc. 122tc; Wendy Stone 231crVince Streano 50bl; Ted Streshinsky 152tl; Keren Su 154tl, 156-157; Sygma; 200bl, 224-225, 277br; Liba Taylor 226b; David Turnley 223b, 230tl; Peter Turnley 128bc, 227bc; Underwood & Underwood 278tl; Horacio Villalobos 131bl; Patrick Ward 69tr, 74bl; David H. Wells 215br; Nik Wheeler 1, 51bl, 182, 194tl ; Oscar White 260cl; Michael S. Yamashita 183bl;

Courtesy of the Colorado Historical Society CHS J.4038: 43b

Denver Public Library, Western History/Genealogy Department: 162bl, 169br

Department of Health and Human Services: 46br

DK: Andy Crawford / Dorling Kindersley (c) Imperial War Museum, London 201bc Lynton Gardiner (c) Dorling Kindersley, Courtesy of The American Museum of Natural History: 16cl, 16cr; Judith Miller/Dorling Kindersley/Lyon and Turnbull Ltd. 258tr

Egan Foundation Collection, Nantucket, Mass " 3,000 Miles To Go...Below Decks" by Rodney J.K. Charman Part of the Irish Collection., 1995, oil on canvas: 144bl

Courtesy of The French Huguenot (Protestant) Church: 64tr

Friends Historical Library of Swarthmore College: 66tl

Germantown Mennonite Historic Trust: Randall Nyce 74tl

Getty Images: 6bl, 34br, 250bl, 264tl, 272bc, 280-281bc AFP/Staff: 33bl, 93bl, 122tl, 180tl, 268bl, 280tl, 281bl ; Erich Auerbach 263tc; Tim Boyle 181br; BWP Media/Stringer 140br; Alfred Eisenstaedt 250br; Hulton Archive: 63tr, 78bl, 107br, 108bl, 109c, 113tl, China Photos/Stringer: 90-91; Andreas Feininger 254; Dirck Halstead 219tr; Yvonne Hemsey 243br 128br; John Kobal Foundation 271br; Arnaldo Magnani: 89br; Mark Mainz 142tc; David McNew: 93tl, 193tr; MPI/Stringer: 124c; NBAE 280tl; Arnold Newman 253tr; Oleg Nikishin 179br, 186br; Spencer Platt 280tr; Louis Requena 279tr; Jacob A. Riis 152bc, 153bl; Time Life Pictures 137br, 155tl, 167cr, 174bl, 185tc, 200br, 220bl, 234-235, 246tr, 248tl, 248cl, 249br, 250bc, 252bl, 256tl, 256br, 257br, 259cl, 276br,; Ben Van Meerondonk 257tr; Mark Wilson 187br

Glasgow City Council Museums: The Burrel Collection Faed Last of the Clan #3366 141tr

Granger Collection: 13, 20tr, 21br, 24tc, 26bl, 27tr, 29cl, 30bl, 30cr, 33br, 35tl, 35tr, 38bl, 39tr, 39br, 40b, 42bc, 62-63bc, 102bl, 102tr, 104tr, 104br, 108tl, 116bl, 138bc, 139br, 148br, 154cr, 168tr, 195tc, 195b, 199tl, 239br, 240tr, 279bl, 279br

Hawaii State Archives: 160bl

Dick Hodgman: 67br

Cover from MY ANTONIA by Willa Cather (Boston: Houghton Mifflin, 1995): 248br

Courtesy of the Huguenot Historical Society: 64bl

Institute of Texas Cultures: 83cl

Kemerovo Oblast Museum of Regional History and Folklife, Kemerovo, Russia: 117bc

David King Collection, London: 252tl

Photo Courtesy of the Krisky Family: 7bl, 82bc

Library and Archives of Canada: 18b, 22br, 23tr, 23tcr, 23br, 38-39b, 64tr, 194bcl

Library of Congress Prints and Photographs - 14bl, 20tl, 28tr, 35br, 36bl, 36b, 42cl, 53tr, 54tl, 66cr, 68br, 70tl, 71tl, 79tr, 107cr, 109tr, 111tl, 111cr, 111br, 113b, 117tl, 142tl, 146c, 146bl, 147tr, 149cl, 161tr, 171tc, 174br, 183tr, 183cr, 193tl, 199tr, 250tl

The Library of the Religious Society of Friends in Britain: 66c, 67bl

Magnum Photos: Cornell Capa Photo by Robert Capa © 2001 251br

Mary Evans Picture Library: 106br,139cr

Courtesy of the Maryland State Archives SPECIAL COLLECTIONS (Tunis Collection) " Margaret Brent" MSA SC 1480: 39c

Müller May © Deutsche Verlagsanstalt: 232tc

The Museum of Russian Art, Minneapolis, Minnesota: 236-237

Courtesy of The Music Center Archives, Otto Rothschild Collection: 264bl

NASA: 240tl, 240b, 241l, 241cr, 241br

National Archives US: 37br, 40bl, 41br, 103bl, 161tl, 169tr, 257tr

National Archives of Canada: 18b, 22br, 23tr, 23car, 23br, 38b, 65tr, 194bc

National Park Service, Colonial National Historic Park: 27br, 138tc

National Park Service, Mormon Pioneer National Historic Trail: 70bl

Photographs Courtesy National Park Service, Statue of Liberty National Monument: 47bc, 48t, 48bl, 48br, 52tl, 52tcl, 52bl, 53tl, 53br. 162cl

Courtesy of New Directions: 113cr

Collection of the New York Historical Society Negative # 77514d: 31cr

New York Transit Museum: 166tc

Northwind Picture Archives: 22cra, 31br

Norwegian American Historical Society: 151tr

The roadside historical marker is a registered trademark of the Pennsylvania Historical and Museum Commission. PHMC owns copyright to the text. Reprinted with Permission: 105tl

Photofest NY: 267tl, 267tr, 270br, 273tl, 274-275

Robert Harding World Imagery: John Miller 138tl

The Royal Archives © 2005 Her Majesty Queen Elizabeth II: 107tl

Seneca Falls Historical Society: 110bl, 110tr

Photograph by Richard Shutler Jr. Image Copyright SFU Museum of Archaeology and Ethnology 2005. Used with Permission: 16bl

The Saint Andrews Golf Club Hastings-on-Hudson. New York: 141br

Science Photo Library/Photo Researchers: 238bc, 238br, 239tr, 241l

Service de la Marine, Vincennes: 18cr

Southern Oregon Historical Society #1603: 181cr

Swiss National Museum, Zurich: 74bl

Tantallon Press: 117cl

Image courtesy of the Touro Synagogue: 81br

© Le Minh Truong/anothervietnam.com; 216bl

Tucson Weekly: Francis Wick 129br

The U.S.ENGLISH Foundation: 43tr

United States Coast Guard: 223tl

U.S. Customs & Border Protection: 50br, 173br

United States Mint Image: 110bc

United States Post Office: 75cr

Courtesy of the Special Collections Department, University of Iowa Libraries: 270bl

Watertown Historical Society: 109br

Yad Vashem: 204tl

From the Archives of the YIVO Institute for Jewish Research, New York: 204tl

Acknowledgments

The author wishes to thank: Christopher Davis and Andrew Heritage, for once again giving me a great opportunity—and additional thanks to Andrew for his editorial vision, his organizational prowess in determining how to tackle this enormous subject, and his guiding hand during the project; Tina Vaughan and Sharon Lucas, for their support throughout; Anja Schmidt, not just for her superlative editorial and project-management skills, but for her excellent contributions to the text; Michelle "Ella" Kasper, for her invaluable help with research and also for her own fine contributions to the writing; Michelle Baxter, Dirk Kaufman, and the rest of the design team for exceeding even their own exacting standards; Chrissy McIntyre, for her diligence in tracking down many an elusive image; and most of all to Rachel Kempster, for being there for me every day and in every way. Finally, thanks to David Grubin and his terrifically talented team for creating the landmark TV series to which this book owes its existence.

This book is dedicated to my daughter, Lauren Elise Wills.

DK would like to thank:

The DK Cartography team for all of the terrific maps in the book.

David Grubin, Bruce Mundt, Alexandria Dionne, and Rachel Buchanen at David Grubin Productions for their enthusiasm about bringing our two projects together.

James Guerra, Brianna Lopez, Melissa Herr, and Kelly Chmielewski at PBS for all their help.